# HOME IN THE CITY

## Urban Aboriginal Housing and Living Conditions

During the past several decades, the Aboriginal population of Canada has become so urbanized that today, the majority of First Nations and Metis people live in cities. *Home in the City* provides an in-depth analysis of urban Aboriginal housing, living conditions, issues, and trends. Based on extensive research, including interviews with more than three thousand residents, it allows for the emergence of a new, contemporary, and more realistic portrait of Aboriginal people in Canada's urban centres.

*Home in the City* focuses on Saskatoon, which has both one of the highest proportions of Aboriginal residents in the country and the highest percentage of Aboriginal people living below the poverty line. While the book details negative aspects of urban Aboriginal life (such as persistent poverty, health problems, and racism), it also highlights many positive developments: the emergence of an Aboriginal middle class, inner-city renewal, innovative collaboration with municipal and community organizations, and more. Alan B. Anderson and the volume's contributors provide an important resource for understanding contemporary Aboriginal life in Canada.

ALAN B. ANDERSON is a professor emeritus in the Department of Sociology and a research fellow in Ethnic and Indigenous Policy in the Department of Political Studies at the University of Saskatchewan.

# Home in the City

*Urban Aboriginal Housing and Living Conditions*

EDITED BY ALAN B. ANDERSON

UNIVERSITY OF TORONTO PRESS
Toronto Buffalo London

ISBN 978-0-8020-9887-0 (cloth)
ISBN 978-0-8020-9591-6 (paper)

Printed on acid-free, 100% post-consumer recycled paper with vegetable-based inks.

---

**Library and Archives Canada Cataloguing in Publication**

Home in the city : urban Aboriginal housing and living conditions /
edited by Alan B. Anderson.

Includes bibliographical references and index.
ISBN 978-0-8020-9887-0 (bound).     ISBN 978-0-8020-9591-6 (pbk.)

1. Native peoples – Urban residence – Saskatchewan – Saskatoon.
2. Native peoples – Dwellings – Saskatchewan – Saskatoon.   3. Native
peoples – Saskatchewan – Saskatoon – Social conditions.   4. Urban
policy – Saskatchewan – Saskatoon.   5. Bridges and Foundations Project
on Urban Aboriginal Housing.   6. Saskatoon (Sask.) – Social conditions.
I. Anderson, Alan B., 1939–

E78.C2H655 2013     305.897'0712425     C2012-906816-0

---

University of Toronto Press acknowledges the financial assistance to its
publishing program of the Canada Council for the Arts and the Ontario
Arts Council.

University of Toronto Press acknowledges the financial support for its
publishing activities of the Government of Canada through the Canada
Book Fund.

# Contents

# List of Tables

# List of Acronyms

| | |
|---|---|
| ABJAC | Aboriginal Justice and Criminology Program (University of Saskatchewan) |
| ACT | Affordability and Choice Today |
| AFN | Assembly of First Nations |
| AHOP | Assisted Home Ownership Program (CMHC) |
| AHP | Affordable Housing Project (Quint Development Corp.) |
| AHURI | Australian Housing and Urban Research Institute |
| AMNSIS | Association of Metis and Non-status Indians of Saskatchewan |
| ANC | Action for Neighbourhood Change |
| ANHDF | Affordable New Home Development Foundation |
| ASAP | Aboriginal Student Achievement Plan |
| ASEP | Aboriginal Skills and Employment Partnership |
| ATASI | Aboriginal Tourism Association of Saskatchewan |
| ATR | Addition to Reserves policy |
| CAHP | Centenary Affordable Housing Program (Saskatchewan) |
| CAP | Congress of Aboriginal Peoples |
| CBR | Community-based research |
| CCDF | Clarence Campeau Development Fund |
| CCJS | Canadian Centre for Justice Statistics |
| CCPA | Canadian Centre for Policy Alternatives |
| CCS | Construction Careers Saskatoon |
| CCSD | Canadian Consultative Council on Social Development |
| CED | community economic development |
| CES | CanSask Career and Employment Services |
| CHBA | Canadian Home Builders' Association |
| CHEP | Child Hunger and Education Program |

| | |
|---|---|
| CHRA | Canadian Housing and Renewal Association |
| CIHI | Canadian Centre for Health Information |
| CIHR | Canadian Institutes of Health Research |
| CMA | Census Metropolitan Area |
| CMAR | Centre for Municipal–Aboriginal Relations |
| CMHC | Canada Mortgage and Housing Corporation |
| CNDC | Core Neighbourhood Development Council |
| CNYC | Core Neighbourhood Youth Co-op |
| CPRN | Canadian Policy Research Networks |
| CUISR | Community–University Institute for Social Research |
| CUMFI | Central Urban Metis Federation Inc. |
| CURA | Community–University Research Alliances program (SSHRC) |
| DCRE | Saskatchewan Department of Community Resources and Employment |
| DTI | Dumont Technical Institute |
| FCM | Federation of Canadian Municipalities |
| FCPP | Frontier Centre for Public Policy |
| FFHI | Family Friendly Housing Initiative (Quint) |
| FNALM | First Nations Alliance for Land Management |
| FNLMA | First Nations Land Management Act |
| FNUC | First Nations University of Canada |
| FSIN | Federation of Saskatchewan Indian Nations |
| GDI | Gabriel Dumont Institute |
| GIFT | grandparents involved full-time |
| HIV/AIDS | human immunodeficiency virus / acquired immune deficiency syndrome |
| HFHC | Habitat for Humanity Canada |
| HOP | Housing Opportunity Partnership (CMHC) |
| HRSDC | Human Resources and Skills Development Canada |
| IMFC | Indian and Metis Friendship Centre |
| INAC | Indian and Northern Affairs Canada |
| IRPP | Institute for Research on Public Policy, Montreal |
| ITEP | Indian Teacher Education Program (University of Saskatchewan) |
| IUS | Institute for Urban Studies (University of Winnipeg) |
| LAPC | local area planning committee |
| LICO | low income cut-off |
| METSI | Metis Employment and Training of Saskatchewan Inc. |
| MLI | Mortgage Loan Insurance program (CMHC) |

| | |
|---|---|
| MNS | Metis Nation of Saskatchewan |
| MUHAS | Metis Urban Housing Association of Saskatchewan |
| NAFC | National Association of Friendship Centres |
| NAHA | National Aboriginal Housing Association |
| NCA | National Children's Agenda |
| NDP | New Democratic Party |
| NHI | National Homelessness Initiative |
| NHOP | Neighbourhood Home Ownership Program |
| NHRC | National Housing Research Committee |
| NORTEP | Northern Teacher Education Program (University of Saskatchewan) |
| NSH | National Secretariat on Homelessness |
| PDF | proposal development funding (CMHC) |
| PRI | Policy Research Initiative |
| RCAP | Royal Commission on Aboriginal Peoples |
| RRAP | Residential Rehabilitation Assistance Program |
| SASAS | Saskatchewan Association of Sexual Assault Survivors |
| SATCC | Saskatchewan Apprenticeship and Trade Certification Commission |
| SHA | Saskatoon Housing Authority |
| SHAC | Social Housing Advisory Committee |
| SHARP | Saskatoon HIV/AIDS Reduction of Harm Program |
| SHC | Saskatchewan Housing Corporation |
| SHIP | Saskatoon Housing Initiatives Partnership |
| SIAST | Saskatchewan Institute of Applied Science and Technology |
| SIEF | Saskatchewan Indian Equity Foundation |
| SIGA | Saskatchewan Indian Gaming Authority |
| SIIT | Saskatchewan Indian Institute of Technologies |
| SNR | SaskNative Rentals |
| SNTC | Saskatchewan Native Theatre Company |
| SOS | Saskatoon Overnight Shelter |
| SPHERU | Saskatchewan Population Health and Evaluation Research Unit (University of Saskatchewan) |
| SREDA | Saskatoon Regional Economic Development Authority |
| SRHBA | Saskatoon and Region Home Builders' Association |
| SSHRC | Social Sciences and Humanities Research Council |
| STC | Saskatoon Tribal Council |
| SUMA | Saskatchewan Urban Municipalities Association |

| | |
|---|---|
| SUNTEP | Saskatchewan Urban Native Teacher Education Program (University of Saskatchewan) |
| SWITCH | Student Wellness Initiative Toward Community Health |
| TIPI | ethical principles of a First Nations research/learning circle |
| TLC | tenant–landlord cooperation group |
| TLEFA | Treaty Land Entitlement Framework Agreement |
| UAED | Urban Aboriginal Economic Development network |
| UAPS | Urban Aboriginal Peoples Study |
| UAS | Urban Aboriginal Strategy |
| UBCM | Union of British Columbia Municipalities |
| UMAYC | Urban Multipurpose Aboriginal Youth Centres |
| WEDC | Western Economic Diversification Canada |

# HOME IN THE CITY

Urban Aboriginal Housing and Living Conditions

## Chapter One

# Introduction

There has been a dramatic shift during recent decades in the Aboriginal population of Canada from being overwhelmingly rural, living on reserves and in northern communities or 'out on the land,' to rapidly becoming predominantly urban, living in larger cities and largely off-reserve or away from traditional communities. Not only are more Aboriginal people now resident in urban places, but also most reserves in Saskatchewan now find far more of their band members living off reserve than on – in some cases more than three-quarters of their members. This pronounced trend toward urbanization has been both continuous and steadily increasing. Demographic analysts still argue over fluctuating rates of urbanization, relative concentration within larger urban centres, return migration back to reserves and traditional communities, and faster population growth on reserve than off; that said, it is clear that the Canadian Aboriginal population has been substantially changing. Increasing numbers of young Aboriginal people are born and raised in cities, with limited or even no acquaintance with life back on reserve or in traditional communities. They are becoming better educated and are entering the labour force in a wider variety of occupations. Only two or three decades ago, there were very few Aboriginal university students; today they number in the thousands. At the University of Saskatchewan, they have increased as much as tenfold in a single decade.

Increasing attention is being devoted on the one hand to the effect that cities have been having on the retention or preservation of traditional Aboriginal cultures, and on the other hand to the impact that rapidly increasing numbers of Aboriginal residents are having on cities. The need to house these residents is paramount. They have tended to be largely concentrated within the poorest neighbourhoods, but this too has been changing as the Aboriginal population disperses throughout the city and gradually moves into the middle class as a result of improved education, occupational diversity, and concomitant expectations of better housing. Housing is central to the quality of life of Aboriginal people, just as it is for the general Canadian population. Respectable, truly affordable, and more than simply adequate accommodation is absolutely vital to healthy living and contentment. Yet across Canada, particularly among Aboriginal people, there continues to be a housing crisis, a chronic failure to meet a serious backlog in demand for affordable housing, although homebuilders, community planners, and municipal, provincial, and federal governments have been making noteworthy, innovative and ambitious efforts to deal more effectively with this situation.

Ten years ago, Saskatoon, Saskatchewan, a mid-sized western Canadian city nearing a quarter of a million population, possessed the largest proportion of Aboriginal residents of any Census Metropolitan Area (CMA) in Canada: almost one in ten residents. Unfortunately, this city also exhibited the very highest proportion of Aboriginal residents in any CMA living below the poverty line (the low-income cut-off calculated by Statistics Canada): close to two-thirds. Yet the city was also becoming the setting for significant advances in Aboriginal higher education, the development of urban reserves, Aboriginal economic diversification, and indeed innovative developments in affordable housing. So with reason, Saskatoon was selected as the focus of a comprehensive study of urban Aboriginal housing and related quality-of-life issues, the Bridges and Foundations Project on Urban Aboriginal Housing. The present book reports the seminal research originally conducted under the auspices of this project, research that was innovative in being community-driven and capturing an Aboriginal perspective. This research is placed in a broader context of up-to-date urban Aboriginal and housing research in Canada.

## The Bridges and Foundations Project on Urban Aboriginal Housing

The Bridges and Foundations Project on Urban Aboriginal Housing, which commenced in 2001 and concluded in 2007, was an initiative of the Community–University Research Alliances (CURA) Program of the Social Sciences and Humanities Research Council of Canada (SSHRC) and the Canada Mortgage and Housing Corporation (CMHC). Collaborating in the Project were several universities: the University of Saskatchewan, the First Nations University of Canada (FNUC), and the Saskatchewan Indian Institute of Technologies (SIIT); provincial and urban Aboriginal bodies: the Federation of Saskatchewan Indian Nations (FSIN), the Saskatoon Tribal Council (STC), the Metis Nation of Saskatchewan (MNS), and the Central Urban Metis Federation Inc. (CUMFI); the City of Saskatoon, particularly the Planning and Development and Community Development branches of the Department of Community Services; home-building and housing associations, including the Saskatoon and Region Home Builders Association (SRHBA), the Saskatoon Housing Initiatives Partnership (SHIP), the Affordable New Home Development Foundation (ANHDF), Sun Ridge Residential Inc., SaskNative Rentals (SNR), and Cress Housing; and local community organizations: Quint Development Corporation and neighbourhood associations. The Project was directed by Alan Anderson, Research Director, a sociology professor at the University of Saskatchewan (and the editor of this book); Keith Hanson, Community Director, President, and CEO of the Sun Ridge Group, including the Affordable New Home Development Foundation in Saskatoon, and currently Chairman of the Board of the Saskatchewan Housing Corporation; and Priscilla Settee, Indigenous Director, Director of the Indigenous Peoples Program, and Associate Professor in the Department of Native Studies at the University of Saskatchewan.

Saskatoon was selected as the setting for this comprehensive project in 2001. Like other western Canadian cities, Saskatoon had a serious shortage of affordable and appropriate housing, particularly for its growing numbers of Aboriginal residents, most of whom were relatively poor. Again, like other cities in western Canada, Saskatoon was the site of a growing problem with Aboriginal street gangs (resulting in rising crime rates) and had a recent history of difficulties in the policing of Aboriginal residents and of poor relations between the police service and Aboriginal residents. Yet at the same time, Saskatoon contained exceptionally large numbers (thousands) of Aboriginal students engaged in higher education at universities and technical institutions. The city was also characterized by the progressive new development of urban reserves, where First Nations organizations and some businesses were located; in fact, the city enjoyed a wide range of Aboriginal commercial developments and a highly developed infrastructure of Aboriginal institutions and services. Moreover, Saskatoon had established a record of innovative and timely Aboriginal research, reflected not only in the increasing research capacity of institutions of higher education in the city (including Aboriginal institutions), but also in the diverse Aboriginal academic programs and research units at the University of Saskatchewan. The Community–University Institute for Social Research (CUISR), based at the University of Saskatchewan, has been instrumental over the past decade in promoting collaboration between the university and the community.

The primary goal of the Bridges and Foundations Project was to build sustainable relationships between Aboriginal and non-Aboriginal organizations to design and develop culturally supportive communities and affordable housing options. The Project research attempted to discern the differences between the availability of affordable housing as well as community services in Saskatoon and what the city's Aboriginal residents actually needed. The Project succeeded in gathering a large volume of pertinent information on urban Aboriginal housing and demographics, living conditions and quality of life, yielding a detailed knowledge of the characteristics and needs of the city's large Aboriginal population. Research was aimed at providing an accurate and updated demographic profile of Aboriginal residents, exploring their living conditions and housing needs, and providing practical analysis of housing design and supply for Aboriginal residents. The many reports of the Project included surveys contracted with First Nations, comprehensive and in-depth neighbourhood surveys, evaluations of Aboriginal and non-Aboriginal collaboration, and studies of the special needs of students and particular challenged populations such as elders. The Project also encompassed housing design workshops, the development of Aboriginal apprenticeships in the homebuilding industry, explorations of financial and funding options for homeownership, re-examinations of community-based research from an Aboriginal perspective, and many other relevant topics.

The Bridges and Foundations Project was innovative in a variety of ways: It focused attention directly on urban Aboriginal housing. It consistently related housing research to quality-of-life research. It concentrated not simply on First Nations residents but also on Metis, and thus on the Aboriginal population in the city as a whole. It acquired fresh (previously unreleased) data directly from Statistics Canada in order to produce an accurate, up-to-date, and detailed analysis of Aboriginal population concentration and distribution within the city. But above all, it sought to hear and learn from the Aboriginal residents themselves; much of the Project's research was community-driven. Thus the Project intentionally sought to redefine the very nature of social research on urban Aboriginal people through developing new perspectives and research methods. The Project succeeded in bringing together, with the common aim of improving housing for Aboriginal residents, a broad spectrum of academic researchers, community and neighbourhood organizations, Aboriginal institutions and organizations, Aboriginal students, urban planners, the homebuilding industry, business people, and financiers. In the process, new collaborative relationships were built and have been maintained on a basis of mutual trust. The Project has been a beneficial learning experience for all participants. The Project as a whole aimed ultimately at policy recommendations, relating both to particular component research projects and more generally to overarching policy changes for all three levels of government (municipal, provincial, federal) and to the implications of these changes for the Canadian homebuilding industry.

The sheer scale of the Bridges and Foundations Project was impressive: more than 3,000 residents were personally interviewed, including over 2,000 Aboriginal residents, and generously provided important information. It is safe to say that never have as many local urban Aboriginal residents – household heads, students, abused women, elders, youth, band members – been interviewed at any time in any particular city. This book is, then, above all, their story, as they experience 'home in the city' (*apiw pihci kihci-itawin* in Cree).

## Purpose and Organization of the Book

This book represents an attempt to accomplish three fundamental goals. First, to present an accurate demographic portrait of the increasing numbers of Aboriginal residents in this particular western Canadian city. Second, to provide a summary of selected research projects conducted under the auspices of the Project as a whole – research findings and recommendations. Third, to draw attention to diverse policy implications for the provision of truly affordable housing for urban Aboriginal residents, not only for governments but also for Aboriginal organizations, local community organizations and service providers, and financial institutions.

The organization of the book follows a sequence of interrelated topics bearing on the urban Aboriginal population's housing and living conditions. The editor's introductory overview to each thematic chapter represents an attempt to place the various specific research contributions comprising the chapter in a broader topical context and to bring the reader completely up to date, mainly through research and media reports. The second chapter focuses on demographics: the complexity and reliability of urban Aboriginal demographic data; urban Aboriginal populations across Canada; the growth, concentration, and distribution of the Aboriginal population of Saskatoon; and a socio-demographic profile of Aboriginal residents in this city. Each of the succeeding chapters (apart from the concluding chapter) commences with a thematic overview of a particular topic relating to urban Aboriginal housing and living conditions; this is followed by more specific case studies reflecting selected research conducted within the Bridges and Foundations Project. For the sake of being as informative as possible, detailed data are provided (especially in the descriptions of demographic trends and housing costs, as well as in reporting research findings in the case studies); yet key points drawn from these data will consistently be emphasized. The third chapter deals more specifically with migration between reserves and the city, as well as the mobility of the Aboriginal population within the city; the chapter contains summaries of two contracted surveys of Dakota and Cree First Nations with a significant proportion of members living in the city. The fourth chapter then probes further into the actual living conditions and health of Aboriginal residents, drawing from three surveys conducted in inner-city neighbourhoods. Next the roles of the family, women, and youth in urban Aboriginal life are discussed; the fifth chapter summarizes research into Aboriginal women fleeing violence, HIV/AIDS among urban Aboriginal women, and the sense of urban belonging among Aboriginal youth. The sixth chapter then delves into the very question of 'affordability' for Aboriginal residents; financial and funding options are described, and the chapter concludes with a description of research on homelessness in Saskatoon. This chapter is followed by a documentary photographic essay portraying Aboriginal life in Saskatoon: both poorer and new affordable housing, living conditions, and institutions. The seventh chapter describes actual housing providers (including 'slumlords'); the clients of two Aboriginal housing providers – SaskNative Rentals (originally primarily Metis) and Cress Housing (catering to First Nations) – are profiled. The eighth chapter, on special needs and housing design, focuses particularly on the problem of accommodating thousands of Aboriginal post-secondary students in Saskatoon, as well as Metis elders. The ninth chapter provides a discussion of Aboriginal participation in economic and community development as well as in the homebuilding industry. Saskatoon has assumed a leadership role nationally in the development of urban reserves, yet to date these reserves have been used primarily for institutional and commercial purposes rather than residential ones; so the tenth chapter provides a thorough discussion of the latter option. Any discussion of the urban Aboriginal population in Saskatoon would be incomplete without taking into consideration increasing types of criminal activity, the problem of youth gangs, relations between the police force and local Aboriginal residents, and more generally race relations in the city; all of these are covered together in the eleventh chapter. The concluding chapter returns to a critical re-evaluation of the Bridges and Foundations Project and provides a final review and overview of housing policies, especially from an Aboriginal viewpoint.

## Overview of Research on Urban Aboriginal Residents and Housing in Canada

The Bridges and Foundations Project represented an intention to contribute toward filling perceived gaps in the Canadian research literature, by focusing on the following: the contemporary urban living of Aboriginal residents in a particular western Canadian city, where they constitute a sizeable and steadily increasing proportion of the population (especially in certain neighbourhoods); the changing distribution and relative concentration of urban Aboriginal population in the city; and the changing socio-economic profile and salient characteristics of urban Aboriginal residents. Most important, the Project itself fostered improved relations and collaboration between Aboriginal and non-Aboriginal institutions and organizations. While the emphasis was by definition primarily on housing issues, housing was seen as very central to urban living and as impacting on many other thematic areas. In a sense, the Bridges and Foundations Project represented a long evolution of research and thought about Canadian – and to some extent comparative – urban indigenous living and housing. The Project set out to identify where more research, information, and improved policies are needed. It is vital, therefore, in reviewing Canadian research in the urban Aboriginal field, not simply to summarize and acknowledge what has been accomplished, but more importantly to critically discern what seems to have been missing; the identification of principal themes leads to an evaluation of the current state of the field and suggestions as to where researchers and policy strategists might profitably wish to head in the future.

General writing on Aboriginal Canadians over the past several decades has occasionally included at least some (usually minimal) mention of the urban context; however, in many books on Canadian Aboriginal peoples in general, there has been little if any mention of their urbanization; coincidentally, many books on specific topics pertaining to Aboriginal people make little or only passing reference to the unique situation of urban Aboriginal residents, although there have been occasional exceptions. Since the 1980s, an extensive literature has developed on the changing nature of First Nations and Aboriginal rights in historical and contemporary contexts and on the political ramifications of those rights; yet remarkably few of these many sources have discussed at any length the political implications of the fact that a majority of Aboriginal Canadians have moved into and now reside in urban places (Peters 1994, 1995).

*The Urban Native as Problem*

Generalized national analyses of urban Aboriginal living and issues have most often been primarily concerned with negative aspects such as poverty, un- and under-employment, inadequate education and preparation for the urban economy, crowding in virtual ghettoes, transiency and maladjustment to urban living, and propensity for criminality, often involving youth gangs. Aboriginal residents have long been regarded as 'social misfits'; this was first reflected in a preoccupation with 'social adjustment' (or a lack of it) during the 1960s and 1970s, yet today to a lesser but still considerable extent these topics are still pursued. Moreover, studies of particular cities have focused on the growth and distribution of the urban Aboriginal population, living conditions and other issues, and again – especially in earlier writing – the presumed failure of these residents to adjust to urban living.

During the 1960s and 1970s, extensive research was conducted on off-reserve Indians in British Columbia, commencing with the Hawthorn reports (1960, 1966). In *Indians in Transition* (1971), G. Walsh noted that there had been a significant movement of Indians off reserves despite the difficulties facing these migrants in urban, industrial Canada; yet many Indians who leave the reserve return when they fail to adjust to urban/industrial life. In his view, this adjustment posed a serious problem to Canadian Indians – particularly youth attracted by the apparent opportunities in the cities – because they lacked the necessary skills to succeed; unable to find employment, they were soon on welfare and living in poor accommodations, thus rendering themselves more liable to prejudice and discrimination. W.T. Stanbury's research, culminating in *Success and Failure: Indians in Urban Society* (1975), was based on a comprehensive survey that probed reasons for living off reserve, adjustment to urban life, demographic characteristics, educational achievement and vocational training, health, labour force participation, poverty and welfare dependence, and the maintenance of Indian identity.

Meanwhile, while this research was underway in British Columbia, other research on urban Native people was being conducted across Canada, including in Saskatoon. Following the earlier attention drawn by Davis (1965, 1968) to Native urbanization in Saskatchewan, Edgar Dosman's study of Indians in Saskatoon, *Indians: The Urban Dilemma* (1972), again portrayed urban Native people as problematic (as the title suggests). Dosman contrasted three categories of urban Indians: the Affluent, the Welfare, and the Anomic. The very small but influential group of Affluent Indians in Saskatoon formed a sort of Native urban aristocracy in the city, exhibiting steady employment, residence in comfortable homes in better neighbourhoods, little intra-city mobility, a high degree of family stability, ready acceptance of public visibility, little evidence of personal disorganization, and self-consciousness about their Indian identity, but little intimate association with Whites. By contrast, the Welfare Indians (by far the majority of Indians in Saskatoon) revealed extraordinarily high job turnover, little interest in either permanent or short-term employment, concentration in the dilapidated inner-city west side, drifting toward hard-core racial slums, little family stability, socializing in several disreputable jobs, and hardly any favourable contact with White people. The Anomic Indians were leading a volatile, unpredictable existence in the city and were constantly aware of their position as outsiders and deviants. Dosman suggested that any development of a more viable, well-adjusted urban Native minority would be dependent upon the successful merging of two basic strategies: first, the provision of expanded opportunities in education, housing, and employment by the larger society; and second, the stimulation of alternatives, essential to develop urban Native institutions that could create a beneficial social, cultural, and political infrastructure.

Mark Nagler authored *Indians in the City: A Study of the Urbanization of Indians in Toronto* (1970), then edited *Perspectives on the North American Indians* (1972), which included a section on 'The Urban Experience,' in which he described status and identification groupings among urban Indians in Toronto, Montreal, and Ottawa. He similarly categorized urban Indians into six principal status and identification groupings and a variety of subgroupings. First, white collars, a small segment of urban Indians who are similar to most other white-collar workers in their professional and occupational pursuits, community participation, and residential patterns. In turn, they are divided into those who admit their Indian identification, those who are ambivalent about their Indian identity, and those who refuse to acknowledge Indian ancestry. Second, blue collars, subdivided into skilled, unskilled, committed (regarding their employment as permanent), and the uncommitted. Third, transitionals, Indians who endeavour to become permanent urban residents, subdivided into students and those entering the city to seek employment. The remaining three categories of Indians do not have any intention of establishing permanent urban residence; rather, these Indians utilize the urban environment for a variety of short-term purposes. Fourth, urban users, who use the urban centre to satisfy short-term needs, subdivided into Indians who enter the city to buy supplies, those who enter for reasons of health and rehabilitation, and those entering for 'entertainment.' The fifth and sixth categories respectively refer to seasonal workers and 'vagabonds.' Then in *Natives Without a Home* (1975), Nagler suggested that given the fact that a very high proportion of Canadian Indians had limited education, many of them would qualify only for the steadily diminishing number of semiskilled or unskilled jobs available; this lack of job opportunities had lessened the attraction of the city for Indians (a questionable assumption, given statistical data indicating that Indians were migrating to the cities in unprecedented numbers). He noted that Indian migrants have not tended to form Native neighbourhoods or ghettoes, although he admitted that such migrants may be found in lower socio-economic districts in relatively large numbers. He concluded that just as poverty limits Indian self-sufficiency on the reserves, so too does it limit the opportunities for Indian migrants' successful adjustment to urban society.

An interesting counterpoint to viewing urban Aboriginals as 'problematic' was provided by Joan Ryan in *Wall of Words: The Betrayal of the Urban Indian* (1978). Yet in his photo essay of urban Aboriginal residents in several western Canadian cities, Krotz referred to them as *Urban Indians: The Strangers in Canada's Cities* (1980). And more recently, such studies emphasizing urban Aboriginal criminality and problems in adjusting to urban living have continued, albeit with more sophisticated methodologies and analysis, exemplified in Carol La Prairie's *Seen but Not Heard: Native People in the Inner City* (1995), which compares two western cities (Edmonton and Regina) and two eastern (Toronto and Montreal); while the Canada West Foundation produced several reports linked with the Urban Aboriginal Initiative (Hanselmann et al. 2001–2), including *Urban Aboriginal People in Western Canada: Realities and Policies*, which described the disproportion of lone parents, high unemployment rates, low income levels, homelessness, and incarceration rates of Aboriginal compared to the non-Aboriginal population (among other topics) in six western cities, including Saskatoon. Yet again, 'The Challenge of Urban Adjustment' was discussed in a chapter in J.W. and V.L. Friesen, *Western Canadian Native Destiny* (2008).

## Demographic Perspectives

Since the 1970s, studies of urban Aboriginal demographics have focused particularly on the growth and changing socio-economic profile of urban Aboriginal populations in Canadian cities, the effect of migration on urbanization, and more recently the changing distribution of Aboriginal residents within these cities (e.g., Price and McCaskill 1974; Gerber 1977; McCaskill 1981; Anderson 1976, 1980, 1981, 1985). With almost all attention being devoted to Status Indians, in an effort to produce more accurate and informative data on Metis and non–Status Indian people, in 1979 A.B. Anderson collaborated with the Association of Metis and Non-Status Indians of Saskatchewan (AMNSIS) in *A Preliminary Socio-economic Survey of Metis and Non-Status Indian People in Saskatoon*. In this research project, a detailed survey of 290 households covered such factors as household structure and family size, education levels and aspirations, actual employment, sources of family income, satisfaction with employment, crowding, homeownership, social patterns, attitudes toward Aboriginal identity and intermarriage, migration and mobility, culture and language, and so on. These findings, collected more than three decades ago, provide an interesting perspective on trends when compared to the information recently gathered through the Bridges and Foundations Project. Then Stewart Clatworthy authored or co-authored reports on *The Demographic Composition and Economic Circumstances of Winnipeg's Native Population* (1980), *The Economic Circumstances of Native People in Selected Metropolitan Centres in Western Canada* (1981), and *Native Economic Conditions in Regina and Saskatoon* (1983) for the Institute of Urban Studies (IUS) at the University of Winnipeg. Most recently much attention has been devoted to migration between reserves and cities, 'ethnic drift' (changing ethnicity), the difficulties in accurate measuring of Aboriginal populations, and the relative distribution and concentration of the Aboriginal population within cities – topics that will be discussed in the next chapter.

*Comprehensive and Policy-Oriented Sources*

Rather than focusing on urban Aboriginal residents simply as 'problematic,' or restricting descriptions primarily to demographic analysis, studies of urban Aboriginal people have become increasingly comprehensive, covering not only demographics but also many diverse and often positive aspects of the changing characteristics of this population; moreover, constructive policy recommendations have gradually gained more prominence. The Ontario Task Force on Native People in the Urban Setting reported in 1981; *The Concrete Reserve: Corporate Programs for Indians in the Urban Work Place*, by Gail Grant (1983) was a rather more focused study; and the following year she collaborated with Raymond Breton to co-author *The Dynamics of Government Programs for Urban Indians in the Prairie* Provinces, published by the Institute for Research on Public Policy in Montreal (1984). Helen Buckley's *From Wooden Ploughs to Welfare: Why Indian Policy Failed in the Prairie Provinces* (1992) included a critique of policies affecting urban Aboriginal people – or the lack of them.

Most significantly, the reports of the Royal Commission on Aboriginal Peoples (RCAP 1993, 1996) described at length the changing situation of urban Aboriginal peoples, with concomitant policy recommendations. The Royal Commission emphasized the urgent need to reduce the large inequalities between Aboriginal peoples and the non-Aboriginal population of Canada regarding socio-economic conditions and quality of life. Focusing significantly on urban centres, the commission recommended increased commitment of all levels of government to close this inequality; and in response, the federal government produced a report, *Gathering Strength: Canada's Aboriginal Action Plan* (1997), which called for collaboration between governments, representative Aboriginal organizations, and local community organizations. Specifically, this action plan advocated four objectives: renewing partnerships; strengthening Aboriginal governance; developing new fiscal relationships; and strengthening community economic development. As a means to meet these objectives, the Urban Aboriginal Strategy was formed the next year by the Department of Indian and Northern Affairs (INAC), with the aim of linking urban Aboriginal communities and building their capacity to affect change. This implied a collaborative approach to improve policy development and program coordination, to provide a foundation for long-term solutions in addressing the needs of local urban Aboriginal communities, while capitalizing on existing programs and policies (Spence and Findlay 2007; Lynch, Spence, and Findlay 2007).

*Not Strangers in These Parts: Urban Aboriginal Peoples* (Newhouse and Peters 2003), a comprehensive volume prepared for the Policy Research Initiative in Ottawa, covers diverse topics with policy implications. The editors have appropriately commented: 'Aboriginal people are now part of the urban landscape and will remain so, most likely in increasing numbers, over the decades to come. Understanding this reality in suf-ficient detail and depth is a major research challenge.' While national analyses of changing urban Aboriginal socio-economic characteristics and economic development have recently been increasing in number, limited attention has been paid to the emergence of an urban Aboriginal middle class (Wotherspoon 2003).

*Aboriginal Peoples in Canadian Cities: Transformations and Continuities* (Howard and Proulx 2011) is a broad edited collection of eleven essays. The introduction discusses emerging urban Aboriginal identities, the trend from traditions to modernities, and the conceptualization of com-munity within the city. The essays are case studies that focus on various diverse topics: a self-reflection on what it means to be middle class, movement between reserve and city, community building processes in Edmonton, a casino in rural Ontario as economic development, an ur-ban Aboriginal secondary school in London, Ontario, criminality and gangs in Saskatoon and Winnipeg, being Inuit in Ottawa, a Friendship Centre in Toronto, and "cultural healing" in Vancouver.

The Urban Aboriginal Peoples Study (2010) surveyed Aboriginal peo-ple living in six western and five eastern cities. The UAPS survey sought to 'fully capture urban Aboriginal peoples as complex individuals and communities.' Claiming to be 'about the future, not the past,' to be 'dif-ferent than any other survey of the Aboriginal population,' the UAPS reports in its background summary that it does not seek to collect a series of economic and social 'facts' about Aboriginal people living in the city; rather it is an enquiry about the values, experiences, identities and aspi-rations of urban Aboriginal peoples – how they see themselves in relation to their communities – both geographically and culturally; which factors are leading them toward greater success, autonomy and cultural confi-dence; what their hopes are for the future, their definitions of success; and what tools and supports have helped them and what barriers have hindered them. The UAPS found that, on average, urban Aboriginal people seem to be just as contented as other Canadians. This is hardly surprising given that for all groups, levels of contentment increase with higher education, better employment, stable relationships, and improved health, and the city generally provides greater opportunity for these than reserves. However, the executive director of the National Association of Friendship Centres has emphasized that urban Aboriginal residents in general remain at the bottom of the socio-economic spectrum in almost every category (*Saskatoon StarPhoenix*, 11 July 2012).

Another goal of this project was to 'investigate how non-Aboriginal people view Aboriginal people in Canada today.' Doubtless the UAPS has contributed interesting information, particularly on Aboriginal self-perceptions of their changing identity within the city, as well as their advances in education (information that will be cited later in this book); yet other studies – including the Bridges and Foundations Project – have also recently researched these topics. Despite the broad geographical range of the UAPS, the study sampled only 2,614 Aboriginal people as well as almost an equal number (2,501) of non-Aboriginal respondents. While probing into the role that education could play in improving quality of life, little attention is paid in the UAPS study to housing and living conditions as vital to a healthy lifestyle. According to the UAPS, 'previous studies have tended to view Aboriginal Canadians largely through a "problem lens" – that is, simply as targets for social services.' Yet other recent studies (notably the Bridges and Foundations Project and the Canada West Foundation project, as well as Newhouse and Peters 2003) have emphasized the importance to urban Aboriginal Canadians of maintaining their cultural identities and strengthening their urban communities, and – not the least – the need for improved social services that respect traditional Aboriginal practices and values. Similar to other earlier research, a major focus of the UAPS was 'to understand how Aboriginal peoples, in the midst of this process of urbanization, feel about living in their cities.' This included determining how long urban Aboriginal people have lived in their cities – specifically, whether they were born and raised here or elsewhere; their connectedness to the city and degree to which it is home to them; what Aboriginal people like or dislike about urban living; and how they might contribute to making the city a better place to live (UAPS 2010, 28).

*Housing*

With the progressive urbanization of the Aboriginal people of Canada over the past several decades, there has been a concomitant increase in studies of urban Aboriginal residents; however, relatively few of these studies have commented on housing, much less focused specifically on it. Rather, attention seems to have been primarily on demographic trends and to a lesser extent on the character and lifestyle of urban Aboriginal residents. There has been sporadic policy-oriented research and analysis, specifically on housing and more generally on other urban Aboriginal issues (dating back to Hawthorn's 1960 report), yet most of this sort of work has been relatively recent, exemplified in the reports of RCAP, the Urban Aboriginal Strategy (UAS), the Policy Research Initiative (PRI), and the Canada Mortgage and Housing Corporation (CMHC). The Canadian Housing Renewal Association (CHRA) and the National Aboriginal Housing Association (NAHA) have been active housing advocacy organizations at the national level.

A Canadian research literature has recently developed on housing in general, much of it in the form of reports published by CMHC, as well as short descriptions of current research projects in the bulletin of the National Housing Research Committee (NHRC) of CMHC (this research literature, especially CMHC and Statistics Canada reports but including many other reports on particular topics pertaining to urban Aboriginal housing, will be cited where appropriate later in this book). Two now-dated general overviews of housing policies in Canada have been: Albert Rose, *Canadian Housing Policies: 1935–1980* (1980) and Novia Carter, *Housing* (1981); while more recently, Alan Finkel has described 'Housing and State Policy, 1945–1980', in *Social Policy and Practice in Canada: A History* (2006). Hanselmann (2003) as well as other researchers have concluded, in debating housing issues in Canada, that there is no coherent national housing policy, much less a policy directed specifically at urban Aboriginal people. Jack Layton, the national leader of the New Democratic Party, authored *Homelessness: The Making and Unmaking of a Crisis* (2000, updated in 2008 as *Homelessness: How to End the National Crisis*). However, none of these general sources on housing policies focus specifically on urban Aboriginal housing. Nonetheless, Layton pointedly described Aboriginal housing – or the lack of it – as a significant part of this national crisis:

> Aboriginal housing and homelessness conditions are a national embarrassment, reflecting the failures of federal, provincial and territorial governments that have allowed poverty, inadequate housing and homelessness to fester on Aboriginal reserves and off-reserve in urban areas. The United Nations has called attention to the disproportionate numbers of homeless First Nations citizens on the streets of Canadian cities. On the reserves,

much of the housing does not even come close to basic standards ... As bad as conditions are on reserves, life for Aboriginal people isn't much better in urban areas.' (2008, 83, 87)

Until the Bridges and Foundations Project, rather limited attention had been paid specifically to the crucial issue of urban Aboriginal housing. Attempts to address this issue had included Peters's studies of Native households in Winnipeg (1984) and Regina and Saskatoon (1991), and particularly the research of Ryan Walker in Winnipeg (commencing with his doctoral dissertation in 2004) and Saskatoon. Community-based research on Aboriginal residents in Winnipeg has included *In Their Own Voices: Building Urban Aboriginal Communities* (Silver et al. 2006), while the research led by Tom Carter (Canada Research Chair in Urban Change and Adaptation at the University of Winnipeg and a director of the Winnipeg Inner City Alliance) has focused to a considerable extent on housing for Aboriginal residents (2006). Similarly, a report on social enterprise in core neighbourhoods of Saskatoon – neighbourhoods with substantial Aboriginal concentrations – probed into social exclusion vs inclusion, investment in social enterprise through training and employment and in social cohesion through the cooperative sector, and political action through the development of policies and programs, including provision of affordable housing (Diamantopoulos and Findlay 2007).

Despite the increasing diversity of the research and writing on urban Aboriginal people in Canada, especially in recent years, until very recently the central issue of adequate and affordable housing, so important to quality of life, has largely been lacking. This is exactly why the comprehensive Bridges and Foundations Project on Urban Aboriginal Housing was initiated in Saskatoon in 2001. Research has continued to focus largely on the transition from reserve and traditional communities to urban living, the disadvantages faced by urban Aboriginal residents, their failure to 'adjust' to urban life, and their concentration in the poorest neighbourhoods. The Urban Aboriginal Peoples Study has probed more into the changing urban Aboriginal identity, as well as the role that education could play in alleviating poverty. However, more research is needed on urban Aboriginal housing in other Canadian cities, its relationship to healthy living, access to and utilization of social services, the development of urban Aboriginal infrastructure, the permanence of Aboriginal settlement in cities, the changing socio-economic profile of the urban Aboriginal population and particularly the emergence of an urban Aboriginal middle class, increasing cooperation and collaboration between Aboriginal and non-Aboriginal

organizations and enterprises, the need for relevant policies at all levels
of government ... the list could go on.

## Comparative Research

It is instructive to compare Canadian research on indigenous populations in urban areas to similar research in other countries, particularly
the United States, Australia, and New Zealand. Obviously a thorough
comparison would be beyond the scope of this book; we will have to be
content with some idea of the utility of comparative research through a
selective review.

### United States

Commencing with the United States, then, relatively few of the vast
number of sources on American Indians have included commentary on
urban Indians; fewer still have focused completely on urban Indians,
and within these few sources there has been only limited specific discussion of housing. Jeanne Guillemin's *Urban Renegades: The Cultural
Strategy of American Indians* (1975), a case study of Micmac Indians in
Boston, focused on urban Indians and the 'tribal community' within
industrial society, the urban tribal network, urban family interaction
and gender relations, and methodology – but apart from analysis of
traditional versus urban households, there was no discussion of housing. *The Urban American Indian*, by A.L. Sorkin (1978), contained a relatively brief mention of housing within chapters on the economic and
social status of the urban American Indian and housing and social services. Joan Webel-Orlando's *Indian Country, L.A.: Maintaining Ethnic
Community in Complex Society* (1991) focuses on historical, demographic,
and cultural profiles of this particular urban Indian community. Ample
attention is paid to skid row; otherwise there is hardly any discussion
of housing. *The Urban Indian Experience in America* (2000), by D.L. Fixico,
does include a chapter on economic conditions and housing and also
discusses the emergence of an Indian middle class.

### Australia

Recent research in Australia has been far more comparable to Canadian
work in this field. There is an extensive literature – much of it recent – on
urban Aboriginal populations and issues, including housing. Much

recent research has been conducted with the support of the Australian Housing and Urban Research Institute (AHURI), which completed *An Audit and Review of Australian Indigenous Housing Research* in 2006. Some AHURI reports pertain to various aspects of Australian housing in general, with implications for the indigenous population, such as housing affordability, household eligibility for public housing, improvement of social housing allocation systems, and enhancing research–policy linkages. Other AHURI reports have focused on specific topics relating to indigenous housing – for example, indigenous access to mainstream public and community housing; helping indigenous families into stable housing and sustainable tenancy; assessing the long-term costs and optimal balance between recurrent and capital expenditure in indigenous housing; social services in urban indigenous housing; crowding of indigenous households in non-remote areas; and Community Land Trusts and indigenous housing options. Other institutions – particularly federal and state governments and university research centres - have also contributed reports on various aspects of indigenous housing and living conditions: housing tenure and infrastructure, housing needs and indicators, homelessness, Aboriginal housing issues in specific cities, Aboriginal migration to the cities and mobility, Aboriginal health, urban Aboriginal disadvantage, race relations, and demographic and geographic dilemmas for indigenous policy. In sum, there is an already voluminous and steadily increasing literature on Aboriginal disadvantage and indigenous–White relations, although until quite recently, little if any attention had been paid in these sources to the urban Aboriginal context. However, there is a rapidly expanding research literature specifically on Aboriginal housing, much of it focusing on urban areas. While there have been occasional examples of community-based research in urban Aboriginal communities, peripheral settlements, and townships, there is increasing evidence of close collaboration between university researchers – especially linked to university indigenous research centres – and local urban Aboriginal communities. Much can be learned by Canadian researchers from all this work in Australia.

*New Zealand*

Similarly, in New Zealand the changing situation of the indigenous Maori population could be of considerable interest to Canadian researchers. General sources have provided informative overviews of the current status of the indigenous population and culture, as well as

New Zealand ethnic identities, including Maori identity in an urban context. There is now an extensive research literature more specifically on Maori housing, including changing Maori housing policies, homeownership, the history of services, issues in the Maori Housing Program, the crisis in Maori housing, the work of the Housing Corporation in meeting Maori housing needs, Maori housing issues, a design guide for Maori housing solutions, urban Maori responses to changes in state housing provision, and emerging trends and issues in Maori housing experiences, Maori urbanization and mobility, the development of research models in housing research, sustainable housing in disadvantaged communities, indigenous deprivation and housing disadvantage, and the relationship between the development of local partnerships and social governance. Canadian researchers on urban Aboriginal housing would clearly benefit from this similar work in New Zealand; moreover, in contrast to Canada, New Zealand has had an explicit national housing policy.

*Systematic Comparison*

Systematic comparisons have been relatively few. Recent comparisons of indigenous policies, including A. Armitage, *Comparing the Policy of Aboriginal Assimilation: Australia, Canada, and New Zealand* (1995), and R. Maaka and A. Fleras, *The Politics of Indigeneity: Challenging the State in Canada and Aotearoa/New Zealand* (2005), have not focused on urban indigenous minorities or on housing issues. Such a systematic analysis specifically of housing policies is found in R.C. Walker and M. Barcham, *Comparative Analysis of Urban Indigenous Housing in Canada, New Zealand, and Australia*, a research report commissioned by the National Aboriginal Housing Association (NAHA) and the Central Mortgage and Housing Corporation (CMHC) of Canada in 2007. This report concisely describes current indigenous housing circumstances in those three countries as it relates to affordability, crowding, state of repair, ownership, homelessness, and residential mobility. The authors summarize urban indigenous housing interventions in the three countries; they then provide examples of innovative indigenous housing initiatives as well as self-management.

The year prior to the production of that report, the Bridges and Foundations Project conducted an invited series of meetings with our research counterparts, government housing agencies, urban indigenous communities, and housing activists in Australia and New Zealand with the intention of exchanging information on urban indigenous housing.

The present research being conducted into service delivery in urban Aboriginal communities in Australia draws explicit comparisons with Canada. These researchers' comparative review of the Canadian experience has led, in turn, to some tentative conclusions about the implications for developing principles for delivering appropriate and effective housing assistance to urban indigenous people in Australia; conversely, Canadians have much to learn from their Australian counterparts in these respects.

## An Aboriginal Perspective on Research Ethics and Methodology

The specific research projects conducted under the auspices of the Bridges and Foundations Project as a whole represented diverse methodologies, including: random sample surveys of neighbourhood residents; neighbourhood community meetings; focus groups; contracted surveys of band members living in the city and off-reserve; contracted surveys of clients of indigenous housing organizations; demographic analysis of original data contracted with the City and Statistics Canada; analysis of secondary demographic data; in-depth interviews with particular respondents on specific topics; studies of specific topics not involving interviews; creation and implementation of innovative programs; workshops and a design charrette; analysis of existing housing programs and market trends; housing field projects; analysis of collaboration and partnering; development of housing manuals; documentary photography; work with the City on race relations; extensive and consistent use of secondary sources and data; and so on.

Three main features of the Bridges and Foundations research were community-based research, community–university collaboration, and an Aboriginal perspective and involvement. First, the Bridges and Foundations Project pre-eminently emphasized community-based research. Community-based research is, by definition, research *done by* the community; ideally it should be research *conceived by* the community, originating in community discussions and meetings; moreover, it should be research *for* the community. Of course, this in turn implies some fairly clear understanding of how 'the community' is conceived; for example, it could represent all residents of a city, or just the Aboriginal residents, or residents of particular neighbourhoods. However, 'the community' may be defined for the purposes of a research project: it is that community which identifies the focus of the study and the issues to be studied or discerned; that establishes the conduct of the research, the recruitment of researchers, and the samples that will be surveyed; and that, after field research has been completed, processes the data, interprets the findings, and, most important, uses the information gathered and disseminates it back to the community.

A recent exhibit of the Centre for the Study of Cooperatives at the University of Saskatchewan explained that 'community-based research aims not merely to advance understanding, but also to ensure that knowledge contributes to making a concrete and constructive difference in the world.' In more traditional research models, the research questions and methods employed tend to be designed completely by the researcher; community-based research differs from this in that it involves researchers and community groups working together on a common problem: Community-based research is a collaboration between community groups of researchers for the purpose of creating new knowledge or understanding about a practical community issue in order to bring about change. The issue is generated by the community and community members participate in all aspects of the research process. Community-based research therefore is collaborative, participatory, empowering, systematic and transformative.

Second, while community-based research may be viewed as an alternative to academic (university-based) research, collaboration between university and community is often the actual reality, as reflected in most of the research conducted for the Bridges and Foundations Project. Indeed, community-based research has often profited from close collaboration with academic expertise, in any number of ways from start to finish in research projects. University academics tend to possess more research capability and methodological training than community personnel (although the latter may have considerable research skills as well as more experience in community-based research). Conversely, university research has been greatly enhanced through such collaboration, which should put universities far more in touch with 'the real world.' This has already been recognized by the Social Sciences and Humanities Research Council (SSHRC), especially through the Community–University Research Alliances (CURA) Program, which during the past decade has supported a large and increasing number of highly relevant social research projects across Canada, including the Bridges and Foundations Project. According to the SSHRC, the purpose of the CURA Program was 'to support the creation of alliances between community organizations and postsecondary institutions which, through a process of ongoing collaboration and mutual learning, will foster innovative research, training and the creation of new knowledge in areas of importance for the social, cultural or economic development of Canadian communities.' Among the specific objectives of the program were to 'promote sharing of knowledge, resources and expertise between postsecondary institutions and organizations in the community' and to 'reinforce community decision-making and problem-solving capacity.' The program emphasized communities and post-secondary institutions working together 'as equal partners in a research endeavour … centred on themes or areas of mutual importance to the partners.' Thus the SSHRC 'expects that partners will develop the capacity to work together effectively (ie., community organizations will develop the capacity to shape research agendas and postsecondary institutions to work with communities).'

Community–university partnerships intersect with multistakeholder approaches to decision making and multidisciplinary research. This intersection has been influenced by several trends in the social sciences, including an increasing appreciation of the role of social scientific inquiry to address pressing human problems by empowering individuals and communities through research, thus facilitating positive social change; growing dissatisfaction with traditional research methods that have consistently failed to produce desired social change; and increasing awareness (if not outright hostility) from marginalized communities after years of traditional research by outsiders has failed to effect positive change in their situation (Williams 2002). In community-based research, collaborative ideals are embedded in the formal relations of university researchers and community organizations. This implies a redistribution of the power balance between the 'observer and the observed': in traditional research methodology, the researcher and subjects are in an asymmetrical relationship wherein the academic researcher is assumed to be in the best position to decide community needs; whereas community-based research is characterized by mutual engagement of researchers with community in all possible steps of the research project. Thus local community members are recognized as possessing valued insights, experience, and problem-solving skills, making them indispensable participants. Most important, the research is viewed as a learning process both for researchers and for community members, and this generates new knowledge that is beneficial to both the university and the local community; moreover, all participants have equal ownership rights over the results of this mutual collaboration (Williams 2002; Kitchen and Muhajarine 2008; Williams et al. 2008; Randall et al. 2008).

Third, it is vital to recognize that a unique Aboriginal perspective may affect community-based research and thereby university–community collaboration in research. Increasing attention has been devoted in recent years to this Aboriginal perspective and to Aboriginal involvement in research; to the operationalization of principles of community-based partnerships when Aboriginal people are involved; to guiding principles in obtaining essential Aboriginal community consent; to involvement of the Aboriginal community in actual conduct of the research; and to that community's subsequent access to and ownership of disseminated information. An effective community-based research partnership should involve agreement on principles and protocols; these should be implicit in research design, facilitate results that are beneficial and significant to the community, and generate policy-relevant research that is supportive of community control and community capacity-building.

Aboriginal people have long been viewed as subjects or objects of research rather than as drivers of research projects. Research has long been perceived – not incorrectly – as benefiting universities and academics rather than Aboriginal people and communities. Research results have not been provided to communities. Aboriginal people have not been involved in project development, approval, management, conduct, and interpretation, or in the communication of results (Anderson and Spence 2008). There has been a lack of Aboriginal involvement in data and contextual analysis, and this has possibly led to misinterpretation of results (although certainly views of participants can differ). There are problematic views of 'Indigenous knowledge' and 'intellectual property' (ownership of information gathered). Aboriginal suspicion and distrust of academic research is well-founded and prevalent in the community. There is a need for 'culturally appropriate' research that satisfies Aboriginal people's perceptions of their needs. Effective partnerships are essential – but how, exactly, do these work at various levels?

The role of university research ethics committees in reviewing research proposals involving Aboriginal people has been re-examined in recent years. Within university bureaucracies, research ethics approval has been problematic. Certain community research projects may not involve the university, at least not directly (except perhaps for funding – although this may also not necessarily be the case). Most important, what exactly has been the Aboriginal involvement in particular projects? Research ethics boards and committees on campus and in the major research funding agencies have few if any Aboriginal members, despite these new ethical guidelines aimed at Aboriginal research, although this may be gradually changing. Well-intended university researchers, ones who are sensitive to Aboriginal community needs, expectations, and protocols, have been frustrated by stringent university ethics committees that have too often required practices that are alien to Aboriginal traditions, with the result that effective community research is disrupted. An example is the requirement that interview consent forms be signed when respondents may expect spontaneity and trust. This has been particularly problematic in subprojects conducted entirely by the Aboriginal community, which may have little use for 'university bureaucracy' or for interference in knowledge gathering that may be more pertinent to the community than to the university. The Aboriginal community may have a distinct understanding of their own traditional protocols but not a formalized approval process. What may be more important to Aboriginal community respondents and participants are respect (*manatsiwin* in Cree), understanding (*nisitohtamawin*), and kindness (*kisewatisiwin*).

Within the Bridges and Foundations Project, then, many of the specific projects were originally conceived by Aboriginal community members and organizations, and/or Aboriginal university professors, as well as non-Aboriginal academics in close collaboration with Aboriginal organizations. Even in some projects originally developed by non-Aboriginal researchers, Aboriginal researchers were employed to collect and analyse data; they were university students as well as neighbourhood residents trained in appropriate research techniques. All projects were initially vetted before the Planning Circle (the Project board), which included representatives of participating First Nations and Metis organizations. A sincere effort was made to ensure Aboriginal representation in every phase of research from start to finish: development, approval, management, actual conduct of research, analysis, and dissemination. This collaboration has been an enriching experience both for the universities and for the Aboriginal community, as well as for our partners in the City of Saskatoon and the homebuilding business. But we still have much to learn.

## Chapter Two

# Demographics

## The Complexity and Reliability of Urban Aboriginal Data

There are a number of problems in compiling and interpreting Aboriginal demographic data, including: the identification of Aboriginal peoples, overestimation versus underestimation of Aboriginal populations, the mobility and urbanization of Aboriginal people, the cultural uniqueness of urban Aboriginal residents, understanding their accommodation, and qualitative versus quantitative research.

There are several different ways of defining Aboriginal Canadians, hence of measuring their numbers. Even in national census data gathered by Statistics Canada every five years, various types of Aboriginal populations are counted in several different ways; so at the very least, census data may be subject to considerable interpretation and qualification (see, for example, Anderson et al. 1991; Kerr et al. 1996, 2003; Norris et al. 1996; Clatworthy et al. 2002; Siggner 2002). Aboriginal people in Canada may identify themselves in the census as primarily Aboriginal – either as 'North American Indians,' Metis, or Inuit, or as some combination of these – or more generally simply as Aboriginal. This will be referred to as 'Aboriginal identity,' which provides somewhat different data than 'Aboriginal ethnic origin.' In the latter case, an individual may similarly respond in the census count as North American Indian, Metis, or Inuit, or a combination of these, or simply as Aboriginal; however, this individual respondent may further indicate whether one or a combination of these is the only ethnic origin indicated (single ethnic origin), or whether other ethnic origins are being claimed in addition to an Aboriginal identity (multiple ethnic origins). Of course, this greatly complicates the counting of the Aboriginal population, for an individual could be entirely Aboriginal or only remotely claiming some sort of Aboriginal ancestry, possibly among many other ethnic origins. In other words, is an individual completely, mostly, half, a quarter, or less of Aboriginal ethnic origin? Moreover, 'Metis' is conventionally regarded as a unique ethnic identity in Canada, yet by definition it represents past mixing of North American Indian/Amerindian identity with European (usually French or Scottish). To further complicate matters, Metis organizations often draw distinctions among 'historic' Metis, the descendants in western Canada of early Native–European mixing (primarily the descendants of the Red River Metis in Manitoba); Metis as mixed Native–European traditional communities elsewhere in Canada; and simply any mixture of Native with European (or even occasionally non-European) anywhere in Canada. Metis have been defined by the Metis National Council as 'a person who self-identifies as Metis, is of historic Metis Nation ancestry, is distinct from other Aboriginal peoples, and is accepted by the Metis Nation.'

Again, another alternative classification (and counting) of the Aboriginal population is by official designation. Thus there is a count of Registered Indians (by Indian and Northern Affairs Canada rather than Statistics Canada, which is responsible for the census). However, 'official' Indians may include Treaty Indians as well as Status Indians who are not covered by particular treaties (as in the case of certain historic western tribes). Both types may have reserves, yet today a majority of band members – Registered Indians – are actually living off reserve; so a distinction can be drawn between on- and off-reserve Indians, both of which are now regarded as First Nations, although the term 'First Nation' may refer either to a particular Indian band, to an entire tribe or people, or to a particular reserve (i.e., a territory rather than a people). Nor are all North American Indians in Canada ultimately based on reserves or registered or in possession of an officially defined status. Many are Non-Status Indians, claiming North American Indian identity or ethnic origin yet counted neither as Registered Indians nor as Metis. In fact, the number of people claiming Aboriginal ancestry but not status is growing rapidly across Canada (*Maclean's*, 7 July 2008); moreover, changing legal definitions could soon mean the loss of status for hundreds of thousands of officially designated Canadian Indians. It is not unusual in Saskatchewan for neighbouring communities to exist, one designated as a reserve and the other as Non-Status and/or Metis. In Alberta there are Metis settlements officially designated by the provincial government, and in Manitoba there are officially recognized Metis communities, but neither of these is found in Saskatchewan (although there are many Saskatchewan communities that are traditionally Metis). To add to the confusion even more, non-Aboriginal or Non-Status Aboriginal women married to male Registered Indians may obtain registered status (Clatworthy 2003). Furthermore, band membership may be counted by particular bands on and off reserve, apart from 'official' INAC data. Still other demographic data may be produced from provincial health data. So for our purposes in this book we will utilize census data on Aboriginal identity as the most comprehensive and reliable for urban Aboriginal populations.

Not surprisingly, Aboriginal populations have been both overestimated and underestimated. They have been overestimated due to respondents to the ethnic origin question in the census claiming Aboriginal ethnic origin among other ethnic origins (multiple ethnic identification). They have also been overestimated for political reasons, such as to inflate a band's size in order to obtain more official recognition and financing. Similarly, in recent Metis elections in Saskatchewan, voter 'inflation' was a controversial issue. Some exaggerated estimations have even suggested that half the entire provincial population may be Aboriginal by 2050 (*Eagle Feather News*, February 2008). Yet Aboriginal populations have also been *under*estimated. In 1996, 77 reserves were either not at all or incompletely enumerated in the census, as were 30 in 2001 and 22 in 2006 (Gionet 2008). Moreover, numerous Metis have not been enumerated as Metis because in the past they have claimed other ethnic origins (such as French) and played down their Metis identity. The Metis Nation of Saskatchewan is of the opinion that many Metis in Saskatchewan are still going uncounted – there could easily be double the number counted by the census, that is, somewhere between 90,000 and 120,000 (*Saskatoon StarPhoenix*, 17 January 2008; *Globe and Mail*, 16 January 2008). Siggner, among other analysts of Aboriginal demographic data, has drawn attention to the problem of individuals changing their ethnic identification, perhaps downplaying any Aboriginal identity when it may be an inconvenience, or re-emphasizing it whenever expedient or due to a regained pride in being Aboriginal (Siggner et al. 2001). In a recent paper (2003a), Siggner has noted an unexpected increase of 43% in Canada's Metis population since the previous census just five years ago. Yet rather than increasing, Metis fertility had been declining – in fact, it has been lower than for other Aboriginal peoples, though still higher than for the non-Aboriginal population in general. Siggner considers it more likely that this increase is due to such non-demographic factors as an increased awareness of Metis issues, together with a corresponding increase in interest in claiming or perhaps rediscovering Metis identification, as well as Metis politicization resulting in what demographers have been calling 'ethnic drift' or 'ethnic mobility,' whereby people tend to change their claimed ethnic affiliations from one census to the next (Guimond 1999, in White, Maxim, and Beavon 2003, in Newhouse and Peters 2003; Norris and Clatworthy 2003; Norris, Cooke, and Clatworthy 2003; Guimond, Robitaille, and Senecal 2008). However, while the intercensal change in Metis identification in Saskatoon has been substantial, it has not been as dramatic as across Canada.

Urban Aboriginal people have tended to be highly mobile, not only in movement between reserves or traditional communities and cities, but also *within* cities. Peters (2009) has argued that there are three myths about urban Aboriginal people: first, that they are abandoning reserves or rural areas and moving into cities; second, that the urban Aboriginal experience is primarily one of economic marginality; and third, that urban Aboriginal people are increasingly segregated. In this chapter an attempt will be made to determine more precisely the character of urban Aboriginal mobility between the reserves and the city, and thereby the extent of Aboriginal urbanization, as well as the relative concentration of Aboriginal residents in the poorest neighbourhoods, concomitant with their increasing dispersion throughout the city.

Still other problems encountered in analysing urban Aboriginal populations pertain to housing. An example is the question of crowding: 'officially,' a rental property may contain only a single family household, yet a not-infrequent reality is that several 'unofficial' persons may also reside in this one accommodation. The 'official' householder may feel obliged to accommodate relatives and even unrelated community members from the original reserve or community. So crowding may in effect be underestimated. Again, much the same could apply to estimates of homelessness: a contrast must be drawn between *absolute* homelessness (where people have no accommodation other than institutional shelters) and *relative* homelessness (where, lacking any accommodation of their own, they may depend on being accommodated in the homes of relatives and friends). Similarly, in data on housing conditions, how exactly are 'major' home repairs to be differentiated from 'minor' ones and in turn from 'regular' home maintenance?

*Qualitative* research is clearly needed in order to probe deeper into the relationship between housing conditions and quality of life. For example, what exactly do residents want and need? What is their own evaluation of quality of life in their neighbourhoods? Where do they wish to live, and why? What is the effect of a perceived lack of amenities and services? Do negative and stereotypical attitudes of the general population toward Aboriginal people have any bearing? What affects mobility? And what affects choice of type of housing? Why do so many Aboriginal residents rent? To what extent do residents really comprehend homeownership? While *quantitative* data are provided throughout this book (especially in this chapter), most of the research conducted under the auspices of the Bridges and Foundations Project was intentionally qualitative, aimed at searching for answers to important questions like these.

## Growth and Distribution of the Aboriginal Population of Saskatoon

*A Growing Aboriginal Population*

Aboriginal people in Canada now number over a million: 1,172,790 people identified as Aboriginal in the 2006 census, including 698,025 First Nations people and 389,785 Metis. Approximately 81% of the First Nations population consisted of Registered Indians; the remainder were Non-Status Indians. The Canadian Aboriginal population now comprises 3.8% of the total Canadian population. In just ten years (1996–2006) the Aboriginal population increased by 45% (First Nations population by 29%, Metis by 91%), compared to an increase of only 8% for the non-Aboriginal population (9% for the general Canadian population). At these present rates of growth, the total Aboriginal population has been projected to increase to more than 1.4 million in another five years (by 2011), while the First Nations population should reach about 800,000 and the Metis population at least 567,000. Between 1986 and 2006, the Aboriginal identity population more than doubled, from 464,655 to 1,172,790. In fact, it has been estimated that over the past decade the Aboriginal population has been increasing six times faster than the non-Aboriginal population (or five times faster than the general Canadian population); between 2001 and 2006, the Aboriginal population of Canada increased 20.1%, compared to just 5.4% for the general population. This increase was due not only to differential natural population growth rates – particularly higher Aboriginal fertility – but also to more Canadians self-identifying as Aboriginal, especially as Metis, as a consequence of ethnic mobility or drift. However, among Aboriginal populations the rates of natural increase as well as fertility rates tend to be considerably lower in urban places than on reserves or in traditional communities.

Currently, Saskatchewan exhibits the fastest rate of growth for any province (an annual increase of 1.53%). According to SaskTrends Monitor, this growth is 'unprecedented' in recent times; however, the provincial population is still barely over 1 million (1,033,381 in 2011, so a relatively small proportion of the Canadian population of over 34 million), and has been gaining an average of just 15,000 a year over the past four years. The current increase is due primarily to immigration (accounting for about 60% of the increase), also to the relatively higher growth rate of the Aboriginal population; however, despite the present economic boom, much of the Aboriginal population is not sharing in these better times. Interprovincial migration is currently contributing slightly to Saskatchewan's population increase; in the past, it usually resulted in a net loss. The Aboriginal population of the province has been steadily and rapidly increasing (e.g., from 130,190 in 2001 to 141,890 in 2006) and now represents at least 16% of the total provincial population (Anderson 2005). At the present provincial rate (+8.2% every five years), the Aboriginal population of Saskatchewan should increase to over 153,000 by 2011; however, at the much higher national rate of Aboriginal population growth (+14.5%), this population would exceed 162,000. The latest projections from Statistics Canada suggest that nearly one-quarter of the province's total population will be Aboriginal by 2031, the highest proportion for any province (*Saskatoon StarPhoenix*, 8 December 2011). By 2006 almost two-thirds of the Aboriginal people of Saskatchewan (64.4%, or 91,400) were people claiming only North American Indian identity (yet the count of Registered Indians was 90,720); they represented 13.1% of all Canadian Indians. The other third (33.9%, or 48,120) consisted of Metis, comprising 12.3% of all Metis in Canada. Few people claimed more than a single Aboriginal identity (just 625) – simply Aboriginal identity in general (1,530) or Inuit identity (215).

*Urbanization*

Rapid urbanization of the Aboriginal population has been apparent across Canada for the past several decades and especially in recent years (Siggner 2003a). Much media attention has been drawn to this rapid increase as being problematic – it has repeatedly been referred to as a population 'bomb' or 'explosion' (e.g., *Maclean's*, 11 November 1996; *Saskatoon StarPhoenix*, 24 and 29 June 2005; *Globe and Mail*, 16 January

2008). Back in 1951, few Aboriginal people were living in Canadian cities. Ten years later, in 1961, only 12.9% of the total Aboriginal population of Canada were urban residents and Aboriginal people still comprised less than 1.0% of the residents in major western Canadian cities, but progressive urbanization was underway. By 1971, 30.7% of the total Aboriginal population of Canada was living in urban places, and the numbers of urban Aboriginal residents were increasing rapidly in western cities. By 1981, while the actual rate of Aboriginal urbanization was slowing, over one-third (36.4%) of Canada's total Aboriginal population was urban. During the previous decade the absolute number of urban Aboriginal residents had doubled in Regina and Calgary, almost tripled in Winnipeg, Edmonton, and Vancouver, and quadrupled in Saskatoon. In 1991, Winnipeg had surged ahead with the largest number of residents claiming Aboriginal ancestry of any city in Canada. By the 2001 census a majority of Canadian Aboriginal people were urban. The 2006 Statistics Canada data revealed that now 53.2% of the total Aboriginal identity population of Canada was urban, forming approximately 10% of the total population of both Winnipeg and Saskatoon (Table 2.1). Winnipeg now contains both the largest number and highest proportion of Aboriginal residents of any CMA. Since 1991, metropolitan Saskatoon, despite its relatively small size in national terms, has been ranked sixth in absolute numbers of Aboriginal residents among CMAs in Canada. Saskatoon's 21,535 Aboriginal residents in 2006 were far fewer, but in terms of proportion, Saskatoon closely followed Winnipeg, with Aboriginal residents forming 9.3% of the CMA population and 9.8% of the city population (Anderson 2005). In fact, five years earlier, Saskatoon had a higher proportion than Winnipeg (9.0% compared with 8.1%); so at the time this was the highest Aboriginal proportion of any CMA in Canada. Of eleven CMAs in Canada with substantial numbers of Aboriginal residents, Saskatoon actually experienced the slowest increase: 6%, compared to 22% in Winnipeg and 60% in Montreal; yet Montreal had several thousand fewer Aboriginal residents (17,865) than much smaller Saskatoon, so its Aboriginal residents comprised only 0.5% of the metropolitan population. At the present rate, in another ten years almost two-thirds of the Aboriginal population of Canada will be urban. According to one recent analysis (2009), the urban Aboriginal population of Canada is now divided between larger cities over 100,000 population (29.1%) and smaller cities (20.4%); the remaining Aboriginal population lives on reserve (31.4%) and in rural places off-reserve (19.1%) – the latter would include traditional Metis and Non-Status Indian communities.

Table 2.1. Growth of Aboriginal population in selected Canadian census metropolitan areas, 1951–2006 (ranked by proportion of Aboriginal population in 2006)

| CMA | 1951 | 1961 | 1971 | 1981 | 1991 | 2001 | 2006 | Total population in 2006 | Aboriginal proportion in 2006 (%) |
|---|---|---|---|---|---|---|---|---|---|
| Winnipeg | 210 | 1,082 | 4,940 | 16,575 | 35,250 | 55,970 | 68,385 | 686,035 | 10.0 |
| Saskatoon | 48 | 207 | 1,070 | 4,350 | 11,920 | 20,455 | 21,535 | 230,855 | 9.3 |
| Regina | 160 | 539 | 2,860 | 6,575 | 11,020 | 15,790 | 17,105 | 192,435 | 8.9 |
| Edmonton | 616 | 995 | 4,260 | 13,750 | 29,235 | 41,295 | 52,100 | 1,024,825 | 5.1 |
| Calgary | 62 | 335 | 2,265 | 7,310 | 14,075 | 22,110 | 26,575 | 1,070,295 | 2.5 |
| Vancouver | 239 | 530 | 3,000 | 16,080 | 25,030 | 37,265 | 40,310 | 2,097,960 | 1.9 |
| Ottawa | – | – | 1,300 | 4,370 | 6,915 | 13,695 | 20,590 | 1,117,125 | 1.8 |
| Toronto | 805 | 1,196 | 2,990 | 13,495 | 14,205 | 20,595 | 26,575 | 5,072,070 | 0.5 |
| Montreal | 296 | 507 | 3,215 | 14,450 | 6,775 | 11,275 | 17,865 | 3,588,520 | 0.5 |

A rapid urbanization of the 'Native Indian' population in Saskatchewan occurred during the 1960s. The urban proportion within this population increased from just 5.5% in 1961 to 21.7% in 1971. Much of this change was in the two largest cities. By 1971, Regina had almost three times as many Aboriginal residents as Saskatoon. Since 1971, the urban Aboriginal population has continued to increase, although at a slower rate each decade. However, the Aboriginal population has been increasing faster in Saskatoon than in Regina, and by 1991, Saskatoon's Aboriginal population exceeded Regina's. Using identity rather than ethnic origin data, one may note that the Aboriginal identity population has increased both in absolute numbers and proportionately during the past decade (Table 2.2). Given the relatively moderate growth trend over the previous five years (2001–6), the number of Aboriginal residents was projected to reach about 23,000 in another five years (2011), although already the city's Aboriginal population has been estimated by Lorne Sully, the former manager of city planning, as 30,000. Today approximately one in every ten residents of Saskatoon is Aboriginal; however, the Aboriginal proportion of the city population is of course relative to the growth of the city population in general. Currently Saskatoon is growing more rapidly than at any time during the past four decades; in fact it is the fastest-growing major city in Canada (*Saskatoon StarPhoenix*, 29 December 2011; 12 January 2012; *Globe and Mail*, 12 January 2012). The Saskatoon CMA grew by 11.4% between 2006 and 2011 (the city

Table 2.2. Aboriginal population growth and proportion, Saskatoon CMA, 1991–2011

|        | Total CMA population | Aboriginal population | Proportion (%) |
|--------|----------------------|-----------------------|----------------|
| 1991   | 209,122              | 11,920                | 5.7            |
| 1996   | 219,056              | 15,550                | 7.5            |
| 2001   | 225,927              | 20,275                | 9.0            |
| 2006   | 230,855              | 21,535                | 9.3            |
| 2011*  | 272,000              | 23,000–30,000         | 8.5–11.0       |

*Projected estimate

proper went from 202,408 to 222,189, a 9.8% increase). However, this is very conjectural: Aboriginal demographic trends may be affected by such factors as in and out-migration, the changing economic situation, reserve and northern development, survival to older age cohorts, changing birth rate and especially a disproportion of youth, and even housing availability.

Yet it is clear that the Aboriginal population is increasing far more rapidly than the general population in Saskatoon. From 1996 to 2001, the city population grew by 3.1%, not the least due to the increasing Aboriginal population, which during the same period had more than double the rate of growth (6.6%), and an even higher rate of growth (7.3%) between 2001 and 2006. Yet the Metis population of Saskatoon increased in this period by 16%, and the First Nations population by little more than 2%. In 2006, 15.2% (21,535) of the 141,890 Aboriginal identity population of Saskatchewan was living within Saskatoon CMA. These Aboriginal residents of Saskatoon were divided mainly between those identifying themselves in the census as North American Indians and those identifying as Metis (Table 2.3). Of the 90,720 Registered Indians in Saskatchewan, 12.1% (10,970) made Saskatoon their home. Between 2001 and 2006, the number of Aboriginal residents was growing – albeit now quite slowly – in all Saskatchewan cities where they comprised a substantial proportion of the population; the proportion was also increasing except in Yorkton and Lloydminster. While it is true that Saskatoon has recently had the highest proportion of Aboriginal residents of any CMA in Canada, Aboriginal residents actually form far higher proportions in three smaller Saskatchewan cities (Table 2.4).

Reasons for the increasing Aboriginal population in Saskatoon include the following. Saskatchewan has one of the highest proportions of Aboriginal population of any Canadian province. This provides a

Table 2.3. Aboriginal population identities in Saskatchewan and Saskatoon, 2006

|  | Saskatchewan (%) | Saskatoon CMA (%) | Saskatoon City (%) |
|---|---|---|---|
| Total population | 968,160 | 230,855 | 202,340 |
| N. American Indian only | 91,400 (64.4) | 11,510 (53.4) | 10,860 (54.8) |
| Metis only | 48,120 (33.9) | 9,610 (44.6) | 8,605 (43.4) |
| All other Aboriginal | 2,370 (1.7) | 415 (2.0) | 355 (1.8) |
| Total Aboriginal | 141,890 (100) | 21,535 (100) | 19,820 (100) |

Table 2.4. Aboriginal identity population in Saskatoon compared with other Saskatchewan selected cities, 2006

|  | Total population | Aboriginal identity pop. | Aboriginal proportion | N. American Indian | Metis | Other Aboriginal incl |
|---|---|---|---|---|---|---|
| Saskatoon CMA | 230,855 | 21,535 | 9.3% | 11,510 | 9,610 | 415 |
| Saskatoon City | 202,340 | 19,820 | 9.8% | 10,860 | 8,605 | 355 |
| Regina CMA | 192,435 | 17,105 | 8.9% | 9,495 | 7,185 | 425 |
| Regina City | 179,246 | 16,535 | 9.2% | 9,265 | 6,855 | 415 |
| Prince Albert City | 39,800 | 13,570 | 34.1% | 6,715 | 6,680 | 175 |
| N. Battleford City | 17,310 | 3,550 | 20.5% | 2,250 | 1,240 | 60 |
| Yorkton City | 17,150 | 1,830 | 10.7% | 1,155 | 635 | 40 |
| Lloydminster, SK/AB | 26,745 | 2,220 | 8.3% | 785 | 1,345 | 90 |
| Lloydminster, SK only | 8,118 | 1,190 | 14.7% | 500 | 685 | 5 |

large pool of potential Aboriginal migrants into the city. The Aboriginal population of Saskatchewan has been increasing much faster than the provincial population: between 1996 and 2001, by 17% compared to 3.7%. Also, Aboriginal people in Saskatchewan have a relatively higher birthrate than the provincial population as a whole. The total fertility rate among Registered Indian women is higher in Saskatchewan than in any other province, while the regional patterns for Non-Status Indians and Metis are similar (although not quite as high). The Aboriginal population is much younger than the non-Aboriginal population in Saskatchewan. By 2001, half (49.9%) of the Aboriginal population of Saskatchewan was under the age of 20, compared to just over one-quarter (26.5%) of the non-Aboriginal population. The relatively higher migration out of Saskatchewan by non-Aboriginals indicates that the Aboriginal population tends to stay within the province. The demographic shift from predominantly rural to predominantly urban that has been occurring among Aboriginal people in Saskatchewan is part of a general trend across Canada. As many as 80% of the population of some First Nations is now living off reserve and especially in cities, and Saskatoon is a natural 'catchment area' for many reserves located in the central region. Thus it is likely that both the absolute number and proportion of Aboriginal residents will continue to increase in Saskatoon. Yet this may depend to some extent on positive net migration of Aboriginal people into the city. Considering that the proportion of Aboriginal residents has virtually doubled in just a single decade, if present trends continue – and if they are not counterbalanced by other factors that serve to substantially increase the non-Aboriginal resident population – then we can expect that in another decade the Aboriginal proportion may double again to approximately 20% (or one in every five residents). However, as we have cautioned, such an assumption could be affected by a complex range of factors.

*Migration into the City*

Movement between reserve and city has been much debated. One has to beware of the facile conclusion that urban Aboriginal populations are steadily growing at the expense of reserve and remote Aboriginal populations. For example, Michael Mendelson concluded in a study released by the Caledon Institute of Public Policy in June 2007 that reserve populations are relatively stable while urban First Nations populations may be slightly declining, but proportionately fewer First Nations people are urbanized than other Aboriginals. And Jeremy Hull of Prologica Research, Winnipeg, found that in 2000–1 more First Nations men and women actually migrated to reserves than left them, while birthrates were falling on reserves. Examination of recent five-year gross migration rates of the Aboriginal population in Saskatoon reveals that in-migration into this city has usually been matched, more or less, by out-migration; yet this may be changing in favour of in-migration. Recent research reveals that an increasing proportion of urban Aboriginal population consists of long-term or 'permanent' residents.

Norris (2002) has pointed out notable differences in migration types between Registered Indian, on the one hand, and Non-Status Indians and Metis on the other. Most striking has been the fact that among Registered Indians, movement between urban places accounted for

37.1% of all moves, compared to 59.1% for Non-Status and 52.5% for Metis (in other words, many Aboriginal migrants into urban places had previous urban experience). Movement from reserves or rural areas to urban areas accounted for 29.3% for Registered Indians, 20.5% for Non-Status Indians, and 19.9% for Metis. Other types of movements included between reserves, between rural places, or between reserves and rural places. Norris found that almost two-thirds of all Aboriginal migrants had actually moved between off-reserve locations. Moreover, reserves and other Aboriginal settlements were experiencing substantial net gains, while urban CMAs were experiencing net losses of Registered Indians, Non-Status Indians, and Metis. In addressing the question of the extent to which migration has contributed to the rapid increase of First Nations populations living off reserve, particularly in urban places, she and previous and subsequent demographic analysts have emphasized the significance of 'churn' – that is, migration to and from urban areas – as being more important than unidirectional population redistribution. This has had the effect of limiting urban growth (Siggner 1977; Trovato et al. 1994; Clatworthy 1995, 2001; Norris 1985, 2002; Norris, Cooke, and Clatworthy 2003; Clatworthy and Norris 2003, Norris and Clatworthy 2003; Norris et al. 2004). During the early 1990s by far the highest Aboriginal in-migration rate into the top ten Canadian cities with the most Aboriginal population happened to be in Saskatoon, which also had, however, one of the highest out-migration rates, giving this city the highest overall gross migration rate (in fact, only Saskatoon and Thunder Bay had positive net migration rates both for Registered Indians and other Aboriginals).

Factors or reasons for migration can be complex and would typically include both 'push' factors (causes of movement away from places of origin) and 'pull' factors (causes of movement into destinations). Migrants are pushed out of reserves and rural areas due to drug and alcohol abuse, suicide, feelings of despondency and dependence, little opportunity for personal advancement, and limited availability of adequate housing; and attracted to cities by reunification of families and friends, education and employment opportunities, access to social services and health care, and improved housing. Yet on the other hand, Aboriginal people may feel driven from cities by crime, drugs, racism, expensive housing and living, racism, and loneliness; and attracted back to the reserves or rural areas by the feeling that it is really 'home,' as well as by culture and cultural activities, friends and extended family, free services, freedom from taxation, and simply acceptance. Of course, there may be other considerations, such as gender – women are more likely than men to move for family and community-related reasons; relative youthfulness – older people may tend to be more reluctant to move; and proximity of a reserve to the city – which could be a particularly important factor determining 'churn.' Among others, Darnell (2011) has commented on 'nomadic legacies' and 'decision-making strategies' in moving between reserve and city. Migrants may be categorized by the frequency with which they move as well as by distance. The overall rates of migration for non-Registered Indians (221 per thousand) and Metis (209) are considerably higher than for Registered Indians (179), yet the rates for all Aboriginal subgroups were declining between 2001 and 2006.

The city acts as an attractive draw to Aboriginal people living in poor conditions with limited opportunities on reserve or in a northern com-munity. The city may seem to promise diverse opportunities. Our interviews with large numbers of Aboriginal residents of Saskatoon revealed that the motives for migration and mobility are very complex indeed. Statistics Canada has recently predicted that Saskatchewan's Aboriginal population may increase by 67,000 in the next decade and that one in five people in the province will be of Aboriginal ancestry (a far higher proportion than in neighbouring Alberta or Manitoba); yet only 12,400 of the 67,000 will live in Saskatoon or Regina – the vast majority of these added people – perhaps as many as 50,000 – will live on reserves, where economic opportunities are limited. Yet some caution must be exercised in concluding from the INAC analysis that a net increase in reserve populations reflects net migration from city to reserve rather than an exodus from reserves. This could be a rather misleading interpretation, insofar as reserve fertility rates are significantly higher than for urban Aboriginal people, and taking into consideration our research findings that long-term return migration from city to reserve may seem to be lessening. Despite certain attractions the reserve may offer, in the minds of most residents these generally tend to be outweighed by positive aspects of urban living.

No less than 42 of the 70 First Nations in Saskatchewan now have more band members living off reserve than on (INAC 2008). On one reserve over 90% of band members are now living off reserve; another two reserves have 80 to 89% living off reserve, eight 70 to 79%, seventeen 60 to 69%, and fourteen 50 to 59%. Increasing numbers of reserves have the majority of their band members no longer living on the reserve. The clear implication is that while reserve populations are continuing to increase, this certainly does not mean that band members are not leaving for the cities, although it is admittedly difficult to estimate the 'churn' effect with any real accuracy. At the least the temporal factor should be considered in any analysis of mobility. That is, how long do given Registered Indians reside in the city, or on reserve, and to what extent are these moves relatively permanent, long-lasting, or only temporary? And concerning the relative proximity of reserves to the cities, one has to be careful about jumping to facile conclusions. While it is true that now just one of the more isolated northern reserves has most band members living off reserve, four more reserves have significant proportions (almost half of band members) living off reserve, although generally these more isolated reserves do have relatively lower proportions off reserve. But the closest reserve to Saskatoon, Whitecap Dakota, is almost equally divided between on reserve (49.2%) and off reserve (50.8%). It does seem that in general, more southern reserves tend to have higher proportions off reserve than more central and northern ones, with most of these people moving into Regina. But the safest generalizations have to be that there is considerable variability in the proportions of band members on each reserve in Saskatchewan currently living off reserve, yet also that the off-reserve populations seem to be steadily increasing.

*Aboriginal Mobility within the City*

Research on residential mobility of Aboriginal residents of Canadian cities has consistently found that Aboriginal people tend to move more frequently than non-Aboriginal people, even twice as often (e.g., Clatworthy 2000; Norris et al. 2000; Norris and Clatworthy 2003). Indeed, in Saskatoon, Aboriginal residents are far more mobile within the city than the general population (Table 2.5). According to the Aboriginal Peoples Survey (2006), one-third of all Aboriginal residents had lived at the same address five years ago (contrasted with 57% of non-Aboriginal residents), and almost 44% had moved at least once within the city in this time period, while another 24% had moved into the city, mainly for family reunification or to seek employment. These data would seem to portray two countervailing trends. On the one hand, the Aboriginal population of Saskatoon is quite mobile within the city, especially over a period of several years. On the other, longer-distance migration is becoming more limited; it is primarily within the province (Clatworthy et al. 1996). The commonly accepted view that Aboriginal people typically move frequently between reserve (or northern/rural

Table 2.5. Migration and mobility of Aboriginal residents and general population in Saskatoon, 2006

| | One Year Ago | | Five Years Ago | |
|---|---|---|---|---|
| | Aboriginal pop. (%) | General pop. (%) | Aboriginal pop. (%) | General Pop. (%) |
| Table 2.5 Total | 21,030 (100) | 228,070 (100) | 19,150 (100) | 217,295 (100) |
| Lived at same address | 13,410 (63.8) | 186,125 (81.6) | 6,305 (32.9) | 118,975 (54.8) |
| Lived at different address within same census subdivision | 5,250 (25.0) | 27,600 (12.1) | 8,330 (43.5) | 59,775 (27.5) |
| Lived at different address in province and different census subdivision | 1,780 (8.5) | 8,455 (3.7) | 3,365 (17.6) | 22,550 (10.4) |
| Lived in another province | 575 (2.7) | 4,010 (1.8) | 1,080 (5.6) | 10,625 (4.9) |

communities/areas) and the city may be increasingly questioned for accuracy. Our several surveys of numerous Aboriginal households in Saskatoon indicated that many Aboriginals have lived in this city for at least several years or longer and remain content to stay here. However, the relatively high rate of mobility within the city may reflect their quest for suitable housing in a satisfactory neighbourhood.

*Aboriginal Concentration and Dispersion in the City*

To determine the Aboriginal concentration in various neighbourhoods in Saskatoon, and dispersion throughout the city, an extensive analysis of all 60 neighbourhoods comprising the City of Saskatoon was conducted, indicative of trends over a five-year period (1996–2001), utilizing data at the neighbourhood (rather than census tract) level contracted with the City and Statistics Canada. A number of interesting conclusions were drawn from this analysis. First, the concentration of the Aboriginal population in almost all inner-city neighbourhoods was continuing to increase (and had reached 48.4% in Pleasant Hill, which soon had an Aboriginal majority, and 43.5% in Riversdale). Second, the increasing Aboriginal population was steadily moving westward and northward beyond the inner city, increasing in most of these neighbourhoods and reaching substantial levels (between 19.8% and 38.3%). Third, Aboriginal residents were starting to penetrate outlying mixed or predominantly middle-class neighbourhoods – in fact, in three of these neighbourhoods, Aboriginal residents had already formed close to 10% of the local population by 2001. Almost all neighbourhoods in the city revealed increases in Aboriginal proportions; and only a couple of neighbourhoods at the time had no Aboriginal residents. Aboriginal people comprised at least 10% in 21 neighbourhoods by 2001. All other neighbourhoods in the city had less than 10% of residents who were Aboriginal; however, these ranged from several that were close to 10% down to three newer neighbourhoods with no known Aboriginal residents at all. In sum, while it remains true that the largest concentration of the Aboriginal population is still found in the poorest inner-city neighbourhoods, Aboriginal residents are increasingly found dispersed throughout the city, with some of the fastest increases in economically diverse west-end neighbourhoods.

Most Aboriginal residents no longer reside in the poorest inner-city neighbourhoods of Canadian cities (Deacon et al. 2001; Gareau et al. 2002; Maxim, White, and Beavon 2003; Maxim, Keane, and White 2003). Evelyn Peters (at the time Canada Research Chair in Identity and Diversity: The Aboriginal Experience, at the University of Saskatchewan) co-produced the online *Atlas of Urban Aboriginal Peoples* in 2005 and has repeatedly challenged the presumed propensity of Aboriginal people to concentrate in the poorest areas of Saskatoon (2007a, 2007b, 2009; Wouters and Peters 2010; Starchenko and Peters 2010). Yet the highest concentration and largest numbers of Aboriginal people in any particular neighbourhood in Saskatoon are in fact here in this area (Iheduru 2004a and 2004b). Moreover, given the greater diversity in housing types in these neighbourhoods than found in more affluent neighbourhoods, who exactly lives in which sorts of housing could be relevant, although there may well be something of a propensity emerging now for Aboriginal families to upgrade their housing type as they increasingly become owners rather than renters, instead of electing to move out of the familiar neighbourhood where they have relatives and friends. But clearly, Aboriginal people are spreading throughout the city. In absolute numbers, at least 4 neighbourhoods already contained over 1,000 Aboriginal residents ten years ago, while another 8 neighbourhoods widely scattered throughout the city had between 500 and 900 Aboriginal residents, and another 34 had between 100 hundred and 500; only 10 had less than 100 and 3 had none at all.

*Implications of Urban Aboriginal Mobility*

Norris (2002) and others (CMHC 1996, 2000) have summarized the implications of Aboriginal mobility in the urban context. The relatively high mobility of Aboriginal residents may have significant implications for their well-being. Across Canada the urban Aboriginal population is in a high state of flux, characterized by family instability and dissolution, a high proportion of female lone-parent families, economic marginalization, and high victimization from crime. Constant 'churn' may lead to residential instability; moreover, high population turnover may affect both urban and rural communities and in turn the provision of services in such areas as housing, health, employment, and education (Beavon and Norris 1999). Norris has argued that implied in the myth that urban growth is largely due to migration from reserves to urban areas is the belief that characteristics of urban Aboriginal populations are those largely associated with migrants. So these misunderstandings could adversely affect policy development. Residential movers and non-movers tend to have differing socio-economic characteristics and service needs. Education can be particularly affected by high mobility; certain neighbourhoods having relatively greater proportions of Aboriginal residents tend to have high turnover rates in students. Moreover, high mobility may adversely affect student performance. A major challenge for urban Aboriginal people is maintaining their cultural identity and developing urban institutions that reflect their Aboriginal values and traditions; urban institutions may often conflict with these values, leading to social isolation. There is a pressing need for urban Aboriginal people to develop their own institutions, which may help foster social cohesion and reduce isolation and marginalization. High mobility or 'churn' leads to weaker social cohesion in communities and neighbourhoods. Aboriginal people living in these areas thus tend to exhibit greater social problems (such as poor educational attainment, divorce, crime, suicide); increased social disorganization leads in turn to greater levels of 'churn.'

The next section of this chapter provides a contemporary socio-demographic profile of Aboriginal residents of Saskatoon and examines in some detail the extent to which such conclusions still seem accurate.

## Socio-demographic Profile of the Aboriginal Population of Saskatoon

This section of the chapter provides a socio-demographic profile of the Aboriginal residents of Saskatoon, successively examining their marital status and family structure, age cohorts, educational attainment, labour force participation, poverty, housing and living conditions, and finally the preservation and recreation of urban Aboriginal culture.

*Marital Status and Family Structure*

The current revised census definition describes a census family as composed of a married or common-law couple (regardless of gender), with or without children, or of a lone parent living with at least one child in the same dwelling. The 2011 census found that average household size has been decreasing across Canada. There are now more one-person households (22.6%) than those consisting of one couple with children aged 24 or younger; 39.5% of families have children but a larger proportion, 44.5%, do not; moreover 13.5% of Canadians aged 15 or over are living alone. Concomitantly, a decline in the number of persons per household in the general Saskatchewan population has become evident, due to decreasing fertility rates (hence average family size), children leaving home later, an aging population resulting in more single-person households occupied by widows or widowers, and an increase in lone-parent families. However, with the exception of the last point, these trends have applied less to urban Aboriginal families, although average family size has similarly decreased with urbanization. Demographers have often attributed lower family size in cities to the higher cost of living; put simply, it costs more to maintain larger families in cities than in rural communities or reserves. Moreover, both parents are more likely to be gainfully employed in urban places, especially compared to Indian reserves.

Looking at marital status, there is still a greater propensity for Aboriginal couples to have common law relationships. In the province as a whole, in 2006 among Aboriginals, 37.9% of currently married and common law couples (excluding separated, divorced, and widowed) were in common law relationships, and 40.1% in Saskatoon (compared to just 12.8% in the general population). Moreover, the incidence of common law relationships among urban Aboriginal people seems to be increasing (Table 2.6).

Back in 1996, the proportion of Aboriginal families in Saskatoon that were headed by lone parents (32.5%) was almost three times as high as the proportion in the general population (11.2%) (see Engeland et al. 1997). Ten years later, only one-quarter (25.3%) of Aboriginal families were headed by lone parents, whereas the proportion in the general population had *increased* to 17.8%. So the propensity of having an

Table 2.6. Marital status of adult Aboriginal population, Saskatoon, 1996, 2001, 2006

|  | 1996 | % | 2001 | % | 2006 | % | Total city population in 2006 | % |
|---|---|---|---|---|---|---|---|---|
| Total Aboriginal population, aged 15 and over | 9,195 | 100 | 11,810 | 100 | 14,060 | 100 | 190,755 | 100 |
| Never married (single) | 5,430 | 59.1 | 7,250 | 61.4 | 8,780 | 62.4 | 69,350 | 36.4 |
| Legally married, not separated | 1,975 | 21.5 | 2,655 | 22.5 | 3,340 | 23.8 | 91,620 | 48.0 |
| Legally married, and separated | 645 | 7.1 | 630 | 5.3 | 575 | 4.1 | 4,975 | 2.6 |
| Common law* | – | – | 1,730 | 14.7 | 2,235 | 15.9 | 13,465 | 7.1 |
| Divorced | 915 | 10.0 | 995 | 8.4 | 985 | 7.0 | 13,875 | 7.3 |
| Widowed | 225 | 2.5 | 275 | 2.3 | 375 | 2.7 | 10,935 | 5.7 |

* In 1996, marital status refers to legal marital status, whereas in 2001, marital status includes common law relationships.

'illegitimate' child (*pakwatosan* in Cree) is far higher for urban Aboriginal people than for the non-Aboriginal population. However, detailed analysis by neighbourhood revealed wide variations in 1996: among Aboriginal families in neighbourhoods having at least 10% Aboriginal population, the proportion of lone-parent families ranged from as high as 68.8% to as low as 23.8%. Also, in three neighbourhoods a majority of Aboriginal families were headed by single parents; in another ten neighbourhoods between one-third and one-half of the families; and in four neighbourhoods between one-quarter and one-third. In Winnipeg it has recently been estimated that as many as 89% of single-parent households are headed by Aboriginal women (Aulinger 2010). The Aboriginal Peoples Survey (2006) found that less than half (46%) of Aboriginal children aged 14 years and older in Saskatoon live with both parents; also, 40% live with a lone mother (compared to 16% in the non-Aboriginal population), 6% with a lone father (compared to 3% in the non-Aboriginal population), 4% with grandparents, and another 4% with other relatives (less than 1% among non-Aboriginal people).

A considerable proportion of Aboriginal females in the city aged 15 and over were engaged in major or substantial amounts (15 to over 30 hours a week) of housework (48.7%) and child care (41.1%); they spent far less time spent caring for seniors, according to Statistics Canada data in 2001 (Table 2.7). Two considerations arise here: first, the

Table 2.7. Aboriginal females in Saskatoon aged 15 and over engaged in housework and child and senior care, 2001 (%)

|  | Housework | Child care: | Senior care |
|---|---|---|---|
| Over 30 hrs/week | 26.7 | 33.8 | 2.8 |
| 15–29 | 22.0 | 7.3 | 5.3 |
| 5–14 | 29.8 | 10.6 | 4.0 |
| Less than 5 | 21.5 | 48.3 | 92.0 |

proportion of seniors among the Aboriginal population is far less than among the general population; and second, in traditional Aboriginal culture seniors themselves play a significant role in the family in unpaid housework and child care.

*Age Cohorts*

The Aboriginal population of Canada is young: according to the 2006 census, almost half (48%) of the Aboriginal population in Canada was under the age of 25 (compared to 31% of the non-Aboriginal population; the median age was 27, whereas it was 40 for the general population. In Saskatchewan almost half (47%) of the total Aboriginal population was under the age of 20. Data from Statistics Canada and the Aboriginal Peoples Survey indicate that in 2006 in Saskatoon the median age of Aboriginal residents was 23 (37 for non-Aboriginals). The proportion of Aboriginals aged under 25 was 55% (34% for non-Aboriginals); Aboriginal residents comprise 28.3% of all residents under the age of 25. Yet in Saskatoon the proportion of Aboriginal youth under 20 has actually been slowly declining: from 49.8% in 1996 to 47.6% in 2001 and 44.9% in 2006. Whereas only 24.2% of the non-Aboriginal population in this city (26.1% of the total city population) were under the age of 20 in 2006. Even more striking is that 35% of all Aboriginal residents were under the age of 15 (compared to just 17% of non-Aboriginal residents). Aboriginal children aged 14 and under comprised 17% of all children in the Saskatoon CMA, and 38% of First Nations children and 30% of Metis children were in this age cohort. Moreover, in addition to this, a significant proportion of Aboriginal residents are relatively young adults; more than another third are in their thirties and forties. At the same time, the proportion of seniors aged 65 and over was far less among the Aboriginal population of the city (only 2.5% or 530 people) than among non-Aboriginal residents (13.3%). Life expectancy rates for the Aboriginal population in Saskatchewan continue to lag behind those for the non-Aboriginal population, though the gap is steadily closing. In 2005, Statistics Canada projected that in little more than ten years, Aboriginal people of working age (15–65) could number 1 million, representing 3.4% of the total Canadian labour force; moreover, the number of young Aboriginal adults in their twenties entering the labour market would grow by 40%, compared to just 9% in the general population. In Saskatchewan, as high as 30% of young adults could be Aboriginal, according to the Urban Aboriginal Peoples Study (UAPS 2010, 25). Other estimates have projected that in ten years as many as half the people under the age of 18 and one-quarter of those in their twenties will be Aboriginal. In 2006 the median age of the Aboriginal population was 26.5 years (compared to 39.5 years for the non-Aboriginal).

An increasing number of young Aboriginal people are born and raised in the city, with little or no familiarity with reserve or rural life. Moreover, the surplus of youth on reserves will lead inevitably to further and perhaps increased migration into the cities. Municipal and provincial investment in education, and encouragement of urban Aboriginal youth to enter the labour force in meaningful positions, are already essential and will become even more so. As Lorne Sully, a past senior urban planner for Saskatoon, has commented, 'This young population needs a renewed confidence in the future. Much has been reported about the past. Now we need to concentrate on future opportunity … Much more work is required if the youth of the Aboriginal community is to fully contribute to the economic life of Saskatoon' (*Saskatoon StarPhoenix*, 27 December 2010). Urban development geared for Aboriginal youth, such as recreational facilities and the existing youth theatrical training program, is becoming increasingly vital. And as we will point out again later, so is the inculcation of Aboriginal culture in urban Aboriginal youth; as columnist Stan Cuthand recently commented, 'Elders tell us that we have to know where we came from so we will know where we are going' (*StarPhoenix*, 18 January 2008). Nationally, some analysts – including the president of the National Aboriginal Achievement Foundation – have predicted that the Aboriginal youth population is expected to quadruple in the next decade, and with that is a looming need to educate and train Native teens, almost 70% of whom drop out of high school, for private-sector jobs. It is noteworthy that 69% of First Nations youths attending high school do so in urban settings (*StarPhoenix*, 22 September 2003). According to Doug Elliott of

*SaskTrends Monitor*, few Indian bands will be able to create enough employment on reserve to build an economy and keep people working on reserves; so the migration of Aboriginal people to large urban centres will continue. Murray Lyons, Business Editor of the *StarPhoenix*, agrees: young Aboriginals will need to settle down in Saskatchewan cities in order to find suitable employment. 'A workforce can't be developed in isolated areas – it has to be where the jobs are' (*StarPhoenix*, 30 June 2005). Leading the way is the Saskatchewan Institute of Indian Technologies (SIIT), an Aboriginal trade school located in Saskatoon, which provides counselling and employment guidance to students through its Career Village.

## Educational Attainment

While there have been indications of an improvement in the educational levels attained by Aboriginal people across Canada, Aboriginal people continue to lag well behind non-Aboriginal Canadians. According to the 2006 Census, over one-third of Aboriginal adults aged 25 to 64 had less than high school education (which was more than double the proportion found among non-Aboriginal Canadians); proportionately fewer Aboriginals had achieved only a high school diploma; and more than two-and-a-half times as many non-Aboriginals had experienced university education (Table 2.8). Further, national data revealed that while off-reserve Aboriginal people have been closing the education gap, First Nations people still on reserves continue to lag far behind the non-Aboriginal population in levels of education attained (Table 2.9). Thus, 40% of Aboriginal people in their early twenties (more like 60% on reserve) lack a high school diploma (compared to just 13% among non-Aboriginals). The Canadian Council on Learning estimates that the cost to society for every person not finishing high school is $4,750 per year in justice costs, social assistance, and forgone tax revenue (*Winnipeg Free Press*, 26 November 2011). The most recent data suggest that First Nations youth on reserves are six times less likely to graduate from high school than the rest of the young Canadian population. In addition, only 8% of Aboriginals have a university degree (compared to 23% of non-Aboriginals).

The total annual operating costs for reserve schools run into hundreds of millions of dollars in some provinces, while especially in more remote reserves as many as one-third of all children continue to be sent to off-reserve schools. Yet reserve schools across Canada are estimated to receive 20% to 30% less financing per student ($2,000 to $5,000) than

Table 2.8. Educational achievement, Aboriginal and non-Aboriginal population aged 25–63, Saskatoon, 2006 (%)

|  | Aboriginal | Non-Aboriginal |
|---|---|---|
| Less than high school | 34 | 15 |
| High school diploma | 21 | 24 |
| University | 11 | 28 |
| Community college/ trade school | 33 | 32 |

Table 2.9. Education attained, Canadian and Aboriginal and reserve population of school age and older, 2006 (%)

|  | Canadian population | Aboriginal population | Reserve population |
|---|---|---|---|
| No certification | 20 | 27 | 54 |
| High school diploma | 25 | 27 | 16 |
| College/technical educ. | 30 | 32 | 23 |
| University | 25 | 15 | 7 |

other schools. Reserve schools in Saskatchewan have experienced years of chronic underfunding. Among Saskatchewan First Nations, frustration and anger are increasing over the perceived delay in the federal government's commitment to reserve schools. This government promised $275 million in 2012, but this funding would be spread nationally over three years, with $100 million earmarked for early literacy programming and $175 million to build or renovate reserve schools, leaving no new funding for operating costs, which is where funding is most needed. Reserve schools in Saskatchewan have an estimated 16,000 children. Provincial schools currently receive over $10,000 per student (Francophone schools $18,800), whereas reserve schools, a federal responsibility, currently receive only $6,400. This gap of $3,600 per student between provincial and federal funding equates to a shortfall of $54.5 million just this present year, in basic funding for school operating costs (excluding new construction and renovation). The FSIN was understandably extremely displeased with this situation, when the federal government then announced further cuts in funding to First Nations administration in order to 'create conditions for healthier, more self-sufficient Aboriginal communities.' The present $1.6 million that the FSIN receives for core funding will be reduced to just $500,000 with a couple of years (*Saskatoon StarPhoenix*, 5 and 7 Sept. 2012).

Some analysts have argued recently that nationally, the education gap between Aboriginal and non-Aboriginal people has actually been widening and that Aboriginals are being left behind in education. John Richards, a professor in the graduate public policy program at Simon Fraser University and a chair in social policy at the C.D. Howe Institute, has suggested in a report titled *A Disastrous Gap – How High Schools have Failed Canada's Aboriginal Students*, released by the C.D. Howe Institute in October 2008, that lagging education of Native students must be addressed:

> Based on the 2006 census, improvement in Aboriginal education over the last generation has been disappointing ... The high school completion rate of Aboriginal students seriously lags that of non-Aboriginals, and the former are not catching up. At all education levels, the gaps between Aboriginal and non-Aboriginal education levels are larger among the younger populations. [Y]et Metis students fare considerably better than those who identify themselves as First Nation or Indian ... A marginalized community such as Aboriginals living in a modern economy can only escape poverty through an educational transformation.

However, the education profile of the Aboriginal population has been changing markedly across Canada in some respects. Already back in 1999, a Statistics Canada report on the educational achievement of young Aboriginal adults (Tait 1999) pointed out that the proportion of Aboriginal college and university graduates had more than doubled in a single decade (1986 to 1996); that nearly one in five young Aboriginal adults no longer attending school had completed college or university in 1996; and that both Aboriginal men and women in their twenties had increased their educational attainment. Still, only 4% have a university education, one-quarter the rate of mainstream society (*Globe and Mail*, 10 April 2012).

In Saskatchewan, the high school graduation rate for Aboriginals remains poor: only about half of Aboriginal people in the province aged 15 and older complete high school (compared to about 80% of non-Aboriginals). Just 38% of Aboriginals who attended on-reserve schools in Saskatchewan had graduated from high school (although this was a higher rate than in neighbouring Alberta, 32%, and Manitoba, 28%). According to the provincial government's most recent education indicators report, 78% of Aboriginal students counted in grade eight in 2005–6 had made it to grade ten two years later; this compares with a general provincial rate of 91%. Also, 6.2% of Aboriginal students had dropped out by grade ten, compared to 3.5% of all students. Saskatchewan Metis also remained more likely than the non-Aboriginal population to have less than a high school education and were less likely to attain high school graduation or post-secondary education: 42.1% had less than high school education, 24.2% had completed high school (and perhaps some post-secondary), 13.6% possessed a trade certificate or diploma, another 13.4% a college diploma or certificate (but not a university degree), and just 6.7% a university degree.

The proportion of all 15 to 19 year olds not currently being educated (i.e., employed, unemployed, and not in the labour force) in Saskatchewan in 2008 was about 23%, compared to 20% in Canada and just 15% in other OECD countries. The Canadian School Boards Association recommended in January 2008 that the federal government consider eliminating income tax for Aboriginals for a set period of time following high school graduation as an incentive to counter the problematic national dropout rate for Aboriginals of almost 50%. Saskatchewan already offers tax savings of up to $5,500 for all high school and post-secondary graduates as an incentive to keep them in the province.

Yet the gap between Aboriginal and non-Aboriginal has been growing rather than decreasing. A study released by Statistics Canada in January 2008 found that off-reserve Indian and Metis adults in Saskatchewan were less literate in 2003 than their non-Aboriginal counterparts: 70% of First Nations people and 56% of Metis were below level 3 (the minimum considered necessary for an individual to be able to function in a complex, knowledge-based society), compared to 37% of non-Aboriginal people; in urban areas, 67.5% of urban First Nations people and 52% of urban Metis were literate, compared to 30% in the general population. A relatively lower level of Aboriginal literacy across Canada and in Saskatchewan is limiting Aboriginal progress, although it has been suggested that 'Aboriginal education is everyone's responsibility.' In Saskatchewan, efforts are being made to improve Aboriginal literacy.

Approximately one in five (20.9%) of Saskatchewan elementary through high school students during the past academic year were self-declared as Aboriginal; similarly, Aboriginal students comprise almost 20% of all students currently enrolled in Saskatoon Catholic schools. The latest data for the City of Saskatoon reveal persistent problems. According to the 2010 Education Indicators Report of the Province of Saskatchewan, both male and female Aboriginal students lagged behind non-Aboriginal students in all subjects measured in grades ten and eleven, as well as on provincial standardized testing of writing skills. Of students who had entered grade ten in 2007–8, 74.1% had graduated as expected within a couple of years; whereas just 32.5% of Aboriginal students had graduated on schedule (we may extrapolate the dropout rate for this cohort of students as 4.3% for all students and 9.4% for Aboriginal students). When a separate Aboriginal high school was founded as the Native Survival School in 1981, the dropout rate for Aboriginal high school students in the city was about 90%; last year (2009), however, only two students out of thirty reportedly graduated from grade twelve (*Saskatoon StarPhoenix*, 10 January 2011). The rates of Aboriginal high school attendance and especially graduation still lag behind the general population average, with boys behind girls.

Yet the cities provide more opportunities for education, and urban Aboriginal youth are clearly becoming better educated. Data on the highest level of education attained in the Aboriginal population aged 15 and over in recent years reveal that significantly higher levels are attained in the urban context than in the province as a whole. For example, in 2001, 48% of the Aboriginal population aged 20 to 24 living off reserve had not completed secondary school, compared to 26% of the general population. The Aboriginal Peoples Survey (2006) reported that 31% of male Aboriginal residents of Saskatoon aged 25 to 64 had not completed a high school education (compared to 14% of non-Aboriginal); among females the proportion was 27% (compared to 10% of non-Aboriginal). Aboriginal youth in Saskatoon are almost equally as likely as non-Aboriginal to be attending school (60% compared to 63%). In fact, Aboriginal people are actually more likely to *return* to school later in life: for example, in Saskatoon 32% of Aboriginal females aged 25 to 34 were currently attending school, compared to just 21% of non-Aboriginal. Reasons given by Aboriginals aged 15 to 34 for not attending school differed somewhat by gender: among males, the most commonly reported reasons were that they 'wanted to work' or were 'bored with school,' whereas for females, pregnancy or childcare seemed more important.

The proportion of the Aboriginal population in Saskatoon that has completed a post-secondary degree, diploma, or certificate has been rising rapidly (Table 2.10). By 2001, one-third of the city's Aboriginal population aged 25 and over possessed a higher education degree, diploma, or certificate; five years later, this figure was 38.8%. The Aboriginal Peoples Survey (2006) went further, suggesting that almost half of Aboriginal residents of Saskatoon aged 25 to 64 have completed a post-secondary education (i.e., a university, college, or trade degree, diploma, or certificate). The proportion among females (50%) was higher than among males: 45%, compared to 63% overall of the non-Aboriginal

Table 2.10. Highest level of education attained, Aboriginal identity population aged 15 years and over, Saskatoon CMA, 1996–2006

| | Aboriginal aged 15 and over | | | | | | Aboriginal aged 35–64 | | Total CMA population aged 15+ | |
|---|---|---|---|---|---|---|---|---|---|---|
| | 1996 | % | 2001 | % | 2006 | % | 2006 | % | 2006 | % |
| Total | 9,200 | 100 | 11,810 | 100 | 14,060 | 100 | 5,725 | 100 | 187,695 | 100.0 |
| No completed degree/ certificate/ diploma | 6,625 | 71.9 | 7,830 | 66.3 | 5,460 | 38.8 | 1,720 | 30.0 | 41,495 | 22.1 |
| Completed high school graduation | 640 | 7.0 | 1,075 | 9.1 | 3,520 | 25.0 | 1,200 | 21.0 | 51,130 | 27.2 |
| Trade certificate/ diploma | 225 | 2.5 | 260 | 2.2 | 1,375 | 9.8 | 820 | 14.3 | 19,440 | 10.4 |
| Other non-university certificate/ diploma | 1,025 | 11.1 | 1,635 | 13.8 | 1,770 | 12.6 | 900 | 15.7 | 31,615 | 16.8 |
| University degree/ certificate/ diploma | 685 | 7.5 | 1,010 | 8.6 | 1,580 | 11.2 | 1,085 | 19.0 | 44,015 | 23.4 |
| Total with completed degree/ certificate/ diploma | 2,575 | 28.1 | 3,980 | 33.7 | 8,245 | 58.6 | 4,005 | 70.0 | 146,200 | 77.9 |

population in these age cohorts. Moreover, 15% of Aboriginals had completed a university degree, compared to one-quarter of non-Aboriginals. Aboriginal women in Saskatoon are more likely than men to complete a university degree: 18% of Aboriginal women aged 25 to 34 and 17% aged 35 to 64, compared to 13% of Aboriginal men aged 25 to 34 and 11% aged 35 to 64. These findings could reflect the fact that Saskatoon is the location of a variety of institutions of higher education with exclusive or substantial numbers of Aboriginal students.

Across Canada, post-secondary educational institutions have been encouraging Aboriginal students to enrol. The Aboriginal Peoples Survey found that in 2006, 16% of post-secondary Aboriginal students were attending universities, 42% community colleges, and 20% technical institutes and trade schools. Many of the 150 main community colleges in Canada were restructuring to meet the needs of Aboriginal students through targeted recruitment, adult education programs, partnerships with Aboriginal communities, specific curriculum, financial assistance, elders on campus, mentoring, and student support services. Several thousand Aboriginal students are enrolled at post-secondary educational institutions in Saskatoon: the University of Saskatchewan, the First Nations University of Canada (FNUC), the Saskatchewan Indian Institute of Technologies (SIIT), the Saskatchewan Institute of Applied Science and Technology (SIAST), and the Dumont Technical Institute (DTI). At former University of Saskatchewan, enrolment of students voluntarily self-identifying as Aboriginal has been increasing rapidly: 3% of students enrolled at this university self-declared as Aboriginal in 2000–1 compared to 9% in 2009–10; today the number of Aboriginal students is approaching 2,000 – approximately 10% of the total student body. The university administration wants this figure to reach 15% by 2020. Peter McKinnon, former university president, has recently commented that 'engaging the young Aboriginal population is the greatest imperative of our time … failing that could be our ruin' (*Saskatoon StarPhoenix*, 6 November 2010). This university contains a wide variety of specific Aboriginal programs and centres: Native Law, the Aboriginal Education Research Centre, the Aboriginal Learning Knowledge Centre, the Saskatchewan Urban Native Teacher Education Program (SUNTEP), the Northern Teacher Education Program (NORTEP), the Indian Teacher Education Program (ITEP), the Department of Native Studies, the Indigenous Peoples Program, the Aboriginal Justice and Criminology Program (ABJAC), the Aboriginal Students' Centre, the Aboriginal Business Administration Program, Aboriginal Public Administration, the Indigenous Peoples Resource Management Program, the Indigenous Peoples' Health Research Centre, and so on. Aboriginal students are now found in academic programs throughout the university, evidenced in the annual graduation powwow to honour First Nations and Metis graduates. Setting aside a temporary decline in Aboriginal enrolment at SIAST Kelsey Campus during the late 1990s, over the past several years enrolment has more than doubled: SIAST now has an estimated 2,500 students of Aboriginal ancestry on its four campuses in the province, and the institute has adopted a new strategy to attract and retain more Aboriginal students – a $5.5 million Aboriginal Student Achievement Plan (ASAP). Enrolment at SIIT has fluctuated recently but is currently the highest ever. So, too, was enrolment at the Saskatoon campus of the First Nations University of Canada and at the main campus of FNUC in Regina, although there have been serious declines in enrolment over the past several years, since this university has experienced administration problems.

The predecessor to FNUC was the Saskatchewan Indian Federated College (SIFC), which was founded in 1976 in an old elementary school building in Saskatoon by the Federation of Saskatchewan Indian Nations (FSIN), as a federated college of the University of Regina. FNUC was established in 2003 by the NDP provincial and Liberal federal governments. A state-of-the-art building was designed by leading Aboriginal Canadian architects and constructed on the University of Regina campus, augmenting other campuses in Saskatoon and Prince Albert. However, after years of accusations of misspending and mismanagement, and frequent dismissals and suspensions of administrators and faculty, the Canadian Association of University Teachers censured the university. Finally, in February 2010, first the Saskatchewan Party provincial government withdrew $5.2 million of annual funding, then the Conservative federal government another $7.3 million. Federal and provincial funding has been restored in stages; even so, the university's operating budget has been reduced by $3 million, which has resulted in 46 job cuts as well as curriculum reductions and an administrative reorganization. The Board of Governors, consisting largely of First Nations chiefs, was dissolved following a vote of lack of confidence led by Chief Lonechild of the FSIN. Senior administrators were dispatched on forced leaves of absence, and an extensive external report on the governance of this university recommended a complete restructuring and depoliticization of the university board. Complete closure of the university was anticipated; in fact, half of the main building on the Regina campus had long been occupied already by INAC offices. In May 2010 it was announced that the Saskatoon campus would close and that the building would be sold; this was bound to affect the active social work program based on that campus (which collaborated with the Bridges and Foundations Project). Serious damage has been done to the aspirations of an Aboriginal-controlled university that had become a model for possible development of similar institutions in Australia and South America. It could take years for FNUC to recover from the exodus of administrators, faculty, and students. Meanwhile, despite or perhaps to some extent even *because of* this disaster, the numbers of Aboriginal students have been increasing steadily at the province's two main universities (the

University of Saskatchewan and the University of Regina), as well as at its main technical institute (the Saskatchewan Institute of Applied Science and Technology) and at the First Nations and Metis technical institutes.

It is interesting to note which subjects at the post-secondary level seem to have attracted male versus female Aboriginal students. In 2001, male and female students were found in equal proportions in the social sciences, whereas males far outnumbered females (by 10 to 1) in applied sciences, technologies, and trades and to a lesser extent (3 to 1) in the humanities; while females far outnumbered males in education, fine arts, commerce, and health (including nursing). Aboriginal enrolment in engineering and the physical sciences had been sparse. But times change fast. The most recent data (2006) reveal that the largest numbers of Aboriginal people in the city aged 15 and over (14,060) have been educated in business management and public administration (1,255), and engineering and related technologies (800), with substantial numbers in health and recreation (585), social and behavioural sciences and law (520), education (510), and humanities, performing arts, and communication (430); whereas fewer have enrolled in physical or social sciences (95) and agriculture and related fields (70).

The increasing urban Aboriginal presence is felt at virtually every level of education but especially at the elementary level. City schools with high Aboriginal proportions are reportedly 'filled to bursting.' In fact, several inner-city schools in Saskatoon already had a majority of Aboriginal pupils by 1998: St Mary's (estimated between 80 to 90%), Pleasant Hill (87.7%), Princess Alexandra (76.1%), and King George (52.1%). St Mary's currently estimates its enrolment to be almost entirely Aboriginal. Apart from several post-secondary institutions run by First Nations and Metis, one high school – Oskayak (formerly the Native Survival School) is designated as Aboriginal. The FSIN announced in December 2009 its intention to create the first separate urban First Nations elementary school, then to expand into a publicly funded separate First Nations school board. This would be similar to existing Catholic and francophone school systems. Such officially designated First Nations schools would emphasize 'faith, culture and traditions.' It is now possible for an Aboriginal student in Saskatoon to proceed all the way from elementary school through high school to university or technical school within a primarily Aboriginal setting.

Despite the marked improvement in education levels attained by the Aboriginal population of Saskatoon, there remain gaps that must be closed with the non-Aboriginal population. Various estimates tell us that between one-third and almost one-half of Aboriginal adults in this city have less than a grade twelve education; moreover, until very recently, certain areas of post-secondary education had hardly been penetrated by Aboriginal people. Education is absolutely crucial for more occupational diversity, which in turn is vital for improved standards of living and housing affordability. Shawn Atleo, National Chief of the Assembly of First Nations (AFN), has observed that 'a good education is one that is owned by the community, that includes being imbedded in culture and identity, that respects the retention of our languages, while accomplishing the education standards that are needed for our young people to succeed' (*Globe and Mail*, 10 December 2010). To which FSIN Vice-Chief Simon Bird has added that education needs to be seen as an investment rather than a cost: 'First Nations and Metis people are the single greatest resource of the province' (*Saskatoon StarPhoenix*, 10 November 2011). Native culture and community involvement must be integral to the curriculum. The culture shock experienced by Aboriginal students, especially those coming into the city from northern and isolated First Nations reserves and Metis communities, can be powerful. Indeed, given the poor learning conditions combined with poverty, high unemployment, and social problems on too many reserves, it is quite remarkable that First Nations students are even able to make it into university. These students often have difficulty adjusting to a campus life that must seem very alien to them. Gaining initial admission may be hard; survival through several years to a degree or certificate may be even harder, though well worth the effort.

Eric Howe, an economics professor at the University of Saskatchewan, has commented that Aboriginal students have among the highest rates of return from education, gaining far more than non-Aboriginal persons: it has been calculated that an Aboriginal person who drops out before graduating from high school loses $525,000 of lifetime income; in terms of university education, the loss is over $1 million. In an economy that increasingly depends on skilled workers, high school education is a minimum for financial independence (*Saskatoon StarPhoenix*, 6 November 2010). And in a later report (Howe 2011), Howe points out that closing the education gap between Aboriginal people and the rest of the Saskatchewan population could yield as much as $90 million in savings overall, combining personal monetary and societal benefits. For example, a Metis male lacking a high school diploma can expect to earn an average $547,000 over a lifetime, but with a university degree that figure triples to $1.67 million. While potash is often emphasized as the province's most valued natural resource, Howe emphasizes that an even greater resource is Aboriginal people, a resource which not been sufficiently developed and which in the longer term is more sustainable than mining. A better educated Aboriginal population would ensure a more skilled Aboriginal workforce and save massive amounts spent on social services, justice, health care and other areas.

According to the Minister of Advanced Education, Employment, and Immigration, Native advancement in education and training has become a high priority of the provincial government, in view of the unacceptably high education and employment differentials between the Aboriginals and non-Aboriginals. Since 2008 the Saskatchewan government has made significant investments in education and skills training, including $40 million in the 2011 budget alone; half of this amount has gone toward a 17% increase in adult basic education to develop fundamental skills (a program delivered on reserve to ten First Nations). The provincial government intends to partner with First Nations and Metis organizations to 'consult widely on long-term solutions to eliminate the current gaps in employment and education outcomes' (*Saskatoon StarPhoenix*, 18 March 2011).

According to the AFN, more and more First Nations chiefs have identified educational reform as the most pressing need in their communities. Recommended and enacted initiatives within Saskatoon's school systems include the following: developing support services to help Aboriginal students deal with socio-economic and academic issues; providing health services; launching literacy initiatives; fostering a welcoming learning environment; providing Aboriginal historical, cultural, and language programs; recruiting resident elders; developing an early learning strategy; increasing the number of Aboriginal teachers (there are currently 667 in the entire province); establishing professional development programs for teachers; developing a community engagement strategy that involves participation in education decision making; and establishing closer collaboration among municipal school divisions, the provincial Ministry of Education, and First Nations and Metis organizations. The Aboriginal Public Administration Program at the University of Saskatchewan uses its students as mentors to high school students at Oskayak, White Buffalo Youth Lodge, and the Core Neighbourhood Youth Co-op (CNYC). CNYC is an alternative inner-city school that offers a holistic education and gainful employment to students from core neighbourhoods that are struggling with poverty and crime; almost all of these students are Aboriginal, and most have been sent there by court order, usually due to truancy (some haven't been in school for several years). Urban Aboriginal residents feel that the most significant motivation for higher education is career goals and that its greatest impact is on feelings of empowerment, especially in terms of learning about and appreciating Aboriginal culture and identity. In this regard, the role of lifelong learning from elders is appreciated (UAPS 2010: 117-118). Funding continues to be the main obstacle in attaining higher education.

*Employment*

Occupation

Given the disproportionately large numbers of Aboriginal residents in the youngest age cohorts, the question must be how these young people will be entering the future labour force, how they will find employment (*atoskewin*). The expectation of improved employment has tended to be a significant factor in Aboriginal people moving into cities from reserves and northern communities; typically, people move to where there are jobs – or perhaps more precisely, to where they expect to find jobs. According to Rob Norris, former Saskatchewan Minister of Advanced Education, Employment, and Immigration, 70,000 to 90,000 jobs in the province will need to be filled within the next five to seven years. Clearly, with urbanization, Aboriginal people have been diversifying within the labour force and earning higher incomes. Almost one-third of urban Aboriginals within the experienced labour force in Saskatchewan are now in sales and service occupations; also, they are becoming relatively prominent in trades, business and finance, and education occupations. However, fewer (although their numbers are increasing) are found in management, health, and applied science occupations. There are gender differences in types of occupations pursued (Table 2.11). In the general Canadian population, women still tend to be concentrated primarily in traditional occupations, though they are increasingly represented in business and finance.

A more detailed breakdown of the total Aboriginal population in the Canadian labour force is provided by data on labour force by industry. These data indicate that the largest numbers are working in accommodation and food services, public administration, health care and social assistance, education, construction, the retail trade, and manufacturing. Construction, agriculture, and the resource industries were almost all

Table 2.11. Saskatoon Aboriginal labour force aged 15 years and over, by occupation and gender, 2001 and 2006

| | 2001 total | % | Male | % | Female | % | 2006 total | % |
|---|---|---|---|---|---|---|---|---|
| Total | 6,800 | 100 | 3,365 | 49.5 | 3,435 | 50.5 | 8,525 | 100 |
| Management | 335 | 4.9 | 210 | 3.1 | 125 | 1.8 | 565 | 6.6 |
| Business/finance/administration | 880 | 12.9 | 210 | 3.1 | 670 | 9.9 | 1,230 | 14.4 |
| Natural/applied sciences | 155 | 2.3 | 130 | 1.9 | 25 | 0.4 | 255 | 3.0 |
| Health | 230 | 3.4 | 35 | 0.5 | 195 | 2.9 | 350 | 4.1 |
| Social science/education/ government service/religion | 705 | 10.4 | 190 | 2.8 | 515 | 7.6 | 825 | 9.7 |
| Art/culture/recreation/sport | 190 | 2.8 | 85 | 1.3 | 105 | 1.5 | 195 | 2.3 |
| Sales/service | 1,950 | 28.7 | 705 | 10.4 | 1,245 | 18.3 | 2,635 | 30.9 |
| Trades/transport/equipment Operators | 1,120 | 16.5 | 1,065 | 15.7 | 55 | 0.8 | 1,535 | 18.0 |
| Primary industry | 205 | 3.0 | 125 | 1.8 | 80 | 1.2 | 405 | 4.8 |
| Processing/manufacturing/utilities | 395 | 5.8 | 320 | 4.7 | 75 | 1.1 | 530 | 6.2 |

male, and wholesale trade and management were also male dominated; gender parity was most evident in the retail trade and in business services; education and health care were female dominated.

Specifically in Saskatoon, more Aboriginal men are working in the 'trades, transport and equipment operators' category, with more women in sales and service, not unlike the non-Aboriginal population. Aboriginal women are more likely than non-Aboriginal to be working in sales and service (37% compared with 30% in 2006), but still less likely to be employed in business, financial, or administrative positions (22% compared to 26%). Between 1996 and 2001 the rate of Aboriginal entrepreneurship was eight times that of the general Canadian population (Howe 2002). Advances are being made in Saskatchewan by Aboriginal people in education and business ownership, including diverse sorts of small businesses as well as larger businesses such as casinos and hotel franchises, and such Aboriginal initiatives are a vital part of the Saskatchewan economy. The question has to be *where* Native people will fit into the prosperous provincial economy and move further into the economic mainstream. Cameco, the international uranium producer headquartered in Saskatoon, has secured the services of former Member of Parliament Gary Merasty in an effort to hire more

Aboriginal people. Cameco has been making a conscious effort to educate, train, and employ Aboriginal people. For example at its Rabbit Lake uranium mine, a majority of employees are now Aboriginal and the mine documents exactly which northern communities they come from; other Aboriginal people work at the main office in Saskatoon.

Not all Saskatchewan companies share Cameco's zeal: in a province where Aboriginal people are at least 15% of the population, in the largest provincial mining company, Potash Corporation of Saskatchewan (owned and operated by the provincial government), only about 1.5% of the employees are Aboriginal (*Report on Business*, January 2010). However, Potash Corp has now developed an Aboriginal strategy directed at increasing Aboriginal employment as well as Aboriginal Awareness Training, and supports the Atoske Camps in urban and rural areas and programming at the White Buffalo Youth Lodge in Saskatoon.

Another Statistics Canada study (Armstrong 1999) cautiously suggested that First Nations communities located within or close to urban areas were more likely to prosper, but there were 'numerous exceptions to the rule ... Although it seems important, location is neither an assured nor only path to socio-economic well-being.' In our surveys, many Aboriginal residents commented on the relative proximity of their home to work and whether this was an issue. So it is instructive to mention specific data on modes of transportation to and from work. A high proportion of both males and females drive to work themselves or are driven; moreover, more walk to work than take public transit. This minimal use of public transit seems relevant. We note that more female than male workers use public transit. Perhaps one could conclude, however, that if public transit were more convenient and accessible in a city where winters can be extremely harsh, more use would be make of this mode.

Income

Across Canada, on-reserve income across remains less than half that of urban First Nations people; moreover, income for all Aboriginal Canadians comes to only about 60% of the Canadian median income. There was an overall shrinking in the gap in median employment income between Aboriginal and non-Aboriginal earners in CMAs from 1981 to 2001 (Maxim, White, and Beavon 2003). However, 2006 census data reveal a continuing disparity, even among earners working full-time for a full year: median income was $34,940 for Aboriginals compared to $41,401 for others. Although the income gap for urban Aboriginals was reduced between 1995 and 2002, Aboriginal earners remained far more likely to be categorized as lower income (41.6%) than the general population (17.7%) (Heisz and McLeod 2004).

Analysing data on total labour force as well as gender differences in average employment income, comparing Aboriginal with non-Aboriginal earners, we can note that Canadian women in full-time jobs earn 73% what males earn; but according to a Toronto-Dominion Bank study, this seems to be partly explicable by motherhood, in that women without children having the same level of education and experience as their male counterparts tend to have commensurate incomes. Income has been increasing for both male and female Aboriginal earners, with males consistently earning more than females; however, Aboriginal income still lags well behind non-Aboriginal. Yet it could also be noted that male Aboriginals lag further behind male non-Aboriginals than is the case for their female counterparts.

The 2006 census revealed that the average income for Aboriginal earners in Saskatchewan as a whole was $19,939 (more than $13,000 less than the average for the non-Aboriginal population). The average household income of Aboriginal residents of Saskatoon grew from $14,256 in 1996 (which at the time was less than one-third of the average income of the general population: $49,032), to $20,267 in 2001 and $24,467 in 2006. The greatest numbers of Aboriginal income earners in Saskatoon were concentrated in the relatively lower income levels: in 2001, 10% of male workers earned less than $1,000 a year, compared to 5.7% of females. Another 13.7% of males earned between $1,000 and $5,000, compared to 15% of females. Two-thirds (65.9%) of potential male members of the labour force (aged 15 and over) and three-quarters (74.9%) of female members earned less than $20,000 a year. Examining the data on median income in 2006, Aboriginal residents were consistently earning far less than the general population, and males less than females (Table 2.12). The Aboriginal Peoples Survey (2006) produced slightly different yet similar data, comparing Aboriginal and non-Aboriginal male and female median incomes: Aboriginal men had a median income of $17,130 (compared to $33,839 for non-Aboriginal), Aboriginal women $16,140 (compared to $21,860). But if we restrict data on median earnings to full-time and full-year, Aboriginal earners in Saskatoon in 2005 made a far larger amount: $33,500 (actually representing a slight decrease since 2000), whereas non-Aboriginal earners were slowly increasing (to

Table 2.12. Median income of general and and Aboriginal population aged 15 years and over, by gender, Saskatoon CMA, 2006

|  | Median earnings ($) |
| --- | --- |
| Population | 25,702 |
| Male | 32,387 |
| Female | 20,643 |
| Aboriginal population | 17,734 |
| Male | 20,358 |
| Female | 15,386 |

$39,800). The relative proportion of Aboriginal to non-Aboriginal earnings was also decreasing: from 88% in 2000 to 84% five years later. However, the data on income distribution between Aboriginal and non-Aboriginal earners is revealing: in 2005 just 18% of Aboriginal residents with income had a total income exceeding $40,000 a year (compared to 31% of non-Aboriginal earners). Yet there were more Aboriginal females in the labour force than males (remember, though, that there is a disproportion of females in the city's Aboriginal population). In the Aboriginal workforce, female workers earn less than male workers, but they also now tend to be better educated, to be more present in the labour force, and to be be in the process of occupying better positions (Howe 2002). However, it should be pointed out here that the substantial proportion of Aboriginal residents in their late teens and twenties who may be students, or who are not working at all, or who are not working full-time, could skew these findings. Close to 10% of non-Aboriginal earners attain an income level of $100,000, but less than 1% of Aboriginal earners do, according to City of Saskatoon data.

A lessening proportion of total income for Canadian Aboriginals (according to an AFN report in March 2009) as well as for the Saskatoon Aboriginal population consists of government transfer payments, which have decreased from one-third (33.5%) of all income in 1996 to one-quarter (25.4%) in 2001 and which are now less than 20%. For Aboriginal residents of Saskatoon, income sources in 2006 were 75.1% from earnings (83.7% for males, 65.6% for females); they received 19.6% of their income from government transfer payments (11.1% for males, 28.9% for females), compared to only 9.8% in the general population (6.4% for males, 14.9% for females).

The importance for Aboriginal people entering the labour force of having a university degree has been re-emphasized in a report of the Canadian Centre for Policy Alternatives released in April 2010, based on 2006 census data (see Macdonald and Wilson 2010). In fact, this report suggests that Aboriginal women with a university degree are earning *more*, on average, than their non-Aboriginal counterparts. An Aboriginal woman possessing a university degree earns on average $2,471 a year more than a non-Aboriginal woman with the same level of education (and $4,521 more with a masters degree); whereas Aboriginal men earn on average $3,667 less than other Canadians with the same level of education. Aboriginal females are narrowing the wage gap with Aboriginal males, in contrast to the trend in the general population. This is partially due to the fact that increasing numbers of Aboriginal women are receiving a university education, although half as many of Aboriginal women (14%) than non-Aboriginal women (28%) have completed a university degree. Just 8% of Aboriginal men have earned a university degree, compared to one-quarter of other Canadians. The same report notes that nationally, the median income for Aboriginal people in 2006 was $18,962, compared to $27,097 for other Canadians (a 30% difference); so at the present rate it will take 63 years to close this gap. The median income gap between Aboriginals and other Canadians was calculated as $7,083 in urban areas and $4,492 in rural. Higher education, the report concludes, is important for closing this gap; however, a more comprehensive approach is needed, one that would replace the prevalent policy of assimilation with consultation and reconciliation. The Canadian Centre for Policy Alternatives reported in December 2010 that the wealthier the Canadian earner, the faster the income differential has been widening. Nonetheless, there are clear indications in Saskatoon and other Canadian cities that an urban Aboriginal middle class is gradually emerging (Wotherspoon 2003; Newhouse 2011).

Labour Force Participation

Aboriginal unemployment across Canada has been rapidly decreasing in cities (e.g., from 24% to 14% between 1996 and 2001), whereas it has barely changed on reserves, where it is double that of the cities; Aboriginal participation in the labour force has been on average little more than half the potential on reserve, compared to 65% in cities (*Globe and Mail*, 6 July 2007). Compared with the current Saskatchewan unemployment rate of 5%, the rate for the Aboriginal population is almost double at 9.4%; moreover, First Nations' jobless numbers show a current rate of increase of 21.3%. However, even these alarming numbers reveal an improving situation, considering that Aboriginal unemployment stood at about 30% as recently as ten years ago (*Saskatoon StarPhoenix*, 10 September 2012). Aboriginal unemployment in Saskatoon, as well as dependence on government transfer payments, while decreasing, is still excessive compared with the rate for the non-Aboriginal population (Table 2.13). Examining data on labour force activity by total population and gender for the Aboriginal population aged 15 and over in the City of Saskatoon in 2001, we can note that although there were more Aboriginal females than males in the labour force (in absolute numbers), proportionally far fewer females than males were gainfully employed. Males actually had a higher participation rate (64.8% for males compared to 51.8% for females). In 2006 the unemployment rate for the core Aboriginal working age population aged 25 to 54 was 13.3% (compared with just 3.4% among the non-Aboriginal population). Moreover, significantly more Aboriginal females (15.8%) than males (11.1%) were unemployed; far less of a discrepancy by gender was found in the rest of the population (respectively 3.6% and 3.3%). Unemployment is higher among Aboriginal youth: in 2006, 27.5% of First Nations and 13.3% of Metis youth aged 15 to 24 in Saskatoon were unemployed (compared to 9.3% of other youth). On closer inspection, Metis employment rates in this city are fairly comparable to non-Aboriginal, First Nations far lower: for example, among Metis aged 25 to 34, 82.1% of men and 72.8% of women were employed in 2006; respectively 89.3% and 81.5% among non-Aboriginal men and women; and 58.2% and 41.7% among First Nations. Aboriginal men are more likely than women to work full time for a full year: 34% of men compared to 24% of women (and in the non-Aboriginal population, respectively 49% and 34%). All together, proportionately far fewer Aboriginal residents (29%) were working full-time for a full year than non-Aboriginal (41%).

Examination of the effect that having young children may have on labour force participation reveals that unemployment substantially increases, and participation in the labour force decreases, particularly among women with young children. The unemployment rate for Aboriginal women with children only under six was 35.1% in 2001; for those with children both under and over six, it was 28.2%.

A study by York University economist Helmar Drost in 1995 for the C.D. Howe Institute found that across Canada, urban Native people were facing much higher unemployment rates than non-Aboriginals,

Table 2.13. Aboriginal and non-Aboriginal employment rates, Saskatoon, 2001 and 2006 (%)

|  | Aboriginal | Non-Aboriginal |
| --- | --- | --- |
| Unemployment rate, 2001 | 22.3 | 4.8 |
| Unemployment rate, 2006 | 14.6 | 3.7 |
| Labour force participation rate, 2006 | 63.2 | 70.6 |
| Employment rate, 2006 | 54.0 | 66.9 |

especially in Saskatchewan, although off-reserve income was considerably higher than on-reserve. Drost suggested that 'how much of the unemployment gap is due to labour market discrimination against Aboriginals is open to question,' because analysing unemployment is complex – variables may include gender, age, family, status, work experience, training, education, type of industry, and especially location. The proportion of off-reserve Aboriginal people in Saskatchewan receiving social assistance was at the time at least four times higher than the comparable rate for non-Aboriginals. John Richards, a professor of business at Simon Fraser University, suggested that federal policies toward Aboriginals were creating a syndrome of unemployment and welfare dependency, compounding problems around urban migration.

Ten years later, by 2006, Aboriginal unemployment rates were still two-and-a-half times the Canadian national average. Aboriginal unemployment rates decreased between 2001 and 2006 yet remained higher than for the non-Aboriginal population. Almost two-thirds (65.8%) of Aboriginal people in Canada were employed in 2006 (compared to 61.2% five years earlier); whereas among the non-Aboriginal population, the proportion increased slightly from 80.3% to 81.6%. Unemployment rates actually declined faster for the Aboriginal (–4.2%) than for the non-Aboriginal (–0.8%) population; yet Aboriginal people were still twice as likely to be unemployed (13.2%) as non-Aboriginal people (5.2%) (UAPS 2010, 25–6). A Statistics Canada report released in May 2010 continued to note a widening gap between off-reserve Aboriginals and other Canadians in employment: the unemployment rate among Aboriginal people aged 15 and over increased from 10.4% in 2008 to 13.9% a year later, while employment rates decreased –3.2% down to 57% in 2009. By occupational sector, there was a 30% employment decline for Aboriginals in manufacturing, compared to just an 8% decline among non-Aboriginals; similarly, there was a drop of 16%

for Aboriginals and of 5% for others in construction. Job losses among Aboriginals exceeded those among other Canadians in most provinces, though not in Saskatchewan.

Yet again, some contemporary analysts have emphasized the possible positive effects that the disproportionately youthful Aboriginal population in Saskatchewan may be having on expansion of the labour force. For example, Brett Gartner, an economist with the Canada West Foundation, has commented recently that 'Saskatchewan must get better at integrating Aboriginal people into the workforce. Arguably, that would have greater impact on the provincial economy than increased immigration' (*Saskatoon StarPhoenix*, 16 February 2007). Some analysts in Saskatchewan have argued that immigration alone is insufficient to fill a need for an increased workforce in certain trades, particularly those tied to the homebuilding industry. The provincial government is anxious to encourage more immigration into Saskatchewan, yet immigrants compete with Native people for scarce employment as well as affordable housing and may possess higher education levels and job skills. Off-reserve Aboriginal employment in the West increased 23% between 2001 and 2005, compared to 11% for non-Aboriginals. The cohort of Aboriginals aged 20 to 27 in Saskatchewan almost doubled in a decade to reach 30% by 2011, up from 17% in 2001. An editorial in the *Saskatoon StarPhoenix* (13 July 2004) suggested that this trend 'inspires hope.' Native columnist Doug Cuthand called it 'encouraging.' Moreover: 'Improving educational outcomes of Aboriginal youth is vital. It is impossible to overstate the role their post-secondary education and skills training will play in Saskatchewan's future economic success. In addition to university, there's tremendous potential to engage these youths in occupations that require a college diploma or certificate or apprenticeship training. A good deal of Saskatchewan's job growth has been in such occupations' (*Saskatoon StarPhoenix*, 16 February 2007). According to SREDA (Saskatoon Regional Economic Development Authority), Aboriginal participation in the Saskatchewan labour force (64% between 2001 and 2005, compared to 75% in Calgary) could be improved. SREDA is advocating an Aboriginal labour force coordinator to work with businesses to better develop the young Aboriginal cohort, 'which has long been considered one of the potential pluses for Saskatchewan' (*Saskatoon StarPhoenix*, 18 July 2007).

Aboriginal employment in Saskatchewan has actually been falling (from 59.6% in 2007 to 57.5% in 2009) and is now well behind Aboriginal employment rates in the neighbouring provinces (according to the

Saskatchewan Chamber of Commerce in June 2010). The proportion of off-reserve employed Aboriginals is currently 64% in Manitoba, 62% in Alberta, and 61% in all of Canada, while the overall Canadian employment rate was 77.7% in 2009. During 2009 the Aboriginal employment rate in Saskatchewan decreased to less than 50% from 60%; during this single year the Aboriginal labour force decreased by several thousand people. Moreover, this recent trend has not abated: the number of employed Aboriginal people continues to decrease. For example, it was approximately 35,600 in December 2010 to 34,400 just a month later. Meanwhile, the Aboriginal unemployment rate increased from 16.5% to 17.3%, and the employment rate dropped from 51.7% to 49.9% (*Saskatoon StarPhoenix*, 11 March 2011). A variety of interrelated explanations have been offered for this: First Nations people have been moving off reserves for employment, only to encounter substantial increases in the cost of housing and renting combined with decreases in the availability of affordable accommodation. These higher costs of housing and living occurred as jobs were becoming lower-paying, leading perhaps to a return migration to the reserves, where employment was even scarcer. The solution to this dilemma clearly lies in education, which in turn would lead to higher incomes. But with one in every five Aboriginal people in the potential labour force, aged 24 to 64, lacking a high school graduation, this makes for chronic underemployment. This has been changing, but is it changing fast enough to suit labour market needs in Saskatchewan?

A recent study by Krishna and Ravi Pendakur (2007), respectively an economist at Simon Fraser University and a sociologist at the University of Ottawa, pointed out that the income gap between Aboriginals and other Canadians is much wider than the gap faced by other ethnic minorities. Using an extensive database from the 2001 census, which covered 20% of all Canadian households and all households on reserves, the research focused on the differential in Aboriginal versus non-Aboriginal earnings both on reserves and in cities. They found that the income of males and females with registered status still living on reserve was respectively 50% and 21% lower than that of non-Aboriginals, while registered males and females living off-reserve had incomes respectively 38% and 23% lower. Specifically in Saskatoon, male registered Indians were earning 63% less than non-Aboriginal men, while the females were earning 44% less than non-Aboriginal women. Comparing Saskatoon with ten other Canadian cities, this city had by far the greatest discrepancy between Aboriginal and non-Aboriginal earnings of men, and with Regina also the greatest discrepancy for women. Even if age and education level are taken into consideration, Aboriginal people are still far poorer on average. In an attempt to remedy this situation, in the southern region of the province the File Hills–Qu'Appelle Tribal Council is collaborating with FSIN and the Regina Chamber of Commerce in a mentorship program to encourage businesses to employ First Nations people.

To put gender differences in labour force participation in a national context, Statistics Canada reports that currently the national labour force participation rate is falling with economic recession, whereas in Saskatchewan participation is substantially increasing; yet the jobless rate for men is actually three times that for women. More than twice as many women as men work part-time; three-quarters of employed women work full-time, but women are more likely than men to work part-time. The current national jobless rate for women is 7%, the highest in six years. Also, 8.1 million Canadian women are employed, representing an employment rate of 58.3%, compared to 65.2% for men.

Glen Hodgson, chief economist of the Conference Board of Canada and author of *Sustaining the Canadian Labour Force: Alternatives to Immigration*, points out that while immigration is the primary source of Canadian labour force growth, especially in western Canada, Aboriginal people are a most significant domestic source of potential workers. The 2006 census reported an Aboriginal population aged 15 and over of 824,000, yet the rate of Aboriginal participation in the labour force was 63%, below the national average of 67%. Increasing the rate of Aboriginal participation would calculate out to 32,000 workers, a significant proportion – perhaps as much as one-third – from Saskatchewan. Moreover, because the gap between Aboriginal and non-Aboriginal participation is higher in Saskatchewan than nationally, we may estimate that 12,500 new workers would be added in Saskatchewan. But this would take time; in effect we are referring to the next generation. Nationally, perhaps 46,000 more Aboriginal workers would be added to the Canadian labour force, significantly complementing the effect of immigration, yet this would represent only a fraction of the actual number of workers that will be needed to sustain economic growth potential, according to Hodgson (*Saskatoon StarPhoenix*, 30 September 2010). This is not to underestimate the future potential of the Aboriginal population to contribute to labour force growth in the longer term. Again, increasing the Aboriginal participation rate will depend on such key factors as increasing educational attainment levels both on and off reserve, together with specific professional and practical occupational skills development, much of which could best be accomplished in an urban milieu.

Canada, and to a lesser extent Saskatchewan, will remain dependent on immigration; the successful Provincial Nominee Program will continue to play a significant role, but the western provinces in particular – notably Saskatchewan – would do well to prioritize the education and skills development of its existing young indigenous Aboriginal population. According to the provincial government, bringing 'newcomers' to Saskatchewan is not to the detriment of opportunities for Native people; but this has increasingly been raised as an important issue. Among others, economist Eric Howe at the University of Saskatchewan recently observed a significant decline in the overall Aboriginal employment rate and a decrease in the Aboriginal labour force in Saskatchewan. Meanwhile, the provincial government is placing emphasis on recruiting immigrants, which could lessen opportunities for entry-level jobs for Aboriginal people (*Saskatoon StarPhoenix*, 11 March 2011). Chief Clarence Louie of Osoyoos, B.C. (chair of the National Aboriginal Economic Development Board), observing that the employment gap between First Nations and others is statistically more than two times higher in Saskatchewan than in the rest of western Canada, adds that 'when First Nations people have the same unemployment rate as the non-native people, then sure the federal government should be looking for workers from overseas.' He has added that 'Saskatchewan has some work to do to include Aboriginal people in the workforce.' In his view, dependence on 'welfare' – social assistance programs that keep Aboriginal people unemployed and undereducated – has been resulted in 'a young, rapidly growing Aboriginal population who threaten to drag down the economy and overburden the country's social safety nets.' (*Saskatoon StarPhoenix*, 7 April 2011). Howe has repeatedly argued that 'this young Aboriginal population that on average is not very well off and on average not very well educated ... absolutely has to be brought into the economic mainstream' (*StarPhoenix*, 4 February 2011). The provincial government minister responsible for employment, recognizing that 'First Nations participation in our workplace is not an option, it is an imperative,' in March 2011 signed a memorandum of understanding between the provincial and federal governments with five Saskatchewan tribal councils. This MOU aims to develop career planning and skills development strategies, basic education and employment skills programs, improved access to short-term training, transitional support such as child care, and recruitment programs. However, specifics have yet to be determined.

*Poverty*

In 2009, Saskatchewan was reported as having the fastest economic growth rate of any Canadian province, surpassing Ontario as the second wealthiest province after Alberta as measured by quantified living standards (*Regina Leader-Post*, 25 November 2009). Yet many continue to argue that a comprehensive anti-poverty strategy is essential for Saskatchewan (Mulvale and Englot 2011). Saskatoon and Regina continue to have the highest proportions of Aboriginal population living below the statistical poverty line of any CMAs in Canada. The low-income cut-off (LICO) has been defined since 1992 as the average (34.7% of total income) that Canadian families spent at that time on basic necessities (food, shelter, clothing), plus 20%, with LICOs adjusted to income levels differentiated by family size and degree of urbanization, updated annually by changes in the consumer price index. In 1996 in Saskatoon, 64% (almost two-thirds) of the Aboriginal population was below the LICO, compared to only 18% of the non-Aboriginal population. Similarly, in Regina, 63% of Aboriginals were below the LICO, compared to 14% of non-Aboriginals. Five years later the situation had improved: in 2001 in Saskatoon and Regina respectively, 52% and 53% (but still more than half) of Aboriginal residents were below the LICO, compared to about 15% of the non-Aboriginal population. And by 2005, 45% of Saskatoon's Aboriginal residents were living below the LICO (compared to just 13% of the non-Aboriginal), but 56% of Aboriginal children aged 14 and under (compared with 14% of non-Aboriginal). August 2004 the Association for Canadian Studies reported that 42.6% of Aboriginal population in Saskatchewan was living below the LICO, compared to only 9.1% of the non-Aboriginal population; while nationally, 31.2% of Aboriginals were living below the LICO compared to 12.4% of non-Aboriginals. It is interesting to note that across Canada, Aboriginal people had average incomes equal to 59% of the general population.

The *Indigenous Children's Health Report* (Health Canada 2009) found that Aboriginal children in Canada are dying at four times the rate of non-Aboriginal children and at a higher rate than in a number of developing countries. Moreover, this study attributed infant and child mortality among the Aboriginal population especially to housing conditions and malnutrition. Disproportionately more Aboriginal families go hungry compared to the non-Aboriginal population: 33% of Aboriginals experienced moderate to severe hunger, compared to only 9% of non-Aboriginal population.

Along with the substantial reduction of this poverty rate among Aboriginal residents in these two Saskatchewan cities, there was a concomitant reduction for the Aboriginal population in all western CMAs during these same five years (1996–2001): Winnipeg from 61% to 49%, Edmonton from 54% to 38%, Vancouver from 49% to 40%. Nonetheless, these two Saskatchewan cities still retain the highest poverty levels. Aboriginal unemployment rates and the LICO rate in all census tracts having the highest Aboriginal concentrations have far exceeded non-Aboriginal rates. Moreover, average income for the Aboriginal identity population has lagged far behind that of the non-Aboriginal population in Saskatoon and Regina. On the whole, then, despite indications of increasing education, occupational diversity, and income among the urban Aboriginal population in Saskatchewan, this population remains disproportionately poor. Despite the gradual dispersion of the Aboriginal population, the highest proportions of Aboriginal residents are still found in the poorest neighbourhoods; moreover, these concentrations are growing. Wide discrepancies persist in median incomes for Saskatoon neighbourhoods, with differences between the most affluent and the poorest ranging as much as sixfold. Furthermore, considering that in some relatively affluent neighbourhoods few or even no Aboriginal families reside, the gulf between these well-to-do non-Aboriginal families and Aboriginal families living in the poorest neighbourhoods is even greater. Poverty in lowest-income neighbourhoods impacts on residents' quality of life, condition of housing, security, and self-respect.

*Housing and Living Conditions*

Housing conditions for urban Aboriginal people are improving, with increasing collaboration between Aboriginal organizations and home-builders, civic government, and community organizations. Among urban Aboriginal people, homeownership is increasing and overcrowding is lessening; however, many families continue to struggle with limited incomes and poor living conditions (Engeland et al. 1998; CMHC 2004a; Carter et al. 2005). Moreover, demand for affordable housing far exceeds availability. For example, the waiting list for 450 units provided by SaskNative Rentals is currently over 800; and Aboriginal housing agencies in the city are of the impression that there is a constant if not increasing backlog of between 1,500 and 2,000 units. The vacancy rate in Saskatoon has declined sharply in recent years to 0.6% (one of the lowest rates of any Canadian city), while the urban Aboriginal population has grown by 6.2%. Moreover, a disproportionately large number of Aboriginal residents are renters rather than homeowners; in fact, according to CMHC, in 2001 Regina and Saskatoon had the highest proportion of Aboriginal renter households among Canadian cities, respectively 18.0% and 17.2%. Of 8,150 Aboriginal households in Saskatoon that year, approximately two-thirds were rented and one-third owned by the occupants. Five years later, of 9,235 private dwellings occupied by Aboriginal residents, 59.2% were rented and 40.8% owned. The overwhelming majority of both First Nations and Metis households were renters rather than owners; virtually all of the Metis elders in our study of their housing needs were renters. For Aboriginal residents in Saskatoon, lower incomes have generally meant that 'affordability' of better or even adequate housing is out of reach; median Aboriginal household income was $26,700 in 2001 and $34,840 in 2006 (compared to $51,169 for the total city population). According to recent census releases from Statistics Canada concerning housing (No. 3: 'Dwelling Characteristics,' 12 September 2007; No. 8: 'Shelter Costs,' 1 May 2008; 'Housing Analysis,' 4 June 2008), more than two-thirds (68.4%) of all Canadian households are now owned by the occupant, in striking contrast to the relatively low proportion of Aboriginal owners in cities. Unfortunately, shelter costs have been rising faster than the inflation rate. An increasing proportion, as many as one-quarter of all Canadian households are at risk of experiencing problems related to housing affordability.

Barriers to finding suitable housing have included higher than average family size, lack of capital in moving into the city from a reserve or northern community, discrimination by landlords, lack of familiarity with financing assistance and mortgaging procedures, reduction of government assistance, difficulty in locating and maintaining regular employment, transiency and homelessness (both relative and absolute), non-familiarity with property maintenance ... the list could go on.

In 2001, 13.8% of all households in Saskatoon were found to be in À'core housing need.' These households typically spent half of their total household income on shelter; this was the second highest ratio for any CMA in Canada. In core housing need were 29.4% of rental households and 5.9% of owners. Among Aboriginal households, 44.5% of renters were in core housing need; among Metis households, 45%; among lone-parent households, 78%. Again in 2001, 4,690 dwellings, representing 6% of all households in Saskatoon, were classified as needing major repair. Among Aboriginal households, though, the proportion needing major repair was 11.9%, while another 34.9% needed minor repair. This grim situation has been slow to change: five years later, 11.8% (1,090 Aboriginal households) needed major repair, 33.3% (3,070) minor repair, and 54.9% (5,070) required only 'regular maintenance.'

The National Occupancy Standard defines overcrowding as exceeding one person per bedroom, excluding such common living spaces as hallways, bathrooms, and rooms used solely for business purposes. The Aboriginal Peoples Survey (2006) found that 9% of all Aboriginal households in this city were overcrowded – nine times the rate for non-Aboriginal households. Moreover, Aboriginal residents were almost three times as likely as non-Aboriginal residents to be living in homes requiring major repairs (requiring, in the opinion of the resident, major repairs to defective plumbing, wiring, or structure): 13% compared to 5% of the non-Aboriginal population. This situation has remained unchanged in recent years. Nationally, 11% of Aboriginals in Canada are living in overcrowded conditions – four times the national rate for the non-Aboriginal population. The greatest decreases in property values have been precisely in west side neighbourhoods with the older housing stock and the highest concentrations of Aboriginal people.

Regarding the composition of Aboriginal households in Saskatoon, in 2001 a high proportion (83.7%) of household members consisted of family members. The remainder (16.3%) consisted of 'non-family persons,' including people living with relatives or non-relatives, or simply alone. Of just 375 Aboriginal residents aged 65 and older, a bit more than half (57.3%) were domiciled with their families, 32.0% were living alone, 9.3% with relatives, and 2.6% with non-relatives.

It is instructive to compare types of housing occupied by Aboriginal residents with types in the general population (Table 2.14). The largest number of Aboriginal households are accommodated in single detached housing, as are the largest number in the general population, but higher proportions of Aboriginal people live in low-rise apartments (five storeys or less), semi-detached housing, or duplexes, than the general population.

Table 2.14. Types of housing, Aboriginal and general population, Saskatoon, 2006 (%)

|  | Aboriginal | General population |
| --- | --- | --- |
| Single detached | 49.2 | 59.7 |
| Apartments in low-rise buildings | 28.5 | 21.3 |
| Semidetached | 6.9 | 3.9 |
| Duplexes | 6.4 | 4.3 |
| Row housing | 5.0 | 4.9 |
| Apartments in high-rise buildings | 2.8 | 5.0 |
| Other | 1.0 | 0.8 |

## Aboriginal Culture in the City

Increasing attention has been drawn to the survival of Aboriginal culture in the urban context (Peters 1996, 2000, 2002). The national Urban Aboriginal Peoples Study found a 'strong sense of cultural vitality among urban Aboriginal peoples in Canadian cities.' This survey learned that Aboriginal culture in Canadian cities is becoming stronger, not weaker, according to most respondents. This was exemplified in increasing participation in Aboriginal cultural activities. Urban Aboriginal people 'maintain great reverence for their heritage and express strong Indigenous pride.' Respondents exhibited a strong sense of family history, survival, tradition, and identity. A very high proportion (80%) of respondents expressed pride in their Aboriginal identity – in fact, a lesser but significant proportion (70%) reported that they were proud to be Canadian. And 60% reported remaining connected to their communities and traditional culture (although some clarification is needed in distinguishing between original communities – in the case of migrants – and urban Aboriginal communities, such as neighbourhoods). A sense of Canadian identity was not necessarily evidence of assimilation into a non-Aboriginal world; those who feel that they belong to a mostly Aboriginal community within the city are just a likely to feel proudly Canadian; moreover, strong Canadian and Aboriginal political identities tend to coincide. Respondents were 'fairly confident' in their ability to retain Aboriginal cultural identity in the city. When asked about their concern over losing their cultural identity, 38% agreed that this was an issue, and 39% completely disagreed (UAPS 2010, 67).

When asked which aspects of culture are most important to pass on to the next generation, the largest number (60%) of respondents reported a traditional language, and 58% 'customs and traditions' (UAPS 2010, 62). But what, exactly, has been the effect of urbanization on Aboriginal culture, identity, and particularly language in the city? In 1999 a Statistics Canada study (Armstrong 1999) suggested that First Nations communities located closest to urban centres have tended to adopt 'mainstream' ways and have improved their socio-economic situation, but at the expense of maintaining their traditional culture. Moreover, a far lower proportion (10%) of more developed communities nearest to cities were still speaking an Aboriginal language at home than less-developed communities farther away (52%). Yet these more developed communities accounted for only about 23% of Registered Indians in Canada in 1996, and were mostly located in southern British Columbia and southern Ontario (only four Saskatchewan reserves were in this category). The steady depletion of traditional Aboriginal languages, especially in an urban context, has been well documented across Canada (Norris 1998, 2000; Norris and MacCon 2003; Norris and Jantzen 2003; O'Sullivan 2003). In 1996, just 26% of Canadians claiming an Aboriginal identity reported an Aboriginal language as their mother tongue and fewer spoke that language at home (Norris 1998). In 2006, census data revealed that only 21.5% of Aboriginal Canadians reported an ability to speak their traditional language fluently (a decline from 24% in 2001 and from 29% in 1996). Cree (*Ininimowin/Nehiyawewin*) is by far the most widespread and most spoken First Nation language both nationally and in Saskatchewan, followed by Ojibwa (*Anishinabe/Nahkawininiwak*) or the mixed Oji-Cree dialect. More than 97% of Metis under the age of 45 in Canada reported in the last census that they do not speak an Aboriginal language, according to a Statistics Canada report released in January 2008. In British Columbia, a study based on community surveys, released in May 2010, found that of 32 First Nations languages identified in the study, virtually all are endangered and three no longer have any known living speakers (*Globe and Mail*, 3 May 2010). In Saskatchewan there is much higher retention of traditional languages, yet a large majority of Aboriginal people are no longer familiar with these languages. As a direct result of the long-standing policy of sending First Nations children away to residential schools, English became commonly spoken by an entire generation and now is by far the most common home language spoken on reserves. Only about one-quarter of the total Aboriginal population of Saskatchewan now recognizes an Aboriginal language as their mother tongue; 38% of First Nations people can speak their traditional language to some extent; just 12% of Metis can speak *Michif* or another Aboriginal language. There may now be approximately

22–26,000 Cree speakers in the province, 6–8,000 Dene (*Denesuline*), and up to 2,000 Ojibwa and Oji-Cree speakers, as well as Sioux (*Dakota and Lakota*), Assiniboine (*Nakota*), and *Michif*-speakers.

Attrition of Aboriginal language use has tended to be most pronounced in urban areas, although less so in Saskatoon than in Regina (Table 2.15). The vast majority of Aboriginal residents of Saskatoon recognize English rather than a Native language as their mother tongue, primary language in the home, and official language. But even in families capable of speaking a traditional Aboriginal language, that language is seldom spoken as the main language of the home. For example, in Saskatoon in 2011, according to the census, Cree was still quite widely spoken by 1,125 residents as their mother tongue, yet by only 250 as their primary home language; Ojibwa and Oji-Cree were viewed by 165 residents as their mother tongue, yet by just 30 as their home language; and Dene by 165 as their mother tongue and 65 as their home language. Other Aboriginal languages spoken in Saskatoon in modest numbers include Michif, Sioux/Dakota and Lakota, Dene, and Assiniboine/Nakota. There have been considerable efforts made across Canada, in Saskatchewan, and in the City of Saskatoon to revitalize the learning of Aboriginal languages. These efforts have included federal funding of a major Metis language conference, held in Saskatoon in 2008; a Cree language teacher in a Cree language camp, a Cree immersion program at an elementary school, and 'language circles'; the Nehiyawiwin Cree Language and Culture Program, made 'permanent' by the Public School Board; and a bilingual Cree program in the Catholic school system, which has been extended through grade three.

The religious affiliations of Aboriginal residents in Saskatoon are extremely diverse. By far the largest number are Roman Catholic (37.8% in 2001). Another 21.9% claimed a wide variety of Protestant affiliations, especially Anglican, and to a lesser extent United Church, Pentecostal, Mormon, Lutheran, Baptist, Presbyterian, and Mennonite. It is interesting to note that in 2001, over 900 residents (4.9%) claimed traditional Aboriginal spirituality. But that same year, a much larger proportion (29.6%) of Aboriginal residents would not claim any religious affiliation. The Catholic church and several evangelical sects have established churches or missions that serve entirely or largely Aboriginal congregations; these may enhance maintenance of Aboriginal cultural identification in the urban environment. Anglican Native congregations have been established in Prince Albert and Winnipeg, but not Saskatoon, although a now-retired Native Anglican priest in Saskatoon, ordained in 1945, recently completed a lifelong work – a translation of the Gospel

Table 2.15. Aboriginal language use, Saskatoon CMA, Regina CMA, and Saskatchewan, 2001

|  | Saskatoon | Regina | Saskatchewan |
|---|---|---|---|
| Aboriginal population | 20,280 | 15,685 | 130,190 |
| Recognizing Aboriginal language as first learned and still understood | 11.8% | 4.4% | 25.5% |
| Still speaking that language at home | 8.2% | 2.0% | 22.4% |
| At least some knowledge of an Aboriginal language | 15.5% | 7.2% | 29.4% |

of Mark into Plains Cree. Moreover, the Anglican diocese of Saskatoon and Prince Albert serves a number of First Nation reserve communities.

The Aboriginal Peoples Survey in 2001 found significant and increasing proportions of non-reserve Aboriginal children in early learning programs specifically for Native children: dance, music, and artistic programs as well as time spent with Native elders. However, off-reserve children's ability to speak or understand an Aboriginal language tends to decline as their parents' educational level increases. For example, 44% of children in non-reserve areas whose parents' education was limited to elementary school could speak or understand an Aboriginal language, compared to 17% whose parents had completed some type of post-secondary education.

Aboriginal businesses and institutions are becoming a common part of the urban scene in Saskatchewan; some of them are located on urban reserves. These serve the needs of the urban Aboriginal population and also reinforce First Nations and Metis identities in an urban context. Specific Aboriginal cultural programs have been initiated – for example, by the White Buffalo Youth Lodge and the Saskatchewan Indian Cultural Centre in Saskatoon, and by Head Start, Red Feather, and Spirit Lodge in the Gathering Place in Regina. The UAPS probed the respondents' use of Aboriginal organizations and services and found that 28% reported using such institutions and services often, 26% occasionally, 22% rarely, and 23% never. Interestingly, only 18% reported using housing services, compared to 42% who used Friendship Centres (UAPS 2010, 68).

Aspects of Aboriginal culture contributing to or representing an emerging unique urban Aboriginal identity include urban art forms (wall murals and graffiti) and music (hip-hop and rap) (Ignace 2011).

An editorial in the *Saskatoon StarPhoenix* (13 July 2004), commenting on a Statistics Canada report on the development of Aboriginal cultural programs in Canadian cities, pointedly argued:

What the Statistics Canada study offers is a basis for sound public policy by governments ... Rather than a dismal future ... this study indicates progress. And rather than dwell on undeniable past injustices and ongoing social problems within the Aboriginal community, this report offers reasons to believe that the futures of young Native people hold great promise ... For Saskatchewan, with its relatively high urban and young Aboriginal population, it is welcome news that thoughtful policies that support these children's education and culture can provide a future workforce the province needs for economic growth and stability ... Along with helping to preserve Native languages, it sends a clear message of inclusion and accommodation to children whose success means so much to the future of this province and Canada.

## Chapter Three

# First Nations in the City

## Reserve Conditions and Migration to Cities

*The Impetus for Migration: Living Conditions on Reserves*

Migration between reserve (*iskonikan*) and city (*kihci-ihtawin*), as well as mobility within the city, were discussed in the previous chapter. Now let us probe more deeply into the conditions on reserves (especially in Saskatchewan) that may stimulate migration into cities (particularly Saskatoon).

While admittedly there is fairly wide variation in living conditions on Saskatchewan reserves, far too many reserves still exhibit deplorable conditions. In a situation on reserves where most extended families live crowded together in homes that are infested with toxic mould and that are too small and poorly constructed, tuberculosis and other illnesses abound (such as severe headaches, asthma, bronchitis, hepatitis, and skin diseases like shingles). So do social and mental problems, including domestic and other violence, sexual abuse, alcohol and drug dependency, depression, and suicide. Crowding is common throughout Saskatchewan reserves: on ten reserves, the average number of residents per home exceeds six. The average number of persons per home on all Saskatchewan reserves is 4.6, compared to a Canadian average of only 2.5; thus reserve homes in Saskatchewan are almost twice as crowded as the average Canadian home, although on some reserves the average is more than three times as crowded. Extended families may include as many as nine or ten children, as well as grandparents and other relatives, not all of whom can be accommodated in one small house. This forces some to reside in other already crowded homes or occasionally even to sleep outside in a tent. Instances have been found where as many as nineteen people share a two-bedroom bungalow, forcing some to sleep on the couch or floor (Warick and Pacholik in *Saskatoon StarPhoenix*, 26 September 2006).

Across Canada, a high proportion (between half and two-thirds) of reserve homes are substandard; 44% are in need of major repairs, compared to just 9% of homes in rural Canada (*Globe and Mail*, 24 November 2005; 25 January 2012). According to FSIN data, of 14,180 housing units on Saskatchewan reserves, 1,875 are in need of major repairs and another 3,395 minor repairs, while 230 need immediate replacement. Homes are often heated by leaving the stove open, which can be a fire hazard; yet bands may not provide fire insurance to cover losses due to fires. Especially on isolated northern reserves, employment is scarce (in Fond-du-Lac, unemployment ranges as high as 90%) and acute poverty is common; yet at the same time, imported foods, goods, and services are far more expensive than down south. As a consequence, large families must survive on a modest monthly welfare cheque that has to cover not only food but also power, telephone, and other bills. Many thousands of reserve residents continue to live in squalor, which fosters abysmal health conditions; they are Canadians living in housing conditions that are poorer than in many developing countries. The problem of mould is so common in reserve homes across Canada that CMHC, in collaboration with Health Canada, Aboriginal Affairs and Northern Development Canada, and the AFN, is developing a First Nations National Mould Strategy aimed at addressing the mould problem in reserve housing more effectively. Doubtless these grim conditions are often a primary motivation for leaving reserves; concomitantly, the promise of improved conditions – better access to health care, further education, employment, and not the least affordable, adequate housing – continues to draw First Nations people into the cities.

In Saskatchewan there is an immediate need for at least 1,000 new, larger homes on reserves to begin to alleviate crowding and to deal more effectively with population growth, but to build them would cost an estimated $206 million, to which could be added another $43 million just to keep pace with the rapidly growing First Nations population (FSIN, cited in Warick and Pacholik). Approximately $22 million a year is allocated for housing from a larger pool of band capital (each First Nation decides the proportion to be allocated for housing), plus $23 million a year of 'stimulus funding' not included in CMHC programs (*Saskatoon StarPhoenix*, 2 December 2011). Across Canada, CMHC is owed large amounts of mortgage debt for reserve housing.

Frustrations abound. Housing contractors not infrequently delay or stop work entirely before a job is completed. Another problem in supplying adequate housing and improving living conditions is simply the long-standing confusion over which level of government should be responsible. The provincial government has claimed that reserves are a federal jurisdiction, given that the provinces were not party to the original treaties; prior to its defeat in 2006, the former Liberal federal government countered that actually, a right to adequate housing was *not* directly stated in those treaties. In turn, FSIN Vice-Chief Lonechild (responsible for housing at the time, later FSIN Chief) maintained that provision of housing – so elementary to health – should be recognized by implication in the spirit of the treaties. The FSIN also expressed scepticism that the federal government would ever fully meet its mandated responsibility to provide adequate housing on reserves. In fact, the Minister of Indian Affairs (at the time, a Liberal) even tended to agree that on-reserve First Nations people had been blocked from homeownership for too long. Saskatchewan's 72 First Nations were collectively given approximately $20 million for social housing construction and home repairs, but this was also meant to cover such other major expenses as fire protection, road maintenance, and waste removal. Provincial collaboration with the federal government has been increasing; for example, although health care on reserves remains a federal responsibility, a new health centre on one reserve has been financed only one-quarter by the federal government and three-quarters by the province. The present Conservative Minister of Indian Affairs has attempted to encourage provincial premiers to end the acrimony between federal and provincial governments that has been a major contributor to the perpetuation of Aboriginal poverty; there should be less tolerance for jurisdictional disputations and more tolerance for action-oriented plans. It has been problematic that while other Canadians can turn to provincial governments for their health care, education, qualifications for employment, road maintenance, and housing, the Canadian Constitution implies that First Nations should look to Ottawa. Moreover, it has been problematic that within some First Nations there has been a history of political favours, fraud, and misappropriation of funds.

For sure, there are examples in Saskatchewan of progressive First Nations homebuilding programs. Fishing Lake First Nation has availed itself of the 'Section 95' program run by CMHC, which provides subsidized loans for new home construction, backed by a 'ministerial loan guarantee' offered by INAC that guarantees repayment of a housing loan if a First Nation defaults. Interestingly, some First Nations – including Fishing Lake, Muskeg Lake, and Beardy's-Okemasis – were becoming involved in building houses or providing housing not only on reserve but also in the cities where band members have been moving. AC Realty, founded in Spiritwood in 2002 by the region's Agency Chiefs Tribal Council, now works with First Nations beyond the region (such as Fishing Lake) to build 'innovative, affordable, durable, national Building Code compliable (mould-free) houses. By 2006, AC Realty was already generating some $7 million in sales. Each home, designed by the Saskatchewan Research Council, sells for an average of $78,000. Another progressive housing scheme is found in the northern community of La Ronge, where homeowners on the First Nation land are granted 29-year leases, which allows them to more easily obtain mortgages; moreover, this First Nation covers down payments, which are financed by a $1.7 million INAC grant. Some reserves have taken the initiative for major self-development. For example, Calgary-based Encanto Resources recently signed an agreement with the FSIN that opened for exploration some 400,000 acres of First Nations land considered to be potash bearing (at a cost of $18 to $25 million); each new mine could cost over $1 billion and potentially employ hundreds of people (*Saskatoon StarPhoenix,* 26 March 2008). The aforementioned Liberal Minister of Indian Affairs noted that Whitecap Dakota First Nation near Saskatoon could be viewed as a model of positive self-development; it was receiving both federal and provincial government assistance for exploring innovative ways to develop land, housing, the community, and business and recreational ventures. In the minister's opinion, it would not be constructive 'to have a circumstance where 617 First Nations across the country are living as collectivities without private property ownership.' However, rather than pressing for individual property rights in First Nations communities, the federal and provincial governments should be working with First Nations to facilitate leases that would allow families to obtain mortgages to build new homes while providing First Nations with adequate funding to meet social housing needs; whatever the cost of making this overdue investment, it cannot be considered in isolation. Coincidentally, support has been growing for a proposed legal reform to the Indian Act that would permit First Nations people to own the reserve land on which they live; theoretically, introducing private property to reserves could encourage improved home construction and ownership, economic development, and more responsible governance – or so the argument goes (see further discussion in chapter 12).

*Resettlement in the City*

Many Native people move into the poorest inner-city neighbourhoods in Saskatoon, where their increasing concentration and presence have resulted in these neighbourhoods being called by their residents 'The Rez,' 'Moccasin Flats,' or 'Alphabet Soup' (referring to west-side avenues being designated alphabetically from A to Y east to west). More than ten years ago the Executive Director of the Friendship Inn in Saskatoon commented that Aboriginal people migrating into the city face an uphill climb. Often it is very difficult for them – they are poorly prepared for urban living and possess few marketable job skills, and there is not a lot of help for them to adjust. As for why they migrate at all, given the conditions they are likely to find in the city, they have little choice. Too often faced with an acute shortage of housing and work, and abysmal living conditions back on the reserve or in northern communities, they do not really have any alternative but to seek a better life in the city. However, the prospects for improved living in the cities are not necessarily better. In addition to facing problems finding employment with limited skills, and finding affordable housing, racism can be a deterrent to becoming active residents of their communities. Having arrived with the best of intentions, they may soon wind up living in rundown housing in poor neighbourhoods. If economics causes poorer Aboriginal people to congregate in the poorest neighbourhoods, racism further segregates them. Yet as we have noted in the preceding chapter, the Aboriginal population of Saskatoon has recently been spreading out into other (generally middle-class) neighbourhoods.

Relatively little recent research has been conducted on the mobility and resettlement of Native migrants. Among informative CMHC reports have been a study of the effects of urban Aboriginal residential mobility conducted by the Saskatchewan Institute of Indian Technologies (SIIT) in 2002–4 (Gareau 2002; CMHC 2004b), which focused on the impact of a high mobility rate on urban Aboriginal populations' access to services; and a report that measured residential mobility of urban Aboriginal people (CMHC 2000), which focused on Toronto and Winnipeg. One ambitious ongoing project on First Nations and Metis mobility and service needs, conducted by the Institute of Urban Studies at the University of Winnipeg (IUS 2009), has aimed at developing a better appreciation of the circumstances, expectations, and experiences of Aboriginal people moving to Winnipeg, as well as developing a better understanding of service needs and the extent to which those needs are or are not being met. This project has targeted people arriving within the previous year; they are interviewed several times over a period of 12 to 15 months, and an exit survey is conducted for those leaving the city. These researchers have found it very challenging to maintain sufficient contact with the migrants. Moreover, they have learned that the 'satisfaction' of respondents with their life circumstances and with various types of services is a very relative concept, one that is affected by housing, services, and neighbourhood context (all of these considerations were explored in detail in the research conducted within the Bridges and Foundations Project).

*Contact with Original Communities*

The national Urban Aboriginal Peoples Study (2010) has added some pertinent information on urban Aboriginal mobility between cities and original communities. This study found that urban Aboriginal people retain a strong sense of connection to their place of origin; yet at the same time, increasing numbers of urban Aboriginal residents have been born and raised in the city and so have little if any familiarity with the original communities from which their families migrated. Most (61%) of the respondents described their connection to their community of origin either as 'very close' or 'fairly close'; especially the first generation reported still feeling close. While the majority of the study's respondents were migrants, a relatively limited number had ever returned to their original communities to live or planned to return permanently. Metis and Non-Status First Nations people are more urbanized than Status First Nations people; they are also the least likely to move back and are often the longest resident in the city. So what demographers call the 'churn' effect – movement between city and reserves or traditional communities – was limited; but of the relatively small minority who had ever moved back, almost half had done so during the past year. Asked whether they planned to return, almost one-quarter of the respondents answered affirmatively; the same number were not sure; the remaining half said they had no such intention. Of urban Aboriginal people interviewed in the study, an estimated 68% were first generation (migrants), 22% were second generation (born and raised in the city), and 9% were third generation (children of the second generation). Interestingly, this national study found that 61% had lived the longest in the city – more than ten years. Asked about their reasons for moving from their original communities, the largest number mentioned work, finding employment, or career consider- ations (46%); family (38%), education (37%), and city amenities (18%) (UAPS 2010, 2, 28–35). It is interesting to compare these results from the UAPS with those from specific surveys conducted in Saskatoon by the Bridges and Foundations Project.

*The City as Home*

Findings from the Bridges and Foundations Project indicated that urban Aboriginal people in Saskatoon have become a permanent part of the city population; increasing numbers of Aboriginal residents, especially those more familiar with the city than with a reserve or traditional community, view the city as home. Later, the Urban Aboriginal Peoples Study similarly supported the permanency of urban Aboriginal settle- ment, emphasizing that Aboriginal communities within urban areas should not simply be viewed as transplanted traditional communities. Clearly, a strong feeling is emerging among urban Aboriginal residents that the city is their final destination; the UAPS found that far more of these residents now viewed the city rather than their original commu- nity as 'home.' A high proportion preferred city living, primarily due to the variety found in city life, proximity of family and friends, and avail- ability of employment and opportunities for career advancement. The most prevalent negative concern, especially in Winnipeg and Saskatoon, was crime. When respondents were asked about their choice of neigh- bourhood, the most frequent responses had to do with proximity to family and friends, work, school, services, amenities, and shopping. Interestingly, housing affordability was expressed as a top concern by 29% of respondents; however, this finding should be subject to careful interpretation, as a lack of affordable housing in other areas of the city could explain why residents may feel obliged to locate in poorer neigh- bourhoods. In fact, the UAPS found that almost half the limited Saskatoon sample felt that they had little choice but to live in the present neighbourhood . Nevertheless, this study emphasized that almost all Aboriginal residents of cities across Canada are generally contented with urban living, especially if they are employed full-time and are very satisfied with their employment. The UAPS study probed into definitions of success, life aspirations, job satisfaction, and hopes for the future (UAPS 2010, 2, 29, 36–40, 105–13).

An editorial in the *Globe and Mail* (12 April 2010) concluded:

> Urban Aboriginals are not in any simplistic way assimilating to broader Canadian society, but they have a sense of fitting in, and indeed of making a positive contribution to the cities – a notable contrast to some conspicuous signs of Native misery on city streets. Many reserves are isolated and provide few ways to earn a living. It is to be hoped that these longstanding communities endure and maintain their traditions. But the future for most Aboriginals is in the cities ... Much like other people, Aboriginals are doing fairly well with the opportunities – and the stresses – of metropolitan life.

This chapter, concerned with First Nations migrants in the city, includes two case studies conducted under the auspices of the Bridges and Foundations Project, respectively of two of the most progressive and most urbanized First Nations in Saskatchewan: Whitecap Dakota/Sioux First Nation residents in Saskatoon (who represented half the total band members), and the Muskeg Lake Cree First Nation (four of five band members now live off reserve, and this First Nation has led the development of urban reserves in Saskatoon). Both of these case studies of urban band members were initiated, contracted, and conducted by these First Nations. These studies inform us in detail of the character, expectations, and present housing and living conditions of migrants from these two First Nations, as well as both their movement between reserve and city and mobility within the city.

## Migration and Mobility between Reserve and City: Whitecap Dakota/Sioux First Nation Residents in Saskatoon

ALAN B. ANDERSON

*Introduction*

Whitecap Dakota/Sioux First Nation Reserve, located 26 kilometres south of the City of Saskatoon, was first selected as a reserve in 1879. Chief Whitecap (Wapahaska) and Chief Standing Buffalo (Tatankanaje) had fled to Canada following the Minnesota Massacre in 1862. For years the chiefs and their bands led a nomadic existence throughout the southern portion of what would become Saskatchewan. The chiefs frequently travelled to Fort Garry (later Winnipeg) in order to secure from government officials protection for their people. In 1866, most of Chief Standing Buffalo's family died in a smallpox epidemic, and the chief himself died that summer fighting the Crow. Both bands were settled on a reserve in the Qu'appelle Valley by 1878; but Chief Whitecap led his band to Moose Woods the following year, where a reserve was eventually surveyed in 1881 (originally just two sections of land but expanded seven times between 1893 and 1941). Band members moved seasonally to Prince Albert as a casual labour force, as well as to meet with other Dakota bands, such as Wahpeton. As the frontier grew, band members found more employment opportunities nearer to Saskatoon and closer to home (details on Dakota/Sioux history in Saskatchewan are provided in Allan 1969; Kehoe 1970; Howard 1984; and Laviolette 1991).

In recent years Whitecap First Nation has gained a reputation as a progressive reserve. When the present chief, Darcy Bear, first became a band councillor in 1991, the reserve was heavily in debt; there was no running water; local fire protection left a lot to be desired; and unemployment was around 70%. Today unemployment is less than 5% and the reserve has to bring in outside labour in order to fill all the positions available – of more than 600 jobs on reserve (soon expected to increase to 1,000), at least two-thirds are held by Aboriginal people who commute from Saskatoon. This turnaround within a short span of time was systematically planned by the chief and council with the assistance of expert outside managers, consultants, and financial planners employed by the band. To deal with the debts a financial management plan was initially developed, then explicit development policies covering housing, education, health, recreation, and tourism. Soon the reserve had a school, a new fire station, a water treatment plant, and affordable and adequate housing. Economic development was planned to bring employment to the community. Business was attracted through implementation of the First Nations Land Management Act in 1999, which now permitted First Nations governance of their own land, including long-term commercial leasehold agreements and real property tax by-laws administered by the First Nation. With the decision of the FSIN to divert a First Nations casino from downtown Saskatoon in August 2003, Whitecap moved quickly to gain this $62 million project, which has been the major employer. Soon afterwards, the $6 million Dakota Dunes golf course opened, making use of the beautiful natural sand hills scenery (this golf course won an award as the best new course in Canada in 2005 and is currently ranked 17th out of 3,500 courses in Canada, and recently hosted the Saskatchewan Open on the Canadian Tour). The golf course was paid off in just six years, half the anticipated time. The First Nation now works closely with the surrounding rural municipalities and nearby city in tourism and recreation development. The highway into Saskatoon has been substantially upgraded and is now being extended southward into a significant tourist/recreation region. The Dakota Dunes Hotel and Convention Centre, a major destination resort hotel and spa adjacent to the casino, together with a high-end resort community of townhouses and condos, will comprise a $100 million development. In an effort to build up housing revenue and attract band members back to the reserve, Whitecap First Nation is contributing $744,000 and the Saskatchewan Housing Corporation $1.7 million to a $2.4 million affordable housing project of twelve units. This would represent the first time the provincial government has funded on-reserve housing (normally a federal responsibility). For its part, the federal government is contributing $3 million to the $26.5 million hotel and spa project. The hotel will be one quarter owned by Muskoday Cree First Nation. It is expected to maintain a $2 million profit each year. The Whitecap Trail Business Park is being planned; this will include aerospace and defence companies (Boeing and Lockheed Martin), with a $150,000 assessment paid by the federal government (the local Conservative MP happens to be Minister of State for Western Economic Diversification) together with the Whitecap Development Corporation. These developments will provide employment for more than 800 people – more employment opportunities than there are residents.

The chief, band manager, and band council agreed during the summer of 2003 to conduct a survey within the Bridges and Foundations Project in order to learn more about band members living in Saskatoon as well as the causes and dynamics of migration and mobility between the reserve and the city. Only very limited generalized information on Aboriginal migration and urbanization was available from government sources such as Statistics Canada and INAC; it was anticipated that this detailed study of Whitecap band members could help fill this void. Relevant information and data would be obtained through personal interviews with Whitecap First Nation urban band members. The survey focused not only on migration but also on the housing needs of urban band members.

The completed sample consisted of 30 households (representing all of the band members living in Saskatoon who could be located and who agreed to be interviewed). Household heads were interviewed;

however, certain types of data were gathered on all household members. A high response rate was ensured by the full cooperation of the Whitecap First Nation and especially by the involvement of the band manager and council in the planning of this survey, as well as by the fact that interviews were conducted by a band member.

*Basic Data on Respondents*

The average number of people living in a home was 3.5, yet there was considerable variation in the number of occupants per household, ranging from one to eight. As four might now be the norm (in general society) for a household consisting of a nuclear family, crowding did not seem to be much of a problem for most respondents, although it should be noted that 30% of household heads interviewed were living in larger households than that level. The respondents tended to be quite young (46.7% were in their twenties, 26.7% in their thirties, 13.3% in their forties, and 10% in their fifties; while a single respondent was over sixty). Other household members typically included spouses and partners as well as sons and daughters; yet they also included grandparents, brothers and sisters, and friends of the family. Considerable variety was noted in types of participation in the labour force; respondents were categorized in a wide variety of occupations, as current students, and as homemakers. Only three respondents were currently unemployed. Again, considerable variety was found in the highest level of education attained: four household heads had completed only grade school, four had at least some high school education; seven had graduated from high school; three had at least some university; two had completed a degree; and seven reported other types of post-secondary education.

*Migration and Mobility*

Residence in the city was generally quite long-term. Asked when they had first moved to Saskatoon, three respondents indicated that they had arrived before 1980, eight during the 1980s, sixteen during the 1990s. This would seem to suggest that movement into the city had been increasing. While many respondents were long-term residents, approximately one-third had moved to Saskatoon during the past 10 years.

We were particularly interested in learning whether this movement tended to be unidirectional or whether people also moved back to the reserve or perhaps back and forth between reserve and city. The results were highly variable: of the respondents who provided information on how many times they have moved between reserve and city, half had moved only once, one-quarter had moved two or three times, and four had moved four or more times, while only two reported that they had never moved (they were born in the city).

The primary motivation for moving from reserve to city was employment opportunities (43.3%), followed by education reasons (33.3%), improved accommodations (33.3%), personal reasons (23.3%), family reunification (20%), or an expressed general dislike of living on the reserve (10%). Surprisingly, only a single respondent emphasized improved access to health care. The decisión to remain in the city was affected by employment (53.3%), education (33.3%), improved accommodations (23.3%), family reasons (20%), or to be close to friends (20%).

Interestingly, in spite of the rapid development of Whitecap, most respondents (60%) expressed no immediate intentions of moving back to the reserve. Of the respondents who provided specific answers as to why they are not planning to move back to the reserve, one-third still believed that the reserve had limited opportunities, and two-thirds said they were more comfortable in the city. However, most of the respondents were not sure whether they would actually ever move back, stating that it would depend on future circumstances; or they answered vaguely, 'perhaps in the next five to ten years.' The reasons given by the few respondents for definitely planning to move back to the reserve were better accommodations at Whitecap, improved highway conditions, and possible employment opportunities and future development on the reserve.

There has been a considerable degree of mobility among Whitecap First Nation residents within the city. When asked how many times they had moved residence during the past five years, 26.7% of the respondents reported having moved three or more times, 40% twice, and 3.3% once; 30% had not moved at all. One-third of the 30 households surveyed had lived in the same neighbourhood for one year or less, another third for two to four years, and the remaining third for more than five years, which points to both relatively high mobility and some propensity to become more sedentary.

### Settlement in City Neighbourhoods

Most band members in the city were living in west side neighbourhoods in which there were an increasing number of Aboriginal residents; several households were located east of the river (closest to the road out of town to Whitecap). When respondents were asked how satisfied they were with the neighbourhood, a significant proportion (70%) were very satisfied with their neighbourhood and expressed virtually no complaints about the area where they were living; just over one-quarter (26.7%) had mixed feelings, both complaints and satisfactions about their neighbourhoods; very few (only 3.3%) expressed only dissatisfaction with their particular neighbourhood. Most respondents expressed satisfaction with access to public transportation, shopping, services, and schools; however, almost one-third believed that their neighbourhood was unsafe. In ranking those factors that determined where they wished to live in the city, respondents tended to emphasize living in a safe neighbourhood (66.7% ranked this first) and proximity to schools (30% ranked this second) and to shops and services (40% ranked this third). Respondents seemed less concerned about proximity to family or friends, nor were they particularly concerned about cultural diversity as a factor in selecting location.

*Housing*

Detailed information was gathered on the types of housing occupied by band members. Most (60%) were living in a single detached house; apartment living was next most common (20%), followed by living in a duplex (16.7%) or basement suite (3.3%). Respondents who lived in a single house had changed their address as frequently as those living in a duplex, apartment, or basement suite. The most prevalent reasons for renting instead of owning a home apparently were the inability to buy the type of home desired, wanting the flexibility of being able to move whenever desired, and the inability to obtain a mortgage.

The band members' two main complaints regarding the condition of their present accommodations were that the home was too small for their family and that the home was in a poor location, although as we have seen, the latter opinion did not necessarily translate into dissatisfaction with the neighbourhood. More than one-quarter of homes were in poor condition or poorly maintained (in the respondents' own opinion). The respondents also expressed their dissatisfaction over inadequate green/recreation space, high rent or mortgage payments, and high utility costs.

If the respondents were buying a home, a large majority preferred a single detached house; the second choice was a townhouse-style condominium, and the third a duplex. One-third of all respondents required a home with more than three bedrooms, one-third opted for three bedrooms, and just under one-third two bedrooms; only one respondent needed a single-bedroom home. Almost all respondents required the same number of bedrooms as the number of people in their home, or less, although some believed they needed one more bedroom than the number of people in the household.

*Reserve and City Living Compared*

Numerous points were mentioned when respondents were asked to compare living in the city with living on the reserve. Responses favouring urban living included the following: better transportation, better services, more opportunities in general (or the reserve had 'nothing to offer'), better employment opportunities (or little employment on reserve), proximity to family/friends, more individualism, a sense of community, and better health care. Also pointed out were the following: the distance, time, and expense of travel between city and reserve; limited accommodation on the reserve; and disagreement with reserve politics. Far fewer responses favoured life on on the reserve. When mentioned, these included more 'peace and quiet,' more sense of community, more chances to maintain traditional culture, the proximity of family/friends, and less crime.

Complex cross-analysis of migrant motivation was revealing. When respondents were asked if they would move back to the reserve if housing was available, 43.3% said no, they would still prefer living in the city; 26.7% supposed that they would; and 30.3% responded that 'it would depend.' The availability of entertainment facilities, transportation, and shops and services in the city seemed to have little influence on whether the respondent would move to the reserve if housing were available. When this study was conducted, Whitecap First Nation was just beginning its rapid economic development; yet urban band members seemed rather ambivalent about reserve development. We were led to conclude that reserve development would not necessarily affect the large proportion of band members who had chosen to live in the city.

This survey of urban band members found a lot of variety in frequency of visits to the reserve – visits doubtless facilitated by the proximity of the reserve to the city. Of the 30 household heads interviewed, 12 reported that they visited frequently (daily to weekly, 'whenever possible,' or 'often'); four visited at least once a month, five annually, and nine rarely or never. When asked how often they attended band meetings, over half never attended them, four attended 'once in a while,' four attended 'somewhat' or 'somewhat often,' two 'very often,' and two 'whenever possible.' Many (almost two-thirds) of the respondents claimed that they kept up to date with Whitecap activities through the newsletter, 'word of mouth,' family contacts, and Whitecap staff. A large majority of respondents said they would be interested in an active band program for housing; however, one household head specified *only* if the housing was in the city.

## Urban Housing Needs of the Muskeg Lake Cree Nation

ALAN B. ANDERSON

*Introduction*

The Muskeg Lake Cree Nation is moving toward establishing an Affordable Housing Program for its band members living in the urban setting. The program would involve three phases: collection of base information, followed by program design and development. In an attempt to meet the first phase, the Muskeg Lake Cree Nation collaborated with the Bridges and Foundations Project . The housing director (*ka-nikanis-kahk waskahikanihkewin*) – officially Chair of the Affordable Housing Program Development Committee of the Muskeg Lake Cree Nation – gained this committee's approval for a research proposal developed by the Research Director of the Bridges and Foundations Project. A questionnaire was then mailed out to all band members living off reserve (more than four in every five band members). The survey was intended to identify the basic parameters required for the design of the Affordable Housing Program; it would determine the wants and needs of Muskeg Lake Cree Nation members in the urban environment, especially Saskatoon. The specific objectives of the research were as follows: to determine why Muskeg Lake Cree Nation members are moving to urban centres; which Saskatoon neighbourhoods they are moving to and why; the types of housing members are currently living in; members' level of satisfaction with their current housing situation; the extent to which members are interested in homeownership; the types of housing members want and need; and members' needs in urban neighbourhoods and communities and the services available or needed. The stated long-term objectives of this research were to understand and address the factors that might be preventing Muskeg Lake Cree Nation families from homeownership; to increase the numbers of Muskeg Lake Cree

Nation families moving into homeownership; and to improve home ownership opportunities for Muskeg Lake Cree Nation families.

## Methodology

The Muskeg Lake Cree Nation, which has a home reserve approximately 90 kilometres northwest of Saskatoon, and an urban reserve in Saskatoon (used for institutional and commercial purposes), consisted at the time of the survey of 1,024 adult voting members out of a total band membership of 1,645. Only an estimated 240 members remained on reserve. Approximately one in five off-reserve households were located in Saskatoon, another quarter elsewhere in Saskatchewan, over one-quarter in Alberta (notably Edmonton and Calgary), about 10% in British Columbia (mainly Vancouver), perhaps 8% in Toronto, and others in Montreal, Winnipeg, the Northwest Territories, and the United States. A mailing list of all band members was compiled from last known addresses. The survey questionnaire was completed finally by 144 household heads living off reserve; however, information was collected on approximately three times that number who were occupants of the respondents' households. The survey had four main purposes: to construct a profile of households and respondents, detailing household size as well as each principal respondent's age, education, and employment; to learn more about the migratory patterns and mobility of band members; to gain a better understanding about the housing conditions of urban band members; and to gain insight into the crucial financial situation of primarily urban band members.

## Profile of Households and Respondents

We learned that the average household was fairly small, usually two to four people (almost three-quarters of the total sample); there were only nine dwellings with six to ten people. Household heads tended to be quite young: the average age of the household head was between 31 and 40. Occupations represented by household heads were diverse. The largest numbers of respondents were employed in sales and services. This was followed by trades; transport, equipment operators, and related occupations; and business, finance, and administration. A significant number of household heads were quite well educated: 35.4% had only a high school education, but one-quarter had a technical/business/vocational school education, 20.8% at least some university education, and another 4.9% a university degree. Regarding family structure, conventional marriages were far more common than common law relationships. Most households contained one or two children, most of them the sons and daughters of the respondent. However, in keeping with the First Nations tradition of extended families, other children included grandchildren, stepchildren, nieces and nephews, and occasionally foster children. Significant numbers of young children as well as teenagers were recorded. Data were collected on the age, education, and possible employment of up to nine other occupants of each household besides the respondent; however, analysing these data proved extremely complex, given the large number of persons recorded – at least 428, including the principal respondents.

*Migration and Mobility*

The Muskeg Lake diaspora is heavily urbanized and mobile: 73.6% of the household heads were living in a city, 12.5% in a town, and 6.9% in a rural area off reserve; also, 6.9% had already moved back to the reserve. Almost two-thirds (64.6%) of the respondents had been where they are now located for more than five years. In the previous five years, 36.8% had not moved, 42.4% had moved one to three times, and 19.4% had moved more than three times. Those situated in a city or town moved the most, accounting for 95% of the respondents who moved three times and for all of the respondents who moved more than three times. Many rationales were given for moving. The most often repeated were as follows: the home was too small; they were moving to a better home; the monthly cost was too high; there had been changes in the family; they wanted to be closer to work; the home was in poor condition; they wanted to live in a safer neighbourhood; they wanted to be closer to shops and services, schools or universities, or public transportation, and to live in an area with more cultural diversity; they had changed employment; they had needed to find less expensive housing, perhaps because of a change in their financial situation; they wanted to live in the country; they had retired. When asked if they had plans to move in the future, 52.1% answered yes, 41.2% no, and 4.2% not sure. Respondents who were already living in a city or town seemed quite divided in their anticipation of moving, whereas respondents who were living in a rural area or back on the reserve were more likely to have no plans to move (60% and 80% respectively). Of the respondents who expected to move, 29.8% wanted to move in the next year and 36.9% in the next three to five years. The main reason why respondents definitely planned to move was to purchase their own home. The next most prominent grounds for moving were financial or related to the size of the present home or to work. Other reasons included affordability, escaping a bad neighbourhood, a desire to move back to the reserve, health care, employment, and family reunification.

## Housing Conditions

Substantial dissatisfaction with housing conditions was found. More than half (57.6%) of households were living in a single detached house, far fewer in an apartment (15.3%), in a townhouse/condo (10.4%), or in a duplex (9%). The remainder were living in a basement suite, fourplex, trailer, suite, or some other form of accommodation. Over half (56.9%) of the respondents were satisfied with their current living accommodations. A high proportion (72%) of those living in a single house were satisfied, whereas very few (8.5%) of those in a townhouse/condo or an apartment were satisfied. Almost half (43.1%) were not satisfied with their current living accommodations; of those who were not satisfied, half asserted that their home was too small, almost one-third (32.2%) that the home was too expensive, and almost another third (32.2%) that the home was in poor condition.

The household heads were divided between renters (a small majority) and homeowners. Slightly more than half (57.6%) of respondents were renting their home. When asked to provide reasons for renting, almost two-thirds (65.1%) of the renters emphasized that they were unable to afford the type of home they wanted, and over half (53%) said they were unable to obtain a mortgage. Other reasons were that they felt uncomfortable dealing with banks, that they liked being able to move whenever they wanted, that they didn't want the responsibility of homeownership, or that they viewed their present accommodation as short-term. Less frequently, respondents said that they just 'weren't ready' to own a home, that no other accommodations were available, that they weren't familiar with the process of buying a home, that they were trying to pay off debts, that they would relocate soon for employment, that they were trying to build up a better credit rating, that their employment situation was unstable, or that they already owned a home elsewhere, and one respondent lived in a seniors home.

Homeowners seemed more satisfied with their housing conditions. Almost half (47.2%) of the respondents owned their own home, and of these homeowners, a high proportion (70.6%) were satisfied with their home. The unsatisfied respondents' two most prominent reasons for lack of satisfaction were that the home was too small and that it was in poor condition. Other reasons given for dissatisfaction were as follows: their home was not close enough to university/college or to schools, to public transportation, or to family and friends; that the neighbourhood was unsafe; and that there was insufficient cultural diversity. Almost all household heads expressed interest in a program that would help them buy a home. The first choice of the majority of respondents was clearly a single house; the second choice, a duplex; the third, a townhouse-style condominium. An apartment-style condominium was the least popular choice. Several individuals required a wheelchair-accessible home. When asked how many bedrooms they would need, 46.5% said three, 23.6% said two, and 23.6% more than three. When purchasing a home, the most important location concerns were as follows: a safe neighbourhood; proximity to work, schools, universities, shopping, other services, public transportation, and family and friends; and a culturally diverse neighbourhood.

*Financial Considerations*

This survey probed the complexities of household finances. The largest number of households (42.4%) had a total annual household income over $42,000; however, one-third earned less than half that amount. Fully three-quarters of the more affluent households were satisfied with their single house; satisfaction tended to increase with income, yet those in apartments, townhouses, and duplexes or fourplexes were generally not satisfied regardless of their income. The total household annual income seemed to have no relationship to the number of moves in the previous five years. A little over half (54.2%) of the respondents were employed full- time, 13.2% part-time; also, 19.4% were unemployed and 8.3% were retired. Of the households containing two or more people, 32.5% reported that the second person identified was employed full-time, 39.7% that the second person was unemployed. Also, 76.4% of all respondents claimed personal property as an asset, 70.1% a saving/chequing account, 43.1% investments, 39.6% a home as an asset, and 16.7% land as an asset. A small percentage (6.9%) of respondents reported having no assets. When respondents were asked about their debts, credit card debt was mentioned most often (50.7%), closely followed by debt with a car loan/lease (48.6%), then personal loans (29.2%), a personal line of credit (26.4%), and a student loan debt (20.1%). A very small proportion (4.9%) reported having no debts at all. The average total monthly debt payment was over $700. Many respondents (36.8%) had monthly housing expenses exceeding $900; 20.8% were paying $700 to $900 a month, 16.0% $500 to $700, and 21.5% $300 to $500. Approximately half the respondents reported that they were able to maintain credit; most of the remainder reported that they were not, except for a very few who claimed that they had never applied for credit. Of the respondents who were unable to maintain credit, most replied that it was due to a bad credit history, and almost one-third said this was the result of not having a high enough income. Some claimed that they had declared bankruptcy, while a very small number did not want to obtain credit at all.

## Chapter Four

# Neighbourhood Living

## Aboriginal Living Conditions and Health

This chapter provides information on living in inner-city neighbourhoods in Saskatoon. First, though, in the introduction it relates urban Aboriginal living conditions to health problems in Saskatoon and more generally in Canada. This introduction first discusses urban Aboriginal poverty, then implications for housing and living conditions, various health issues, and, finally, quality-of-life research and its policy implications. The specific research from the Bridges and Foundations Project described in this chapter includes three separate surveys of residents of particular neighbourhoods. The first survey gathered detailed data on Aboriginal residents in a wide variety of west-side Saskatoon neighbourhoods, profiling their occupations, employment, education levels, cultural identity, family composition, housing, migration and mobility, and integration into their neighbourhood communities. The second survey interviewed over a thousand residents of five inner-city neighbourhoods to hear their concerns as well as their impressions of their issues and needs. The third survey focused on a single neighbourhood, Pleasant Hill, which is the poorest neighbourhood in the city and contains the highest proportion of Aboriginal population, to ascertain the residents' main concerns for their neighbourhood and to contrast homeowners with renters.

### Urban Aboriginal Poverty

For many Aboriginal residents of Saskatoon, poverty, poor housing conditions, and health are closely interlinked. International research studies, such as a 2010 UNICEF report *The Children Left Behind,* as well as recent Canadian research (Ross 2004), have emphasized that income inequality has a significant impact on population health; moreover, that poverty leads to marginality and exclusion (PRI 2005). According to a poll conducted by Environics for the Canadian Centre for Policy Alternatives (CCPA) in 2006, fully half of all Canadians feared that they were excluded from economic well-being; almost two-thirds of the people polled across the country felt that any benefits from recent economic growth had gone to well-off rather than average Canadians (CCPA 2006). In fact, this perceived gap between rich and poor has been increasing rather than diminishing, especially in view of the economic recession. In 2007, even before the present economic downturn, approximately 637,000 children – 9.5% of all Canadian children – were living in poverty. The national child poverty rate was 12% for non-immigrants, whereas it was 34% for Aboriginal people, according to Statistics Canada data in November 2009. Since the federal government pledged to eliminate child poverty, with the formation of the National Anti-Poverty Organization back in 1971, poverty among seniors has nearly doubled even while the Canadian GDP has more than doubled (*Saskatoon StarPhoenix*, 26 November 2009).

A report of Poverty Free Saskatchewan, released in October 2011, estimates that 140,000 people in Saskatchewan, including 44,000 children are poor. The CCPA reported in 2006 that the top 10% of Saskatchewan families were receiving 28% of all income, the bottom half only 18%; the wealthiest 10% had an average income of $206,922, the poorest 10% an income of $14,696. In the province, 13% of women and 9% of men live in poverty. Based on 2004 data, it was estimated that approximately $352 million was needed to raise all poor Saskatchewan families to the poverty line (*Regina Leader-Post*, 25 November 2006). As the *2004 Report Card on Child Poverty in Saskatchewan* put it, tens of thousands of children in the province "go to bed hungry, cold and deprived of the necessities most people take for granted." The *2008 Report Card on Child and Family Poverty in Canada* reported that the child poverty rate in Saskatchewan was now the second highest in Canada. Saskatchewan's child poverty rate (the proportion of children living below the statistical poverty line) has fluctuated from 21.7% in 1989 to 18.7% in 2001 and 19.9% in 2006, but consistently has been higher than the Canadian national child poverty rate, which has remained relatively unchanged: 15.1% in 1989, 15.6% in 2001, 15.8% in 2006.

Moreover, Aboriginal people constitute a disproportionate share of the poor and of children living in poverty. Approximately half of First Nations children younger than six living off reserve in Canada are in low-income families (compared to 18% of non-Aboriginal children of this age; moreover, 57% of Aboriginal children in larger cities live in low-income families; and at least one-third of all Aboriginal children are in families where access to healthy food is a concern (*Vancouver Sun*, 8 November 2011). Aboriginal children are about four times more likely to be living in poverty than other children; it is estimated that between one-quarter and one-half of all Aboriginal children in Saskatchewan are living in poverty. The most recent estimate is that 51% of Aboriginal children under the age of six in Saskatchewan live in low-income families, compared to 15% of other children.

Infant mortality is closely related to child poverty. Saskatchewan now has the highest infant mortality rate in Canada; children under the age of one year die more frequently in Saskatchewan than in any other province (the infant mortality rate in Saskatchewan is 8.3 per 1,000 live births, compared to a national average of 5.4). Mark Lemstra, Saskatoon health researcher and columnist, suggests that child poverty in Saskatchewan could be virtually eliminated for $178 million a year. In his view, Saskatchewan could lower the incidence of infant mortality by as much as 73% by redirecting and reprioritizing provincial health funding. He argues that 'the ultimate measure of a society is how many children are allowed to die unnecessarily when there are known preventive measures ... and the second most important measure is how many are allowed to live in poverty' (*Saskatoon StarPhoenix*, 23 December 2010; 22 December 2011).

Almost one in every five residents of the City of Saskatoon lives in poverty (39,955 in 2006, i.e., 18% of the population); and the proportion may be as much as three times higher among Aboriginal residents, according to the Saskatoon Anti-Poverty Coalition and a variety of recent research (MacDermott 2003; Grosso 2003; Jackson 2004; CUISR 2006). A majority of Aboriginal residents of Saskatoon and Regina are living in statistical poverty, which compounds their marginalization. The gap between rich and poor is widest in these two largest Saskatchewan cities, according to a report of the Canadian Institute for Health Information (CIHI 2008b); compared with major cities across Canada, Saskatoon and Regina have repeatedly been ranked first and second for the greatest discrepancies in hospitalization rates, especially for substance abuse, chronic obstructive pulmonary disorder, diabetes, and mental health problems.

Residents of the poorest neighbourhoods suffer disproportionately from illness and depression. For most indicators used in the research, there was a gradient in all of Canada's fifteen largest cities showing that the lower the socio-economic status, the higher the rates of injuries, chronic diseases, and high-risk health behaviours. Socio-economic status was defined as a combination of material means (income, education, employment, housing) and marital/family status. In Saskatchewan a large disproportion of single-parent (usually female-headed) families is Aboriginal, and it is noteworthy that nearly half (47.5%) of children living in female-headed lone-parent families are poor. That is four times the prevalence of poverty among children in families with two parents (*Saskatoon StarPhoenix*, 24 November 2008).

As Lemstra has pointed out (*Saskatoon StarPhoenix*, 13 January 2011), income is a major if not *the* main predictor of almost all infectious and chronic diseases in Saskatoon, as across Canada, with few exceptions. The poor health of low-income residents is assumed to be due to their unhealthy lifestyle, yet if high-risk behaviours as causes of poor health outcomes are statistically removed, low-income residents still exhibit far higher rates of disease and premature mortality; these risk behaviours account for less than one-third of higher disease rates among lower-income residents. Aboriginal residents have higher rates of virtually every disease, disorder, and risk behaviour monitored; but actually, their relatively lower levels of income, employment, and education together contribute to disparities in health, which are thus explicable more by social environment than by cultural heredity. Both Lemstra (2012) and Meili (2012) make the important point that health disparities among disadvantaged groups are entirely preventable. Poverty does not simply cause poor health; rather, the inability to participate fully in urban society negatively impacts health. In his view, the most controversial notion to confront may be that health care services have a limited impact on health outcomes. Governments disproportionately allocate much of their budgets toward health care services when they could be investing in initiatives that promote education, employment, and social services. Expanded social assistance, subsidized housing, and day care are needed for residents to participate successfully in educational and employment initiatives. It follows that the principal factors predicting health outcomes – income, education, employment, and housing – cannot be adequately funded without reducing expenditures in health care services through evidence-based protocols. A national and a Saskatchewan provincial anti-poverty strategy are urgently needed and entirely feasible (Mulvale and Englot 2011).

Poverty, especially child poverty, may relate closely to health problems and to an ability to feed families adequately (Lemstra 2009b). Over 18,000 people per month use food banks in Saskatchewan, and this number is currently increasing 9% a year for the province and at an even faster rate – 12% - for the City of Saskatoon (this is still far less than the 61% increase recorded in Alberta). Aboriginal people are disproportionate users of food banks – 12% nationally but 62.5% in Saskatoon. An estimated 12,000 people use the Saskatoon food bank at least twice a month and another 8,000 once a month (*Saskatoon Sun*, 22 November 2009; Bowditch 2003; Woods 2003). A national survey of food bank users counted in March 2011 revealed that 38% of 851,014 users were under the age of 18; 43% of 20,665 users counted in Saskatchewan were children. Nationally 10% were Aboriginal: 63.3% were living in market/rental housing, 22.1% were living in social/subsidized housing; and 7.2% were homeowners. Some 40% were living alone; however, relatively few were staying 'temporarily' with family or friends (3.3%), or in shelters or group homes (1.8%), or were homeless out on the street (0.7%) (*Globe and Mail*, 11 November 2011). In his research on food security in Winnipeg, Max Aulinger (2010) emphasizes that food is not simply a product; rather, it needs to be considered a relationship. With at least 2,300 families (most of them Aboriginal) waiting for social housing at a time of declining availability, less and less is available in family budgets for food – the family food budget is stretched to the utmost limit as accommodation costs increase. So housing directly impacts food security, and poor families become less healthy. The Child Hunger and Education Program (CHEP), a community agency in Saskatoon dedicated to building community through working with children, families, and core communities to improve their access to healthy food, has partnered with First Nations and Metis organizations (including the Saskatoon Indian and Metis Friendship Centre) to ensure food security, which is viewed as particularly hard hit by rising housing costs. The Smart Cities, Healthy Kids: Food Environment research project that commenced in Saskatoon in September 2010 is examining access of families with children to healthy food in their neighbourhoods; the distribution of supermarkets and restaurants in the city; the availability of nutritious food to neighbourhoods; the links between healthy food environments and families' socio-economic levels; and how this may affect food choices for families with children, and thus children's health. For many residents, it is easier to get to a fast food restaurant and convenience store than to an adequate grocery store. Less than half the entire city population lives within reasonably short walking distance of a supermarket, whereas three-quarters can easily walk to a fast food outlet. Only an estimated 17% have more than a single supermarket within easy access by foot, but the average resident has at least three fast food choices nearby. In particular, inner-city neighbourhoods where the Aboriginal population is most concentrated have become 'food deserts,' with the poorest access to healthy food. Ready access to a food store (*micim-atawewikamik*) is fundamental to a local community.

## Housing Conditions

Poor housing conditions (including poor state of repair, overcrowding, involuntary residential mobility, monthly expenditure on housing a cost of living, and insecurity of tenure) are closely related to poverty and health problems (Walker 2010). Research for Habitat for Humanity commissioned by CMHC reports that safe and affordable housing improves residents' physical and mental health; for example, a child living in decent housing is ten times less likely to contract meningitis, asthma, or respiratory complications, and this effectively reduces dependency on social services. Moreover, improved housing clearly results in children's improved school performance, behaviour, and well-being (*Saskatoon StarPhoenix*, 26 November 2010). Both adults and children in poor or inadequate housing typically exhibit a wide range of physical and mental health problems. Provision of suitable, affordable housing would in the long run save governments many millions of dollars in health costs. Social assistance payments to families in need fall far short of accommodation costs, and this in turn seriously affects the ability to maintain a healthy diet and lifestyle.

In assessing housing conditions, CMHC distinguishes between 'adequate,' 'suitable,' and 'affordable' dwellings: 'adequate' dwellings are those reported by their residents as not requiring any major repairs; 'suitable' dwellings have enough bedrooms for the size and make-up of resident households, according to National Occupancy Standard requirements; 'affordable' dwellings cost less than 30% of before-tax household income. By definition, a household spending 50% or more of its income on shelter would fall below the affordability standard. A household is defined as being in 'core housing need' if its housing falls below at least one of these adequacy, suitability, or affordability standards and if it would have to spend 30% or more of its before-tax income to pay the median rent of alternative local housing that would meet all three standards. 'Shelter costs' refers to household expenditure on housing each month. 'Severe housing affordability problems' refers to households that spend half or more of their income on shelter and that are in core housing need. In 2001, 6.5% of all Canadian households were spending 50% or more of their income on shelter, and 20.2% were spending 30% or more on shelter. Affordability is the main reason for falling into core housing need; it follows that households in core housing need have significantly lower incomes than other households. According to CMHC data in 2005, more than 80% of households in core housing need and spending more than half their income on shelter have annual incomes of less than $20,000, and 30.2% have incomes under $10,000; whereas only 15.6% of all Canadian households reported an income of less than $20,000 and just 2.9% an income of less than $10,000.

It is important to note that a higher proportion of Aboriginal households living outside reserves are in core housing need and are spending more than half their income on shelter costs (8.5%) than is the case for non-Aboriginal households (5.2%). In 2001, almost one-quarter of all Aboriginal households in Canada outside reserves were in core housing need: 24%, compared to 13.5% of non-Aboriginal households. At the time, Aboriginal households comprised only 2.8% of all Canadian households but 4.8% of all households in core housing need; specifically in Saskatchewan, Aboriginal households made up a far higher proportion both of all households (9.2%) and especially of households in core housing need (22.9% – which was the highest proportion in any Canadian province, though not as high as in the territories). The housing conditions of off-reserve Status Indian households have continued to slowly improve, with slightly more than half (54.7% in 2006) of households nationally living above housing standards, compared to 52.4% in 2001 and 47.4% in 1996 (NHRC, Spring 2010).

Public complaints over 'problem properties' in Saskatoon are now estimated to number more than six hundred. The fire department is responsible for the city's property maintenance bylaw: tickets for offences range from $250 for the first offence, $500 for the second, and $750 for the third. However, just five staff are dealing with problem properties while the backlog of complaints steadily increases (*Saskatoon StarPhoenix*, 11 July 2012).

Poor housing and living conditions have a direct bearing on children's health and educational advancement. Children living in overcrowded homes may suffer from anxiety, depression, and behavioural problems, which in turn are likely to affect their educational achievement. Residential mobility, too, has a significant impact. Adequate, affordable housing with security of tenure can contribute to a healthy family and learning environment (Walker 2010). Some Aboriginal families with children are living in boarded-up houses slated for demolition. Such houses, of course, lack any services – heating, electricity, gas, water, waste removal. Other families continue to live in houses condemned by health inspectors as 'unsanitary and unfit for human habitation.' While these homes may be clearly posted, they are also clearly occupied; yet tenants may not be evicted immediately unless the domicile is considered 'life-threatening' – theoretically, occupants may remain at least until the end of the month despite unsanitary conditions. In one such case, a Metis man was paying $500 a month to live with his aunt and five children in a condemned house. He expected the landlord to clean up the place, but 'things kept falling apart.' Typically, such houses feature non-functioning plumbing (toilets that don't flush, sinks and bathtubs that don't drain), rusted and leaking pipes, exposed electrical wiring, cracked walls, heaving floors, damp carpeting, crumbling foundation walls mixed with rodent droppings. In one home, several children were sleeping on soiled mattresses on the floor of the unfinished basement, next to an old furnace, the only source of heat to offset the gaping holes in the disintegrating walls, which offered easy passage to stray cats, who at least might help control the vermin. In another house, a family with young children and grandparents lived in overcrowded conditions; they were dismayed that the family of squatters in the boarded house next door had stolen the kids' bikes and now had just hung their dog on a fencepost. Pest control services in the city note a multiple increase in reported bedbug infestations.

Fire (*iskotew*) is all too familiar to families living in poor as well as subsidized affordable housing. Fires have repeatedly devastated inner west side homes and apartment buildings. Many such fires have been the result of poor rental property maintenance by landlords (as we will see further in chapter 7); others have been the result of deliberate targeting by gang members (one such house accommodated seventeen people), or reported negligence by smoking renters, as was the recent case for an apartment building run by the reputable Quint Development Corporation, which has done much to provide affordable housing in the inner city. In this latter case, the fire displaced twenty-two families and resulted in $1.5 million in damage.

*Implications for Health*

The close relationship between inadequate housing and poor health has been extensively examined in Canada (Moloughney 2004; CMHC March 2004; CIHI 2006), and more specifically for Aboriginal residents (CMHC, August 2004; Stokes 2004). Aboriginal Canadians too often become familiar with the hospital (*ahkosiwikamik*), and they continue to suffer from poor health at far higher rates than the general population: 19% from arthritis and rheumatism, compared to 11% in the general population; diabetes 8.3% compared to 2.9%; high blood pressure 12% compared to 8.7%. Aboriginal adults are twice as likely to consider their health below the Canadian average; specifically, 38% of Aboriginal Canadians between 55 and 64 rate their health as poor to fair compared to 19% of Canadians in general. In fact, half of off-reserve First Nations people report chronic health problems. Health declines more rapidly for adult Aboriginal people than for Canadians in general; mortality rates for the Aboriginal population, while declining, still tend to be far higher than for other Canadians, with the inevitable result that relatively fewer Aboriginal people than non-Aboriginals survive into older age cohorts. On average, Aboriginal Canadians can expect to live a decade less than other Canadians; moreover, Native people have higher rates of disability and live about 12 more years with a disability. Members of Aboriginal communities suffer traumatic injuries at four times the rate of the general Canadian population. It seems surprising, then, that funding for the national Aboriginal Health Organization (NAHO), which amounted to almost $5 million a year, has been cut by Health Canada, causing its demise at a time when the 'abysmal health' of Canada's Native population has been described as 'Canada's greatest shame' (*Globe and Mail*, 10 April 2012). According to Health Canada, for people living at least to the age of 25, life expectancy for First Nations males is 4.4 years below that of other Canadian males; among females, the differential is 6.3 years. And the disparity in life expectancy rates is much greater if we consider people from birth, due to the far higher rates of infectious diseases, chronic illnesses, accidents, suicide, and infant mortality among Aboriginals. Compared to other Canadian women, First Nations women are 434% more likely to die prematurely from infectious diseases, 400% more likely from an endocrine disorder, and 266% more likely from external causes, including accidents (Lemstra in *Saskatoon StarPhoenix*, 3 February 2011). Older Aboriginal women have the poorest health. The infant mortality rate for indigenous babies in Canada, the United States, Australia, and New Zealand is up to four times that of other newborns; moreover, the infant mortality rate for Canadian children on reserves is double that of non-Natives. And the obesity rate for on-reserve children is 36%, compared to 8% for Canadian children overall (Smylie 2009). According to the Aboriginal Peoples Survey in 2001, one-quarter of Aboriginal children under the age of 15 live in unhealthy, overcrowded conditions (more than one person per room) – twice the rate for Canadians in general; moreover, Aboriginal homes are far more likely to need major repair and to have their water supply contaminated. Regardless of education level, poorer children in Canada are at greater risk of growth retardation due to malnutrition (Séguin 2009).

Statistics Canada data have revealed that more than half of Metis youth and adults aged 15 and over have been diagnosed with chronic health conditions (lasting over six months). In these age cohorts, 21% of Metis suffer from arthritis (compared to 13% of the general population); 16% from high blood pressure (compared to 12%); 14% from asthma (compared to 8%); and 7% from diabetes (compared to 4%) (cited in *Saskatoon StarPhoenix*, 8 June 2007 and 20 February 2009). Research by the University of Saskatchewan in collaboration with the Metis Nation of Saskatchewan (MNS) and the First Nations University of Canada (FNUC), released in October 2010, examined the health status of 1,500 Metis and found that Metis generally seem to have poorer health than the average Canadian; that they lack access to programs and services provided to First Nations; and that they exhibit high rates of chronic illnesses, including diabetes (26%) and high blood pressure (13%).

In the Aboriginal Peoples Survey conducted by Statistics Canada in 2006, 21% of First Nations respondents and 12% of Metis considered their health poor to fair, and just over half of both First Nations and Metis respondents aged 15 and over reported chronic health issues. Similarly, the Urban Aboriginal Peoples Study (UAPS 2010, 114–15) reported that urban Aboriginal people generally seem to have positive views about their personal health: 79% of the Aboriginal respondents to this survey considered it to be 'good to excellent.' Moreover, a large majority emphasized outlook on life, reduction of stress or anxiety, diet, spirituality, and 'being part of a healthy, vibrant community' as most important to overall health. Surprisingly, housing was not viewed as a factor.

The suicide rates for First Nations youth aged 15 to 25 are five to seven times the rate for the general population. Suicide (*nipahisow*) accounts for one-quarter of all injury deaths among First Nations people and for between 22% to 33% of all deaths of Aboriginal youth aged 10 to 19 (*Saskatoon StarPhoenix*, 4 February 2009, 21 August 2009, 27 August 2009). Between 2000 and 2005, Saskatchewan averaged over 100 suicides a year. These high Aboriginal rates are affected by living conditions, perceived lack of opportunity, high unemployment, and drug and alcohol abuse (60% of Aboriginal suicides occur while intoxicated). A report of the Royal Commission on Aboriginal Peoples (RCAP) refers to 'cultural stress,' the 'loss of confidence in the ways of life and living that have been taught within a particular culture,' leading to the internalization of inferiority and a loss of self-esteem. As Lemstra has pointed out, suicide tends to decline markedly among Aboriginal residents of Saskatoon as income levels increase: research has revealed that 33.1% of lower-income residents harboured suicidal thoughts, compared to only 3.8% among those with incomes over $75,000 a year. One Saskatoon study found that 27.9% of Aboriginal residents sampled had suicidal thoughts, compared to 9.7% of other adults (Lemstra in *StarPhoenix*, 3 February 2011). The major risk factors have been identified as poverty, younger age, residence in poor neighbourhoods, and extreme stress levels.

Conversely, research has indicated that self-determination and control over health services and education among Aboriginal peoples – as is found, for example, in British Columbia – seem to be a deterrent to suicide; reserves with limited control over decision making exhibited far higher suicide rates. In fact, RCAP similarly concluded that Aboriginal control over their own services is one of four key policies needing to be adopted to reduce health disparities. However, a survey of 5,000 Saskatoon residents during 2008 revealed that only about half the respondents favoured more Aboriginal control over health and social programs (Lemstra in *Saskatoon StarPhoenix*, 27 August 2009). Health Canada has supported the placement of health promotion coordinators in predominantly Aboriginal northern Saskatchewan communities through the Aboriginal Health Transition Fund, and also in collaboration with the Metis youth suicide prevention program. Native affairs columnist Doug Cuthand has commented:

Today the children and grandchildren of the stolen generations are rebuilding our societies as best they can. But serious damage has been done and we see jails replacing residential schools, gangs replacing families, and television replacing the teachings of the elders ... The suicide epidemic, like so many of our issues in Indian country, has its roots in colonialism, thrust on us from the outside. But ultimately, it is our problem. We must address it and put a stop to this senseless loss of life. (*Saskatoon StarPhoenix*, 6 February 2009)

Diabetes is the sixth leading cause of death in Canada, killing more than 7,000 Canadians a year; it is also a contributing factor in another 41,500 deaths a year . Diabetic patients with lower incomes are dying at a much higher rate than more affluent ones; in fact, the risk of death due to low income has increased 40% in just eleven years, according to data released by the Institute for Clinical Evaluative Sciences in Toronto in December 2009. Lower-income patients are less able to afford the necessary treatment. Moreover, the Diabetes Association of Canada has recently estimated (December 2009) that the number of people diagnosed with diabetes in Canada has doubled in the past ten years, from 1.3 million in 2000 to 2.5 million in 2010; an additional 5 million may be at risk due to sedentary lifestyles combined with excessive consumption of sugar and fats. Soon one in ten Canadians could have diabetes. Among First Nations people, diabetes (*kawaspinew*) is reaching epidemic proportions, affecting women to such an extent that almost half of them are developing the disease, often at a young age (Dressler 2004). First Nations women and their children are increasingly caught in a 'potentially accelerating process,' with the rates increasing with each generation, according to research conducted at the University of Saskatchewan (Dyck 2010). Diabetes was rare in Aboriginal populations 70 years ago but today has become very common for First Nations people in their forties. Numerous First Nations women develop the disease between the ages of 20 and 50, and by age 60 almost half of them – as well as more than 40% of men – have the disease. Dyck's research also found that 20% of women and 16% of men living in Native communities in Saskatchewan already had Type 2 diabetes in 2005 – much higher percentages than 25 years earlier, when the figures were 9.5% and 4.9% respectively (during the same period, rates rose from 2% to 5.5% among non-Aboriginal women and 2% to 6.2% among men). Overall, among Aboriginals, the incidence and prevalence of diabetes have both increased – approximately fourfold among women and two-and-a-half times among men. Among the factors in this disproportion are significantly higher rates of obesity among Aboriginal populations, and higher rates of gestational diabetes among pregnant Aboriginal women.

HIV and AIDS (*misiwaspinewin*) are also increasing rapidly among the Aboriginal population. Saskatchewan now has the highest HIV rate in Canada – double the national one. By 2009 this amounted to approximately 900 confirmed cases of HIV and 250 of AIDS (however, these are only the known cases – it is estimated that at least one-quarter of actual cases have not yet been diagnosed). Moreover, Aboriginal people accounted for 69% of all new HIV cases, while Aboriginal women comprised 79% of diagnosed HIV cases (*Saskatoon StarPhoenix*, 13, 14, and 17 May 2010). In the Saskatoon area the number of new confirmed cases of HIV rose from just 16 to 94 between 2004 to 2009, according to data from the Saskatoon Health Region. A current research project of the Saskatoon HIV/AIDS Reduction of Harm Program (SHARP), which has been following 1,000 drug users and sex trade workers in Saskatoon over two years, is attempting to determine why HIV and AIDS are spreading so quickly. A profile of respondents to this survey indicated that as many as half of those at risk of contacting HIV had been sexually assaulted as children; also, they have limited education – three-quarters have less than high school graduation; almost all are unemployed or have limited incomes; and one-third are homeless, with almost all of the rest not living in their own home or apartment. At least half the respondents viewed a lack of adequate and affordable housing as a major problem interfering with accessing care. A high proportion (87%) of the respondents are Aboriginal. The implications for difficulty in finding suitable housing are enormous (CMHC Feb. 2003).

Saskatchewan First Nations infants with breathing problems are hospitalized at a rate two to three times the Canadian average. An extensive five-year study is currently being conducted into respiratory health problems of the First Nations population there. This research, with $1.5 million funding from the Canadian Institute of Health Research (CIHR) and the Institute of Aboriginal's People's Health, represents a partnership between the University of Saskatchewan, University of Regina, and first Nations University with the Montreal Lake and Beardy's/Okemasis First Nations. Respiratory problems relate especially to poor living conditions – overcrowding and poor air quality from dampness and mould – as well as diet and obesity (*Saskatoon StarPhoenix*, 25 April 2012).

A report of the Public Health Agency of Canada, released in March 2010, indicated that the tuberculosis infection rate per 100,000 people in 2008 was 0.8 for non-Aboriginal population, 2.1 for Canadian-born, 4.8 for the entire Canadian population, 8.0 for Metis, 27.8 for Status and

Non-Status Indians, and 157.5 for Inuit. The rate among Status Indians was 31 times that of non-Aboriginal Canadians. More specifically in Saskatchewan, almost all 127 victims of tuberculosis ('chest sickness' – *naskikan-ahkosiw*) in one year were Aboriginal people who had been living in overcrowded homes, especially on reserves. This represented the highest tuberculosis rate in ten years. Even on reserves with vaccination programs, reportedly less than half of the residents actually used this opportunity (*Saskatoon StarPhoenix*, 26 September 2006). High incidence of tuberculosis in traditional Aboriginal communities, especially in isolated northern areas, has been related to the prevalence of pneumonia (*cahkatamow*). During the past year, Canada has contributed close to $140 million to global efforts to combat tuberculosis and other diseases in selected developing countries, compared to only $10.8 million within Canada, where the disease ravages Native communities. Because Canada tends to be viewed as quite an affluent country, this perception hides the fact that so many indigenous communities have serious health problems. In fact, the *Winnipeg Free Press* reported in 2009 that certain First Nations communities in Manitoba exhibit some of the very highest tuberculosis rates in the entire world, up to 100 times the Canadian average. Again, it is impossible to treat this disease without addressing the underlying social conditions that cause the illness to spread (*Globe and Mail*, 13 December 2010).

Canadian Aboriginal people are far heavier smokers than other Canadians. Statistics Canada reported that in 2007–8, the rate of smoking for First Nations people was virtually double that of non-Aboriginal people: 45.3% compared to 23.3% (*Saskatoon StarPhoenix*, 26 March 2010). Recent research specifically on Metis health in Saskatchewan has found that 54% of 1,500 respondents were regular smokers, double the estimated provincial average but slightly less than First Nations (60%). According to Lemstra, Aboriginal people are more likely to smoke: 44% smoke daily, compared to 18.6% of Whites; also, 44.1% of residents in poor neighbourhoods compared to 18.5% in more affluent neighbourhoods; and 29.5% with annual incomes under $25,000 compared to 13.6% with incomes over $75,000 (Lemstra 2009a). Recent research has indicated that smoking starts very early on Saskatchewan reserves: more than one-quarter of children in grade six were already smoking, and more than half before high school; and almost half of these youth were permitted to smoke at home (Lemstra in *StarPhoenix*, 29 December 2011).

Drug and alcohol addiction (*ka-sakinikot / ka-tipenmiikot*) continues to be a problem among the Aboriginal population. An estimated 5,000 people in Saskatchewan are injection drug users; they use over 1,000 needles a day, according to a provincial review of needle exchange programs released in December 2008. Just in Saskatoon, about 1 million needles for drug intake are distributed annually, according to data of the Saskatoon Health Region. In 2009, 11,216 discarded needles were collected (actually significantly less than the previous year), as reported by the Saskatoon Fire and Protection Services. A recent study in British Columbia found that more than one-third of young Aboriginal drug users in that province are now infected with hepatitis C (*Globe and Mail*, 11 February 2010). A recent Saskatoon Health Region study found that 16.7% of Aboriginal children aged 10 to 15 abuse alcohol, compared to 5.4% of other children in that age cohort (Lemstra in *Saskatoon StarPhoenix*, 3 February 2011).

*Health Disparity in Saskatoon: Analysis to Intervention*, a revealing study conducted for the Saskatoon Health Region (Lemstra and Neudorf 2006), compared six poorer west side neighbourhoods (having the highest concentration of Aboriginal residents) with five affluent east side neighbourhoods (where average income exceeded $100,000 a year). It was found that the poor west side neighbourhoods had 16 times more hospitalizations for suicide attempts, almost 15 times more cases of chlamydia, almost 13 times more hospitalizations for diabetes, and over four times more hospitalizations for mental disorders. Residents of these poor neighbourhoods were 34 times more likely to have hep C and 3 times more likely to have heart disease. These neighbourhoods also had a five times higher rate of infant mortality. Residents of inner-city neighbourhoods were 1,186% more likely to require hospitalization for diabetes than residents of other neighbourhoods in the city, while infant mortality rates were 448% higher in core neighbourhoods than elsewhere in the city. This research is supported by other Canadian research on the links among poverty, poor housing, and mental health (CIHI 2007, 2008a) and on the social disparities in health rates. In fact, Aboriginal residents of Saskatoon have worse health outcomes than other residents in virtually every outcome that has been monitored, primarily due to social conditions.

Moreover, the gap between richer and poorer has actually been widening, especially for infant mortality (e.g., between 2002 and 2006, there was a 110% increase), HIV and sexually transmitted diseases, and life expectancy. In fact, the HIV rate in Saskatchewan increased 40% just in a single year (2008), with the largest increase in cases recorded at the Westside Community Clinic in Saskatoon, which serves the neighbourhoods having the largest concentration of urban Aboriginal population; one-third of these new cases were found in women under 29 (the youngest was just 15), and many were Aboriginal. In Saskatoon, 6.4 times as many poor as rich are hospitalized for substance abuse (the differential is even higher in Regina – 8.5 times as many). And other research by Lemstra has indicated that poverty leads more Aboriginal youth to drink alcohol and smoke marijuana (Lemstra 2009a). Among Canadian cities, Saskatoon and Regina exhibit the greatest gap between rich and poor for substance abuse, chronic obstructive pulmonary disorder, and mental health problems (CIHI 2008b).

## Quality of Life

Despite all these depressing statistics on poverty, living conditions, and health, the extensive quality-of-life research being conducted in Saskatoon through the Community–University Institute for Social Research (Dunning 2004; Sun 2005; CUISR 2006, 2008) has revealed that this city is generally regarded as a good place to live. As part of this research, eight 'domains' pertaining to neighbourhood quality of life were explored: housing, health, employment/income, land use and environment, crime and safety, education, social environment and services, and community participation. In a recent survey conducted by the City of Saskatoon, the vast majority of residents (92%) rated the quality of life in Saskatoon as 'good' to 'very good'; moreover, a large majority of residents felt that the services they were receiving from the city were good value for their tax dollars. The largest number of residents expressed crime and policing as their foremost concerns; however, the proportion listing this as their top concern had dropped sharply, from 35% the previous year (2006) to 19%. Many residents felt that the city was doing its best to provide clean drinking water, fire protection, electrical services, and waste disposal. In certain respects, Saskatchewan enjoys the best health in Canada (e.g., a relatively lower cancer rate, as well as an overall life expectancy rate equivalent to the national one); moreover, the province still has the lowest proportion of people living in cities of any province west of the Maritimes.

More generally, Statistics Canada data revealed that between 1996 and 2006 – which was prior to the present recession – a strong economy, an open job market, and generous government benefits had lifted more than 1 million Canadians out of the low-income ranks. The number of Canadians living in poverty was decreasing. The poor, it seems, did not always get poorer. This conclusion was based on data indicating that median after-tax income seemed to be rising, while the proportion of poor families was concomitantly falling. The 'enduring myth' that child poverty is worsening in Canada is countered by data suggesting that in fact, child poverty has been declining quite rapidly: for example, 1.3 million children under 18 lived in low-income families back in 1996, compared to approximately 865,000 by 2004. However, that same year the low-income rate for children in female lone-parent families was 40%, five times the rate for children in poverty in two-parent families.

The decline in child poverty nationally has been affected by a combination of more employment for mothers and generous benefits and transfer payments, so that working-age adults without children now constitute the preponderance of the poor, with after-tax median incomes of $21,300; many remain stuck in minimum-wage jobs or depend on welfare, with limited prospects for improvement. Between January 2005 and January 2006 – that is, in a single year – average weekly earnings increased by 4.85%, well above the inflation rate. So, the statisticians conclude, a thriving market economy, combined with generous social programs, has clearly benefited the poor (*Globe and Mail*, 1 April 2006).

Indeed, the urban Aboriginal population has been changing quite rapidly in a variety of respects that suggest a more positive picture. Recent trends among urban Aboriginal residents have included a declining high school dropout rate, increasing high school and university or technical school graduation, greater occupational diversity, corresponding increasing income, access to improved housing, and better health care.

A recent report commissioned by the Human Resources Department of the newly elected Conservative federal government in 2007 went a lot further in recommending new and very different policy options to address Native poverty (Mendelson 2007). The report, authored by Michael Mendelson of the Caledon Institute of Social Policy in Ottawa, challenges a number of assumptions about the situation of Aboriginal people, not the least that First Nations people are increasingly fleeing their reserves to seek a better life in Canada's cities. Also, the economic and educational gaps between Aboriginal and non-Aboriginal Canadians are not as great as widely believed; the Aboriginal participation rate in the workforce is higher than expected and close to the Canadian average; and Aboriginal high school graduates are just as likely to complete post-secondary education as other high school graduates – in fact, Aboriginal people in some provinces are actually *more* likely to complete non-university post-secondary education than non-Aboriginals. The report contends that it is essential to correct misconceptions through a careful review of empirical data. Furthermore, it suggests, misconceptions about Aboriginal data are having an impact on social policy, and the federal government should rethink spending billions of taxpayers' dollars on First Nations. Specifically, Mendelson makes it clear that the federal government may need to rethink approaches to improving both the education levels of Aboriginals and their economic opportunities. Yet the report does recognize that 'all the socio-economic indicators ... reviewed ... with only a few exceptions are much worse than for the Canadian population as a whole.' It adds that the Aboriginal labour force does face an extremely high unemployment rate, that almost half of working-age Aboriginal people have not completed high school, and that a larger proportion of Aboriginal incomes comes from transfer payments than for non-Aboriginals. The same report suggests that policy emphasis should be on helping Aboriginal people obtain the necessary skills and knowledge for well-paying jobs rather than on incentives to get Aboriginal people to work.

A reality check is needed here: many of Saskatoon's Aboriginal residents remain in overcrowded, unhealthy housing conditions in the poorest neighbourhoods. Also, although advances are being made, too many Aboriginal residents still lag well behind non-Aboriginal ones in many respects. As Ed Broadbent, former national leader of the NDP, pointedly commented: 'This poverty was not inevitable. Mostly it is the product of governments that have neither shared nor cared ... Canadian politicians have failed our children.' He has argued that during the previous decade, the federal government virtually abandoned a leadership role for the country's poor by unilaterally cancelling the Canada Assistance Plan with the provinces, eliminating all low-cost housing programs, and failing to pursue a national child-care program (*Globe and Mail*, 24 November 2009).

And Jim Harding, a former professor of environmental and justice studies at the University of Regina, has commented: 'The life-chances of children born into poverty are greatly lowered. Poverty has long been associated with higher incidence of diabetes, heart disease, suicide, etc. So why do we tolerate poverty as a society?' (*Saskatoon StarPhoenix*, 26 November 2009). A co-chair of the Saskatoon Anti-Poverty Coalition has suggested that 'the primary hallmark of a poverty reduction or elimination strategy would be that it is developed through consultations with citizens – especially the poor themselves.' Even the Saskatchewan

Social Services Minister has admitted that 'the government's focus on economic growth as a solution to poverty is misguided' (*StarPhoenix*, 17 October 2009). Cuthand has pointed out that according to a 2008 Auditor General's report, First Nation child welfare agencies were receiving 22% less per capita in funding than corresponding provincial agencies, while there were approximately 27,000 First Nation children in care; yet for more than a decade the federal Department of Indian Affairs has placed a 2% cap on budget increases for services, thus effectively starving First Nations of the resources they need to deal effectively with child poverty (*StarPhoenix*, 4 December 2009). The Saskatoon Health Region has adopted a strategic direction, 'Partnering for Improved Health for Aboriginal People'; however, this partnering has been criticized for including neither the Saskatoon Tribal Council nor the four rural First Nations contained within the health region.

The Minister of Health for the relatively new Saskatchewan Party government of Saskatchewan has suggested that the provincial government has already made changes – including increased housing allowances and rental supplements – aimed at closing the gap between rich and poor in Saskatoon. One of the many recommendations in the report, *Health Disparity in Saskatoon: Analysis to Intervention* (Lemstra and Neudorf 2008), is that specific poverty reduction goals be set, such as doubling the social assistance allowance for food, shelter, and clothing. Social assistance could be indexed to inflation rates to keep recipients above the poverty line. Funds could be paid directly to landlords (not a particularly good idea, as we will see in a later chapter) or through vouchers for healthier foods. The estimated $178 million a year this would cost taxpayers could be covered through the new Child Poverty Protection Plan, modelled after the Canada Pension Plan. Moreover, the report has argued that an investment of $300 million from Saskatchewan taxpayers could actually *save* the province $1 billion in the long run. CIHI research has estimated the additional cost from people living in poverty as in excess of $640 million every year in Canada. While the Saskatchewan Party government has raised the basic personal income tax exemption to nearly $13,000, it has not funded this tax break for low-income people by eliminating the exemption for high-income earners. Nor has the government followed the precedent set by Sweden – which has a very low rate of single-parent families living in poverty – by extending parental leave pay and initiating child care reform (the authors of the disparity report have recommended raising parental leave from 55% to 80% of income) (CIHI 2008b).

To provide more accessible health care to inner-city residents, the Westside Community Clinic, centrally located in Pleasant Hill, has been served by university medical students through the SWITCH (Student Wellness Initiative Towards Community Health) program since 2005. Under this program, 85 local residents walk through the clinic's doors on an average day. A sign on the clinic's wall reads: 'Take care of your body. It's the only place you have to live.' SWITCH (which is only one of eight similar student-staffed health care clinics in Canada) is helping start similar student-managed primary health care clinics in Australia. The clinic provides local residents not only with readily accessible physical health care and dental services, but also social work counselling and nutrition advice. Many of its clients are Aboriginal people who face poverty, homelessness, and the never-ending struggle to find affordable housing and make ends meet, while suffering health problems. CHEP has helped ensure that elementary school students on the inner west side are being adequately fed at lunchtime.

## Meeting the People: Aboriginal Residents Speak Out

ALAN B. ANDERSON

*Introduction*

The Saskatoon Aboriginal Neighbourhood Survey was intended to gather essential information not available from census data or the City of Saskatoon Aboriginal Neighbourhood Profiles. Information was gathered from Aboriginal residents of selected inner-city neighbourhoods on age, occupation, employment, and education of respondents and household members; on cultural identification; on household composition; on housing types, costs, and needs; on migration and mobility; and on the community – that is, on the services, ethnic relations, and problems or issues in each neighbourhood. This survey was an opportunity for Aboriginal residents to explain their personal views and share their individual experiences.

*Methodology*

As a result of the relative difficulty of approaching residents anonymously door to door, community organizations assisted in identifying participants. The first problem facing each interviewer was the need to quickly gain the confidence of a respondent. This involved explaining accurately the point of the project and the survey, as well as guaranteeing that the information gathered would be used to recommend policies that could benefit the community and eventually improve the housing situation. It was explained that every respondent's anonymity would be ensured, as well as that of other household members. In accordance with ethical guidelines, each respondent signed a consent agreement prior to being interviewed. Also, respondents were completely free not to respond to any questions with which they felt uncomfortable (although inevitably this policy affected the completion rate on certain items of information).

Many of the interviews were conducted in poorer inner-city neighbourhoods where crime rates were increasing. These neighbourhoods had the city's highest rates of prostitution, break and entry, and violence – in fact, among the highest rates in Canada. Youth gangs were rapidly becoming a significant problem. So on the one hand, residents tended to be increasingly fearful or at least wary of strangers; on the other, the interviewers (especially the female ones) were at risk, so they usually worked in pairs during longer daylight hours in summer and avoided evening interviews (except by appointment).

Overall, the residents were interested in the survey and quite receptive and open once entry into the home had been permitted. However, it was often difficult to gain entry – many refusals were encountered, and these increased with media reports of criminal activities. Female interviewers tended to gain access more readily; male interviewers felt less at risk. Completed interviews, while hard to obtain and relatively few in total number, were in-depth, taking at least an hour to complete. The interviewers appreciated the cooperation, courtesy, and openness of the respondents. Most of the interviewers were Aboriginal, First Nations (representing several First Nations of Saskatchewan), and Metis, and most were themselves longtime residents of inner-city neighbourhoods. This allowed some interviewers to address Aboriginal residents in their traditional language, which quickly facilitated rapport. In all, 87 in-depth household interviews were completed; these households included approximately 300 occupants. A 'respondent' was considered to be the principal household head.

*Basic Data on Respondents*

The sample population was relatively young: 47.1% of the respondents were between the ages of 20 and 29; 21.8% were 30 to 39; 19.5% were

40 to 49; and 11.4% older than 50. Regarding occupation, most respondents reported that they were students, 'homeowners,' or in sales/service occupations; but virtually all other occupational categories were represented in the sample. A substantial proportion (17.2%) of respondents reported that they were currently unemployed. Slightly more than one-third (35.6%) of the total sample said they were employed full-time; 13.8% said they were employed part-time or seasonally.

Regarding the highest level of education attained by household heads, 6.9% reported only an elementary school education; 34.5% some high school education; 19.5% a high school diploma; 14.9% some university education (but not yet a degree – this most likely would include current university students); 5.7% a university degree; 2.3% at least some technical training (but not a diploma – again, this would include current technical students); and 8.0% a technical diploma. In sum, the respondents seemed quite well educated: 54.0% had either graduated from high school or had at least some high school education, while an additional 30.9% had gone further, into post-secondary education.

*Cultural Identification*

When asked about their Aboriginal identity, 34.5% of respondents identified as First Nations and 14.9% as Metis, while 17.4% claimed various other Aboriginal identities. The remaining one-third would not select a specific Aboriginal identification (although they would not have been interviewed unless they initially self-identified as Aboriginal). A minority of respondents – albeit a large one (39.9%) – claimed familiarity with an Aboriginal language; the largest number (20.7%) spoke Cree, while several spoke Saulteaux, Dene, or Michif. However, few of the respondents who provided further details on their familiarity with an Aboriginal language claimed to be literate or 'somewhat literate' in that language: some thought they spoke the language well, others 'only a bit.' When asked which language they spoke in the home, most respondents seemed unsure how to answer: 41.4% reported English, while the rest reported variable uses of English and an Aboriginal language or a mixture of an Aboriginal language with English. Of the 43 household heads who provided information on generational differences in language use, a large majority suggested that English would be the preferred language of subsequent generations. When asked about the value placed on preserving traditional Aboriginal culture, 24.3% placed 'a lot' of value on it, 9.2% claimed 'very little,' and 3.4% said 'none.' But fully half the respondents did not express any opinion. When asked whether they still participated in traditional Aboriginal gatherings and ceremonies such as powwows, sun dances, round dances, smudges, and dancing and singing, just over half the respondents were unsure, approximately one-quarter to one-third said not at all, and the remainder reported variable participation, ranging from occasionally to often. Participation in Native community organizations was also quite variable: approximately one-quarter of the respondents did participate (most of them often), slightly more than half were unsure how to answer, and the remainder did not participate. When asked about Aboriginal culture in the city, almost one in five interviewees said it was strong, but an almost equal number said it was becoming weaker, and a few thought that it was currently in limbo. We can conclude, therefore, that at least among this sample of inner-city residents, aspects of Aboriginal culture – such as traditional language retention – remain fairly strong, although there may be concern over a perceived weakening of culture in the city, if not considerable indifference.

*Household Composition*

Interestingly, more respondents claimed a common law marital status than claimed they were legally married. More than half (57.5%) of the respondents said they were single, almost one-third (32.2%) single with dependents, and one-quarter (25.3%) single with no children. Of the married respondents, about two-thirds were married to an Aboriginal spouse, one-third to a non-Aboriginal spouse.

Crowding may be an issue for a substantial proportion of households: 8% of households contained just a single occupant, 25.3% had two occupants, 23% had three, 8.4% had four, and 21.6% had five or more. Analysis of shared accommodation proved complex: 77.0% of households were single family; 4.6% reported sharing accommodation with nuclear family members (including, for example, grown children, or siblings); 11.5% reported accommodation shared with extended family (typically grandparents of their children, but also possibly uncles/aunts, nephews/nieces, grandchildren, foster children, cousins, in-laws and their children, and so on). Adding to this complexity, 12.6% of accommodations were shared by more than one family, or with outsiders (such as boyfriend/girlfriend, other friends, or boarders). Moreover, this sharing ranged from occasionally to always. Although 40.1% of households reported children under 10 years of age living at home, very few had more than three children. Similarly, 31% reported children aged 10 to 19 living at home, but mostly just one or two. Fewer still household heads (10.3%) reported young adults aged 20 and over still living at home.

*Housing*

Sufficient data were obtained from 60 households on exact type of housing. Of these households, 58.3% were apartments, 28.3% single detached houses, and 8.3% semi-detached/duplexes; the rest were basement suites, condos, or townhouses. Most respondents (61.6%) said their preferred home would be a large, single detached house; 12.8% said a duplex, 8.1% said a larger apartment. The majority of respondents (74.3%) required either a two-bedroom home (31.1%) or a three-bedroom (43.2%); fewer (20.3%) needed four or more bedrooms, and even fewer (5.4%) needed only one bedroom. Where sufficient data were obtained on the number of bedrooms per household, we learned that half were two-bedroom and almost one-third were three-bedroom. Only seven households commented on special needs to accommodate extended families. Also, four desired special considerations for elderly residents, and one for a physical handicap (although another 16 mentioned such problems as learning disabilities, back pain, and brain injury).

Almost all households had a single bathroom. One in five homes lacked a separate kitchen. Almost all had a living room (or equivalent space, however small). Slightly over one-third possessed a separate dining room. Seventeen homes had a finished and/or occupied basement; however, this question was irrelevant in the case of apartments. Also, 52.9% of households reported at least one television set, 18.4% a personal dishwasher, and 9.2% a clothes washer/drier (compared to 13.7% reporting a shared washer/drier in the home/building). Another 23% simply claimed use of a washer/drier without being more specific.

A very high proportion (86.2%) of households surveyed consisted of renters. Of these renters, just over half (56.3%) were paying $400 to $600 per month for these accommodations. Just under one-quarter (23.8%) were paying less ($200 to $400 per month), while even fewer (16.3%) were paying more (over $600 a month). These costs are generally paid by the individual respondent (46.3%) or shared with another person (36.3%). A small proportion of home costs were being paid by social services. Usually, rent did not include utilities, or only certain types of utilities were included; moreover, there was wide variation in the actual amount paid for utilities.

Almost half the households were spending around half their total household income on rent or mortgage payments. Respondents were generally very reluctant to provide information on their annual household income. More than half the respondents who were willing to provide this information made under $10,000; about one-quarter made $10,000 to $19,000; and very few made over $20,000. The average total amount of social assistance received was approximately $700 a month (including family allowance, transactional allowance, welfare, and Employment Insurance).

Many respondents named 'private' landlords, but a wide range of property-holding companies were also identified. Relatively few of these companies were community-based or Aboriginal. Fewer still were properties managed by the City of Saskatoon or the Saskatoon Housing Authority. The most numerous property holders were a variety of real estate, investment, contracting, and property management companies. The renters we interviewed were more satisfied than dissatisfied with the rental arrangement: 38.2% were very satisfied, 22.4% somewhat satisfied, 9.2% undecided, 13.2% somewhat dissatisfied, and 17.1% very dissatisfied. In fact, almost half the renters did not identify any particular problems and believed that their landlord was keeping up with maintenance and tended to be understanding. However, one-quarter of the renters believed that the landlord was unsatisfactory, primarily because he or she was failing to keep up with maintenance issues, or was not understanding. Comments on landlords included the following 'differing opinions on what needs replacing'; 'does nothing he promises to do'; 'charges more because I have kids'; and 'is very intrusive or rude at times,'

Many factors were mentioned when respondents were asked what was blocking them from homeownership. A high proportion of respondents said that financial reasons were the most prominent barrier. The issues mentioned included affordability, limited income, credit problems, inability to meet down payments, difficulty saving, and lack of a credit rating. Other factors mentioned by respondents included high mobility, as well as employment problems. Some viewed their stay in the city as only short-term (e.g., they were here as students); others did not want the responsibility of homeownership. Other constraints mentioned in this regard were racism and prejudice, lack of opportunities, living with grandparents, other 'family problems,' 'government bureaucracy,' and fear of vandalism.

Familiarity with the affordable housing programs available to home occupants was quite limited. Of those who provided their opinion (one-third of all households surveyed), over three-quarters believed that these organizations do not assist enough. When asked to indicate specific problem areas regarding assistance, many gave informative critical responses. Some of these pertained specifically to Aboriginal issues: there were more Aboriginal people than available housing; overcrowding was a problem; more places were needed where young Aboriginal people could go; the Aboriginal population was mostly poor and lacked financial resources and assistance; 'what finances there could be seem to be diverted into casinos'; 'people are helped on reserve but ignored in the city.' Other respondents emphasized that affordable housing agencies could do more to help Aboriginal residents: such agencies were unknown, and were not promoted enough; 'they try to help, perhaps, but people need to help themselves more'; 'social services don't really help'; more programs were needed; long waiting lists were a problem; only 'people on the inside' received assistance; agencies were there 'only for face value'; agencies 'don't care about us personally.' Some responses focused on community needs: 'we need to work on unemployment to combat housing problems'; too many people were living in substandard housing; 'we need to be more open and up front'; bad and unscrupulous landlords were a problem.

Many problems were identified by informants when it came to finding satisfaction in a suitable home. These problems included a low personal/family income, limited availability, difficulty in finding a suitable location, and prejudice and discrimination. Respondents expressed their frustration over the competition for limited housing: 'when going to see a specific house, we find it's already rented.' From their perspective, a lot of housing was just too expensive, and the demand for affordable housing was getting stronger every year. So they were having to look for cheaper housing in the worst areas of the city. This was a problem for Aboriginal university and technical students, who were living in less than adequate accommodations in poor inner-city neighbourhoods where the rents were cheaper. Some identified family growth as a problem: 'a large family can be a problem when trying to save'; 'too many people are having kids.' Many respondents emphasized prejudice and discrimination as a problem in finding housing. They pointed out that some landlords prefer non-Native tenants, or they believed that 'because I am Native I won't care for the home.' They suggested that 'we're grouped together because we aren't as well off.' Nonetheless, satisfaction with specific accommodation was quite high: 38.1% of respondents were very satisfied, 27.4% were somewhat satisfied, 8.3% had mixed feelings, 10.7% were somewhat dissatisfied, and 15.5% were very dissatisfied.

Areas of satisfaction included the condition of the home, the stability associated with having a home, the location, and their neighbours. Of those dissatisfied with their home, the majority stated problems with the upkeep of the dwelling. Other sources of dissatisfaction related to the neighbourhood's location, high crime in the area, inadequate accommodation for the size of the family, the home 'being smashed up because of gangs,' and the landlord's rules being too strict. Just 28.7% of the respondents believed their home to be in poor condition, and one-quarter indicated that only regular maintenance was needed; yet 16.1% of homes were described in interviewers' notes as in need of major repairs and 62.1% in need of minor repairs.

*Migration and Mobility*

Of those respondents who originally came to Saskatoon from an Aboriginal community or reserve, a significant majority (61.3%) did not plan on returning to that community or reserve. However, 29% indicated that they would be returning; and 9.7% responded that they might return 'some day.' Many reasons were given for returning: to hunt, to be with family and friends, to work, to obtain a home on reserve, to visit. In other cases, the respondent already had a home there, or felt no connection to the city. But more reasons were given to *stay* in the city: the respondent 'didn't want kids to grow up on reserve'; living standards on reserve were poor; the respondent felt comfortable in the city; the respondent anticipated starting a business in the city; employment opportunities were better in the city (and worse on the reserve); the respondent wouldn't return until the reserve 'cleans up with drinking and drugs'; the respondent had no family left on reserve; better housing could be purchased in the city; the respondent had family and friends in the city or was going to school there. One respondent explained with irony that she had left the reserve because of a lack of adequate housing, because there was 'nothing to do' (e.g., no work), and because the reserve was beset with alcoholism and drug problems; but in the city she had encountered difficulty finding a house and a job, and crime and gangs were ruining the neighbourhood.

These residents were not necessarily new to urban living: 44.6% had never lived in another city, 55.4% had lived in one other city, and 25.3% have lived in two other cities (especially Prince Albert, Edmonton, Regina, Vancouver, and Calgary). Very few had lived in smaller centres. Time spent in other urban places ranged from very short (less than one year) to 'most of my life.' The most popular reasons for moving included family reasons, education, and employment. Many did not know how long they would be living in Saskatoon: 19.8% saw themselves as permanent residents, 18.6% saw themselves residing there for five or more years, and 12.6% expected to be there for less than five years. The Aboriginal residents this survey interviewed exhibited high mobility: during the previous five years, 15.1% had not moved, 24.4% had moved once or twice, 37.2% three to five times, 14% six to nine times, and 8.1% ten or more times.

Clearly, it would be incorrect to view the Aboriginal residents of these neighbourhoods as transitory. Most of the household heads interviewed were long-term residents of Saskatoon. When asked how long they had lived in Saskatoon, one-quarter said most of their life, another 28.6% ten or more years, 16.7% 6 to 9 years, 8.3% 4 to 5 years, and 21.4% less than 3 years. Almost two-thirds (64%) of the respondents had been born on a reserve or in a Metis community. Reasons for changing residences within the city included the following: the previous home had been too small; it had needed maintenance; or it had been in an unsafe or an undesirable neighbourhood; or shops and services, educational facilities, and/or family and friends were too far away. Factors mentioned less often were rising crime rates, rising rents, and poor public transportation. Most respondents expected to move again in the near future or eventually; only a little more than one-quarter did not plan to move. Typical reasons for these moves included the desire to live in a better home or to leave a 'bad' neighbourhood. Some respondents said they wanted a place where the kids could play safely in the backyard.

## The Community

Satisfaction with the present neighbourhood was moderately reserved (31% of the respondents were satisfied, 22.6% had mixed feelings, 10.7% were somewhat dissatisfied, and 9.5% were very dissatisfied). The majority of respondents found some satisfaction in their neighbourhoods, yet most also recognized that their neighbourhood was unsafe and had high crime rates and that prostitution was a problem. More positively, the respondents commented that their neighbourhood was near their workplace, schools, shops, and services, parks, and family and friends. While many believed that few or no improvements were needed in their neighbourhood, a larger number wanted to see certain improvements, particularly in security, in terms of improved policing and stronger efforts to combat prostitution, gangs, vandalism, and drug and alcohol abuse – generally, 'cleaning up the neighbourhood.' Some suggested a neighbourhood crime watch program. Other possible improvements mentioned included specific shops and services, recognition of ethnic diversity, fines for negligent landlords, and more concern shown by parents for their children. Yet most respondents said they hoped to remain in their relatively poorer or mixed west side neighbourhoods.

Interestingly, a large majority of respondents did not have a preference when it came to living in an 'Aboriginal' neighbourhood. A small number actually desired a lower proportion of Aboriginals in their neighbourhood; an equal number desired a higher proportion; and several respondents advocated a mixture of ethnic groups. One (Aboriginal) respondent even desired a home 'in a nice area with no Aboriginals.' Most respondents did not state a preference when it came to socializing with Aboriginals; however, some preferred to socialize only with Aboriginal people. Half the respondents described their relations with their non-Aboriginal neighbours as 'frequent and sociable'; 17.6% described them as 'seldom' and/or 'difficult'; 31.8% did not really care. Also, 74.4% of respondents interacted with non-Aboriginal people 'a lot' or 'somewhat'; only 20% said very rarely or never (these latter reported that they did not interact at work, in their communities, in educational facilities, or simply wherever). Respondents' beliefs about the attitudes of non-Aboriginal people toward the growing Aboriginal population seemed, then, to be mixed: one-quarter did not believe this trend mattered to non-Aboriginals; another quarter believed that 'it bothers some [of them]'; 15.8% believed that it bothered non-Aboriginals a lot; and 17.1% did not comment on the subject. Finally, on the question of whether urban reserves should be used for housing, almost two-thirds (65.5%) of the respondents commented that they should definitely be used for that purpose, while 18.4% believed they should not, as it might contribute to ghettoization.

## Community Voices: Assessing Capacity and Needs within Inner-City Neighbourhoods

ALAN B. ANDERSON

*Introduction*

The Bridges and Foundations Project conducted an extensive survey to ascertain the needs, issues, and concerns of the residents of five inner-city neighbourhoods in Saskatoon (Riversdale, Pleasant Hill, Caswell Hill, King George, and Westmount). This project was developed and coordinated by a couple of local community activists (one with training in public administration), with the support of SaskNative Rentals and the Saskatoon Police Services and the collaboration of the five neighbourhood community associations. The present paper represents an attempt to summarize the full report of this project (Burk 2004) – the salient findings and concluding impressions. While a variety of organizations and agencies serve residents of these neighbourhoods, limited collaboration has been evident in identifying the issues and concerns of these residents. Assessments of needs has tended to be mandate-oriented and too narrowly focused. Residents therefore saw a need to conduct a more comprehensive capacity and needs assessment. The specific objectives of the assessment were first, to identify the emerging issues, concerns, and strengths of community members; second, to assess the level of knowledge and frequency of use of existing agencies/ organizations by community members; third, to determine what was preventing citizens from using local services and organizations; and fourth, to move research into action.

*Methodology*

The comprehensive data collection method used consisted of a detailed questionnaire distributed randomly door to door. The primary focus of the survey was to capture the 'true voice' of a broad cross-section of residents in all five inner-city neighbourhoods. The project succeeded in interviewing a sample of at least 200 residents in each of the five neighbourhoods – that is, 1,000 residents in all. Local residents were recruited and trained to assist with interviewing. The project gathered information not only through this community-based survey but also by utilizing focus groups to identify and discuss specific issues. A steering committee consisting of local residents helped the researchers to identify focus group topics and select focus group participants, in addition to designing and field-testing the community survey and interpreting feedback and formulating recommendations. Ten focus groups of six to ten residents were organized, totaling 74 participants. These focus groups lasted approximately two hours.

In keeping with the Tri-Council Policy Statement on research ethics (2003), which points out that 'in developing ethical standards and practices, Aboriginal peoples have rights and interests, which deserve recognition and respect by the research community,' the research team consistently made a sincere attempt to review ethical issues, to discern good practices, and to conduct research in respectful ways, with the intention of contributing to the well-being of neighbourhood communities.

Analysis of the basic characteristics of the survey sample revealed that 36% of the respondents self-identified as Aboriginal, First Nations, or Metis. 62% were female. The largest age cohort consisted of respondents in their thirties. Of the survey sample, 14% reported less than a high school education, whereas 41% indicated post-secondary education. Over half the respondents reported that they were employed outside the home. One-third reported their household income level as between $20,000 and $29,000 per year, and 27% less than $20,000 per year (the remainder ranged from $30,000 to over $60,000).

## Quality of Life and the Neighbourhood

This particular research project anticipated providing residents as well as those working in service delivery with a detailed 'grassroots' community analysis of the needs, strengths, and capacity of inner-city neighbourhoods. The length of residence of the participants in the inner city was highly variable, from as short as one month to an entire lifetime. One-quarter of the respondents had resided in their current location for less than two years; 47% had lived in the same or another inner-city neighbourhood; 22% in other west side communities, and 17% in other communities and reserves throughout Saskatchewan. Finally, 2% had moved from outside the province (the remaining 12% did not identify exactly where they previously resided).

As for their impression of their neighbourhood, on the positive side, residents commented that they enjoyed the mature trees and parks in their communities, the character homes, the location (i.e., being close to downtown), and the cultural and ethnic diversity. Relatively lower cost of housing was a major inducement: rental housing was more readily available in the inner city, while among homeowners, the purchase prices for housing in the inner city tended to be lower than in other areas of Saskatoon, which allowed some families to purchase their first home sooner. On the negative side, participants identified their foremost concerns: crime and community safety, rental housing (dilapidated, overcrowded, and unsafe), addiction issues, aging community infrastructure, by-law infractions (failure to comply with the City of

Saskatoon's Property Maintenance and Nuisance Abatement By-law), increasing taxes, parenting and life skills issues, a pervasive lack of business/commercial diversity, poverty issues (e.g., food insecurity, a lack of resources to adequately manage their households and meet their children's basic needs, physical and mental health issues), and race relations and stereotyping.

Most participants expressed contentment that they were living in a community that had so much ethnic diversity. Racism exists in the inner-city communities; however, very few respondents stated that they were discouraged with the ethnic composition of their community. One Aboriginal participant stated: 'We all have to find our own way in which to respect ourselves and one another.' Another resident commented: 'As a White female, I often find most things are heavily weighted toward "Aboriginal" and though I am not prejudiced, it can be "too much of a good thing," and I feel excluded, and often even unaccepted.' While racism does exist, most participants had found that cultural and ethnic diversity is a strength for these communities.

Residents pointed out that there was a clear shortage of recreational facilities, cultural centres, and outdoor activities in their communities, as well as a lack of affordable day care and limited opportunities for individuals to continue their education and training at the local level. They suggested that programs and services needed to be socially inclusive so that all members of the community would be welcome regardless of ethnicity (the one centre with the most comprehensive programs and facilities, centrally located in Pleasant Hill, is the White Buffalo Youth Lodge, which caters primarily to the Aboriginal youth). Seniors or elders expressed a desire to share their wealth of knowledge with other members of the community, and suggested that they needed a place where they could gather to 'decrease the overwhelming sense of isolation that they experience living in the inner city with the social problems that exist.' Residents commented that 'we all live together in the community, and it is time we all come together as a community.' Aboriginal residents added: 'Our Saskatoon elders always share in their teachings, that one must know who they are and where they come from in order to move forward in life.' Many residents wanted to see positive, family-oriented development that would be inclusive for all residents regardless of socio-economic status.

The survey found that the negative stereotypes associated with the inner west side of Saskatoon were extremely frustrating for residents. Almost all respondents felt that the media misrepresented their

communities; yet almost all respondents also expressed a positive willingness to 'get involved' in community betterment (the few remaining
participants indicated that they had already done their part and weren't
willing to get involved outside of their own current family situation).

The researchers emphasized that sharing of knowledge and views
among residents is invaluable. Neighbourhood communities must be
valued for their strengths and capacities. Communities need support
and resources if they are to assume responsibility for addressing the
social issues in their communities without relying on inflexible systems
with limited mandates. New ways to engage and empower communities to begin the processes of reclaiming themselves need to be found.
Participants repeatedly stated that they were not being heard: decisions
continued to be made on behalf of the community with little or no input
by the residents on issues that affected their quality of life. As Burk
(2004) has emphasized, this lack of voice and choice for those who are
labelled (as poor, senior, Indian, west side or inner-city resident, etc.) or
marginalized and isolated in the community of residence is unfortunate
for many inner-city residents.

*Housing*

Many participants expressed serious concerns about housing; they identified an urgent need to address the poorest housing in their neighbourhoods. Specific issues here included rundown rental units fostering an
unhealthy environment for families, and absentee landlords who failed
to show respect. Homeownership was key: 'As our seniors move out,
landlords move in.' A way needed to be found to encourage residents
to purchase these older homes, so that they would invest in them and
remain in the communities. Seniors commented on their inability to
meet housing renovations adequately on their limited income. A flexible
program would need to be developed to help them address necessary
renovations so that they could remain in their own homes; moreover,
they would need assistance in retaining their independence. Cost,
awareness, and availability were mentioned as barriers to accessing
daily living assistance.

Yet most residents (especially homeowners) stated that they were
more or less satisfied with their present housing situation. When respondents were asked if they intended to stay in their current home,
they were divided between those who definitely planned on leaving the
inner city (14%) and those who had no intention of leaving (13%).

The research found that many residents – both homeowners and renters – had experienced difficulties in housing themselves and/or their families. Affordability was increasingly the foremost concern of residents – the limited number of affordable units for sale or rent. Also important, though, were the small size and poor quality of available properties, and aging and deteriorating housing stock. Participants shared many stories about discrimination in housing: more than three-quarters (78%) of renters felt that they had been discriminated against in one form or another while looking for a place to live.

Most homeowners reported that the quality of their home was adequate to good, with some repairs and minor maintenance required. They identified a lack of financial resources as hindering their ability to maintain or renovate their existing homes; they feared that they might have to spend more on their home renovations than their home was worth, so that it might be cheaper to sell the house than to address the deficiencies.

Among renters, 87% pointed out that they did not have the required down payment to become homeowners, largely due to a lack of credit. A large majority said they would be interested in becoming homeowners, though almost three-quarters did not want to purchase a home in the inner-city community where they were currently residing. Renters felt a high level of frustration with regard to the maintenance of the properties they occupied. They did not feel that their landlords were willing to address the deficiencies in their properties. For example, when they asked a landlord to address a mould problem, they were told that 'all houses are this way … All old houses have mould … It's normal.'

Residents repeatedly mentioned the number of 'slum housing' units in the inner city as a major problem. Homeowners believed that this was negatively impacting their quality of life and the value of their homes; tenants were concerned about the impact it was having directly on their family's health, quality of life, and level of inclusion with neighbours and the community. Many respondents stressed the need for outside help. In particular, seniors suggested that they required assistance with household work, home health assistance, and transportation, and families commented that they required safe, affordable child care services.

According to the National Children's Agenda (NCA), safe, adequate, and reasonably priced housing is vital to child health and safety, educational attainment, and social engagement. The quality, cost, tenure, and stability of housing, along with the neighbourhoods and communities in which children/families reside, all play a role in the achievement of desired outcomes in the areas of health, safety, education, and social engagement. For example, income obviously affects the quality and type of housing a family can afford; spending a disproportionate amount of income on housing means that less is available for other necessities. Risk factors associated with neighbourhoods containing a disproportionate share of poor housing interact with low family socio-economic status, which in turn contributes to unfavourable child outcomes. Inadequate housing, frequent relocation, and financial instability cause parental stress, which can contribute to dysfunctional family relationships, which in turn can result in domestic violence, separation, and divorce, all of which have been identified as among the most common reasons for frequent moves and housing disruptions. As Cooper (2001) has pointed out, while housing improvements serve as an effective intervention to prevent and redress certain problems, such improvements are both de-pendent on and a step toward the satisfaction of the three enabling con-ditions for good child outcomes: adequate income, effective parenting, and supportive community environments. It is difficult to achieve these conditions when children are poorly housed. Moreover, the chances that children will be well housed in the absence of these conditions are lower than when these conditions are present.

*Agencies, Organizations, and Service Providers*

A significant part of the research was designed to gauge the participants' current awareness of services and service providers operating in the five core neighbourhoods. The researchers found an overwhelming lack of awareness among residents as to what services were available; even some local community associations didn't know. The inevitable conclu-sion was drawn that this lack of awareness would have to be be ad-dressed for healthy community development.

Additional comments made by respondents may be summarized as follows: Community residents viewed systems and agencies as meeting their own needs first and *then* those of families or communities based on their mandates. Family supports were limited after traditional work hours, with limited after-hour resources available. Services for families were mandate-focused versus needs-focused. Services in inner-city communities were fragmented and inaccessible to those who needed them. With the urban migration of First Nations and Metis people to core neighbourhoods, and inadequate numbers of homeowners, most neighbourhood residents were living in poverty. The homeowners – the true community stakeholders – were frustrated, for their community and family needs were not being adequately met.

## Concluding Observations

A number of pertinent concluding observations were made by the project coordinator (Burk 2004), drawing on the community development literature: This community capacity and needs assessment provided an excellent example of engaging the citizens to participate in the identification of issues, concerns, and the development of potential solutions and goals. An assessment of this nature provides a process for citizen involvement where people learn more about the situation, and feel that they have had the opportunity to have their voice heard. Communities must be valued for their strengths and capacities, and the participants from five inner-city neighbourhoods for this assessment showed exemplary capacity. Their knowledge of their community and the issues that are affecting the quality of life is invaluable. This is a positive strength, which must be recognized and built upon.

As one First Nations elder explained, living a 'good and productive life' as an individual in a strong and caring community depends on whether these strengths are used, developed, and strengthened. Individuals and communities who are recognized and valued develop a positive view and continue to grow, thus laying a foundation for sustainable community development.

Respectful relationships already existing within the community should be further developed. Local communities need to recognize that they possess resources and strengths that can be relied upon within the community; outside intervention may not always be appropriate to deal with issues within a local community. Issues may be addressed by engaging residents and recognizing their strengths. Organizations, agencies, and service providers must be willing to work closely with communities in a collaborative and respectful manner (Barter 1996).

Community members repeatedly stressed to the research team that their voices were not being heard or respected. The full report of the project (Burk 2004) therefore emphasized that the identification of issues, concerns, needs, capacities, and strengths should be ongoing. Programming that brings residents together around common concerns and that encourages them to coordinate their efforts to solve community issues contributes the most to strengthening and supporting the community. Community members, working together to lessen the isolation of individuals, help develop respect for others and for property. They learn to work together, bridging differences, enhancing community spirit and a sense of belonging.

Aboriginal and other residents of inner-city communities must seek empowerment to make social policy change through citizen participation and voice. As Roberta Jamieson, Chief of the Six Nations, has commented, this 'presents a challenge for [all] our levels of government, including our First Nations ... The "cost of doing nothing" weighs heavily on us as well as Canada.' (Jamieson 2004).

It is important for local communities to build a solid foundation on which the partners can develop a collaborative vision, goals, and commitment. Working with the community needs to be inclusive and open; community partnership development should be built on a solid foundation of mutual respect and trust (Panet-Raymond 1992).

As we have noted, many poorer inner-city residents were aware that outsiders tended to view them as problematic troublemakers who were never satisfied. Progressive social change is enhanced through the direct participation of individual citizens collaborating to envision improved living conditions, then mobilizing to bring recommendations forward to promote vibrant and tolerant communities. The goal of social change is to strengthen the capacity of marginalized people to influence the social, economic, and political structures that govern their lives (Murphy 2009).

Burk (2004) has emphasized that our governments must look at the role of housing in social policy and further, how housing policy must be integrated with other sectors of children's policy and social policies in general. While community supports are of little value in the absence of housing, the presence of housing alone does not guarantee that all objectives and outcomes will be realized anytime soon. To date, there have been numerous attempts of intersectoral dialogue and policy development among a select group of decision-makers of all levels of government and community representatives. Yet each policy sphere has tended to make decisions in isolation; no coherent approach has evolved even though stakeholders have stated their commitment to work this way.

Three principles to govern the direction of social policy are common purpose, a focus on citizens, and collaboration (Cooper 2001). When neighbourhood communities are valued, this is an opportunity to respect the importance of process, to engage in collaborative relationships, to be innovative, and to build community and social justice for the common good (Barter 1996). Collaboration, like empowerment, is a people process. It is important to believe in people's abilities to change as well as to believe that people are, and always will be, the experts in themselves, their situation, their relationships, and what they want and need (Smale 1995). Burk has concluded, 'For agencies and organizations wanting to work in community, they must be prepared to revisit their values and beliefs; their work practices must reflect that as professionals they must be supportive of community.'

## Patterns and Influences of Home Ownership and Renting in Pleasant Hill

DARLENE LANCELEY with the Saskatchewan Indian Institute of Technologies

### Introduction

The purpose of this research project was to gather information on patterns of housing and renting in the Pleasant Hill neighbourhood of Saskatoon, a residential and commercial area on Saskatoon's inner west side, which has the highest Aboriginal proportion and lowest average family income of any neighbourhood in Saskatoon. Pleasant Hill had the lowest rates of homeownership in the city, as well as high rates of medium- to high-density rental housing (City of Saskatoon 2002). Many neighbourhood residents spend a large portion of their income on meeting the necessities of life. Mobility greatly affects the residential patterns of Pleasant Hill; this is demonstrated by the flux in numbers of enrolled school students. Factors affecting mobility rates include access to stable housing, employment, and income opportunities for families.

### Methodology

Interviews, focus groups, and thematic analysis enabled the research team to describe the patterns of homeownership and renting and the provision of services (Merriam 1999; Hopkins 1994). Participatory research, incorporating a 'community in research' process, is action-oriented in that it seeks recommendations on issues and problems as revealed by the community. The primary goal of this research in the Pleasant Hill neighbourhood was to capture the voice of the people to determine patterns and influences of homeownership and renting. Research participants answered structured as well as open-ended questions regarding any possible solutions to the issues.

The research team focused on low-density housing in the neighbourhood, specifically on single and double units. Out of 939 homes, researchers visited a random sample of 469; however, only 128 interviews were completed (65 residents voluntarily withdrew from the study after interviewing had commenced, and 276 homes were noted as unsuccessful 'call backs'). Limitations that prevented researchers from collecting the data included residential mobility (respondents moving during the research), fear and apprehension of residents, and potentially dangerous situations for the interviewers (the researchers were obliged to avert plans to conduct research at residences that posed a potentially dangerous or overly difficult situation). The proposed ideal number of participants in the residents' focus group was 20. The research team decided to conduct an additional focus group of community service providers in order to develop an additional perspective on the research findings. The research team was comprised of Aboriginal researchers who already possessed experience conducting community-based research. The residents' questionnaire, developed by the project team, was designed to obtain specific information about demographics, current housing situations, and perspectives on the neighbourhood. Residents' focus group questions were then developed, following analysis of the residents' questionnaires. Individuals selected for the residents' focus group self-identified during the interview process. Community agencies were identified through existing networks and invited to participate in the other focus group, which focused on service providers.

*Characteristics of Homeowners and Renters*

The 128 households interviewed were evenly split between 64 homeowners and 64 renters. 87 respondents were females and 41 were males. Of the females, 71 indicated they were the head of the household, compared to 35 males; the remaining 22 indicated that they shared the title of head of household with another individual in the household.

The ethnicity of the respondents approximated the ethnic breakdown of the total neighbourhood population: 28% were First Nation and 16% Metis (plus one undifferentiated Aboriginal); the remainder represented very diverse ethnic origins. It was particularly interesting that Aboriginal respondents constituted 73.4% of renters but only 15.6% of homeowners.

Respondents ranged widely in age. Of the total respondent pool, 17.1% had less than a grade nine education, 26.5% some high school education, and 21.8% a high school diploma, while 14.8% had at least some post-secondary education. Strikingly, one-quarter of the homeowners had not yet graduated from high school, compared to 62% of the renters.

Asked what their total annual household income from all sources (before deductions) was, 24.2% of the respondents had an income under $10,000 per year; 17.9%, an income of $10,000 to $19,000; 19.5%, $20,000 to $29,000; 10.1%, $30,000 to $39,000; 7%, $40,000 to $49,000; and 7%, over $50,000 per year (the remainder did not provide information on household income). Most significant was the finding that 17% of homeowners had a household income under $20,000 a year compared to 83% of renters. Moreover, one-third of the Aboriginal home-owning households had an annual income under $20,000 a year, compared to 89.3% of the Aboriginal renting households. Clearly, poverty was an important problem for many, especially Aboriginal respondents. Slightly more than one-third of the respondents (just over half of the homeowners but only 11 of the renters) were currently in some form of employment (full-time, part-time, or casual, or self-employment). Almost one-third were receiving social assistance, pension benefits, or student assistance as their primary source of income. The remaining respondents had a combination of sources of income. For example, 41% received child tax benefits for children residing in their household.

*Mobility and Housing*

Residents were asked how long they had lived in the neighbourhood. Households were approximately equally divided between shorter-term residency (less than five years) and longer. As expected, homeowners seemed less transitory than renters: 34.4% of homeowners compared to 64.1% of renters had lived in the neighbourhood less than five years. Higher mobility among Aboriginal residents was evident: 40% of home-owners and 57.4% of renters had resided in the neighbourhood for less than five years.

When asked more specifically how long they had lived in their current accommodation, responses ranged from less than two years to over 20 years. Again, we found that homeowners were far more sedentary than renters: among homeowners, 39.1% had lived in their present home for less than five years, compared to 84.4% of the renters; whereas

60% of the Aboriginal homeowners had lived in their present home for less than five years, comparable to 60.9% of Aboriginal renters.

Residents were asked where they had lived before moving to their current residence. The majority of homeowners and renters had already been Saskatoon residents. Three-quarters of the homeowners had already lived in Saskatoon; the remainder had lived elsewhere in Saskatchewan or out of the province. A higher proportion (81.3%) of the renters had already been Saskatoon residents. We found that almost one-third of the homeowners had not been living in a house prior to their present home; moreover, almost half had not been previous home-owners; rather, they had rented their accommodations. Among renters, just over half had previously lived in a house, and just under one-quarter in an apartment, but 88% of current renters had rented their previous accommodations.

In contrast to the data gathered on actual length of occupation of their present abode, when asked how long they intended to stay at their current home, homeowners tended to be fairly equally divided between very short-term (several years) and longer. Renters were more mobile, but some uncertainty was noted; for example, they would move 'when an affordable place could be found,' or 'when something else comes along,' or they would stay 'as long as possible.'

When asked whether their current home met their household's overall needs, 88% of homeowners and 78% of renters responded affirmatively. The homeowners' concerns were that they needed a bigger place, required more bedrooms, needed a smaller place, needed more security, and needed repairs. The renters' main concerns were that they needed more space, more comfort and security, bigger appliances, better carpeting, and repairs. Almost all renters said they were interested in owning their own place. Most residents had not taken any training (including self-education) to learn how to maintain their place; homeowners were actually less willing than renters to take training on home maintenance.

When renters were asked whether they would buy a place in Pleasant Hill, responses were almost evenly split between those who would and those who would not. More than one-third of the homeowners and half the renters commented that they would be moving in the near future. Reasons for moving included the following: to get away from the neighbourhood, or from undesirable neighbours, or from criminal activities; concerns about physical safety and property safety; the need for a different place, or space; to be closer to family; to enter a retirement home; to obtain employment; to return to the country or reserve; to be closer to better schools; to pay lower utility costs; or to have a landlord who would take better care of the place.

*Household Size*

Crowding did not seem to be as much of an issue as expected. The homeowners reported that the number of rooms in their homes ranged from two to twelve; most homes ranged from four to nine rooms, and the majority had five rooms. The number of bedrooms ranged from one to five, with almost half having three bedrooms. Over three-quarters of the renters were living in a house, the remainder in a townhouse, duplex, suite, or fourplex. Among the renters, the number of rooms ranged from three to eight; most residences ranged from four to six rooms. The number of bedrooms ranged from one to four, with most residences having either two or three.

Residents were asked how many adults and children usually lived in their place. Surprisingly, more than two-thirds of the homeowners had no children, and for the remainder, family size was relatively small. Yet the adult residents consisted of homeowners, spouses, parents, roommates, and boarders. The children under 18 years of age were either children of the homeowners or foster children who lived with the homeowners (more common among Aboriginal people). Of the rentals, 37.5% contained no children, another 26.6% just one child, 26.6% between two and four children, and 9.3% five or more children (one household contained nine children). The children under 18 were either children of the renting respondent or grandchildren and foster children living with the respondent (seven households indicated that they had grandchildren living in their household). The adult residents consisted of renters, spouses, siblings, friends, parents, and roommates.

*Housing Costs and Conditions*

Most homeowners (58%) owed on a mortgage for their home. Those respondents who owed on a mortgage were asked when their mortgage would be paid in full; responses were evenly spread across the range of less than five years to twenty-five years. Just 10 respondents indicated that they had obtained assistance from a program to purchase their home.

When asked what percentage of the household gross monthly income (before deductions) was used for household-related payments (mortgage, insurance, and taxes), homeowners' responses ranged from less than 10% to 90%; more than two-thirds of homeowners were paying less than one- quarter of their household income. With regard to monthly utilities (electricity, heat, water), homeowners' payments typically ranged from less than $200 to $500 per month. One-quarter of the home-owners reported that they shared the costs of household payments with someone else in the household.

Homeowners generally considered the condition of their house to be either fair (48.4%), suggesting that their home could use some minor repairs, or good (46.9%), suggesting that their home did not need re-pairs. Interestingly, a very small number (just three respondents) indi-cated that their home could use major repairs; however, this could reflect an unwillingness of the respondent to admit to living in poor conditions. Yet homeowners described a wide variety of types of repairs that they considered were needed to their homes. When homeowners were asked whether they would make the required repairs, three-quar-ters of them felt that a professional contractor was not required to make them. Residents were asked if they were satisfied with the condition of their place. Homeowners had surprisingly high levels of satisfaction with their homes: 90% indicated that they were satisfied (but again, 'satisfaction' can be highly relative).

When we investigated the percentage of household gross monthly income being used for household-related payments, renters' responses ranged from less than 10% to 100%; 37.5% of renters were paying over half of their income. With regard to monthly utilities, renters' payments ranged from less than $200 to $1,200 per month, with slightly more than half (57.6%) paying less than $300. Only eight renters reported subsi-dized rent. As well, 27% of renters shared the costs of household pay-ments with someone else in the household.

Most renters considered the condition of their accommodation to be either fair (54.7%) or good (42.2%). Just two renters admitted that their homes could use major repairs. When the interviewers inquired whether the renters would make the required repairs, they were divided between those who said they would, those who would not, and those offering no response. When renters were asked if they thought their landlord would make the required repairs, more than two-thirds replied affirmatively. The minority who said their landlords would not make the required repairs offered the following explanations: the landlord checks the re-quired repairs but never makes the repairs; the landlord reimburses the resident for repairs and supplies; the renter is afraid of the landlord and the landlord's threats; the landlord supplies materials for the resident to make required repairs; the landlord is a large company (owning a lot of property); the landlord lives out of city and does not know what's wrong with the property; the landlord simply does not care; or the landlord repairs what he can repair. A high proportion of renters said they would feel comfortable asking their landlord to make the repairs in their homes. Renters offered the following explanations regarding their landlords' unwillingness to make repairs: the resident does not have a good relationship with the landlord; the landlord does not like to spend money on repairs; the landlord is too busy; the renter is afraid to say anything (i.e., of getting evicted for requesting repair work); the landlord does not care; the renter does not have a landlord; the landlord is not reliable; the renter has to keep the house clean at all times for repair people to come in; or the landlord repairs what he can repair. Renters had a surprisingly high level of satisfaction (86%) with the condition of their accommodations.

*Evaluating the Neighbourhood*

Respondents identified a broad variety of services available in the Pleasant Hill neighbourhood and were generally of the opinion that most services were easy to access; however, some services were lacking or difficult to access.

A high proportion of residents reported evidence of criminal or disruptive activities in the neighbourhood: prostitution, drug use, vandalism, alcohol abuse, gang activity, child neglect, the street sale of alcohol or drugs (with evidence of needles), noisy parties, stabbings, murders, bullying, animal abuse, frequent verbal abuse, car theft, elder abuse, neglect of property, a lot of violence … A highly prevalent perception among residents of Pleasant Hill was that there was too much negative activity in the area and they did not feel safe. Yet 78% of residents cautiously indicated that they liked living in their neighbourhood. The remainder, when asked why they did not like living there, offered these explanations: there was too much criminal activity, such as prostitution, vandalism, and drug use/abuse; they used to like the neighbourhood but it had declined badly and they didn't understand why this was happening; there were too many social problems and issues of general safety; and the area had become too noisy. Almost two-thirds (63%) of residents interviewed had family or close friends in the neighbourhood, indicative of fairly strong attachment to Pleasant Hill. When asked what they would need in order to stay in their home for the next five years, residents suggested a cleaner neighbourhood, increased security and police presence, less crime and fewer gangs, localized employment, improved health, improved upkeep of property by the landlord, lower taxes, sufficient finances to make improvements or to buy a house, and/ or more affordable homes. Some respondents mentioned the need to make personal changes.

*Reflections on Affordable Housing*

The numbers of renters in Pleasant Hill are relatively high compared to owner-occupants of houses. Living conditions are often overcrowded. Rental units must be maintained and rents sustained at affordable levels for low- and moderate-income families (City of Saskatoon 2003c). The seniors population requires affordable housing as well. A number of organizations in the city provide services to seniors, yet there remains a need for housing choices.

Strategies identified by the residents from the interviews and focus groups for helping people obtain 'adequate' and 'affordable' housing include the following: creating a Tenant–Landlord Cooperation Group (consisting of tenants, landlords, and community residents), which would develop minimum criteria for rental accommodations in the community, and not just regarding maintenance; creating a list of affordable housing units; investing in land and real estate in partnership with organizations, with the goal of building houses; offering an alternative form or better blend of culturally relevant housing units; involving the public, in that people need a active voice as opposed to being told what to do (people know what they need in order to be a true community and meet the cultural needs of their community); and encouraging more homeownership (because homeowners will then do better maintenance on the homes they have purchased). Utilities are expensive, especially in older houses. The rent may be low, but people are displaced because the cost of utilities is too high. There are a lot of older furnaces, and the SaskEnergy program is regarded as ineffective due to the reliance on credit ratings – that is, people with a poor credit rating cannot access the program. Seniors are disproportionately victims of crime (break and enters); also, they are affected more by high utility bills, including, sometimes, the loss of utilities when they cannot pay their bills. Strategies such as by-law amendments, tax incentives, rental controls, standards for rent, and grants for energy should all be explored; similarly, incentive programs would enhance existing housing (the updated community plan for Saskatoon specifies that an established quality for construction and maintenance be followed). Developing adequate and affordable housing for residents will clearly be a long and complicated process.

Residents identified many gaps in the various affordable housing programs and suggested ways to fill them. They suggested investigating slum landlords, as well as social services organizations that pay lip service to community development but seem to have other agendas. They also suggested an information campaign to remove negative perceptions about the neighbourhood (as one focus group participant put it, 'potential employers don't like an address here – living in this neighbourhood can be a hindrance despite a resident's work experience, education, and ability to work'). Subpopulations such as young people, the physically disabled, those with special needs, those with unidentified needs, and seniors all have specific housing needs. Regarding home-ownership, the residents provided the following recommendations: offer low-income homeownership programs geared toward singles, seniors, and families; develop cooperative housing options, 'rent-to-own' options, and a 'sweat equity' program; provide rental controls, and/or caps on both rent and rent increases as well as on utilities; provide a central resource centre that includes a library and housing information, advocacy, and support and that provides supportive housing opportunities in conjunction with coordinated services and programs; and create new, affordable housing units to meet the needs for adequate and affordable housing.

*The Search for Community*

The Pleasant Hill residents have created a community whose members watch over one another, their homes and property. For a brief time, we observed the neighbourhood's daily activities and the impact these have on the residents' personal safety. We observed many negative activities: criminal and gang activity, prostitution, the sale of drugs, drug and alcohol use and abuse, children not in school, children being left without adult supervision, and needles and condoms in schoolyards and public spaces. Yet we also noted positive activities, such as individuals and families gathering in schoolyards and public spaces with their children, families playing together, and residents providing ad hoc advocacy and support for one another. We repeatedly heard from the residents that they wanted the criminal activity to leave their neighbourhood so that they could resume normal day-to-day activities of the kind that most citizens take for granted, such as going to the park, walking in the neighbourhood, visiting neighbours, taking the bus, walking from the bus stop without fear, and feeling safe in your own home without fear of a home invasion or a break and enter. The residents also wanted to have their voices heard, for they knew what the solutions were for their community.

Residents in the focus groups and personal interviews identified the need for strategies to help families stay in their homes and neighbourhood. These included establishing better amenities in the neighbourhood such as a grocery store, schools, parks, a library, and recreation opportunities, and developing advocacy and support systems for students and seniors. The updated Saskatoon Community Plan recommends a community support centre to provide services for the diverse ethnic groups found in Pleasant Hill. The residents have devoted much attention to community building. They would like a central gathering place – a true community centre that would serve as a multisector facility. If services in the neighbourhood were centralized, people could access more easily the services they need. The residents contended that the Outreach Program of the Saskatchewan Health Region had been brought into the community without its consent. There has since been an increase in the number of needles and condoms found in parks and other public areas – a clear danger to health. They also pointed out that community schools and facilities have already reached maximum capacity. They suggested that social, cultural, and recreational activities should be incorporated into the schools so that children will not be lured so easily into dangerous alternatives. They also called for a culturally supportive Aboriginal housing centre to accommodate the rising Aboriginal population. Capacity strengthening for Aboriginal organizations would improve the delivery of adequate and affordable housing. Cultural awareness and sensitivity to traditional values are requisite to the provisioning of services to the Aboriginal community.

Regarding education and training, the city offers free resources, but they are all are located downtown. Some local community programs have been innovative and well received. The Bent Nail Tool Cooperative has provided access to maintenance workshops and tools at low or no cost. According to one focus group participant, one program, the 'Wrap Around Program,' worked well, but it was cut after three years. That program focused on building community and community-based programs. It was about values, voicing choices, and integrating services. It fitted well with the Aboriginal paradigm and world view, working on the front line with families that had been marginalized.

More support for youth seems necessary: Said one resident: 'Young children are often left alone. The inner city has the highest rates of poverty and no day care. Poverty is a big industry in this neighbourhood.' Another issue is sexually exploited girls: 'The girls go back to school in the morning after they work the corner.'

Participants identified the need for strategies to help families attain a better quality of life. Cultural education should be available for everyone; the neighbourhood consists of residents of diverse cultural backgrounds and has the highest Aboriginal proportion in the city. Transportation services are restrictive due to location and the cost of riding the bus. As well, residents indicate that some taxi drivers will not go into the Pleasant Hill neighbourhood. People have to leave the neighbourhood to access needed services such as food and laundry, while pharmaceuticals are limited, which has an impact on low-income households. It is difficult and often dangerous to walk with children to distant services. Better coordination between service providers is required. Then there is the issue of children who come from impoverished, drug-addicted families. 'We see three generations of "weakened families," for example, grandmothers working to support and raise their grandchildren,' as a focus group participant explained.

Increased police presence is needed in the community. Residents were of the opinion that police are biased. There is a sentiment that they do not respond quickly enough in the area or treat the residents with respect. One resident commented: 'The inner city needs more Native officers involved and they should be on foot, which would allow them to see more.' Community policing should include a 'safe walk' program as well as specific measures to deal with the sex trade. Residents were anxious to see prostitution moved out of residential areas. There is a correlation with certain residences and gangs. There are thirty-one active gangs in the area. According to one focus group participant, 'We need to enhance the community, in activities such as "meet your neighbour" events. We need to maintain contact with each other.' Another commented, 'We need a safer neighbourhood. Part of the issue is weakened families. We need to build families and build the sense of community'.

Residents of Pleasant Hill are especially concerned about the crime in their neighbourhood; in fact, the foremost issue identified by the residents is that their neighbourhood is unsafe. Criminal activity has damaged the neighbourhood. Children, youth, and women cannot walk around the neighbourhood or even sit on their front doorsteps because 'johns' approach them. Seniors are afraid to walk to the bus for fear of being attacked or robbed. Children and youth are victims or perpetrators of criminal activity. Most residents want to remain in their neighbourhood, but want the criminal activity to leave.

Many residents recommended intelligent solutions for their community. They told us that homeownership needs to be supported and encouraged and that rent controls should be considered as a way to encourage adequate and affordable housing. The residents saw homeownership as a means of stabilizing their neighbourhood by helping those with low incomes (including single people) obtain a stable environment. Renters and homeowners who had been living in the neighbourhood for quite some time wanted to remain there and in their current homes. The majority of renters wanted to own their own place and would buy in the neighbourhood if they could afford it.

Residents in the community offered numerous insights and recommendations for their community. As experts on their community, their voices and their experiences comprised the bulk of the content of this study. Their commitment to their community, their resilience in the face of fear and crime, and their strength impressed the research team.

## Chapter Five

# Family, Women, and Youth

## The Role of Family, Women, and Youth in Urban Aboriginal Life

This chapter explores how urban Aboriginal families, women, and youth are all closely linked. It discusses a number of contemporary salient issues: changing family structure, housing initiatives as they pertain to women and families, the provision of family services, the protection of women, the disappearances of Aboriginal women and children, the adoption of Aboriginal children, and the situation of Aboriginal youth in the city. Several case studies from the Bridges and Foundations Project probe more deeply into particular topics affecting urban Aboriginal residents: the chronic problem of domestic violence; increasing HIV/AIDS among urban Aboriginal women; and the integration or alienation of youth within the city.

### Family

There has been relatively limited research specifically on the effects of changing family structure on housing among urban Aboriginal residents since Peters's suggestive study 'Family Values, Household Structure, and Housing Needs: Indian Households in Regina and Saskatoon, Saskatchewan, 1982' (Peters 1991). Yet there have been some pertinent recent trends deserving of our attention. In 1999 the City of Saskatoon Neighbourhood Profiles indicated that the annual family income of Aboriginal residents was lagging far behind that of non-Aboriginals: once the over-$30,000 level was passed, the proportion of Aboriginal families earning higher incomes trailed off markedly compared to other residents. A high disproportion of Aboriginal families

were in the lower-earning cohorts; more than one-quarter of all
Aboriginal families were earning less than $10,000, compared to ap-
proximately 5% of non-Aboriginal families; almost 40% of Aboriginal
families were earning between $20,000 and $30,000, compared to only
about 10% of non-Aboriginal families. National data on changing family
structure from the 2006 census were also noteworthy. For example,
among Canadians as a whole in the past 20 years, the proportion of
common law couples with children aged 24 and under had grown from
2.7% to 6.8%, and of those without children from 4.5% to 8.7%; whereas
far higher proportions were typically found in urban Aboriginal populations. The national proportion of lone parents with children had increased from 10.5% to 12.4%, of those without children from 2.1% to
3.5%. Yet these rates were far below the rates found in urban Aboriginal
populations. According to Native affairs columnist Doug Cuthand,
'today we have an epidemic in family breakdown, with a plethora of
single-parent families' (*Saskatoon StarPhoenix*, 7 May 2010). *Blind Spot:
What Happened to Canada's Aboriginal Fathers?*, a CBC documentary film
which aired January 14, 2012, points out that Aboriginal boys who grow
up without fathers are 80% more likely to wind up in jails, and sons of
teenage mothers in fatherless homes ten times as likely. The proportion
of young adults still living at their parents' home has been increasing,
from 27.0% to 28.4% in just the previous five years; but again, more family members tended to live in a single domicile in the extended family
situation still quite commonly found among urban Aboriginal residents.
While this may be lessening over time in crowded urban conditions,
typically the Aboriginal concept of 'family' consists not only of the nuclear family – husband/father, wife/unwed-spouse/mother, and their
children – but also potentially many other relatives, possibly including
grandparents, uncles, aunts, nephews and nieces, cousins, in-laws, 'illegitimate,' adopted, and foster children and relatives' children (First
Nations languages have numerous separate terms designating each of
these relationships). So to some extent, even in the urban milieu, a particular Aboriginal household could include any of these relatives, not
infrequently to a far greater extent traditionally than in most non-
Aboriginal ethnic cultures. Approximately 9% of all Canadian families
have five or more people in a single household, while we have seen that
overcrowding remains a significant problem on most First Nations reserves and in many urban Aboriginal homes. Finally, another observ-
able general trend has been the increase in household spending. The
Province of Saskatchewan actually recorded the fastest growth rate in

household spending in 2007 – a 7.7% increase in a single year, more than double the Canadian average rate of increase – although the Saskatchewan rate was still below the Canadian average. That represents more than $5,000 a year more spent on such expenditures as shelter, household operation, health care, transportation, tobacco products, and alcoholic beverages. Yet the province had the lowest average shelter costs nationally, with Regina residents spending $1,411 less than Saskatoon on average. The average annual household expenditure in Saskatchewan was $63,940 in 2007, compared to a national average of $69,950. Suffice it to point out again that much of the Aboriginal population does not have sufficient assets to meet this housing expenditure without ample government subsidization.

The provision of family services to Aboriginal residents has been an important development in Saskatoon. An initial effort to develop a counselling service for Aboriginal families in 1994 lasted less than a year; the main purpose of Wihcihitik (Saulteaux for 'helping each other') had been to reunite children taken away by Social Services with their original Aboriginal families. The Saskatoon Tribal Council (STC) opened a modest Family Centre in a house in the inner west side in November 1996 'to improve the quality of life for urban First Nations and Aboriginal families.' This centre intended to

> provide a model of service delivery that will emphasize traditional First Nations concepts of parenting and of healthy childhood growth and development, rebuild the First Nations concept of community childcare, thus eliminating the need for the systematized apprehension of children, organize community and in-home support for families in crisis so that over time the number of First Nations children going into care will be reduced, and reunite children in the provincial child welfare system with their birth family, extended family, and/or First Nations care providers. [Thus First Nations] children will remain within their family/community environments, children and families will have access to cultural teachings and ceremonies, children and families will be more connected to their communities, and urban communities will have First Nations representation.

The Centre would provide family support services, advocacy, practical assistance, referral services, consultations with elders, healing circles, interest groups, and workshops. Then four years later the STC established its expanded Child and Family Services Agency, with parent education programs, parent aides, child protection, family support homes, self-help groups, healing circles, and other community development initiatives. The agency is funded by the federal government through Indian and Northern Affairs Canada as well as the provincial government.

## Women

The unique situations faced by urban Aboriginal women have drawn limited attention by academic researchers. Again, Peters, a geography professor, has addressed this in her paper titled 'Subversive Spaces: First Nations Women and the City' (1998), commenting that 'there is little work which explores how the definition of the city, particularly in colonized countries, excludes indigenous peoples and cultures.' So she turns 'critical attention to the cultural meaning of urbanism by focusing on the complex geographies of identity and resistance which characterize the meaning of the term "urban" in relation to First Nations women in Canada.' In the process she refers to First Nations reserves as 'masculinized spaces,' then describes the 'alternative geographies of rights and identity imagined by urban First Nations women.' This may be a useful theoretical perspective in keeping with both women's and gender studies and geography, yet there are specific issues that need to be addressed. This has been accomplished most recently by Priscilla Settee, who has collected a variety of short essays recounting the personal impressions and experiences of Aboriginal women (Settee 2011).

In 1999, the then-Liberal Minister of Indian and Northern Affairs referred to the Indian Act as 'outdated' and 'offensive' and promised $2 million to groups representing Native people living off reserve. But the president of the Native Women's Association of Canada, which was to receive 10% of this funding, expressed her dismay that her association was usually excluded from federal funding and left out of critical negotiations. In response, the minister said he would name a 'special representative' to 'study' the role of Aboriginal women as the government worked toward 'modernizing' its relationship with Native people (*Saskatoon StarPhoenix*, 12 December 1999). Recent research reports of the Prairie Women's Health Centre of Excellence have included *Telling It Like It Is: Realities of Parenting in Poverty* (Green 2001), a Saskatoon-based study that responds to myths of parenting in poverty – myths such as 'poverty is the failure of the individual,' 'the poor don't want to work – they're just lazy,' 'welfare rates are too generous,' 'poor people need to be taught basic life skills like budgeting,' 'cheating and fraud are common among those on welfare,' 'poor families are poor because they have too many children,' and 'we cannot afford the social programs needed to end poverty.' These opinions are all too familiar to urban Aboriginal people. Other research conducted by the centre has included a study of affordable housing of women in Winnipeg (McCracken and Watson 2004) and a study of women's health, poverty, justice, and income support in Manitoba (Wiebe and Keirstead 2004).

Aboriginal women who have moved to the city within the past ten years are now assisted by the Tawow Women's Welcoming Circle in finding housing, employment, health services, and day care facilities. This new initiative developed in partnership with the Indigenous Peoples' Health Research Centre at the University of Saskatchewan.

A central issue has been the protection of urban Aboriginal women, especially in poorer inner-city neighbourhoods. These women have repeatedly been subjected to domestic abuse (*wikimakana notinew*) and violence. On the one hand, Aboriginal women have arguably enjoyed more success than their male counterparts in achieving higher education and career success; as many as three-quarters of Native post-secondary graduates are women, and their presence is increasingly being felt in professions and in leadership roles in First Nations government. Aboriginal women play a key role in maintaining and passing on traditional cultures. They are also contributing significantly to community economic development (Findlay and Wuttunee 2007). Yet on the other hand they continue to lag behind the general population in suffering from poverty, racism, sexism, and domestic abuse – too many Aboriginal women live in pain and fear because of domestic violence. The report of the Manitoba Aboriginal justice inquiry in 1999 indicated that the rate of spousal abuse in Aboriginal households was a shocking one in three, compared to one in ten in the general Canadian population. The problem has persisted because a large majority of First Nations band councils are male dominated and the people accused of abuse could be their friends or relatives.

A report of the Native Women's Association of Canada (2010) informs us that Aboriginal women continue to be the most at-risk group for violence in Canada. Aboriginal women between 25 and 44 years of age on reserves are five times more likely to die a violent death than are non-Aboriginal women in Canada; moreover spousal violence affects 54% of Aboriginal women annually, compared to 36% of non-Aboriginal women (Cuthand in *Saskatoon StarPhoenix*, 13 July 2007). Aboriginal women are twice as likely to experience violence or sexual assault as

Caucasian women, according to Statistics Canada; yet it has been estimated that only about one-third of the incidents of violent crime against
Aboriginal women ever get reported (*Saskatoon StarPhoenix*, 19 Dec.
2011). Aboriginal women constitute 3% of the national population yet
10% of reported homicides; almost half of these remain unsolved, even
though the overall clearance rate for homicides in Canada is 84%.
Saskatchewan actually has the best clearance rate (78%) of any province
in solving cases of murdered Aboriginal women, at least partly because
it is one of the few provinces with a comprehensive disaggregation by
race of cases of murdered and missing women (*StarPhoenix*, 24 April
2010). The homicide rate for Aboriginal women is almost seven times
greater than the rate for non-Aboriginal women. There have been
393 recorded murders of Aboriginal women in Canada since 1974, three-
quarters of them just during the past ten years, yet nobody has been
charged in 150 confirmed homicides. More than two-thirds of these
cases have occurred in the western provinces (*Canwest News Service*,
22 April 2010).

The need of Aboriginal women in Saskatoon for culturally sensitive
and appropriate shelter when fleeing this oppressive situation is explained in a case study included in this chapter. The YWCA conducts its
annual Rose Campaign aimed at eliminating violence against women
and calling for increased federal government funding for women's
social housing so that they won't have to face possible homelessness
when they decide to leave their abusers. The YWCA estimates that
100,000 women and children are forced to leave their homes for emergency shelters every year; moreover, 30% of them are repeat clients
(*Postmedia News*, 26 November 2010). The Saskatchewan Association of
Sexual Assault Services (SASAS) now operates a website to provide
women with easier access to information and services.

A chronic problem in western Canadian cities has been the disappear-
ance of numerous Aboriginal women and the murder of many prostitutes. The Sisters in Spirit project of the Native Women's Association,
which commenced in 2005 with $5 million in funding from Status of
Women Canada and another $10 million promised in the 2009 federal
budget, has been developing a database based on a wide array of variables, including suspect information; it is anticipated that some of this
funding will go toward housing, services for abused and battered
women, and improved education for police services to better understand Aboriginal issues. Data gathered to date reveal that across Canada
in the past three decades, at least 582 Native women have gone missing

or been murdered. Most were under 30 years of age, and many were under eighteen. Since 1980 more than 70 Native women have gone missing or been murdered in Manitoba alone. Winnipeg has the largest number of Aboriginal residents of any Canadian city; its Aboriginal families are disproportionately poor, their children too often reliant on an overburdened provincial child welfare system that tends to leave youth at risk even while it shelters and protects them (*Globe and Mail*, 7 September 2009; 6 January 2010). According to data from Saskatchewan included in an Amnesty International report, *No More Stolen Sisters* (2009), 60% of the long-term cases of missing women in the province are Aboriginal, even though these women comprise only about 6% of the province's population.

Aboriginal women in the city have also been disproportionately involved in the sex trade, which has in recent years contributed to a significant rise in HIV/AIDS among this population. Nearly half of the murdered and missing women recorded in Saskatchewan have been involved in the sex trade. The Native Women's Association argues that far more attention must be paid to preventing young Aboriginal women from being coerced into a life of prostitution, and that more assistance should be given to those who want to escape. Coincidentally, it was on the International Day for the Abolition of Slavery (2 December 2009) that the Calgary police charged a 38-year-old Aboriginal woman under the Alberta Protection of Sexually Exploited Children Act with trafficking in persons, procuring persons to become prostitutes, and living on the avails of prostitutes under age of 18. Three of the four Aboriginal girls involved, aged 16 and 17, had been lured to Calgary from Saskatoon with the pretext of modelling and forced into the sex trade (*Saskatoon StarPhoenix*, 3 and 4 December 2009). The perceptive research by Romanow in conjunction with the Bridges and Foundations Project on HIV/AIDS among urban Aboriginal women, summarized in this chapter, tells the personal life stories of 22 women and describes the close links between HIV/AIDS, involvement in the sex trade, and physical abuse.

*Youth*

Urban Aboriginal children, too, have been disappearing. Commenting on one unresolved case – that of a young child who suddenly vanished in Regina in 2004 – columnist Doug Cuthand wrote that 'this story underscores the importance of developing proper services for our urban citizens ... We can no longer allow our people to exist in poverty and isolation in cities' (*Saskatoon StarPhoenix*, 3 September 2004). Indeed, child poverty has been a central dilemma in the urban Aboriginal population (as we noted in the Introduction to the previous chapter). The federal government created the First Nations Child and Family Services Program in 1990; today this program supports over 100 First Nations agencies, serving approximately 160,000 children and youth. Yet a report in March 2009 of the Standing Committee on Public Accounts reiterated that Indian Affairs was not treating First Nations children equitably. That committee noted that 'it would be reasonable to expect First Nations agencies to receive greater funding, given their unique and challenging circumstances.'

The confiscation of Aboriginal children by Social Services, and adoption into non-Aboriginal homes, particularly common during the 1960s, has generated a great deal of controversy, especially with the release of a report on the province's child welfare system in December 2010. Today there are still more Aboriginal children in care than at the height of residential schools – a policy that First Nations spokespersons regard as the perpetuation of 'cultural genocide.' The Saskatchewan Social Services Ministry reports that there are 3,600 First Nations children in care off reserve; 17 First Nations child and family service agencies; 63 First Nations foster homes; and about 1,200 children in foster care on reserves. There is a progressive movement to keep First Nations children needing special care within a First Nations setting, evidenced in a new contract in December 2010 between the large Lac La Ronge Indian Band Child and Family Services and the provincial Social Services Ministry. But these First Nations care homes are hardly capable of caring for the large number of children living in poverty in overcrowded, substandard housing. A very high proportion (currently 80%) of children in care in Saskatchewan are Aboriginal. The disproportion of First Nations children in care (about 10%, compared to just 1% of other children) is incredible. The Canadian Incidence Study on reported child abuse and neglect has explained this disproportion by pointing out that First Nations children come to the attention of child welfare authorities because they are more likely than other children to experience child abuse (*awasisiwi wanitotamowin*) and neglect driven by poverty, poor and inadequate housing, caregiver substance abuse, family neglect, and sexual abuse and domestic violence (which are the more common reasons for other children).

First Nations child care programs are seriously underfunded, especially considering Aboriginal population growth. Moreover, the quality of Canadian child care programs and services has been lagging in comparison to other developed countries; a recent report by the UNICEF Innocenti Research Centre found that Canada met only one of the ten minimum standards for protecting the rights of children. There are 2 million Canadian children under the age of six requiring day care, yet only 800,000 are enrolled in regulated programs. Moreover, Canada has no national standards or national accountability, according to the president of the Canadian Child Care Federation (*Saskatoon StarPhoenix*, 11 December 2008). The Conservative federal government recently did announce support for First Nations child and family services ($105 million aimed at helping families on reserve to prevent their children being placed in foster care), but this funding excludes urban families. While appreciating this funding, past FSIN Chief Lonechild has emphasized that the FSIN is determined to reduce the excessive number of First Nations children in care, commenting that 'today we think it is time to put the Indian back into the child' (*StarPhoenix*, 23 July 2008). Cuthand has written:

> After the school closed and the missionaries moved on, it was time for the social workers to move in ... Social workers made life-changing decisions and removed children from their parents. Families were dismantled and scattered ... anywhere but to another Indian family. Out of control social workers played God ... The program preserved the interests of local racism ... First Nations families are not islands. They are networks of aunts, uncles and grandparents. This is our great strength and it must be seen as such. (*Saskatoon StarPhoenix*, 25 July 25, 2008)

One-quarter of First Nations youth aged 10 to 15 on reserves in Saskatchewan experience depression (compared to less than 10% of Caucasian youth in Saskatoon, according to research conducted in 2008), so we may conclude that on-reserve youth may have triple the propensity for depression as urban Caucasian youth; an environment of poverty and limited opportunities found on many reserves tends to have a strong influence on depression among youth (Lemstra in *Saskatoon StarPhoenix*, 21 July 2011).

However, increasing numbers of Aboriginal youth are born and raised in the urban context. Often they have virtually no acquaintance with a reserve or rural community, except perhaps for occasional visits 'back home' to relatives remaining there. This is especially true for Aboriginal children adopted into or placed in foster care in non-Aboriginal families in the city. Native people use the expression 'apple' – red on the outside but white inside – to describe such children. Concern over the loss of Aboriginal culture in the urban context has been significant. To what extent do urban Aboriginal youth living in Aboriginal families now view the city as 'home'? This is explored in the final case study in this chapter. What is the differential experience of young men (*oskinikiw*) and young women (*oskinikiskwew*)? Home can be a geographic location, of course, but it can also have symbolic, social, cultural, or psychic meaning (Driedger 2010, 334).

Urban Aboriginal youth may be integrated into urban life or alienated from it. Among the initiatives aimed at giving purpose to urban Aboriginal youth have been the Core Neighbourhood Youth Co-op (CNYC) and Urban Multipurpose Aboriginal Youth Centres (UMAYC). The CNYC in Saskatoon teaches basic skills to local youth, then gives them the opportunity to provide city residents with services and produce. Established in 1996, and reflecting the desire of residents of the Riversdale neighbourhood on the inner west side to 'address self-sufficiency, cooperative principles, and environmentalism,' CNYC provides 'at-risk' inner-city youth with opportunities to learn economic and marketing basics. Youths in the program have been involved in tree banding, compost bin construction and sales, bicycle repairs, recycling, organic gardening, and selling fresh produce (Tupone 2004). The UMAYC initiative was developed by the National Association of Friendship Centres (NAFC) in 1998 as a five-year program to provide urban Aboriginal youth with a wide range of culturally based programs, services, and activities that are locally controlled. It was intended to 'empower Aboriginal youth to address the challenges they face and determine their own future with a sense of pride in a safe and culturally relevant environment' (NAFC 2001). Research has also drawn attention to elder mentoring of youths.

Quint Development Corporation operates a Youth Lodge with the objective of providing a safe, supportive environment for males aged 16 to 22 who are in need of assistance to get back into school or into the workforce; 'case plan management is conducted with an emphasis upon a holistic medicine wheel approach which recognizes the interdependency of mental, physical, emotional and spiritual elements – the Youth Lodge intends to provide a supportive environment with focus on education and employment.' One individual attempt to counsel Aboriginal youth in Saskatoon about the dangers of street life – notably drug use and prostitution – was initiated by a former pimp who had spent much of his own youth in prison (*Saskatoon Free Press*, 19 December

1996). The EGADZ youth centre in Saskatoon works with exploited teens trying to leave the sex trade while recovering from years of abuse and neglect. Father André, a retired Catholic priest inducted into the Order of Canada in 2010, has long served Native youth attempting to find themselves in the city.

According to a survey released by Statistics Canada in 2004, urban Aboriginal youth across Canada seem to be quite active in sports (71% participated at least weekly), in clubs and cultural activities (31%), in helping out in the community or school (21%), or in spending time with an elder (34%). To this, Cuthand has responded that in Saskatoon, affordability of recreational activities can be an issue and that an increasing majority of youth actually 'live in English immersion' and have little familiarity with Aboriginal culture. Moreover, the once healthy Aboriginal diet of natural foods has been largely replaced by an atrocious diet leading to obesity, malnutrition, and a whole series of long-term effects including heart disease and diabetes. Most disturbingly, he adds, the general public image of Aboriginal youth (fostered by the media) is that they are violent, addicted gang members; moreover, the police are quick to suggest that a small segment of the population is responsible for a large percentage of criminal activities (*Saskatoon StarPhoenix*, 16 July 2004).

## Aboriginal Women Fleeing Violence

SHELLEY THOMAS PROKOP and JOAN SANDERSON

*Introduction*

This report reflects the voices of 25 Aboriginal women fleeing violence in Saskatoon, 14 agencies and organizations that work with or refer Aboriginal women fleeing violence, and 3 elders. Our main objective in this study was to find out more about the current capacity of Saskatoon to shelter Aboriginal women fleeing violence and about the specific shelter needs of Aboriginal women fleeing violence. We initially found that while there is a fairly extensive research literature pertaining at least partially to Aboriginal women fleeing abusive situations, there was limited research indicating the current capacity of Saskatoon to house Aboriginal women fleeing violence; nor was there much information on the specific needs of a shelter for Aboriginal women. What we were able to find was an abundance of people interested in discussing the capacity of Saskatoon to meet the needs of Aboriginal women fleeing violence, and in discussing the physical components needed in a shelter for them. This report addresses and voices their opinions, concerns, and recommendations.

## Methodology

The two main researchers, employees of the First Nations University of Canada (FNUC) at the time, both endorsed community-based methodologies that build capacity in the community and that encourage individuals to speak for themselves in the research process in the community. Research assistants hired for the project were social work students of this university.

This research project was based on the principles of community-based research, which include the community being involved in the development, implementation, and analysis of the project. Therefore, throughout this project many efforts were made to include participants in the research process and to develop activities that sought their input in a welcoming and non-judgmental way. Focus groups and personal interviews were conducted to gather most of the information for this project.

The ethics that guided the project included the ethical guidelines outlined by the University of Regina (with which FNUC was affiliated) as well as the TIPI teaching principles. The TIPI principles of the First Nations research–learning circle emphasize that we strive to live in harmony with one another and with all creation around us in this circle of life. In a circle, no one is above another. There is a sense of belonging to a family and to a community.

Qualitative methods of focus group and personal interviews were used to encourage and nurture the voices both of Aboriginal women fleeing violence and of organizations and agencies who work with those women.

## The Shelters

All agencies indicated that the women were desperate, in crisis, scared, and confused. An agency shared that 'women who are entering a shelter are doing so as a last resort.' One elder indicated that when she sees women going into the shelter, 'they are fearful for their life, the kids are upset and they are in crisis.' Awareness of the traumatized state of mind of a woman and children in these circumstances has to be continually considered.

Within the research we found only one shelter that was required to keep statistics on Aboriginal women. All other shelters and organizations kept statistics, or some form of recording, but did not distinguish ethnicity among the women clients. This resulted in some difficulty in ascertaining the capacity of Saskatoon to meet the needs of Aboriginal women fleeing violence. However, when agencies were asked to approximate how many of the women they served were Aboriginal, their answers ranged from half to virtually all (these numbers came from agencies that specifically serviced Aboriginal women and those that serviced all women). The one agency that shared specific data with us indicated that in the previous year, they had turned away 892 women (excluding their children) who had called. With each woman coming with an average of two children, this number jumped to 2,676 people who could not be sheltered at one particular shelter in the previous year. This number is alarming and speaks to the need for more shelters in Saskatoon, a relatively small city of just over 200,000 population. In discussion with agencies about how long it took to shelter a woman and what happened if they could not be sheltered, the agencies all responded that if they could not find immediate accommodations, and had exhausted family and other emergency options for fleeing violence, then the women would likely be obliged to return to the situation they had just left.

Only one shelter was conducting a post-shelter evaluation. However, other agencies and organizations mentioned having discussions with the Aboriginal women staying in the shelter on what would meet their needs while in the shelter with their families. Moreover, the one agency that conducted post or exit evaluations indicated that it had a voluntary evaluation form that women could choose to fill out at the end of their stay. Such activities are potentially important in determining the value of services and in helping the women find a voice in the service they are receiving.

When we asked agencies about the wait period to enter a shelter, we again found that they kept minimal statistics. However, participants indicated that they were full most of the time and were constantly turning clients away. Each woman was encouraged to call the shelter each day to find out the current status. If someone left unexpectedly or if their 30 days were up, then a space became available. In some circumstances the Salvation Army houses the women temporarily, one or two nights, at a local hotel; this is a temporary solution, however, and does not include professional assistance or support while staying at the hotel.

Most shelters in Saskatoon have a 30-day stay period. This time period is linked to funding for women and families to stay in the shelter. The time limit poses problems for many women who are in crisis and who may not be able to coordinate resources to leave the shelter in 30 days. This limit is complicated with other issues for Aboriginal women, particularly for Aboriginal women who are moving from a rural to an urban environment. Their knowledge of services and programs available to them in an urban setting is limited; and given that women are entering the shelter in a crisis situation, they may be scared for their lives. This time limit is simply not feasible for all Aboriginal women fleeing violence. Suggestions given by the participants to remedy this problem included stages of housing, such as an emergency shelter for 30 days and then second-stage housing for another period of time until the women and children feel they are ready to move on. However, respondents noted that only emergency shelters are funded; second-stage housing tends not to be funded in Saskatchewan. All agencies and victimized women felt that more options for shelters should be available for those who are at different stages.

The original full report provides many constructive suggestions on the physical components and programming components of an ideal shelter, summarizing the comments made by respondents in the focus groups and through personal interviews.

*Holistic Approach*

An interesting finding of this study was that '[rehabilitation] could be grounded in holistic healing.' During one of the focus groups, a participant commented, '*Ati-mino-ayaw* ... Men need a place to heal, too. My partner looked for help, and couldn't find much that worked for him.' This comment was followed by an outpouring of ideas and support that focused initially around men healing, then relationship healing and family healing. There was a lot of positive energy around this conversation, and many comments reflected the desire for holistic approaches when dealing with the issue of family violence: 'Men need support if they are willing to work on the relationship.' The need was expressed not only for a safe, secure place for women and their children who are in danger; but also for a lodge for men who wanted to heal and work on themselves and the relationship. The possibility of housing for men who have been part of domestic violence is perhaps an unexpected vision to arise out of research that has focused on shelters for Aboriginal women fleeing violence, but it is a potent and powerful vision.

*Recommendations*

In sum, it was recommended that future stages of development toward shelters for Aboriginal women should continue to have the participation of the Aboriginal community. The results of this research should be widely disseminated and published to address the issue of limited information and knowledge of the shelter needs of Aboriginal women. Statistics and evaluations should be conducted by agencies to further contribute to the development of shelters for Aboriginal women. Continual support should be given to Aboriginal women fleeing violence and to organizations servicing these women. It was recommended that more statistics be collected that reflect the waiting periods faced by Aboriginal women entering a shelter. There should be several types of shelters meeting the needs of women, specifically crisis shelters, transition shelters, and long-term shelters. The programs in shelters should reflect Aboriginal women's needs of those of their families. Shelters should not discriminate service based on women who have or have not money. Shelters should be set up for a variety of family sizes, accommodating women with or without children. The physical components and programming components suggested by participants should be implemented to better meet the needs of Aboriginal women and family: day care, prayer room, cultural programs, elders counselling, and so on. Cultural programming should be a foundation for shelters, and both female and male elders should be involved in this program development with the women. Children's programs should be developed, and there should be a search for funding from a variety of sources that could accommodate this. The elders recommended that the services should be consistent with First Nations cultural and spiritual principles, philosophies, and traditions. It was recommended that a holistic approach be used as a foundation for further development of a shelter for Aboriginal women. There should be a focus on family healing, specifically for men. There has been limited attention paid to men's role in healing the family; research on this is needed. To support and meet the needs of Aboriginal families, shelters for Aboriginal women fleeing violence should be created with the input and knowledge of the needs of the women, children, and partners.

The responses from the women and the agencies that took part in this research have been very supportive of Aboriginal shelters that meet the specific needs of the Aboriginal women who enter them. Although there are specific services in Saskatoon for Aboriginal women, many Aboriginal women are still unable to access the shelters because they are full, or are not meeting their programming needs, or are not large enough to accommodate their family size. There has been considerable support for an Aboriginal men's shelter that would lend itself to a holistic approach, which many Aboriginal people use to treat the family – that is, to also treat the man. This philosophy resonated throughout the research as women worked toward healing for themselves, their children, and their partners.

What should a shelter look like? The responses were suggestive of a highly inclusive and harmonious physical structure – one that would nurture growth, provide sufficient privacy, offer large rooms to accommodate large families, offer a visitors' space, and – this is important – include a prayer or quiet room where women could have quiet time or a smudge and practise their culture in a comfortable space. Also, programs should be plentiful and project a 'holism' for clients – that is, they should include programming for the women in physical, mental, emotional, and spiritual domains, and they should be available to children and men as well.

Overall, this particular research project collected an abundance of data, experiences, and stories that supported another shelter and very specific components that are reflective of the needs of Aboriginal women accessing a shelter.

## HIV/AIDS and Urban Aboriginal Women

CAROL ROMANOW

*Introduction*

Women in general and Aboriginal women in Saskatchewan in particular, who have contracted HIV/AIDS, face numerous obstacles. The fear and stigma attached to HIV/AIDS keeps many Aboriginal women from disclosing their status, and this has led to a lack of adequate treatment and support. Family members who would normally support a person dealing with grief and loss stay away from the person touched by AIDS. Societal discrimination creates an environment of increased risk for anyone who experiences it. Saraswati and Sahas (1996, 7) contend that 'only to the extent that we as a society can reduce discrimination and promote respect for rights and dignity, will we be successful in preventing HIV transmission, be able to care for those who are infected and ill and advance the health of all people.' The quality of life of stigmatized Aboriginal women in Saskatoon with HIV/AIDS and/or hepatitis C can be enhanced when they belong to a community that accepts them and their families for who they are – that is, a community that does not reject them in response to the disease they have contracted.

HIV infection rates are interrelated with the general health conditions facing Aboriginal communities in Saskatchewan. Many of the factors that contribute to a higher risk of HIV infection – such as unemployment, poor housing, low income, and poor sanitation – are associated with economic and social disadvantage. The high incidence of physical, emotional, and sexual violence experienced by Aboriginal women is an additional indicator of the general social conditions in Aboriginal communities in Saskatchewan.

To prevent the spread of HIV/AIDS effectively, one must look at why Aboriginal people are overrepresented in high-risk groups for HIV transmission. Why are there more Aboriginal people in Saskatchewan using drugs? Why are Aboriginal women in Saskatchewan more prone to becoming involved in prostitution and drug use? Why are more Aboriginal people in Saskatchewan involved in substance abuse and violence (Health Canada 1996, 3)? One would think that the number of AIDS cases would be in proportion to the number represented in the general population. In fact, the overall infection rates for HIV/AIDS cases among Aboriginal women in Saskatchewan are on the rise while in non-Aboriginal populations the numbers have started to level off.

What this information emphasizes is how important it is for each individual to protect him/herself by making healthier choices, in order to reduce the risk of infection. There are social and economic factors that increase the chances of becoming infected. Especially important risk factors here are low levels of education and high levels of unstable housing and poverty; to stem the spread of disease, both must be addressed along with other risk factors. In order for Aboriginal women in Saskatoon to protect themselves from the social and health-related ills of society, they must be provided with the opportunity to enhance their own quality of life, including a stable home in which to raise their children.

Saskatchewan Aboriginal communities have long faced other major social and health concerns, such as youth suicide, solvent abuse, and violence, on a scale far higher than the broad Canadian population. HIV/AIDS is still a very new challenge in Aboriginal communities in Saskatchewan. Advances have been made in raising awareness of the disease in Canadian society, and a broad range of services to combat it have been developed in the past decade; but too few of these initiatives have focused on the specific needs of Aboriginal communities and on the specific ways in which effective care, education, and support must be approached in those communities. For example, significant numbers of Aboriginal people in Saskatchewan live in remote and marginalized areas; these can and do include places such as correctional facilities, rooming houses, and the street (RCAP 1996, III:12).

Women living in poverty face an increased risk of HIV infection because they have restricted access not only to health information but also to health services. Poverty affects attitudes toward risk in complex ways. When too much energy is expended on basic survival, people tend to ignore a disease that may or may not materialize for seven to ten years. The contending issues resulting from poverty can crowd out the seriousness of HIV/AIDS (Easton 1992, 16). This, according to Mariasy and Thomas (1990, 36), can result in 'a lack of economic, social, cultural, sexual and technological options to lead vulnerable women to concentrate on addressing the more immediate risks in their lives: poverty, homelessness and the frequent disruption of socioeconomic support systems.'

As the spread of HIV among heterosexuals increases in Saskatchewan, the relationship between social and economic advantage and risk behaviour becomes clearer. Many of the factors that contribute to a higher risk of HIV infection are associated with economic and social disadvantage. Saraswati and Sahas (1996, 10) contend that 'HIV infection rates are interrelated with the general health conditions of communities.' The general health of Aboriginal people in Saskatchewan indicates that there is a very high risk of HIV/AIDS transmission. De Bruyn (1998, 11) points out: 'The cumulative effect of HIV/AIDS-related stigma and discrimination is to objectify, marginalize, and exclude people with HIV/AIDS. Those who were already objectified, marginalized and excluded are pushed even further from recognition of shared humanity and from the support of human society.'

Aboriginal women, who have already been discriminated against with respect to employment, housing, and health care, are further discriminated against because they are HIV-positive. The majority of Aboriginal women in Saskatchewan live in poverty. De Bruyn (1998, 18) argues that 'those people who were marginalized, stigmatized, and discriminated against before HIV/AIDS arrived, have become over time those at highest risk of HIV infection.' Regardless of where it began, the leading edge of the epidemic has inexorably moved toward those who bear the greatest societal burden. In Saskatchewan, the epidemic has increasingly targeted ethnic minority populations in inner cities, intravenous drug users, and women.

Groups whose rate of HIV/AIDS infection is already high, such as street youth, prostitutes, and the prison population, include a significant number of Aboriginal women. Even more troubling, many Aboriginal people in Saskatchewan apparently do not think of AIDS as a disease that affects them. Some think of it as a gay disease, imagining that homosexuality is rare among Aboriginal people; or as a city disease, imagining that it will not follow them into small or isolated communities; or as a white man's disease, imagining that it can somehow be restricted to non-Aboriginal people. These are false hopes (RCAP 1996, III:12). The results of this research illustrate Health Canada's contention that HIV/AIDS and hepatitis C do exist in Aboriginal communities in Saskatchewan, mainly because of low condom use, high rates of STDs, low self-esteem, and increasing violence, sexual abuse, prostitution, and intravenous drug use (Health Canada 1998).

*Profile of the Respondents*

Of the 22 women interviewed in this study, the majority were interviewed while they were in provincial or federal custody in Prince Albert (13 at the provincial women's detention centre, one in the federal penitentiary, and a couple at the clinic for sexually transmitted diseases); the remainder were interviewed in Saskatoon. Most of the women interviewed supported themselves and their children through prostitution. Many had never completed grade twelve, had been incarcerated more than once, had no permanent address, abused alcohol and/or intravenous drugs, had contracted one or more sexually transmitted disease, had contracted HIV/AIDS and/or hepatitis C, and had been sexually, physically, emotionally, and/or spiritually abused.

A number of the respondents had never been married but had lived common law. Nineteen of the women maintained that their priority was their children, even if it meant raising them as a single parent. Almost all of the respondents noted that the father of their children had moved on without committing any psychological or financial support, not long after the children were born. It can be argued strongly that these issues were a prominent factor in the lifestyles of these women, who felt that their only recourse was prostitution.

Some of the women lived with their children and common law partner; others lived by themselves, because their children had been removed by social services. Most of the women did not remain at the same address for any length of time, mainly for financial reasons (a shortage of funds). Most of the urban Aboriginal women in this research engaged in prostitution and alcohol and/or intravenous drug use, due in part to the reality that these vices were more common in the larger urban areas than on reserve. Some of the women profiled in the study were now or had once been incarcerated at Prince Albert's correctional centre but had lived in southern or central as well as northern Saskatchewan.

Sixteen of the women were currently prostitutes or had been in the past. They stated that this was mainly because it was the quickest and easiest way to get money. Yet the rationale they offered for choosing a life of prostitution was more than economic. Other 'encouraging' factors included the cycle of alcohol and/or intravenous drug use as well as the sexual, physical, emotional, and spiritual abuse they faced at home. Most of the women had prostituted themselves from a very early age. Sixteen of the women were still working as prostitutes at the time of the study; the remaining six identified their occupations as housewife, labourer, elder, corrections officer, or unemployed.

After listening to the personal stories of the respondents, it was not difficult to understand why they had so little self-confidence or self-respect, and why they lacked any belief that they were just as deserving of a decent and happy life as the rest of humanity. Growing up, these women had aunts, sisters, and mothers who were already working on the street as prostitutes or drug dealers and who were addicted to alcohol and/or intravenous drugs. These other women were obviously not good role models for 10- and 11-year-old girls, who ran away looking for the love they did not receive at home. Typically, the money these women made through prostitution was not all theirs to keep: most of the women profiled had to share their earnings with a pimp. Through their pimps, they were involved in money laundering, intimidation, assault, attempted murder, fraud, loan sharking, extortion, prostitution, and the trafficking of illegal weapons and drugs, including cocaine, marijuana, and ecstasy.

Aboriginal street prostitutes are the most marginalized of sex trade workers and are more likely to be arrested and incarcerated for soliciting. The HIV and hepatitis C crisis has both heightened and exposed the vulnerability of Aboriginal prostitutes to discriminatory attitudes, attention, and regulations. The 22 Aboriginal women profiled in this research made it clear how HIV/AIDS and hepatitis C had affected their quality of life as well as the lives of their families. The respondents who continued to be street prostitutes had all been diagnosed with HIV and/or hepatitis C.

For many of the women, having children at a very young age and being responsible for those children did not make education an option. Four women had less than any high school education; ten had some high school (grades none to eleven); seven had completed high school; and one had some post-secondary education. All but two of the women also stated that more education did not seem plausible, because they were required at home to help raise their younger siblings. All of the respondents had a dysfunctional and unstable family life, and as a result, they gravitated toward their friends who were already on the street. Approximately one-third of the respondents had attended residential school. Many Aboriginal families had been torn apart as a result of the residential school system in Saskatchewan.

Almost all of the respondents have suffered from some form of abuse: sexual, physical, emotional, or spiritual. The abuse took place either at home or on the street. Of the 22 women, all but one had been a victim of physical and emotional abuse, all but two of violence, and all but three of sexual abuse. Family members – including their fathers, grandfathers, uncles, foster fathers, ex-boyfriends, and common laws, as well as customers – had violated the respondents. These women had suffered a whole range of abuse, including rape, beatings with a weapon, hospitalization for broken bones, and intimidation, resulting in a cycle of violence for most of them.

*Conclusions*

Women are the greater part of the urban Aboriginal population in Saskatchewan, as well as the majority of migrants from reserve to urban neighbourhoods (RCAP 1996, IV). For all of the respondents, the urban centre was where they spent the majority of their time. Aboriginal women also play a crucial role in, and assume much of the responsibility for, the welfare of Aboriginal people in urban communities. Their initiatives have been essential in ensuring the day-to-day survival of Aboriginal communities in Saskatchewan's cities. Aboriginal women's position in society must be recognized and their needs met.

It is Aboriginal women who determine the developing relationship between Aboriginal people and urban institutions. Yet there is overwhelming evidence that urban service delivery groups are not meeting

the specific needs of urban Aboriginal women, and endeavours to resolve this situation are key to advancing Aboriginal women's health
and well-being (RCAP 1996, IV).

An effective community-team approach would involve Aboriginal
women who reside in urban centres; it would also recognize the importance of Aboriginal community dynamics and the need for more
sharing of information. It would instil a sense of competency in
Aboriginal women when it comes to dealing with HIV/AIDS and
hepatitis C infection, along with an understanding that their traditional methods for dealing with life – including crisis situations – can
be modified and integrated. This competency would in turn give
Aboriginal women in Saskatchewan the confidence to handle the issues that surround HIV/AIDS and hepatitis C and the credibility that
they will require in their respective communities to garner support for
their efforts.

An increasing number of young Aboriginal women in Saskatchewan
are living with HIV/AIDS and hepatitis C. There is a strong need for
improved education and prevention programs in affected Aboriginal
communities. But effective HIV/AIDS and hepatitis C strategies can no
longer only be about HIV/AIDS and hepatitis C prevention and education; they must also be about improving and enhancing the quality of
life of Aboriginal women and their families living with HIV/AIDS and
hepatitis C. Many infectious diseases are more common in the Aboriginal
community; overall rates of violence and self-destructive behaviour are
high; and rates of welfare dependency, conflict with the law, and incarceration all point to imbalances in the social conditions that are shaping
the quality of life of Aboriginal women (RCAP 1996, IV; Health Canada
1998). Many factors that contribute to a higher risk of HIV/AIDS and
hepatitis C in Aboriginal women in Saskatchewan relate directly or indirectly to their quality of life and living conditions. These factors include high rates of sexually transmitted disease and teenage pregnancy,
which point to a lack of safer-sex practices and a higher risk to Aboriginal
youth; low self-esteem and high rates of sexual and physical violence,
as well as drug and alcohol abuse; a lack of access to health information
and facilities; and an inferior quality of life.

The long-term problems faced by Aboriginal women in Saskatchewan
include the psychological impact of colonization, racism, poverty, and
marginalization, and now HIV/AIDS and hepatitis C. Taken together,
these factors have resulted in Aboriginal people in general, and
Aboriginal women more specifically, having the poorest overall health

and socio-economic status of any group in Saskatchewan. HIV/AIDS and hepatitis C and the responses to these diseases are not merely medical issues; they are simultaneously economic, social, cultural, political, and more importantly spiritual issues (RCAP 1996 IV: 4).

HIV/AIDS and hepatitis C rates for Aboriginal women continue to rise; yet denial and intolerance remain prominent with respect to those living with these diseases. This intolerance has taken a variety of forms – for example, Aboriginal women living with HIV/AIDS and hepatitis C are being forced to stay away from their home communities. Mobility between urban and reserve communities is recurrent, and Aboriginal reserve communities generally make collaborative health education and prevention strategies extremely difficult.

Some key principles need to be taken into account when proposing an agenda that is specific to the needs of Aboriginal women in Saskatchewan who have HIV/AIDS or hepatitis C. Respect for community autonomy and diversity, as well as for Aboriginal women and their families, regardless of status, residency, gender, or sexual orientation, must be maintained. Also, any agenda must be community-based in design, development, and delivery and include direct participation by both male and female Aboriginal youth and Aboriginal elders / spiritual advisers. It must also respect Aboriginal history and promote positive Aboriginal traditional values. It should involve Aboriginal women who are living with and affected by HIV/AIDS and hepatitis C. It must utilize an Aboriginal community-based evaluation process and acknowledge and respect an Aboriginal woman's choice of programs and services. It should also respect their right to privacy and their freedom to make decisions concerning their own healing and care. Finally, it has to provide opportunity and encouragement for Aboriginal communities in Saskatchewan to maintain adequate support that is safe and secure for Aboriginal women living with and affected by HIV/AIDS and hepatitis C.

Indisputably, the most efficient way to fully comprehend how Aboriginal women have been affected by HIV/AIDS and hepatitis C, and what programs and services would improve their chances of not contracting infection, would be to involve Aboriginal women. This research has made it abundantly plain that the best person to talk to young Aboriginal women in Saskatchewan about the risks of HIV and hepatitis C infection is an Aboriginal woman who has been there and who has lived the experience. This research has also made it clear that most of the infected women felt they had no choice but to lead a life of prostitution in order to survive. Contracting HIV/AIDS and hepatitis C involves high-risk behaviour and the inability to make healthy life choices.

Aboriginal women in Saskatchewan are markedly disadvantaged relative to their non-Aboriginal neighbours. The experience of urban Aboriginal women in Saskatchewan has been one of isolation and enhanced risk for substance abuse and HIV/AIDS. More services that address HIV/AIDS, hepatitis C, and substance abuse are being made available in Saskatchewan cities, but these services are sometimes provided in ways that are discriminatory, particularly toward those who are at greater risk of HIV and hepatitis C infection, such as Aboriginal women who are intravenous drug users and/or prostitutes. One obvious approach to treating Aboriginal women – including those with HIV/AIDS and hepatitis C – with dignity is to offer them services of the same value as those provided to others in Saskatchewan who have the same needs. Another positive approach would be to affirm the insights and practices of Aboriginal cultures in Saskatchewan when developing and delivering programs and services; this would include incorporating traditional Aboriginal healers and healing practices into those programs and services (de Bruyn 1998).

This research offers many examples of urban Aboriginal women in Saskatoon and other urban centres in Saskatchewan who serve as explicit illustrations of what it is like to live in a low-income neighbourhood. The quality of life of Aboriginal women in Saskatchewan is affected by lifestyle, socio-economic status, gender, and the physical environment. This research has revealed that for the most part, urban Aboriginal women live in poverty. Applied social research could have a tremendous impact on the quality of life and the living conditions of the Aboriginal women studied in this research. Aboriginal women and their children form a substantial segment of low-income families in Saskatoon, and few of these families can afford even low-income accommodations. This research reveals the extent of the specific needs facing urban Aboriginal women and their families.

In relating these experiences of the 22 Aboriginal women, who so openly and caringly entrusted their stories to me, I have underscored the explicit needs and life issues of urban Aboriginal women and their families living with HIV/AIDS. I hope this research will lead to changes that help these women establish a foundation on which they can build the rest of their lives – a foundation that includes a permanent home for themselves and their families and a community where they are not discriminated against because they are Aboriginal and have HIV/AIDS; where they can obtain some control over their own lives and how they live; where they feel secure and safe and have a sense of belonging and do not have to worry about violent pimps and customers; where they can raise their children and not have to fear social services removing them and placing them in foster care; where they can get a 'real' job and not have to work on the street prostituting themselves; where there is no overcrowding and poor sanitation; where their children can go to the same school on a regular basis; where their spiritual needs can be met by community elders; and where they can, one hopes, attain some sense of self-esteem, self-respect, and self-worth.

## The City as Home: The Sense of Belonging among Aboriginal Youth

GAIL MACKAY

*Introduction*

This particular research project interprets 16 Aboriginal youths' reflections on their relationships with and within Saskatoon's urban landscape. Topics include identity, a sense of belonging, and youths' identified needs to be protected, nourished, nurtured, and challenged. The research set out to ascertain what contributes to Aboriginal youths' sense of belonging in the city, and to report this in the form of relevant policy recommendations.

This researcher contends that age alone is not a sufficient common denominator and that experiences, levels of maturity, independence, and responsibility should be among the criteria for inclusion in the category of 'youth.' This research used a working definition of youth based on criteria of chronological age, life experiences, and self-realization. In this report the term 'youth' refers to a stage in life and a category of individuals. Youth is characterized by an age range between 15 and 29 years and by the individuals' efforts to establish themselves in the social and working world as self-actualized and self-reliant persons. This definition operates from the premise that youth is a stage of life, a crucial period of development graduated by individual efforts, achievements, and experiences.

Identity is the sense of oneself as an individual and the sense of oneself belonging to a collective. A person gains a sense of him/herself as an individual by increasing awareness of his/her spiritual, physical, and social being. This view of identity conforms to Johnston's (1976) presentation of an Anishnawbe perspective of the human being as a composite of corporeal and incorporeal substances, one that strives for self-understanding and that is trained to function in society.

The factors that contribute to a sense of self as an individual may be synonymous with or separate from the factors that contribute to a sense of oneself belonging to a collective (Mihesuah 2003). The Royal Commission on Aboriginal Peoples (RCAP) identified the elements of Aboriginal identity as including spirituality, language, a land base or ancestral territory, elders, traditional values, family, and ceremonial life (1996, IV:524). Statistics cannot adequately capture this complexity of identity formation. Indeed, academics and demographers have identified phenomena such as ethnic mobility and discrepancy between Aboriginal origin and Aboriginal identity that defy a definitive category of identity. Furthermore, the context, audience, and purpose may influence a person to choose one identity over another as master status. These terms of identity are labels that could be applied by the individual or by outsiders to ascribe identity, belonging, exclusion, and/or ineligibility. Depending on the context, audience, and purpose, a person may use one or all as a master status to self-identify.

Each subsequent generation of Aboriginal youth who live in an urban centre must come to terms with it on an individual basis. As youth, they must gain an intimate understanding of who they are as individual beings, and they must gain the recognition of a community of people to affirm their belonging. Youths' sense of self as belonging to a collective is vulnerable to many influences that can undermine their sense of identity and self-worth. The shared experiences of real or assumed poverty, racism, and victimization can lead a person to resign him/herself to this plight or to reject belonging. Societal attitudes that dismiss contemporary or adapted Aboriginal cultural expressions as less authentic, non-traditional, or unworthy weaken individual and collective identity. Representations of Aboriginal people in the media, which are very limited in range and depth, foster a mistaken assumption of a narrow collective experience and confine insider and outsider ascriptions of identity.

An individual youth's sense of belonging to a collective is strengthened by his or her own *subjective* and by outsiders' *objective* recognition of cultural competence. Competence is broadly defined as the functional and instrumental skills required to perform adult tasks within a particular culture. There are particular knowledges, skills, and attributes that adults consciously nurture in the upcoming generation to ensure their competence and survival. Although the topic of identity formation merits greater contemplation than this cursory description provides, this model of identity formation meets this research project's objective of making recommendations that support Aboriginal youths' sense of identity and belonging in an urban setting.

*Themes in Research Relevant to Aboriginal Youth
in Canadian Cities and Saskatoon*

A review of recent literature reveals common themes to describe the context of Aboriginal youths' lives in Canadian cities. These themes are low income and education attainment, unemployment and poverty, core housing need, mobility and homelessness, and exploitation and alienation. Indeed the Standing Senate Committee on Aboriginal Peoples concluded in 2003 that of all issues affecting urban Aboriginal people, some of the most pressing and urgent are the needs of Aboriginal youth. The committee was struck by the absolute necessity of addressing their needs – particularly the needs of those estranged from their cultural heritage and the broader community in which they reside. In addition, although the vast majority of programming is geared to the social pathology of being urban and Aboriginal, the committee was told by youth that they wanted a supportive place to go where they could tap into their interests and develop and nurture their leadership abilities: a place where they were more than just the sum of their problems. Building on youths' participation in their own deliverance is common to recommendations for addressing the needs of Aboriginal youth in cities. Youths' optimism, desires, and self-confidence in their ability to direct change are natural resources to be used when reconstructing the urban landscape.

Most Aboriginal youth in Saskatoon live under stressed conditions and face daunting societal obstacles on their path to gain equal social and economic status with their non-Aboriginal counterparts. Aboriginal youth are among the most economically and socially disadvantaged: statistics for Saskatchewan have indicated that Aboriginal people have been victims of violent crime at a disproportionate rate. The majority of urban Aboriginal youth, who comprise the majority of the city's Aboriginal population, were living in poverty (CCSD 2003: 1; LaPrairie and Stenning 2003, 185).

Education and mobility are two significant factors when describing youths' experiences of the city. The 2001 Census showed that 42.3% Aboriginal adults in Saskatoon had not finished high school and that

24% of Aboriginal adults who had completed high school had done so through a High School Equivalency program. The most frequently selected reason for not finishing high school was 'pregnancy / taking care of children' at 17%, followed by 'wanted to work' at 15% and 'had to work' at 11%. It has been noted in numerous research reports that Aboriginal people change residence at a higher rate than non-Aboriginal people. Norris and Jantzen (2003, 111) refer to this urban–rural mobility as 'churn' and argue that this is a consequence of people moving to maintain family and cultural relationships. This idea is further supported by the fact that 42% of adults who moved to Saskatoon selected 'family' as the reason to move.

Such data represent the hindrances that Aboriginal youth struggle against in their efforts to set the trajectory of their lives. Youth is a crucial stage of development and vulnerability. The conditions associated with poverty are among those that contribute to overrepresentation in the criminal justice system. LaPrairie and Stenning (2003, 187) conclude that

> there is no question that the particular demographics of the Aboriginal population of Canada (a higher proportion of people in the high-risk 15 to 24 age group, lower education levels, higher unemployment, higher rates of substance abuse and addiction, etc.) lead to their over-representation in these vulnerable neighbourhoods, and hence to their overall over-representation in the criminal justice system. There can equally be little doubt any more that these 'particular circumstances' of many Aboriginal people are reflected in Aboriginal involvement in both crime and the criminal justice system, both as offenders and victims.

LaPrairie and Stenning (190) go on to state that the rate of representation of Aboriginal people in the justice system is similar to that of other groups with similar social and economic factors. Put another way, involvement in the justice system is a consequence of poverty rather than Aboriginal identity or heritage. The numbers show the social consequence of maintaining things as they are.

*Methodology*

The researcher received the support of the Metis Nation of Saskatchewan and the Saskatoon Tribal Council, as well as that of the general manager of the Saskatchewan Native Theatre Company (SNTC), the coordinator of Quint Male Youth Lodge, and the director of Infinity House, all of whom granted permission for the researcher to contact the youth in their respective programs and invite the youth to participate in focus group discussions. Participants were to be selected by the criteria of being Aboriginal youth living in Saskatoon who were currently involved in programs that were assisting them with life skills, employment training, and/or housing. This group of respondents would be likely to have experience and insight into young Aboriginal people's perceptions of adequate, affordable, and culturally supportive housing in an urban setting. Infinity House, Quint Male Youth Lodge, and SNTC have programs that offer youth support and direction in their efforts to gain life skills, employment, and housing. Infinity House is a supportive housing facility for Aboriginal women and their children who are homeless or at risk of becoming homeless. The Central Urban Metis Federation Inc. (CUMFI) has twelve transitional housing units and three emergency accommodation units. Through the Circle of Voices program, SNTC provides Aboriginal youth with professional theatre training and life skills development as they prepare and present a live theatre production.

Focus group discussions involved between five to twelve youth participants at each of the sites. The researcher moderated each focus group discussion, following set questions aimed at eliciting information about youth perceptions of home, what is needed for a home, what is beneficial to the sense of belonging in the city, what is detrimental to the sense of belonging in the city, and what would make the city a better place for them. Before a focus group discussion, participants were asked to complete a demographic profile questionnaire that elicited information about identity, housing, family, and life experiences. Following each focus group, the researcher summarized what she had heard the participants say and invited them to add and or clarify information. After the focus group the researcher and a research assistant compared their impressions of the discussion and identified prominent themes.

The discussion and the questionnaire responses highlighted youths' perceptions that the researcher had not anticipated. Themes that were repeated often related to family, collective and individual identity, and home as a place of belonging that meets the particular maturation needs of people in the youth stage of life. Youth talked about safety, stability, a social network of family and community, nourishment of body and soul, and education and training to be independent and resourceful.

*Review of Findings*

This project was designed to solicit urban Aboriginal youths' perceptions of what a space required in order to be worthy of being called 'home.' The researcher assumed that youths' sense of belonging would relate to home as a physical, social, and emotional reality and anticipated they would describe their actual and ideal domicile, neighbourhood, and community in expressing their sense of belonging. In fact the youth described a sense of belonging that was primarily in the social sphere and secondarily in the physical sphere.

*Demographic Profile of Participants: Age, Education, Mobility, Health*

The participants in the focus groups ranged in age between 18 and 27. Sixteen participants, nine male and seven female, participated. The males ranged in age from 19 to 26 with a median age of 21, the females from 18 to 27 with a median age of 24. A factor in the older age range may be the selection criterion of involvement in programs to assist in skills training and/or housing. Participants' maturity and life experiences contributed to the richness of their discussion.

Participants' level of education ranged from completion of grade eight to studying at a university undergraduate level. On average, male youth participants had completed more years of schooling. Male participants had attained a higher level of education with a median of grade twelve, while female participants achieved a median of grade ten. However, female family members were identified as the person with the most education in their family by eleven participants, compared to male relatives identified as the most educated by five participants. In reporting the highest level of education in their family, two participants reported a university graduate degree, six an undergraduate degree, six high school graduation, and one grade eleven. Participants consistently expressed that they placed a high value on education. When one participant expressed a sense of having been defeated by the rules that said she was too old to attend high school without paying for each course, other participants encouragingly shared their knowledge of alternative ways to achieve high school level and gain entrance to college programs.

Six participants had lived only in Saskatoon; the rest, besides living in the city, had also lived in a variety of rural settings (on reserve, in a small town, or 'out in the country' or 'in the bush'). Female participants had a shorter average stay in all types of domiciles: on average, the females had stayed in an apartment for one year, in a house for four years, and in a shelter for three days; whereas the males had stayed in an apartment for two years, in a house for ten years, and in a shelter for six months. Five participants reported that they had lived 'on the street' for varying lengths of time, ranging from a single night (1), to a couple of weeks (2), to longer than a month (2).

In discussion, some participants talked about having more than one home, meaning they lived with one relative for a time and then stayed with another for an extended period. The literature refers to this as 'hidden homelessness,' yet the youth viewed it in the most positive of terms – as building social networks and maintaining family bonds. They expressed the instability of living with people whose lifestyles differ from their own. Other causes of instability mentioned were high rent, wanting to escape a dangerous neighbourhood, and conflict exacerbated by alcohol and drug use.

Tobacco use in the past year was reported by fifteen of the sixteen participants, alcohol use by thirteen, and drug use by ten. This is consistent with Statistics Canada reporting of youths' tobacco smoking and of higher smoking incidence among Aboriginals. It is noteworthy that in the previous year, 22% of the males and 11% of the females had not used alcohol and 66% of the males and 11% of the females had not used drugs. Fifteen participants responded that drugs or alcohol had affected some aspect of their lives. Thirteen participants responded affirmatively to the question 'Does anyone in your family have a problem with drugs?' The participants repeatedly expressed the value and importance of sobriety when referring to their young adult lives but also to their childhood memories of when times were bad and when things turned around for the better. The participants' commitment to making the effort to improve their situations is evidenced by their level of sobriety, their interest in learning traditional teachings about self-care, and their participation in programs to develop their skills and independence.

*Experience of Gangs*

Four (two male and two female) participants reported that gangs had not affected them in any way. Three male participants reported that gangs had affected them in positive ways: by giving them someone they could depend on, connecting them with people, and adding to their Native identity. However, ten participants indicated that gangs had affected them in negative ways: by violence toward them, a relative, or a friend. Two male participants and three female participants had experienced intimidation by gangs. Two participants had been affected by committing crime. And one participant (who had also mentioned positive ways that gangs had affected him) added that gangs had blinded him of his identity. In these focus groups, a large majority had experienced the negative impact of gangs. Male participants, more often than female participants, had been the target of gang violence and gang activity. The mothers in the groups expressed great concern about the real danger their sons would be facing beginning at a very young age. One young mother reported that her seven-year-old son had already been approached numerous times to join a gang. Mothers worry about choosing a good neighbourhood and school, fearing their children are vulnerable to 'swarming,' intimidation, and gang initiation.

*Perception of Economic Status, Identity, and Belonging*

The participants were characteristically optimistic about their economic status. Four participants thought that when they were growing up they thought their families were 'poor … we didn't have what we needed'; eight participants that their families were 'doing okay, not poor but working hard to get what we needed'; four participants that their families were 'doing good, not rich but we could easily get what we needed.' To the preamble 'Right now I think I am …,' fourteen participants selected 'doing okay, not poor but working hard to get what I need,' and two selected 'doing good, not rich but I can easily get what I need.' No participant selected the response 'poor, I don't have what I need.' These responses seem to suggest that well-being has more to do with social networks than with material possessions.

Often, when Native people meet, the questions exchanged in getting to know each other include, 'Where are you from?' and 'Who is your grandmother/grandfather?' This sense of belonging is not about a physical place of birth, but about a social network. In talking about their sense of belonging, participants identified their extended families, reserve communities, friends, and social network in the city. Aboriginal identities are complex in the city because the various situations, audiences, and purposes demanding self-identification presuppose that an individual will identify with categories of people that may be legal, constitutional, linguistic, cultural, or historical.

The participants' answers on the questionnaire confirmed the researcher's idea that identity may be variously defined by the individual and by outsiders. In identifying their roots, nine participants identified ancestors from a single Aboriginal group, seven identified ancestors from multiple Aboriginal groups, and one identified ancestors from non-Aboriginal groups. Eleven participants identified a single Aboriginal group and five more than one group as the most important to them. This supports the discrepancy between the census numbers for people of Aboriginal *origin* and the numbers for people with Aboriginal *identity*. To the question of how they are 'officially' identified, eight participants selected 'First Nations,' three selected 'Metis,' and one selected 'Non-Status Indian' (the remainder could not differentiate). A person's sense of him/herself is in part formed by knowledge of ancestral heritage, but it is also formed by aligning oneself with a significant group or groups. Nonetheless, the power of outsider ascription can disregard, overshadow, or distort a person's individual self-identity. Evidence of the uneasy coexistence of insider and outsider ascription was in the contrast between the participants carefully describing in detail who they are and then unequivocally checking the box next to the government's designation of a single legal definition of their identity.

The participants' identity was defined by their sense of belonging to a collective. This at times is an uneasy fit for people who belong to more than one group. Self-doubt, exclusion, rejection, and dismissal are powerful threats to youths' self-concept as they negotiate their relationships with multiple groups in the city. A sense of belonging develops out of one's sense of relationship to a collective. Belonging is strengthened when the individual engages in activity that builds reciprocal relationships. Kindness, sharing, and selfless labour strengthen the family and community ties that bind the group together. The questionnaire and the participants' discussion, which highlighted the important social relationships in Aboriginal families and communities, suggested to the researcher that the Aboriginal concept of family is not understood or appreciated by mainstream institutions. Helping family and friends, caring for children, and providing a haven for relatives are examples of the principle of sharing that defines people's belonging to a group. But viewed from outside the culture, this help is sometimes misconstrued as dependence and dysfunction. A hopeful sign of change is in the expanded definition of family in the 2001 census. Previously a significant number of children had been classified as 'non-family persons.' The census definition has been changed to take into account three-generation households as well as caregivers who are relatives other than parents.

The demographic questionnaire revealed bonds of relatedness in family and community. The youths' answers on the questionnaire and their discussion in focus groups together suggest that the family extends beyond the nuclear unit of two generations – parents and children. For them, family and belonging are much broader. Because the focus of the research was on 'youths' sense of belonging,' it would have been no surprise had the participants named someone from their sibling age group to finish the statement. Instead, nine of sixteen participants identified relatives a generation older than themselves and once removed.

Another indication of family ties concerned the participants' caregivers until age 16. Four participants lived in two-parent households for their first 16 years. Five participants never lived with their father. Two participants never lived with either their mother or father. Eleven participants reported living with between two to six caregivers for periods between six months and sixteen years. Family members who cared for them included grandparents, aunt/uncle, adult sister, adult brother, step-parent, other relatives, and foster parents. Bonds of relatedness are shown in participants' answer to the question 'Tomorrow, if I were having serious trouble, whom could I count on for help?' The responses were extremely varied: friends were selected by twelve participants, sister or brother by twelve, mother by eleven, elder by eight, girlfriend or boyfriend by seven, father by six, aunt or uncle by five, cousin by four, a counsellor by three, grandparents by two, step-parent by one. This suggests that most youths' bonds of belonging and relatedness had been nurtured by relatives who cared for them for varying lengths of time. Clearly, the sense of belonging of Aboriginal youth in Saskatoon depends upon the strength of their social network of family, friends, and community kinship.

*Perceptions of Home*

Participants described 'home,' a place of belonging, principally as a social and emotional environment. The youth conceived of home as a community first, a neighbourhood second, and a physical structure last. The researcher identified four key aspects of home as a place of belonging that contributes to youth's self-knowledge and self-actualization: protection, nourishment, training, and nurture. Candid scenarios and images described by participants indicated that the urban environment is not providing an adequate solution for Aboriginal youths' needs for the city as home.

Fundamental issues of safety reverberated in the discussions. All participants expressed concern about safety in the neighbourhood. Violations of the security and harmony of family relationships are closely tied to alcohol and drug use. Participants spoke of childhood experiences of the chaos and drama when drinking went on in their homes. Participants said life was better when their parents quit drinking and that there are conflicts and trouble when people in the home are drinking. Participants expressed that the ideal situation is sobriety within in the family and neighbourhood. Youth need a place where they can live with stability, without an authority judging their lifestyle and evicting them. Participants talked about the need to have people respect their space, not to use it as a shelter for people who are transient or needing a party place. One participant made an oblique reference to escaping from a violent boyfriend and protecting her children; she talked about the need to learn how to resolve disagreements without violence.

The physical environment contributes to the danger for youth and children. Specifically, participants identified the following as typical danger zones to be avoided: rundown buildings; too few or burnt-out street lights; idle kids unsupervised, hanging out in groups and vulnerable to gang initiation; dirty needles littering the ground; sex trade workers; far too easy access to drugs; and police don't and can't protect them in every situation they face. The participants talked about how frightening the youth gangs are. They spoke of how the gang members are ruthless and have no fear of consequences. Even those participants who are striving for stability, health, education, and employment experience first-hand the violence of poverty.

In the sense of home as a place of belonging, nourishment is for physical, social, and emotional well-being and strength. An individual who is nourished in these aspects of his or her being is taught to be resourceful and independent. The physical environment may be constructed to nourish youth. Education should prepare youth to be involved in work that enables them to support themselves and their children. Education and work experience should give youth the opportunity to develop their competence as young adults. There need to be good role models of people who are independent and resourceful and who are willing to help youth find opportunities to work and apply their skills. A place of belonging is where one is nurtured to fulfil one's purpose.

There appear to be two significant differences for male and female participants in this aspect of their individual and social growth. Males are more vulnerable to gang activity. They reported more frequently violence directed toward them and being approached or initiated by gangs. The danger for males is physical injury or incarceration that would derail their efforts to achieve their goals. Females were less frequently targeted for gang violence. Young women in the groups often spoke of their role of mother. This suggests that this role provides coherence to their social relationships and gives them a purpose: to nurture and protect their children. However, young parenthood is often the reason for interrupting school completion and has a negative effect on the young woman's options and opportunities.

Participants described physical, emotional, and spiritual wellness and stressed the importance of elders and counsellors who can offer traditional teachings for children, youth, and young parents. Participants talked about the elders at the SNTC and how they as youth had an opportunity to work with the elders and have meaningful interactions with them. The elders helped them in their decision making. Some participants mentioned that for some youth, traditional ceremonies and beliefs are not that important to them until they are in a crisis situation. But all participants spoke of the value of having traditional people as part of the community and in their programs. One person spoke of cultural boot camp to save youth by withdrawing them from a poisonous environment; other participants disagreed with this, saying that people have to come to cultural beliefs and practices on their own.

*Recommendations*

The ideal environment is a place where parents and children can spend time together. A strong neighbourhood would have free programs year-round to involve the children and youth in sports, cultural activities, tournaments, and competitions. There would be parks with walking and jogging paths. Streets would be in good repair and well lit at night. Housing would be affordable. Private and rental properties would be maintained and clean. Youth would be safe and not targeted by predators and gang intimidation. Pawnshops, liquor stores, and pornography shops would be absent from the neighbourhood. An ideal environment would have services in the neighbourhood such as schools, day care, preschool, a grocery store, doctors' and dentists' offices, a library, a community centre, access to counsellors, and traditional healers and elders.

For youth to achieve their full potential, city planners and policy makers should incorporate the idea of the city as home – as a social, spiritual, and physical environment that provides a place of belonging. Recommendations for policy changes and increased funding and programs have a greater chance of success if the youth have an active role in redefining the cityscape, to make it a place where they may challenge their limits and test their mettle.

The physical environment needs to be safe. It must provide for the maintenance of social relationships. The concept of family and neighbours should contribute to building spaces where there is opportunity to interact, work together, and support one another. Those spaces need to be clean and have services that contribute to the well-being of individuals, families, and communities.

The social environment needs to provide support systems and community programs. This would provide opportunities for youth to learn and be active in relationships with community members, elders, children, and adults. It should provide opportunities for youth to learn practical skills. A family treatment program for substance and alcohol addiction would contribute to the social wellness of families and community. Involvement with elders should be a meaningful activity wherein elders help youth learn and test their potential. There need to be spaces for ceremonies such as socials, feasts, and round dances.

Recommendations for further research could include the following: first, it is noteworthy that female participants generally reported having fewer social supports (between one and five people) than male participants reported (between two and ten people). This merits further inquiry in future research to understand the gender difference. Second, the role of males in Aboriginal communities is a topic worth exploring. Of interest would be how young men are socialized to masculinity and relationships. This could provide insight into how to prevent young men's alienation and help them find alternatives for testing their courage. Third, a longitudinal study that examines family planning patterns of Aboriginal youth and how these relate to social and economic status in the short and long term could draw qualitative data to trace changing perceptions from youth to adulthood.

*Conclusion*

This research concluded that some Aboriginal youth express a view that the urban environment could be improved to better meet Aboriginal youths' needs of the city as home. Aboriginal youth who described their sense of belonging in a Canadian prairie city gave researchers and academics ideas about how a Native perspective might be used to conceptualize remedies to urban poverty and youth alienation. The youths, in defining their needs for survival and self-realization, conceptualized home as a physical, social, and spiritual sphere. Home, a place of belonging, is where one is protected, nourished, and taught to be independent and resourceful. It is where one is trained to fulfil one's purpose for individual and social growth, where one is nurtured for physical and inner well-being. The findings of this research are consistent with the recommendations of the Standing Senate Committee on Aboriginal Peoples for the establishment of urban Aboriginal youth centres. Recreational and sports facilities are important. But there needs to be more in the city for youth: more interface, practice, and involvement with meaningful activity that is constructive, that promotes growth in their efforts to test the bounds of their abilities, and that expands the horizons of their dreams.

Who has a stake in the development of Aboriginal youth in urban centres? Without exaggeration, it is safe to say *all* citizens. There is a need to challenge the present foreboding about the social and economic implications of the growing Aboriginal demographic and the impending labour shortage. First, it would ease apprehension if Aboriginal youth were seen as a resource rather than a social liability. Second, it needs to be understood that Aboriginal youth desire the opportunity to fulfil their dreams, that they wish to be challenged to test their limits and to be rewarded and celebrated for their efforts. Third, finding innovative ways to aid youths' self-actualization would free their creativity and focus their passion to achieve. These premises underlie recent academic research that has introduced a new view of urbanization and policy responses. There has been a move away from the focus on individuals and from policies that promote the cultural adaptation of individuals in an urban context. Recent research is moving toward a focus on the development and sustainability of Aboriginal communities and identity in urban centres (Newhouse and Peters 2002).

This research is significant because it recorded Aboriginal youths' reflections on their relationship with their urban landscape. The youth were forceful in asserting their power and capacity to do something significant in the community. Youths' place in the city need not be peripheral and transitional; it can be central and permanent.

## Chapter Six

# Affordable Housing

## Affordability and the Housing Crisis

The introduction to this chapter, as a theoretical overview, begins by questioning the very notion of 'affordable housing' in examining trends in the average cost of housing and relating those trends to provincial economic growth. The actual availability of affordable housing is analysed, and urban Aboriginal housing conditions are described. This is followed by a more general discussion of poverty and social housing, and finally by policy analysis and related commentary. The chapter includes a concise description of financial and funding options for urban Aboriginal homeownership in Saskatoon, drawn from a workshop involving homebuilders, financial institutions, and Aboriginal organizations, conducted by the Bridges and Foundations Project. The chapter concludes with a summary of recent and ongoing research in Saskatoon on homelessness, drawing attention particularly to Aboriginal homelessness.

### The Question of Affordability

'Affordable housing' is a frequently used term. But what, exactly, does it really mean? 'Affordable' to whom? The standard definition of affordability used by CMHC is that 'affordable dwellings cost less than 30% of before-tax household income.' Shelter costs include, for renters, 'rent and any payments for electricity, fuel, water and other municipal services'; for owners, it includes 'mortgage payments, property taxes, and any condominium fees, along with payments for electricity, fuel, water and other municipal services.' *Affordability*, together with *adequacy* ('adequate dwellings are those reported by their residents as not requiring any major repairs') and *suitability* ('suitable dwellings have enough bedrooms for the size and make-up of resident households'), constitute a measure of *core housing need*.

According to National Occupancy Standard requirements defined in 1991, 'enough bedrooms means one bedroom for each cohabiting adult couple, unattached household member eighteen years of age and over, same sex pair of children under age eighteen, and additional boy or girl in the family, unless there are two opposite sex siblings under five years of age, in which case they are expected to share a bedroom.' Very few Canadian households are crowded; in 2001, 93.9% of Canadian households lived in dwellings considered suitable. However, there has been a far higher propensity for Aboriginal homes to be crowded.

Approximately one-quarter of Canadians rely on housing subsidies or experience periods when they spend more than 30% of pretax household income on housing (*Saskatoon StarPhoenix*, 17 December 2010). A CMHC study in 2004 learned that over 70% of Canadian households living in housing that did not meet the affordability criterion were unable to obtain acceptable housing. Moreover, renters were having much more difficulty finding affordable housing than owners; two-thirds of renter households were living in affordable housing, compared to 86.6% of owners. The inability to access acceptable housing was far more pronounced among renters, with 28.5% of renter households paying 30% or more of their income on shelter and unable to access acceptable housing, while 5.3% were below the affordability standard yet able to access acceptable housing (CMHC April 2004a).

CMHC also uses the term *severe affordability problems* for households spending half or more of their income on shelter (CMHC 2007). In 2001, 6.5% of all Canadians households were in this situation, compared to 20.2% spending 30% or more. Renter households were more than four times as likely as owner households to be in core housing need while facing severe affordability problems. Again, limited income was a dominant issue, with over 80% of households with severe housing affordability problems reporting an annual income of less than $20,000 (compared to 15.6% of all Canadian households reporting such an income). The most vulnerable residents spending half or more of their limited income on shelter were those without jobs or that were largely dependent on government transfer payments, and youth.

A distinction must be made between affordable housing and social housing. Social housing is defined as 'subsidized housing targeted to low-income households who would otherwise not be able to afford safe, secure shelter.' The key difference between social housing and affordable housing relates to the income level that is targeted and the degree of ability to access the private market. Affordable housing focuses on individuals with low to moderate incomes who have difficulty accessing housing in the private market, not just shelter in general (SIIT 2000, 10–11). The market's current focus is primarily on building high-end 'empty nesters' rather than affordable homes for families. The Saskatoon Housing Initiatives Partnership (SHIP) estimated in 2004 that an income level of $39,500 was the minimum point of access to market housing options. Yet 42.3% of Aboriginal renters, 45% of all Metis people, and 78% of Aboriginal lone-parent families in Saskatoon were in core housing need. In Saskatoon at the time, only 28.5% of homes for sale were affordable for households earning less than this amount (Foss 2004).

According to the Canadian Home Builders' Association, back in 1945 the average house size in Canada was approximately 800 square feet; thirty years later it was 1,075 square feet; and today it is more like 1,700 square feet. But while homes have been getting larger, the average number of people per household has been declining (Walker 2010). In 2005, housing may have been becoming more affordable, but 1.7 million Canadian families (more than one in seven) were still living in housing that was overcrowded, too expensive, or in significant need of repair. The proportion of families in core housing need had declined to 13.7% by 2001 and 12.7% by 2006. The proportion of households in housing need was decreasing in every province; it was 13.9% in Saskatchewan, which placed that province ninth out of thirteen provinces and territories. However, by 2006, Saskatchewan was the only province not experiencing a reduction in core housing need. Data for 2006 confirmed that homeowners were much more likely to live in acceptable housing (77.3%) than renters (51.8%), given owners' higher incomes (approximately double that of renters) (NHRC 2009). Data in the *Wealthscapes 2010* report of Environics Analytics indicated that Saskatoon was actually above average among Canadian CMAs in average household income and average household investments, but below average in average household net worth and average household debt, and at the very bottom in average household savings. Of course, these data are for the general population; a very different picture emerges for the Aboriginal population.

*Globe and Mail* columnist Doug Sanders has commented, 'If there is a global problem, this is it: there is not enough housing, to rent or buy, at a price that people with decent but ordinary employment can afford. We have come to think of this as a natural state of affairs. In fact, it makes no sense at all. Housing is a basic, easy to create amenity. If there is a large demand, and people are willing to pay ... it should be one of the world's most basic markets. But it isn't.' (*Globe and Mail*, 28 April 2012).

*Trends in Housing Costs*

Housing in Saskatoon had long been regarded as more affordable than housing in other, larger Canadian cities; however, with the rapid increase in housing costs in recent years, this situation was destined to change quickly. The average price for various types of housing in Saskatoon now actually exceeds the average in a number of larger Canadian cities and is comparable to the Canadian national average.

Analysing recent trends in housing costs can be a challenge. Let us examine two sets of data: average costs of houses sold, and average costs of *new* homes, both in Saskatoon and across Canada. Three distinct periods can be discerned during the past several years: a period of substantial increase in housing costs both in Saskatoon and nationally (2004–7), followed by an economic recession characterized by decreases across Canada and a slowing of increases in Saskatoon (2007–9), then a rebound, with national increases and very rapid increases in Saskatoon (since 2009).

There was a dramatic increase in the average monthly price index for Saskatoon, from $136,501 in June 2004 to a peak $340,000 in April 2008 (data from reports of the Saskatoon Region Association of Realtors). The average value of a new home in Canada increased by more than 10% a year between 2005 and 2007), and 60% overall in just five years (*Macleans*, 31 December 2007). In Saskatoon the average house price had topped $200,000 by March 2007, peaking at $310,386 for a new home in June 2008. Saskatoon was now leading the entire nation, with the fastest-ever new housing annual average price increases: 58.3% between February 2007 and 2008. The increase of 11% in the house price index in Saskatoon just between April and May 2007 represented the largest increase in any Canadian city, when national average housing prices were now declining –10% a year (according to CMHC data). In Martensville, a northern suburb that was once a small Mennonite community, housing costs escalated 264% in a single decade (*Saskatoon StarPhoenix*, 4 June 2008).

The fluctuation in housing costs may have seemed to benefit affordability, at least temporarily with the ensuing economic downturn, with housing costs in Saskatoon increasing far more moderately (12.5% from November 2007 to a year later, then just 7% between June 2009 and May 2010). However, the recession also affected the homebuilding industry as well as the real estate business, both nationally and in Saskatoon. While average housing prices and sales continued to decrease across Canada, and housing sales across the country declined by an average –24% during 2007–8, this trend was not as pronounced in Saskatoon, where prices remained high: the average cost of a new home in this city decreased to $224,800 in November 2008, while the average cost of a resale home declined to $275,000 in 2009, representing a –4.4% decrease from the previous year.

Yet this lull was very short-lived – the Saskatoon housing industry has rebounded with incredible speed, which may affect housing avail-ability in general but not necessarily affordable housing. At a time when most Aboriginal residents of Saskatoon were already having consider-able difficulty affording adequate and suitable housing, the very rapid escalation of housing prices put most housing completely out of reach for them. The average cost of a house in Canada had increased from $282,583 in October 2008 to $341,079 just a year later and was now in-creasing by about 24% a year (according to TD Bank data released in December 2009, a significantly higher rate of increase than the national rate of 19% calculated by the Canadian Real Estate Association). On average, then, housing in Saskatoon was still substantially less expen-sive, and even less expensive (about $250,000 on average) in Regina (as estimated by Re/Max). According to the Saskatoon Region Association of Realtors, a steadily increasing number of houses were being sold, now at an average cost of $299,214 (April 2010), compared to $275,455 a year before. Statistics Canada data suggest that the cost of a new home in the Saskatoon region was still rising faster (an annual increase of 3.3%) than nationally (+1.9%). Yet CMHC data indicate that nationally the current annual increase in average house prices (not necessarily newly constructed homes) comes to +6.5%. Similarly, in Saskatoon the average selling price of residential homes has been increasing 8% a year; the average home price has approximately doubled in five years, reach-ing $328,297 by mid-2012, while the average cost of newly constructed homes also increased rapidly from $278,000 in 2009 to $296,000 in 2011. The average price of a home in Canada reached $365,192 in 2011, repre-senting an annual increase of 8.8% (*Postmedia News*, 18 March 2011). TD housing experts estimate that Canadian housing prices are currently overvalued by 10% to 15%.

On average it now takes 39 days to sell a home in Saskatoon. The City has contributed to the availability of 1,818 housing units – affordable homes, rental accommodation, secondary suites – just during the past three years, at a time when housing costs have been increasing rapidly while incomes have not. Just a few years ago, a family required an income of $48,000 in order to buy an average home in the city; a couple of years later, that amount had risen sharply to $75,000, far in excess of the median income of $60,000 (which was far more than the average income earned by Aboriginal residents). In other words, fully half the city's residents (and a far higher proportion of Aboriginal residents) were unable to afford a home. Moreover, the City estimates that for every percentage-point rise in the interest rate, the annual income needed to buy a home increases by $5,000 (Klein in *Saskatoon StarPhoenix*, 10 March 2011). At the time of a provincial election, the NDP argued that 'the market is simply not taking care of the needs of families' (*StarPhoenix*, 15 October 2011); whereas the Frontier Centre for Public Policy suggested that the NDP's advocating subsidizing both homebuyers and homebuilders constituted a 'flawed approach,' leading to 'unintended consequences' (*Saskatoon StarPhoenix*, 21 October 2011). Yet according to the provincial government's new housing strategy, with both the average cost of a new home and resale prices rapidly rising, homeownership is becoming 'less and less a likely option for low to moderate income families' (*Saskatoon StarPhoenix*, 9 August 2011).

*Variation by Types of Housing in Saskatoon and Other Canadian Cities*

An RBC report in December 2009 found housing in Saskatchewan on average to be in the mid-range of affordability. But for how long? Also, different conclusions can be drawn when we compare the *rates of increase* in average housing costs in various Canadian cities – which have tended to be highest in Vancouver, Toronto, and some smaller cities in other provinces – with the actual *cost* of housing. For example, currently Alberta has a much slower rate of increase than Saskatchewan, but a far higher cost: an average home in Alberta cost $339,000 in 2009 compared to $233,000 in Saskatchewan, according to CMHC data. Moreover, Canadian homes were being overvalued by as much as $87,000; in Saskatoon, housing prices were overvalued anywhere between 15% and 35% (*Saskatoon StarPhoenix*, 9 September 2008; 19 December 2009).

By 2009 the cost of housing was increasing approximately 41% a year in Saskatchewan for a detached bungalow, a rate that was slower than in Vancouver (67%) and Toronto (49%) but faster than in Ottawa (39%), Montreal (37.5%), and Calgary (37%). In Saskatchewan, on average, the cost of a two-storey home was increasing 44% a year, a standard townhouse 34% a year, a condominium 27%.

The average cost of a two-storey home in Saskatoon is currently $379,500, representing a cost increase of 4.1% over the previous year (2010). That is more than the average cost today in Regina ($282,500), Halifax ($291,000), Winnipeg ($296,750), St John's ($327,627), Edmonton ($334,286), Ottawa ($354,083) or Montreal ($375,222); but less than the average cost in Calgary ($404,622), Victoria ($480,000), Toronto ($594,231), or Vancouver ($1 million), according to data from Royal LePage Real Estate Services. Throughout Canada, at least a 3% annual increase is forecast in the average cost of a two-storey home, to $348,000 in 2011.

By 2008 the average cost of a standard detached bungalow in Saskatoon had increased to $340,000, which was now actually higher than in Edmonton ($330,000), Regina ($237,138), Winnipeg ($229,125), and Montreal ($227,799). Indeed, it was higher than the national average ($336,834) (Royal LePage data, 4 April 2008). Data for increasing housing costs in Saskatoon vary somewhat, depending on source and annual quarters compared: for example, according to a Royal Lepage House Price Survey, in July 2012 standard two-storey homes averaged $379,500, an increase of 7.3% from the same quarter the previous year; detached bungalows averaged $351,125, an increase of 6.0%; and standard condominiums, $255,667, an increase of 5.6%. However, in October the same survey showed more modest calculations with average increases at about 4%. Comparing Saskatoon with national data shows that all three housing types currently cost less  in Saskatoon than the national average, but the prices seem to be increasing faster.

Approximately 3,000 homes were sold in 2012 in Saskatoon, representing an increase of 17%. Approximately a quarter of these sales were in the $300,000 to $400,000 range, about 180 sold for more than half a million dollars, and 6 for over a million dollars. But this pales in comparison to Calgary, where sales of high-end homes increased by 25% in some areas of the city; in 2010 there were 8,198 single-family residential homes and condos assessed at over $1 million (a substantial increase from 6,496 just a year ago). The most expensive home (since 2008) has been assessed at $22 million, the second most expensive at $10.2 million.

*Variation by Area of the City*

There has been considerable variation in housing costs by area of the city. For example, while the average annual price increase was 29% in Saskatoon for the first quarter of 2007, it was actually as high as 40% in some neighbourhoods (City of Saskatoon 2007c). Houses even in the relatively poor inner west side neighbourhood of Riversdale, which has a substantial Aboriginal population, were now selling for as much as $164,000; out of 540 properties listed in this area, 480 sold for an average $121,000. This had been the lowest-selling neighbourhood in the city, averaging $86,000 the previous year (2006). Also, a standard detached bungalow on the west side in general, where most of the Aboriginal population was concentrated, cost approximately $300,000 in April 2008, compared to $345,000 in the north, $350,000 in east-central, and $365,000 farther east. Yet by January 2009 the average cost had declined to $270,000 in the west, $300,000 in the north, $310,000 in east-central, and $320,000 farther east. A two-storey home ranged from $290,000 in the west, to $330,000 in the north, $335,000 in the east-central, and $360,000 farther east; and a condominium averaged $199,500 in the north and $189,000 in east-central (data cited in *Saskatoon StarPhoenix*). The most rapid expansion of Saskatoon is to the south. Here, in Stonebridge, one typical 43-unit development features three-bedroom townhouses of 1,200 to 1,300 square feet, costing between $289,900 and $309,900.

*Rental Accommodation*

Saskatoon has recently exhibited the third-highest increase in rental rates on record (according to CMHC data in December 2009). Average monthly rent for an apartment in Saskatoon increased $66.33 a year between 2005 and 2011, from $585 to $936. However, there are indications that this rate of increase has been abating. Currently, monthly rent for all apartments comes to $881: $632 for 'bachelor' units, $787 for single-bedroom, $966 for two-bedroom, $1,075 for three-bedroom. All of these average rates have been increasing, but moderately by $28 to $116 a year. Increasing rents are a problem throughout Canada. One property investment company informed tenants that their monthly rent in an inner-city apartment building would almost double within just three months, to a level well beyond tenants' maximum shelter allowance ($385/month), together with a provincial Disability Rental Housing Supplement ($165/month). Moreover, the City was considering raising the property tax by 8.3% (*Saskatoon StarPhoenix*, 13 March and 17 April 2008). A considerable debate has developed over the issue of rent control: the provincial premier views it as potentially 'dangerous,' insofar as it could negatively impact long-term supply, whereas the NDP opposition views rent control as necessary in the current climate of rapidly increasing rent charges and decreasing vacancies.

*Affordability*

While average housing costs are lowest in the west side, they still have very rapidly risen far out of reach of most Aboriginal residents, making homeownership virtually impossible without ample subsidization. Aboriginal residents are facing a crisis in home affordability and are limited almost entirely either to renting or to purchasing older homes with the possibility of renovating. According to the Demographia International Housing Affordability Survey, released by the Frontier Centre for Public Policy in January 2009, housing affordability had eroded dramatically over the past couple of years. Saskatoon was now classified as 'seriously unaffordable,' with an index of 4.6 years that it would take to buy a new house on an average household income. (Just two years earlier, the index had stood at 2.6.) Moreover, most Aboriginal residents were lagging well below this average city income and so would be classified as 'severely unaffordable' (CMHC 2004a; August 2004). No other city surveyed in six countries had experienced such a rapid increase in this index in just a couple of years.

According to an RBC study, as recently as 2003, on average, homeownership in Saskatchewan consumed 28.9% of pretax household income, and the province was still ranked as one of the most affordable. However, RBC pointed out in May 2010 that a steadily increasing amount of household income in the province is going toward homeownership. Saskatchewan posted some of the largest quarterly increases in homeownership costs in Canada. For example, a detached bungalow was now consuming 41.4% of pretax household income, a standard townhouse 33.9%, a condominium 28.7%, a two-storey home 44.8%. The annual report of the Vanier Institute of the Family, released on 16 February 2010, showed the highest debt-to-income ratios ever recorded; also, a survey conducted by that institute revealed that one-quarter of Canadians believed that it was likely that someone in their household would lose their job in the coming year. The crucial factor is affordability – that is, the proportion of a household's income required to afford a home. When housing price increases begin to exceed income gains, the inevitable result is reduced housing affordability. The traditional approach taken by banks, according to the RBC in May 2010, is that mortgage payments, property taxes, and utilities should not exceed

32% of household income, assuming a 25% down payment. However, a reality check: the percentage of a typical Canadian household's income required to carry an average bungalow is currently calculated at 39% nationally for long-term average (but has reached as high as 53%); moreover, there is considerable variation across Canada, with long-term averages of 57% in Vancouver (and an all-time high of 81%) and 49% in Toronto (and an all-time high of 73%).

The actual cost of living can be quite complex; the cost of housing is just one factor. For example, in Saskatoon in 2009, per single person earning $25,000 total income, average rental housing costs came to $8,100; add to this $1,772 for total average household utility costs and another $1,277 for total average provincial taxes and health premiums. This totals to $11,149, which is actually higher than in Montreal ($11,124) and Winnipeg ($10,342), though lower than in Toronto ($16,156), Calgary ($15,371), and Vancouver ($14,071), according to the Saskatchewan Department of Finance. Compared to nine other Canadian cities, residents of Saskatoon pay relatively less in taxes and utilities. But again, the very notion of 'affordability' could be seriously questioned from the standpoint of urban indigenous populations, which are largely poor in relative terms.

According to a recent report of the International Monetary Fund (December 2010), the Canadian economy is facing serious obstacles, including high levels of household debt, which has increased to a record 148.1% of disposable income in Canada (*Globe and Mail*, 14 December 2010; *Financial Post*, 23 December 2010). Noting that Canada is facing a $56 billion deficit, the federal finance minister (a Conservative) has suggested that these record high debt levels are leading to a tightening of the lines of credit that people can back with their homes. In his view, the government is obliged to closely monitor the housing market, ready to intervene if necessary. Market demand, driven by very low interest rates, has been leading residents to buy homes that they are not really able to afford. A precedent for increased government control has already been set in the United States: since 2008, the US Treasury Department has twice raised the standards that homebuyers must meet in order to qualify for a government-backed mortgage. These standards relate, for example, to minimum down payments required to qualify for such a mortgage. Also, limits have been placed on the amount of cash that homeowners can free up by refinancing a mortgage. In Canada, many homeowners could be affected if interest rates increase more rapidly than expected. During an address to the Economic Club of Canada on

13 December 2010, the Governor of the Bank of Canada emphasized that householders and lenders alike have a responsibility to have solid grounds for expecting that consumer-borrowers will be able to service their debts.

## Household Net Worth and Household Expenditures

Across Canada, household debt is rising and is now estimated at $1.5 trillion, according to the Certified General Accountants Association of Canada in June 2011. In other words, if household debt were distributed evenly among all Canadians, a two-child household would owe $176,461 (including mortgage costs). Approximately 27% of working Canadians are not saving; households having an income of less than $50,000 (notably including single-parent families and retirees) are six times more likely to be financially vulnerable in terms of their debt-service ratio (*Globe and Mail*, 15 June 2011).

Household net worth across Canada has actually been decreasing in recent years – for example, it fell by 6% between June 2008 and June 2009. This amounted to $360 billion, or $10,500 per person, according to Statistics Canada. Home equity is difficult to analyse. According to Statistics Canada, household net worth can increase even while home sales and residential mortgages are decreasing. The Saskatchewan government suggests that housing costs are the main contributor to a rising inflation rate +2.0% per month).

Moreover, while household expenditures have been slightly decreasing nationally (overall –0.3% in 2009), in Saskatchewan they have been substantially increasing (by 1.9%, the third-highest provincial rate). Household expenditures in Saskatchewan were below the rate of increase in personal incomes in 2009, according to *SaskTrends Monitor*. Currently in Saskatchewan, 17.9% of household expenditures are on shelter costs, compared to 19.8% nationally. Statistics Canada reports that energy costs are increasing 6.7% a year, gasoline 7.2%, electricity 5.9%, and food 1.5% to 2.2%, while clothing and footwear expenditures are decreasing at 3.2%.

## Availability of Affordable Housing

Given that a much higher proportion of Aboriginal residents than non-Aboriginal are renters rather than owners, availability of rental units is a particularly crucial problem for Aboriginal people. Keith Hanson,

Executive Director of the Affordable New Home Development Foundation and Community Director of the Bridges and Foundations Project, recently commented that there may be 1,600 homes for sale in Saskatoon on the multiple listing service system, but many people cannot come close to affording these houses. Yet they still require shelter, so governments and the housing industry must ask themselves what the need for housing is and find ways to meet that need. Saskatoon residents, especially Aboriginal residents, need more accessible housing.

Saskatoon's average vacancy rate in 2006 was 3.2%, which wasn't bad at the time, considering that the national average stood at 2.6%, while in Vancouver it was 0.7% and in Calgary 0.5%. However, rental property availability was seriously imbalanced in Saskatoon. In the relatively more affluent east side neighbourhoods – Nutana and Lakeview – the vacancy rates that same year were 0.7% and 0.8% respectively. Compare this to the generally poorer west side neighbourhoods, where the rates were 12.9% in the southwest (including Riversdale and King George) and 4.7% in the west-central area (including Caswell Hill and Mayfair). Yet by the following year (2007), vacancy rates for rental apartments were plummeting, down to a city average of 0.6% by October, when the rate had been 3.2% the year before, according to CMHC. Vacancy rates since then have slowly been increasing, from 1.9% to 2.6%. The current apartment vacancy rate in Saskatoon is 2.6%.

CMHC suggested in December 2010 that apartment rentals in Saskatoon were easier than they had been the year before; however, the same agency also admitted that this could be a result of increasing rents, which can have the effect of crowding people together or pushing them into homeownership.

The shortage of 'affordable' housing has been conservatively estimated at no less than 3,500 units. More than one-quarter of Saskatoon Food Bank clients – many of them Aboriginal – report that there is a strong probability that they would be requiring emergency shelter during the winter for themselves and their families. The city's pledge to provide 500 new units to low-income families 'over the next five years' is clearly insufficient. The provincial government's new initiatives, such as a modest increase in the housing allowance for individuals and families on social assistance, do not come close to meeting increasing housing costs, which were now doubling every six months, nor the shortfall of truly affordable housing. Nor is Saskatoon alone: according to the Cooperative Housing Federation of Canada, as of December 2007 at least 1.5 million households containing over 4 million men, women, and children were in 'core housing need.' A report released by the Federation of Canadian Municipalities in January 2008, *Trends and Issues in Affordable Housing and Homelessness*, pointed out that despite an increase in home-ownership across Canada, of all the housing starts reported between 2001 and 2006, fewer than 9% were for rental units.

The recent and growing trend toward converting rental properties into condominiums has effectively blocked access to them for Aboriginal and other residents. Hanson observed that in the face of large numbers of condos being sold and taken off the rental market, hardly any afford-able rental properties were available. The vacancy rate for rental apart-ments dropped drastically during 2007; meanwhile, through March 2008 the city received applications to convert a 1,634 apartment units into condos (*Saskatoon StarPhoenix*, 19 April 2008). Columnist Randy Burton wryly commented: 'City councillors might be forgiven for hav-ing trouble figuring out what to do about this circumstance, simply be-cause they have never had to face it before ... [Yet] the debate about condo conversion is only one aspect [of the housing crisis], albeit an important one' (*StarPhoenix*, 17 April 2008).

There can be no doubt that in recent years there has been a housing boom in Saskatoon; but this has had little effect on Aboriginal residents' access to affordable housing. For example, the number of housing starts in a single month, April 2007, was almost triple the number the previous year. Early the following year, housing starts hit a 30-year high, with the units almost evenly split between single-family homes and condo-style dwellings. Saskatoon and Regina were experiencing the strongest de-mand for new housing in decades. By July 2008 there were 2,628 homes currently under construction, especially multiple units – semi-detached homes and condos. By October the city had issued 3,215 current build-ing permits with a total value of $550 million. The most recent CMHC data indicate that starts of single family detached homes in Saskatchewan are currently increasing 18% a year; yet within the Saskatoon region an overall increase in single family starts is expected to be as much 44%, according to the CHBA-Saskatchewan. (Although CMHC is forecasting a general moderation in the Canadian housing market.) Despite the boom in housing construction in Saskatoon, demand, especially for af-fordable housing, has tended to increase more rapidly than supply, put-ting upward pressure on housing costs.

Despite the recent economic recession, Saskatchewan has maintained strong economic growth; in fact, the province currently leads the coun-try in economic growth with an annual growth rate of almost 5% due to a strong economy and increasing in-migration. However, Native people must compete for jobs and affordable housing. According to the RBC Financial Group (2 June 2010), the Saskatoon population will continue to grow steadily. The city population grew by 11.4% between 2004 and 2011 (when it reached 261,000); during this period this represented the third-fastest growth of any CMA in Canada (after Calgary and Edmonton), and it is currently the fastest. Saskatoon has a history of steady growth even when the provincial population has been slowly declining or relatively stable.

However, just as there have been fluctuating trends in housing costs (discussed above), so too have there been fluctuations in housing starts and home sales, which affects availability. The recent economic downturn resulted in a temporary decline in housing starts, which was very much part of a national trend. Between September 2007 and September 2008, single detached starts decreased 64.2% in the CMA and 81.9% in the City of Saskatoon proper, while multiple-family starts actually increased 4.1% in the CMA and 19.4% in the city; overall, total starts decreased 30.3% in the CMA and 22.3% in the city. During the first quarter of 2009, housing starts in Saskatoon plummeted 85% compared to the same period a year ago. A report by CMHC (February 2009) expected that residential construction in the city would fall 43% during 2009, owing to an oversupply of new homes on the market during a time of economic recession; moreover, the decline in housing starts was attributable to developers working to finish the houses they had started building earlier and selling them in difficult financial times.

Population growth is continuing in Saskatoon, yet a significant part of this growth has been due to seniors, and this has interesting implications for housing. With affordability dropping dramatically with the recent increase in prices (a detached bungalow may now eat up nearly half a family's income), higher prices inevitably led to a decrease in demand for new homes; this likely halved the number of housing starts during 2009. CMHC further suggested that demand for homeownership and rental units would lessen in 2009–10, as fewer people moved into the urban region and the economic slowdown placed pressure on the homebuilding and rental accommodation industries. The Saskatoon region home sale rate decreased 15.3% between 2008 and the same month in 2009 (about 3,000 sales a year, back to the same number recorded five years earlier). In Saskatoon in 2008–9, home sales had been increasing at the rate of 41% a year and new listings by 16% (Saskatoon Region Association of Realtors, 2 December 2009). But then a 37% *decrease* in home sales was recorded between January 2009 and January 2010 (Re/ Max, 24 February 2010). Data reveal a decrease in actual housing starts between 2008 and 2009, including in single-detached and multiple-family homes (CMHC, 12 January 2010). Home sales decreased 18% in a single year, July 2009–10. Overall there was a 7% decrease in Saskatoon home sales in 2010; however, more specifically, sales of homes priced over $300,000 *rose* 14% whereas sales of homes priced less than that *dropped* 18%. There had been a 'cool-down' in the entry-level market, as people with lower incomes were simply unable to afford the increasing cost of housing, much less step up to a higher-priced home. CMHC data indicate that home sales in Saskatoon were approximately 3,500 a year in 2010, representing a decline of 8.7% from the previous year.

But this decline was destined to change markedly. Nationally, CMHC has pointed out that Canadian housing starts should increase by approximately 175,000 units a year in order to keep pace with population growth. Single-family homes are leading these increases by 3.4% a year (or some 69,800 units) (reported by CMHC, 8 December 2009). In Saskatoon, Alan Thomarat, CEO of the Saskatoon and Region Home Builders' Association, commented on the rising demand for new housing that was resulting from the inventory built up during 2007–8 finally being absorbed by the market. Housing starts were expected to increase from 3,800 in 2009 to over 5,000 the following year (RBC, 3 June 2010). CMHC reported a 28.8% increase per month in home construction in the Saskatoon region in July 2010 compared to the same month a year earlier. Saskatchewan urban housing starts increased 63% in one year (May 2009–10), the third-highest rate among the provinces; but 140% during the first five months of 2010, the fastest rate for any province; and by 251% in Saskatoon during this same period. Building permits in Saskatoon, now valued at a record $1 billion a year, increased 65.1% in February–March 2010, again the highest rate of increase in Canada; at the same time, nationally there has been a decline in housing starts (for example, –13% in November 2011). Saskatoon CMA saw an 80.5% increase in building permit values between March 2009 and March 2010. At the time of writing, during the past year (2011) building permits issued for new homes have almost doubled, as have permits for new apartment buildings, and more than four times as many as the previous year have been issued for row housing. During summer of 2010, for example, 365 new homes a month were under construction in Saskatoon. Factoring in the winter slowdown in construction, the current annual average could be calculated as approximately 2,346 starts (the CMHC had projected 2,125), which would be almost double the average for the previous year. By 2010, 72.9% of new homes were single detached; these have proportionately been decreasing but still well over 1,500 are constructed a year. The number of new multiple-family homes more than tripled, with approximately 1,500 starts during 2011. Homebuilders suggest that this trend should improve affordability, but for whom exactly? Entry-level homebuyers are becoming increasingly concerned over high home prices, so are seeking smaller, more affordable homes. The homebuilders need to recognize this.

Meanwhile, the city population was increasing in the range of 5,000 to 7,000 a year. There was an estimated 20% to 30% increase in housing inventory in 2010. The residential construction industry now contributes $2 billion a year to the Saskatoon GDP (which represents 45% of the provincial GDP).

Saskatoon has quickly become per capita one of the most spread-out cities in Canada. South of the city, for example, the new development of Stonebridge, consisting primarily of medium-density townhouses, is attracting young couples searching for a first home as well as 'empty nesters' who are downsizing in retirement ... but in either case, few Aboriginals. One single suburban development currently being planned will house around 11,000 people – but again, all of this development will likely be too expensive for the vast majority of Aboriginal residents to afford. Thomarat emphasizes that government and the homebuilding industry must keep working closely together in order to fill both short-term and long-term housing needs (*Globe and* Mail, 11 August 2010). Meanwhile, the provincial government suggests that an estimated 10,000 immigrants are expected 'in the near future.' At least 4,000 of them are likely to settle in Saskatoon, and this influx could compete with Aboriginal people seeking affordable housing.

*Urban Aboriginal Housing Conditions*

A disproportion of urban Aboriginal households have serious affordability problems. In the never-ending search for *waskahikanihkewin* (housing), most Aboriginal residents are resigned to rest content with just *waskahikanis* (a small house) or small apartment, which may be overcrowded and entirely inadequate for a large family. A higher proportion of Aboriginal households outside of reserves (8.5%) than non-Aboriginal households (5.2%) were in core housing need and spending half or more of their household income on housing. Generally across Canada, urban

Aboriginal people significantly lag behind non-Aboriginals in total household income. Status Indians had the highest incidence of falling into core housing need and encountering severe affordability problems (10.4%) (CMHC 2005a). In Saskatchewan, housing conditions have been especially problematic among the First Nations and Metis populations: almost two-thirds (65%) of on-reserve and almost half (49%) of off-re-serve Aboriginal people in Saskatchewan were living in substandard housing in 2002 (Anderson 2002). Bearing in mind that the Aboriginal residents of Saskatoon are disproportionately poor, the question of affordability becomes all the more pressing. Affordable housing is an on-going and ever-increasing concern for the residents of Saskatoon, especially First Nations and Metis, who experience extreme difficulty in accessing affordable and appropriate housing for their needs (Foss 2004). There is a need for thousands of new housing units to accommo-date the already large and growing Aboriginal population in Saskatoon. As Hanson has commented: 'the general reality is that there is not enough appropriate, affordable housing in Saskatoon. The big issue is affordability … The financial institutions and mortgage insurance com-panies need to adjust their criteria in order for people to be able to ac-quire appropriate housing, and that creative financing needs to be put in place.'

Despite indications that Aboriginal poverty is steadily decreasing, more still needs to be done to find suitable housing for Aboriginal resi-dents. The Aboriginal unemployment rate at the time of the project was 22.3% but may have been as high as 35% in families with young children. With the Aboriginal population of the city growing at twice the rate of the general population, and half of the approximately 20,000 Aboriginal residents under the age of 20, the biggest issue need-ing to be addressed clearly is housing, which according to Hanson is not given enough attention even though it is the root of many problems in the Aboriginal community: 'The thing I find most difficult is that health is on the public agenda, and we talk about health all the time, but hous-ing for some reason is missed. The research is clear; the single biggest determinant of health is housing. Housing needs to be on the public agenda' (*Saskatoon StarPhoenix*, 19 February 2005).

The National Housing Research Committee (NHRC) documented the changing housing conditions of off-reserve Status Indian households (almost half of which were in Canada's 33 metropolitan areas) during the past ten years (NHRC 2010, 19–20) and found that there have been many improvements: from 1996 to 2006 the proportion of households living above the housing standard (as defined by CMHC) increased nationally from 47.4% to 54.7%; conversely, households below this living standard decreased from 52.6% to 45.3%; below affordability from 33.6% to 27.1%; below sustainability from 18.7% to 13.5%; and below adequacy from 15.6% to 15.2%. In 1996, 34.4% of households were in core housing need, compared to about one-quarter (24.8%) ten years later. The proportion both in core need and below affordability fell from 28.1% to 19.7%; in core need and below sustainability from 11.0% to 6.4%; and in core need and below adequacy from 7.9% to 6.5%. In comparison to non-Aboriginal households, off-reserve Status Indian households tend to have lower homeownership rates (47% compared to 70% in 2006). Yet the homeownership gap has been gradually narrowing, just as the income gap has been. A significant proportion (22%) of these First Nations households were headed by lone parents, particularly women (83%). The absolute number of off-reserve Status Indian households has been growing at a rate of approximately 22% every five years, so that although core housing need has been decreasing, this decrease has been offset by a marked increase in the absolute number of households in this population. Of these households, 27.1% reported spending in excess of 30% of their before-tax household income on accommodation; 13.5% lacked suitable housing – that is, housing with sufficient bedrooms for the household's size and composition; and 15.2% reported that their housing was inadequate, needing major repairs. As in the general population, living conditions, homeownership versus rental accommodation, and income were closely interrelated. The NHRC concludes that this research reveals a housing profile for off-reserve Indian households that is steadily improving yet remains far below national averages.

With the vacancy rate down to 0.6% in Saskatoon, moving into the city from a reserve or northern community was becoming a daunting task. A vice-chief of the FSIN emphasized that there were three main reasons for the surge of rural Aboriginal migrants to the city: the lack of housing in First Nations communities; limited opportunities for education on reserves; and high unemployment rates. The 2006 census concluded that an Aboriginal resident of Saskatoon was nine times more likely to be living in an overcrowded dwelling than a non-Aboriginal person; moreover, 12% of First Nations and Metis in the city were living in homes in need of major repair. The chief of One Arrow First Nation, north of the city, commenting on the acute shortage of housing both on reserve and in the city, has explained that on One Arrow 'there's a huge shortage and we're getting overcrowded … We just keep building and building, but we can't keep up with the number of young people … The crowding [in the city] isn't necessarily a racial issue ... You just have to take what you can get.' By 2008 the Central Urban Metis Federation Inc. (CUMFI) was reporting more than 300 people on their waiting lists for housing; SaskNative Rentals recorded over 800 people waiting for the 450 units handled by the agency.

A few innovative projects for First Nations and Metis have succeeded. In August 2007, La Maison Mamawe-Atosketak, a 70-suite Metis housing development, was completed in Caswell Hill. The provincial government contributed $3.3 million through the Saskatchewan Housing Corporation (SHC) and the municipal government $357,000 for this project. The project is managed by SaskNative Rentals. The local provincial MLA commented: 'We are working with local people and local groups to help lower-income families get the quality, affordable housing they need and the independence they deserve' (*Saskatoon StarPhoenix*, 17 August 2007). Then in March 2009, CUMFI announced its new Coming Home program for mothers with children in foster care; they would now be given an affordable place to live and to raise their own children under the supervision of a mentor parent. This 12-suite renovated apartment building would be part of a complex of low-income housing projects developed and run by CUMFI in Pleasant Hill. The project's estimated $1.2 million cost was to be shared by all three levels of government, with the federal government contributing $206,000, the provincial government $924,000 through the Saskatchewan Housing Corporation, and the municipal government $125,000. The complex would be drug and alcohol-free, and residents would have access to addiction counselling, child care services, and a communal kitchen.

The entire CUMFI complex included three renovated apartment buildings containing 36 apartments, intended for low- to middle-income families, many of whom would be single-parent families. For the $1.8 million project, completed in 2004, more than $1.4 million was supplied by the Centenary Affordable Housing Program (CAHP) and most of the remainder by the Residential Rehabilitation Assistance Program (RRAP), though the city contributed up to $180,000 toward the CAHP funding. CUMFI itself contributed approximately $100,000 to the project from donations. Interestingly, helping bring this project to fruition was the successful development of a work education program in which CUMFI partnered with other Metis organizations – the Dumont Technical Institute (DTI) and the Metis and Employment Training Saskatchewan Inc. (METSI), as well as the Saskatoon Tribal Council and Career and Employment Services (CES).

Several blocks away in Pleasant Hill is a new $1.1 million housing project developed by One Arrow Cree First Nation, which contributed $125,000, while the province donated $891,000 through SHC. The city and federal governments were also partners in the project. The One Arrow chief commented that many First Nations young people need to move into the city to further their education. He hoped the project would help them cope with the rising costs of shelter and tuition.

*Poverty and Social Housing*

Poverty, so prevalent in the Aboriginal population, and the need for social housing are closely related. Faced with an unprecedented housing crisis, the Alberta government imposed controls on landlords in May 2007, limiting the number of times they could increase rents and forcing reviews of the amount of those increases. This reflected a housing industry that had even left some middle-class families facing the prospect of homelessness as they felt the pressure of the housing shortage combined with rapidly increasing prices. As a result, although the City of Saskatoon had just rejected rent control, city councillors asked civic officials whether the city could afford to double its contribution to social housing to 10% of the difference between housing costs and what people who qualify might be able to afford; they also asked the city to encourage the provincial government to similarly increase its contribution. At the time, the average new housing price was increasing faster in Saskatoon than in Calgary (approximately +42% a year compared to +25%).

The gap between Canada's richest and poorest has widened steadily in recent years (Green and Milligan 2007), not the least exemplified in the housing crisis. Bluntly put, the rich have become richer while the poor have stayed poor. This trend has been readily apparent in Saskatoon. A city councillor who had been a former director of the Saskatoon Food Bank commented in 2007 that the number of post-secondary students needing assistance had increased 30% in a single year, while the number of seniors receiving food hampers had jumped from 240 to 520; the primary reason for these drastic increases at the Food Bank had been the cost of housing, with rents rising all over the city and rental properties changing hands (*Saskatoon StarPhoenix*, 11 July 2007). The director of the Child Hunger and Education Program (CHEP), a community organization attempting to improve access to healthier food and ensure food security, commented that poor people – including student families and grandmothers obliged to return to work – were being forced to choose rent over food. They reported going to soup kitchens and the food bank more often to supplement the groceries they were able to buy. They were also eating less and buying less healthy foods of the sort that are inexpensive and filling (such as cases of noodles), and they were seldom eating fruits and vegetables. 'A person's whole health – physical, mental, emotional, and spiritual – is affected by inadequate nutrition ... It also affects people's behaviour, their ability to learn and their participation in the community' (*StarPhoenix*, 13 June 2009).

*Policy Implications*

Finally, there are all sorts of policy implications in affordable housing. A report of the Institute for Research on Public Policy (IRPP) (Walker 2008) drew the obvious conclusion that poor housing for urban Aboriginal people in Canada is a problem that keeps growing. The study focused on the growing gap between the housing needed by urban Aboriginal people and the supply offered through low-rental projects. The report pointed out that a well-established group of organizations are working hard to deliver affordable housing to Aboriginal residents, but they are lacking a commitment from various levels of government to expand their work so that it can meet the community's needs.

Housing is the single largest user of developed urban land in Canadian cities (Hodge and Gordon 2008). Zoning can relate to housing affordability. Zoning and other building restrictions effectively reduce the supply of land that can be developed; thus, these restrictions tend to push prices upward (CMHC, September 2005b). The Frontier Centre for Public Policy blames restrictive land development for driving up housing prices so rapidly.

In fact, the very notion of 'development' can be challenged – 'development' in whose interest? For example, one of the poorest neighbourhoods in Saskatoon was McNab Park, originally constructed in 1952 to provide base housing for the RCAF near the Saskatoon airport. A group of Calgary investors has bought title to the entire 50-acre site and plans to convert it from a social assistance residential area into an upscale business park, Aero Green. The approximately 400 low-income residents living in 148 units were given short notice to leave (mostly three to six months, but shorter for 'newer' tenants). In this and other cases of 'development,' land would seem to have more value than poor people.

Housing design can bear on affordability. It is entirely possible to build adequate and appropriate housing economically, and there is beginning to be some – although far too little – interest in this in Saskatoon. For example, Alberta-based CCL Communities has recently been expressing interest in the Saskatoon housing market. Their dwellings aim to be well crafted and full of useful features and will use inexpensive but attractive materials. The Saskatoon and Region Home Builders Association seems inclined to agree that affordable housing needs to be built, not so much for profit (although this is to some extent simply good business) as for actual affordability to various segments of the population. Creating a well-constructed, truly affordable home is not just possible – it is necessary and even profitable. Housing is, of course, an investment. While Saskatchewan's economic upswing has been producing a crisis in housing affordability, leaving many people desperate for a solution, Saskatoon's real estate prices tell people in the business that there are profits to be made. According to David Seymour, Saskatchewan policy analyst at the Frontier Centre for Public Policy, more intelligent solutions would encourage more supply of more affordable housing and target those most affected by the affordability crunch (Seymour 2009; 2011). Furthermore, apart from new home construction and condo conversion, affordable home renovation could and should be an important solution. The January 2009 federal budget included a novel home renovation credit program with an estimated cost of $2.5 billion over the following fiscal year, aimed at supporting the now-faltering housing market; this plan offered a tax credit for 15% of the cost of qualifying home renovations in the $1,000 to $10,000 range, yet the maximum payment per household would be only $1,350 (*Globe and Mail*, 28 January 2009).

Recent changes in mortgaging may negatively affect affordability. In July 2008 the federal finance minister announced that CMHC would be shortening the maximum amortization period to 35 years from 40 and, more important, would now be requiring a down payment of at least 5% of the value of a home. These new regulations, which took effect in October of that year, effectively made it more difficult for prospective homeowners to receive government-backed mortgages. Housing policy analysts are legitimately concerned that homeowners may now take on more debt than they will be able to afford when interest rates rise again.

Well-known politician and former Governor General Edward Schreyer, who is also an international board member of Habitat for Humanity, has pointedly argued for a Canadian strategy to house its neediest citizens. To summarize his comments, Canada is now the only G8 country lacking a national housing policy, but this has not always been the case. Before the mid-1990s, Canada ranked among the most progressive countries in providing affordable housing to those in need; however, budget cuts and shifting priorities have taken a devastating toll: 'The consequences of this inaction are self-evident and sad. Across Canada, too many families are in need of simple, decent, affordable housing. Too many women and men, mothers and fathers, each month are being forced to choose between adequate shelter and food, clothing and the necessities of life. Too many children know only a life of transience, shelters and stress.' In March 2010 the UN Special Rapporteur on the Right to Adequate Housing released a report that found Canada to be in urgent need of a 'comprehensive and coordinated national housing policy.' Other reports have described the lack of affordable housing as a 'national emergency.' Schreyer concludes: 'It is a fact that having a proper place to live leads to improved health outcomes and job prospects, and ultimately a decreased reliance on the state. A broad housing strategy is therefore an investment in a stronger and more stable society – and in the health and vibrancy of our communities. It is a direct and effective way to fight poverty' (*Saskatoon StarPhoenix*, 24 June 2010).

More specifically addressing housing costs in Saskatchewan, in an article in the *Globe and Mail* (28 December 2009), Saskatchewan writer Patricia Dawn Robertson commented that 'many Saskatchewan low-income people who have been punted from the rental market are not laughing. Forget about Saskatchewan home ownership. That dream died when housing prices soared in the past three years.' Saskatoon and other Saskatchewan cities, she continued, 'have all seen a remarkable rise in prices due to economic gains and speculation prompted by our previously undervalued real estate market ... Affordable housing in Saskatchewan has now exceeded the reach of low-income renters.' Condo conversions were now dominating the skyline. 'What remains for Saskatchewan renters are over-priced ghettoes ... No one should have to choose between paying the slumlord and buying groceries, yet many do. Affordable housing, public health and food security are all interconnected ... Yet I hear no ... excited talk [from the federal government] about affordable housing, co-operatives or homelessness.'

This chapter includes two case studies pertaining to aspects of affordable housing, particularly for urban Aboriginal people. First, Val Sutton, Project Manager of the Sun Ridge Group, provides a detailed description of financial and funding options for affordable homeownership for Aboriginal people in the city, together with recommendations from an informative workshop that brought together diverse Aboriginal, financial, business, and academic participants.

In other research conducted for the Bridges and Foundations Project, Katriona Hanna and Lori Hanson, of the Department of Community Health and Epidemiology at the University of Saskatchewan, studied the possible relevance of Saskatoon Habitat for Humanity to urban Aboriginal people (Hanna and Hanson 2004). Habitat for Humanity Canada (HFHC) was founded in 1985; since then, through its 73 affiliates across Canada, it has helped 1,800 Canadian families build and purchase affordable, well-designed homes. HFHC utilizes 50,000 volunteers a year. The international Habitat organization now operates in 93 countries and has built over 350,000 homes. After this informative study in Saskatoon was completed, a national survey conducted in 2004 was successfully completed in a total of 163 homes in 30 HFHC affiliates. This ambitious (but in the end limited) national study found that respondents reported positive aspects of HFHC (including affordability of payments and improved housing costs, security of tenure, changes in children's behaviour and scholastic achievement, further adult education and upgrading of job skills, new community relationships, and homeownership partnering). Yet the project summary made no mention of any Aboriginal residents (CHMC 2004b, April), while the earlier Saskatoon study found that at the time, just three homes had been occupied or built by Aboriginal people; moreover, it suggested that there were implicit reasons within the Saskatoon HFH organization and modus operandi for this lack of stronger Aboriginal involvement. HFHC established its Aboriginal Housing Program in 2007 with CMHC support, to facilitate homeownership for low-income Aboriginal families, particularly by increasing the access of Aboriginal families, both on and off reserve, to Habitat homes. Yet by 2011 just one home in Saskatoon had been constructed under this program, and none were being built or planned in Saskatchewan; of 31 homes built across Canada, two-thirds were in Manitoba (Thakur 2011).

The chapter concludes by focusing on those Aboriginals who cannot afford *any* housing – the homeless. Recent and continuing research in Saskatoon indicates that a disproportion of the homeless – in fact almost half – are Aboriginal. Moreover, the rapid increases in rent have put many residents – especially Aboriginal – at risk of 'virtual' homelessness. The NHRC identified seven basic factors contributing to the risk of homelessness: first, gross rent spending (50% or more of household income); second, social housing waiting lists; third, rental housing starts; fourth, incidence of low family incomes; fifth, vacancy rates; sixth, lone-parent families; and seventh, unemployment rates (NHRC

2009). Approximately 30,000 Saskatoon households were reported to be at risk of homelessness due to financial pressures, according to the city's 2007 Community Plan on Homelessness and Housing. An estimated 400 people were already living on the street, and 6,000 more comprised the 'hidden homeless' (*Saskatoon StarPhoenix*, 4 June 2008).

## Affordable Home Ownership for Aboriginal People: Financial and Funding Options

VALERIE SUTTON

*Introduction*

Over the past ten years housing costs have increased at a much faster rate than most household incomes. The result has been an ever-widening gap between what many can pay for housing and what is being offered in the marketplace. Often, households qualify for a mortgage but cannot find a home in their price range. Single persons, lone-parent families, Aboriginals, and seniors find it especially hard to afford decent and suitable housing. The objectives of this research were to develop financing and funding options that would make it easier for Aboriginal people to purchase housing, and to develop those options so that they could be implemented quickly.

*Home Financing*

The capacity of an individual or family to purchase a home is influenced by personal income, employment, credit history, debts, utility rates, and tax assessment; while house prices are influenced by land costs, zoning, development costs, construction costs (materials and labour), and design and technical innovations (e.g., improvements in energy efficiency, which have increased the cost of construction). Various options can be implemented to close the gap between the capacity of individuals/families to purchase a home and the price of homes. *Financing* options include modifying underwriting criteria, establishing alternative lending strategies, finding equity partners, and establishing benefactor funds. *Funding* options include homeowner grants (offset by tax equivalents such as GST, PST, and income tax) and government grants in general. These existing options, as well as other potential options, need to be discussed by creative, knowledgeable, and influential people, including individuals from the financial community such as lenders and insurers;

builders and developers; municipal and provincial housing authorities; and Aboriginal organizations.

## The Affordable New Home Development Foundation: First Homes, CAHP, Transition Entity Cooperative

The Affordable New Home Development Foundation (ANHDF) targets individuals and families with annual household incomes of $40,000 or less. Families and individuals in this income range are often paying rents roughly equivalent to monthly principal and interest payments; however, because of real or perceived barriers, they are unable to purchase a home through normal channels. The ANDHF works with people to help them overcome these barriers, leading to the purchase of a new home.

First Homes is a program of the ANHDF designed to help families become the owners of new, quality first homes in Saskatoon. The program targets families that are tired of paying rent, want to own their own home, and hope to benefit from the tax-free increase in value of their home while enjoying a better life. The First Homes Program is designed for families and individuals who are ready to make a commitment to work toward homeownership. Participants are expected to contribute an agreed-upon amount per month to a special savings account leading toward a down payment. They also agree to meet monthly rental obligations and to participate fully in the education portion of the program. In return, the foundation agrees to provide a Centenary Affordable Housing Grant as well as preferential access to special financing programs and to new housing options. The First Homes program includes an educational component that provides information about credit and debt, mortgages, the process of buying and selling, home maintenance, home styles, and types of housing availability. Participants learn about the benefits and responsibilities of being a homeowner. Mentoring and individual help are also provided to help improve the participant's credit and debt situation.

The ANHDF has been approved as a sponsor of the Centenary Affordable Housing Program (CAHP) under the Homeownership Option. CAHP provides forgivable equity loans to approved households; this enables them to purchase a home through the foundation. Approved households are then responsible for contributing the difference between the purchase price and the forgivable equity loan. The difference may be funded through mortgage financing or a combination of mortgage and owner/sponsor equity. The foundation recruits applicants and helps them obtain the mortgage lending approval and CAHP loan approval. Eligible households must meet certain criteria, including these: the total gross household income from all sources must be at or below $39,500; and the applicant must be able to obtain mortgage and other funding equal to the difference between the purchase price and the equity loan. Priority is given to families with dependents, Aboriginal households, and persons with disabilities. Forgivable loan amounts, which are income dependent, range from $3,500 to $19,500. The foundation has been given approval to sponsor 50 households. These loans are to be used only for new affordable housing within the City of Saskatoon in the form of single-family dwellings, attached dwellings (with a separate title to each unit), and condominiums.

The Transition Entity Cooperative utilized by the ANHDF is a legally incorporated body under provincial laws. It is designed to help families that are close to qualifying for a mortgage under normal lending requirements but who presently fail to qualify because they do not meet all the required criteria – however, within a relatively short period (two to five years), they *will* be able to qualify. Reasons why they do not presently qualify include these: bankruptcy has been discharged for more than two years, but credit has not been re-established; the family is in debt, though it may be receiving debt counselling; or a family head has not yet received an expected raise. A board of directors makes sure that the common payments are made every month; receives the funds from the occupant members; and ensures that when someone leaves, a replacement is found and the property is cleaned up and repaired. To protect the lender and the mortgage insurer against default, a contingency fund has been established. This is composed of contributions made by a benefactor and by the families within the co-op (i.e., each household contributes $25 per month). All interest earned is retained in the fund. Financial mentoring – keeping a budget, managing debt – is another support; yet another is mentoring on how to keep the home maintained. Potential members must be able to qualify for a mortgage fairly soon, and they must have the desire to become a homeowner with all the associated rights, privileges, and responsibilities. The co-op purchases a number of homes, which can be located in different areas. A contract is drawn with a family that has the ability to purchase the home as soon as the barriers to mortgage qualification have been removed. That family provides a 5% down payment. Mortgage insurance is provided by a mortgage insurer, such as CMHC. The co-op then makes the payments to the lender and collects the amount from the family. Once a family is able to qualify for a mortgage, it assumes full responsibility for the mortgage and becomes a homeowner. Once a mortgage has been assumed, a new family can be brought in to replace it. Equity in the home is accrued only when ownership is turned over from the co-op to the family. Families that move or that do not wish to stay in the co-op will not accrue equity.

SHIP Housing Investment Fund: Land Trust, Revolving Equity Fund, and Community Investment Deposit

A central objective of the Saskatoon Housing Initiatives Partnership (SHIP) is to raise equity for affordable housing. A housing fund is essentially a locally based not-for-profit organization that has secured revenue and is committed to using that revenue to help low- and modest-income households acquire appropriate, affordable housing. Housing funds have emerged primarily to fill gaps in available funding. They provide a mechanism for governments to commit resources to affordable housing and have succeeded in generating needed funds from private sources, thereby creating new public–private partnerships to build a long-standing environment supportive of new housing initiatives. Basically, a housing fund acquires money to provide gap financing to low- and modest-income households to help them become homeowners. Repayment of these funds is deferred for the term of the first mortgage, or until sale, transfer, or refinancing of the home, or until another amount of time predetermined by the housing trust fund. The housing fund is directed at reducing the initial financing costs that create a barrier for lower-income households. A second mortgage is provided, with the security for this financing in the form of a second mortgage on the house for which the fund is providing financing. It is expected that at the time of repayment, the participating household will have built up equity in the home and the value of the home will have increased. The participant will then refinance the home, and the investment will be repaid in full to the housing fund, often with a return. The key source of revenue for a housing fund is a permanent or dedicated source that provides ongoing revenue to it. Most funds also receive other monies from public, private, and charitable sources. These monies add to the funds already available for affordable housing (i.e., they do not divert or replace them). Income for the fund is also derived from the repayment of loans. In the past, most housing funds received government support through allocations from government programs. Typically, these allocations were given to start up the housing fund until the dedicated revenues came on stream or to supplement the dedicated revenues when inadequate. Money may be acquired through various sources, such as public funds, capital investors, or industry contributions. Housing funds that provide purchasers with loans, as opposed to grants, are viewed more favourably because they are not perceived as 'giving money away.' Through a cyclical deferred-loan mechanism, monies that are paid back are returned to the fund to be disbursed again to other purchasers. Also, a return on investment is expected as equity in the house increases; the fund will receive a portion of that equity increase upon repayment. An initial responsibility of the housing fund's administrator or sponsor is to explore ways to protect the fund's security. When a mortgage is provided, a risk is created that the property's value will decline and that the fund will thereby incur a loss. So the administrator confers with mortgage insurers and lenders to ascertain whether mortgage insurance will be available to the fund. When mortgages are insured, there is less risk of loss and investors view their investments as secure, which in turn makes it easier to attract further investments in the fund.

The Housing Investment Fund of SHIP helps build much-needed housing in Saskatoon in three ways. First, it can provide land through the SHIP Land Trust. The purpose of the trust is to improve the economics of affordable housing construction by deferring the cost of the land to the project. SHIP solicits land and property, or cash donations to purchase land for the trust. This land is then available free to proponents of affordable housing projects for a period of time. A land trust is a legal entity that can purchase, hold, and sell land. A house is built on land owned by the trust, which then leases it out. A mortgage is taken out on the building only, and the owner pays a fee for leasing the land. This reduces considerably the required mortgage amount. Equity may be shared between the occupant and the trust. The land trust will need to acquire funding from various sources in order to purchase the land (e.g., grants from financial institutions, CMHC, or CAHP; from federal or provincial governments; or from Aboriginal Affairs and Northern Development Canada (AANDC). Once a funding source is secured and land is acquired, the land trust can deal directly with the long-term cooperative, the transition entity cooperative, or some other form of tenure.

The second way relates to the Revolving Equity Fund. SHIP recognizes that financing affordable housing often involves an equity gap. The Revolving Equity Fund supplies 'patient capital' to projects that serve Saskatoon families in need of housing. SHIP solicits investment from corporations, foundations, and governments and makes it available for the development of affordable housing through a second-mortgage mechanism. Projects can be made more affordable if a portion of the debt can be deferred. Monthly payments are not required until enough equity has been built up in the project through its regular mortgage payments.

The third way involves the Community Investment Deposit. This is a Guaranteed Investment Certificate (GIC) with RRSP eligibility. The GIC product may offer 1.5% interest where 1% goes to the investor (return) and 0.5% to SHIP (unencumbered). SHIP is working with a financial institution to manage the certificates and work on the sales training and marketing materials. A number of terms can be available with varying rates. RRSP eligibility comes from the Self-Directed RRSP provisions.

Other Options

Other options for funding and financing homes include the following. A sponsor may give an *Equity Loan* to purchase a home. The occupant will then be required to repay the loan in one of two ways: over time (monthly payments), or in one lump sum. A *Limited Equity Co-op* allows the building of equity but not the capture of appreciation. *Shared Ownership* provides households with an opportunity to own a part share in their home; applicants can buy a share (minimum 25%) in a property according to their means, then rent the remaining 'unsold' share from a housing association, but can normally purchase further shares until they own the home outright. With *Government-Backed Mortgage Securities*, mortgages are purchased, packaged, and sold as securities to investors to generate a pool of capital. With *Community Bonds*, the community borrows money from the people to invest in a project or activity that is in line with the stated purpose of the bond; while *Tax-Exempt Municipal Bonds* may be structured to appeal to either institutional or individual investors, with the attraction being the tax-exempt nature of the return – a higher after-tax yield. A *Supportive Investment* involves an investment pool, such as a charitable foundation or pension fund, investing 1% of its total endowment in affordable housing at 0% interest over five years; the principal is repaid after five years, and the capital can be protected through mortgage insurance, a benefactor guarantee, a contingency fund, or a government guarantee. Finally, *Bank Initiatives* provide 'cashback' without any 'clawback'; more flexible underwriting criteria; administration of a housing fund; and financially supported education and training initiatives.

### Recommendations

There is a pressing need for First Nations and Metis organizations, homebuilders, financial institutions, and municipal and provincial governments to work together to make housing more affordable for Aboriginal people. The following priority actions are recommended: first, develop an aggressive mentoring and education program for lenders, builders and developers, governments, clients, and user groups; second, lobby the municipal government to provide land at appropriate prices and locations; third, create a housing fund and find funding for it; fourth, recommend changes to underwriting criteria, and lobby for the changes; and fifth, develop capacity to move ahead collaboratively.

## Aboriginal Homelessness

ALAN B. ANDERSON

The final portion of this chapter focuses on research on homelessness in Saskatoon, particularly research recently conducted by the Community–University Institute for Social Research (CUISR) at the University of Saskatchewan, as well as other research more specifically on Aboriginal homelessness in Saskatoon and other Saskatchewan cities. Collectively this research found that Aboriginals comprise a disproportionate share of the homeless.

### Definitions of Homelessness

In any attempt to arrive at a more accurate estimate of the numbers of homeless, distinctions should be drawn between *absolute*, *relative*, and *hidden* homelessness, as well as 'at risk of homelessness.' Absolute homelessness refers to those individuals who visibly lack shelter; relative homelessness to those who are among the hidden homeless or who are at risk of becoming homeless; and hidden homelessness to those who are temporarily living with friends and family or who are 'couch surfing' because they do not have their own shelter. 'At risk of homelessness' refers to those individuals who currently have housing but who are at imminent risk of becoming homeless. Factors that are thought to contribute to the precarious housing situations of those at risk of homelessness include living in substandard or inadequate housing that is physically unsafe and in need of repair; living in overcrowded conditions; living in housing that is unaffordable (i.e., more than 30% of a household's income is spent on rent); being at risk for eviction, without having any new housing possibilities in sight; and living in a household where family conflict or violence is prevalent (Springer 2000; Deacon 2001; Distasio et al. 2005; IUS 2005; Fiedler et al. 2006; Wilkie and Berdahl 2007; Peters and Robillard 2007; City of Saskatoon 2007a; McMurtry 2009). At risk of homelessness reflects the largest proportion of individuals who are affected by homelessness.

*Determinants of Homelessness*

Jewell (2008) and Chopin and Wormith (2008) have concisely summarized the close relationship between homelessness and housing affordability. The rapid change in Saskatoon's economy and housing market over the past several years has seriously affected housing affordability and availability. As a result of these increasing accommodation costs, the average Saskatoon resident is now paying 40% of his/her income on housing, which places many individuals in the category of at risk for homelessness, as housing is considered affordable only when a household is spending 30% or less of its income on shelter (CMHC 2007). Moreover, by 2008 at least 9,000 households were thought to be in core housing need. Saskatoon has also experienced a rapid rise in the cost of rental accommodation and a decline in vacancy rates. The vacancy rate in Saskatoon reached an all-time low in 2007, though it had previously enjoyed one of the highest vacancy rates nationwide. The City of Saskatoon (2003c, 2007c) has estimated that 667 households have multiple families living under one roof, which suggests that many families may be living in overcrowded conditions because they cannot find or afford adequate shelter. Yet community workers have informed us that data on overcrowding invariably tend to be underestimated, due to homeowners or renters not wishing to report any extra occupants of a particular residence. Moreover, the number of safety inspections that failed has been increasing at a rate of 15% a year, which in raw numbers comes close to 5,000 a year (City of Saskatoon 2006). Almost three-quarters of the failed inspections occurred in Pleasant Hill and Riversdale, the neighbourhoods with the highest Aboriginal density. And up to 64% of the properties that were reinspected in 2005 due to their failure to pass safety standards the previous year failed the inspection again, indicating that many landlords had not taken action to improve the condition of these buildings. Living in substandard or inadequate housing is an important factor for being at risk of homelessness (Jewell 2008).

Other factors that may contribute to hidden homelessness include these: poverty; poor physical and mental health; drug and alcohol addiction; domestic violence; and discrimination directed against Native people. Also, people released from correctional services, health care, and foster care may find it difficult to locate stable, adequate accommodation (Hill 1994; Beavis et al. 1997; SIIT 2000; Distasio et al. 2005).

## Aboriginal Homelessness

Much attention has been paid in recent years in CMHC research reports to various aspects of the problem of homelessness in Canada. These reports have touched on, for example, housing for people with mental illness at risk of homelessness (March 2002); innovative housing for homeless youth (December 2002); tenant exits from housing for homeless people (May 2003); transitional housing (February 2004); developing methodology for tracking homeless people over a long term (September 2004); homeless applicants' access to social housing (April 2005b); and housing for homeless people with substance abuse issues (September 2005). An extensive report on mental health and homelessness for the Canadian Institute of Health Information (CIHI 2007) suggested that on any given night, more than 10,000 Canadians are homeless. In Toronto alone, more than a decade and a half ago, growing housing shortages were already contributing to a significant proportion of the homelessless confronting an estimated 65,000 Native people (*Globe and Mail*, 2 January 1995). Across Canada there has been increasing activism to reduce and resolve homelessness, as evidenced in the collaboration between the National Secretariat on Homelessness (NSH), the National Homelessness Initiative, and Action for Neighbourhood Change (ANC 2004). Yet relatively limited national attention has been devoted specifically to Aboriginal homelessness (Beavis et al. 1997; Layton 2000, 2008). CMHC did produce one report on *Housing, Long-term Care Facilities, and Services for Homeless and Low-Income Urban Aboriginal People Living with HIV/AIDS* (February 2003), and there have been several recent studies of Aboriginal homelessness in Saskatchewan cities.

The Homelessness Community Advisory Committee has estimated that as many as 400 individuals in Saskatoon are absolutely homeless, that between 2,000 to 6,000 are struggling with hidden homelessness, and that perhaps 30,000 are at risk of homelessness. Nearly 14,000 of this at-risk population were receiving income supports that were inadequate relative to rent increases, while 9,000 lacked suitable housing (City of Saskatoon 2007b). According to the Saskatoon Overnight Shelter (SOS), 20 to 30 men are experiencing chronic homelessness (over a year); 200 to 400 people – many of them youths – absolute homelessness; and 11% of the total city population hidden or relative homelessness.

Several recent studies have focused specifically on homelessness among Aboriginal people in Saskatchewan cities. Two studies were released in 2000, one on Metis (Rivard et al. 2000) and the other on First Nations (SIIT 2000). The latter project consisted of 472 personal interviews with homeless individuals in Saskatoon, Prince Albert, and Regina. Two-thirds of these respondents could be considered relatively homeless. With respect to the condition of the housing in which the participants lived, 50% stated it was fair, while 12% indicated that they lived in poor conditions and 16% in very poor conditions. Approximately 44% were living with immediate family, 15% with extended family, and 7% with friends. Furthermore, 15% of the participants stated that they had inadequate space in their accommodations. The majority of the participants (57%) indicated they were on social assistance; 17% were unemployed, 6% received student assistance, and 6% were on pension. Participants cited many barriers to accessing programs and services intended to help them with their housing needs; these included a lack of appropriate programs, staff shortages at existing programs, transportation, employment, references for attaining housing, addictions, long housing waitlists, having a large family for whom to find housing, and a lack of money for initial start-up costs. The results from this study, then, provide insight into the characteristics of individuals who are among the hidden homeless, the factors that may contribute to their homelessness, and the barriers that may limit an individual's ability to find housing (Jewell 2008).

In another project, Distasio and colleagues (2005; IUS 2005) surveyed 129 Aboriginal persons who were considered to be hidden homeless in Saskatoon, Regina, and Winnipeg. In Saskatoon, all but one of the 25 participants reported that they were 'temporarily staying with friends.' The respondents as a whole seemed quite mobile: approximately 52% of the sample had lived in three or more accommodations in the last 6 months, 24% had lived at two places, and 24% had lived at the same place. Roughly 21% indicated that they stayed, on average, two weeks at each accommodation; 33% stayed for 0 to 3 months, 25% stayed for 3 to 6 months, and 21% stayed for 6 to 12 months. Furthermore, 36% reported that their temporary shelter conditions were somewhat crowded, and 32% that they were very crowded; also, 52% were unsatisfied with their shelter. In addition, 15% had no annual income, 65% earned $10,000 or less per year, and 20% had an income less than $20,000. Regarding education, 24% had attained grade eight or less, 57% grade nine to twelve, and 19% higher than grade twelve. Regarding housing specifically, 80% had never received subsidized housing, 88% were not on a waiting list for housing, 80% had encountered barriers to securing shelter, and 29% had stayed in an emergency shelter over the past year. Jewell (2008) concludes that the hidden homeless individuals in this study constituted a highly mobile group that often lived in unsatisfactory accommodations and were unlikely to utilize services intended to help them obtain housing.

These studies confirmed that hidden homelessness is a problem in Saskatoon. However, they did not attempt to systematically estimate the prevalence of hidden homelessness in that city (Jewell 2008). A study by Robillard and Peters (2007) described hidden homelessness among First Nations people in Prince Albert; for this, 143 interviews were conducted. These respondents lived in rental accommodations, had minimal incomes (less than $690 per month), were unemployed, received their main income from social assistance, had less than a high school diploma, and had moved at least once in the past month. Roughly one-third of these individuals suffered from alcoholism or drug addiction, and 60% reported that a traumatic experience (e.g., living in a foster home, attending a residential school, or spending time in a correctional centre) contributed to their current lack of housing. Only 31% had accessed services to help them find a place to live in the previous six months. It appears that multiple factors contributed to these individuals' homelessness, including low income, lack of education, and past victimization (Jewell 2008). Since the completion of this study, information has been released indicating that Prince Albert now has over 900 homeless people: 40 out on the street, approximately 600 to 700 hidden, 100 in shelters, and 80 in 'supportive housing.' Possibly, another 700 are at risk (*Saskatoon StarPhoenix*, 24 December 2008).

CUISR conducted the first count of Saskatoon's homeless population during May 2008. The project had two components: an enumeration, which counted the number of homeless individuals staying in emergency shelters and transitional housing (hereafter service providers) and outdoors; and a street needs assessment, which examined homeless individuals' service use patterns as well as their needs (Chopin and Wormith 2008). Data were collected at emergency shelters and transitional housing service providers; outdoor survey areas were identified in consultation with community groups that work with homeless individuals. The number of individuals reporting no fixed address was collected from a campground, a detox centre, and an interval house. The number of referrals by the Salvation Army to hotels on the evening of the count was also collected. The purposes of the CUISR study, which was funded through the Homelessness Partnering Strategy, included these: to estimate the number of individuals in Saskatoon who are at risk of homelessness; to obtain quantitative and qualitative information about the experiences of individuals who are currently among the hidden homeless; to obtain qualitative information about hidden homelessness from service providers, landlords, and the business community who are affected by issues related to hidden homelessness; and to review existing policies that affect the ability of Saskatoon citizens to find and retain housing (Jewell 2008). The research revealed that of 261 homeless individuals counted in Saskatoon in May 2008, half were Aboriginal (in the shelters, 46% self-identified as Aboriginal, while half of the outdoor survey respondents were Aboriginal). Given that Aboriginal residents comprise about one in ten residents of the city, Aboriginal people were far overrepresented among the homeless who were counted. One-quarter of the entire count was female, and thirty-two children were counted, almost all in shelters (Chopin and Wormith 2008). By 2011 a subsequent city report estimated 290 people were currently living in shelters and at least another 500 in transitional housing. Then a detailed recount by more than 130 volunteers in September 2012, conducted by CUISR in conjunction with the Saskatoon and Area United Way, found 372 homeless, including 78 children. This represented an increase of 40% since the previous detailed count in 2008. Despite adding more beds and facilities during the past four years, there were still about 100 people sleeping outdoors.

*Dimensions of the Problem*

Population increases have driven up housing costs and reduced the stock of affordable, adequate housing. Commenting recently on this 'totally unacceptable' situation, staff of the Westside Community Clinic in Saskatoon were emphatic that insufficiencies in the housing and the rental markets were forcing residents into inadequate housing situations characterized by homelessness, crisis shelters, overcrowding, and 'couch surfing.'

Between 150,000 and 300,000 Canadians are now homeless. By 2011, 146,726 individuals were counted who were using homeless emergency shelters in Canada (NHRC 2011). Additionally, for every person sleeping on the streets, another twenty-three may be at risk of homelessness, living in unaffordable, overcrowded, and unsafe conditions. The 'vulnerably housed' include thousands of Canadians – perhaps 400,000 – who are just a step away from homelessness and who face the same devastating health risks as the homeless out on the streets. This is according to a report released in November 2010 by the Research Alliance of Canadian Homelessness, Housing, and Health, after a two-year study funded by the Canadian Institute of Health Research (CIHR) of 1,200 homeless and vulnerably housed in Toronto, Vancouver, and Ottawa. Numbers like the ones found in that report point to 'a hidden emergency that is being ignored.' Homelessness is being underestimated because of the blurry line between the homeless and the vulnerably housed. Many of the latter have, in fact, been homeless. Together with the actual homeless, most have suffered from mental illness and harsh physical health problems and have had difficulty finding adequate, healthy food.

On average, Saskatoon's 'soup kitchens' feed more than 400 people every day, and each of these may represent another ten who are 'couch surfing' or who have found temporary accommodation in shelters. So suggests the documentary film Nowhere to Go: Homeless in Saskatoon, made in 2010 by Passion for Action Against Homelessness (founded in 2008) with funding from the Saskatoon Health Region and the province's Regional Intersectoral Committee. Passion for Action estimates that as many as 30,000 residents of Saskatoon find themselves in a 'housing-stressed situation.' At any given time some 6,000 people may be relatively homeless, that is, 'couch-surfing' (Saskatoon Sun, 27 March 2011). An estimated 300 women a month are currently turned away from the 38-bed YWCA shelter, and city shelters seem to be constantly full. At a meeting of social workers on 'Saskatoon's housing crisis,' held on 23 March 2010, a representative of SOS estimated that that there was a 3,500-unit shortfall in adequate shelter in the city. The Mental Health Commission of Canada has recently reported that as many as half of Canada's homeless have mental problems; and now CMHC reports that middle-class as well as low-income residents are having problems finding appropriate housing in Saskatoon. Between 2008 and 2010, Regina saw an increase of 44.5% in the average number of shelter beds occupied on a daily basis. The average daily capacity of 19 service providers using the HIFIS (Homeless Individuals and Families Information System) is 92.9%. The average individual stays in these shelters for 56 nights; more than 40% of Saskatoon shelter stays are three months or longer. Of 3,164 people discharged, the vast majority (83.7%) had no alternative place to go (*Regina Leader-Post*, 8 October 2011).

Being Aboriginal has seemed to compound the problem of homelessness. Columnist Janice Acoose once commented on the prevalent view that many urban problems in Saskatoon can be blamed on homeless young Native people (*Saskatoon StarPhoenix*, 6 August 1993). The managing editor of *Issues Network* later emphasized that 'the federal government must get serious about a major Aboriginal problem – the poverty, sickness and unemployment of off-reserve Indians in our cities ... The problems of Aboriginals in urban centres are mounting ... and it's a situation that, if neglected, will only get worse with time because of growing Aboriginal populations' (*StarPhoenix*, 27 December 1996). A study during the fall and winter 2008 of Metis and First Nations homeless people described a 'grim life on the streets' of Saskatoon (*StarPhoenix*, 9 May 2009). More than ten years ago, Jack Layton wrote that Saskatoon had 1,600 households on the waiting list for social housing; also, that 7,000 people had stayed in the city's eight emergency shelters in one year (1998) – over one-quarter of them children. He praised the 'creative minds' and innovations in the affordable housing field in Saskatoon (Layton 2000, 107–9). Let's hope he is still right. Saskatoon has repeatedly been touted as 'among the best places to live' (*StarPhoenix*, 16 September 2008) – that is, assuming that individuals and families have a roof (*apahkwan*) over their heads.

*Homelessness Policies and Initiatives*

It is the responsibility of all levels of government to deal with homelessness. There is an urgent need to improve the quality and availability of truly affordable housing. An All-Party Commons Committee has recently commented that 'all Canadians have a right to adequate shelter and a comprehensive long-term national housing strategy is essential to making this happen.' However, housing is primarily a provincial jurisdiction with municipal involvement.

The public cost of homelessness can hardly be overstated. Research has revealed the following: mortality rates among the homeless are as much as ten times those among the housed population; health supports for mental as well as physical problems tend to be less effective because of the stress caused by homelessness; about one in five chronic homeless account for half the total homeless service capacity; and it is four to ten times more costly per day to deal with homelessness on an emergency basis than to house and support the homeless (Walker 2010).

The federal government announced on 19 December 2008 that it would be contributing $1.7 million to homelessness projects in Saskatchewan (including a new Salvation Army emergency women's shelter in Saskatoon); but social agencies trying to cope with increasing homelessness point out that a 'crisis point' has already been reached. In addition to the initiatives implemented and supported by various levels of government, many community-based organizations in Saskatoon have dealt with issues related to homelessness and affordable housing. The Central Urban Metis Federation Inc. (CUMFI) provides emergency and transitional housing for Aboriginal women and children, as well as for men; the YWCA and Interval House provide crisis shelter services to women and their children; the Salvation Army provides emergency shelter for single men; the Saskatoon Overnight Shelter (SOS) provides 20 to 40 shelter beds during the winter months; Cress Housing and SaskNative Rentals provide safe and affordable housing accommodations to Aboriginals; Quint Development Corporation rents affordable apartment units to families and promotes cooperatives leading to homeownership; the Rainbow Housing and Terra Housing Cooperatives offer affordable housing alternatives to families and singles; CUMFI and the YWCA maintain rental units for at-risk families; and the Affordable New Home Development Foundation (ANHDF) and Habitat for Humanity Saskatoon (HHS) have implemented assisted homeownership programs. Community groups have emerged to achieve various advocacy goals related to homelessness. One such group is Passion for Action Against Homelessness, which is calling for the federal and provincial governments to work together to offer incentives and funds that favour affordable housing, and for them to engage in long-term strategic planning with respect to affordable housing and homelessness. Governments at all levels in Canada spend more than $4.5 billion a year providing homeless people with services such as shelter and food, emergency health care, mental health assistance, legal aid, and law enforcement. If people were provided housing at the outset rather than having to fend for themselves until they are in a crisis situation, taxpayers would be saved more than half this money, according to a report released in September 2012 by the Canadian Homeless Research Network (*Saskatoon StarPhoenix*, 25 Sept. 2012). Passion for Action believes that three-quarters of the people occupying city shelters may actually be working full time. Housing First in Calgary could become a model for Saskatoon. This new initiative, whose objective is 'rapid re-housing,' aims to find permanent accommodation for the homeless; 2,600 of an estimated 4,000 homeless have been assisted, including more than 500 families.

Homelessness is about much more than people without shelter – it has a serious impact on health, including psychological health, and it leaves people more vulnerable to violence and criminal activity. That is why it is so important to move people into housing that is appropriate and truly affordable, that is supported by community health and social services, and that offers access to education and justice – social costs decrease as security and stability increase.

## Chapter Seven

# Housing Providers

## Who Provides Housing for Urban Aboriginal People?

The provision of housing to urban Aboriginal people ranges from the very positive to the extremely negative. On the positive side, the federal government and other national organizations – notably the Canada Mortgage and Housing Corporation (CMHC) – as well as provincial and municipal governments and organizations have all played active roles in promoting and making available affordable housing to all Canadians with low to moderate incomes. On the negative side, Saskatoon has experienced a problem of pervasive 'slumlords,' who operate numerous properties in the inner west side neighbourhoods that have the highest concentration of Aboriginal residents. The introduction to this chapter describes affordable housing policies and initiatives at the national, provincial, and municipal levels; then it discusses the controversial role of 'slumlords' in providing cheaper housing. The chapter includes two case studies conducted within the Bridges and Foundations Project. Both are surveys of the clients of two Aboriginal housing organizations: SaskNative Rentals, originally a Metis organization; and Cress Housing, affiliated with the Saskatoon Tribal Council, which serves First Nations residents.

### National Housing Policies and Initiatives

Housing policies in Canada, and thus Saskatchewan and Saskatoon, are very complex. They are determined by three levels of government – national, provincial, municipal – and by related organizations at these levels. National housing policies and programs can be divided into three basic sorts: those developed and enacted by the federal government; those by autonomous government agencies; and those by non-government organizations.

## 1. The Government of Canada

While Canadian federal housing policies have been described and analysed in historical perspective (Rose 1980; Carter 1981; Finkel 2006), the discussion here will be limited primarily to the most recent several years. During the 1980s, federal support for housing focused mainly on housing supply, especially construction of social housing; the federal government was a primary funder of housing projects involving all levels of government as well as not-for-profit organizations. However, by 1996, federal government involvement began to decline as concern increased about deficit financing for social programs and as the provinces renewed their pressure on the federal government to withdraw from areas that the provinces and municipalities considered to be under their jurisdiction, including housing. In 1996, devolution agreements with most of the provinces culminated in the federal government transferring responsibility for most social housing programs to the provincial governments (PRI 2005, 21; Carter 2000, 1–6). After that year, the federal government's presence in social housing was largely curtailed, except as it related to cooperative housing and to programs providing limited initial funding for the construction of social housing by community groups.

Yet within three years, under provincial government pressure, the Government of Canada began to re-enter the field of social housing and homelessness through the National Homelessness Initiative in 1999 and the Affordable Housing Program in 2001. The latter actually involved joint funding by the federal and provincial governments to develop affordable housing through both new construction and rehabilitation. The Government of Canada also created the Residential Rehabilitation Assistance Program (RRAP) to provide financial resources to homeowners intending to renovate existing substandard housing stocks (CMHC 2005a). In 2004, the Liberal government in Ottawa, recognizing the affordable housing crisis facing Canadians, made fiscal contributions to housing that included $1 billion to create new affordable housing as well as investments of $384 million in renovation assistance to preserve and make better use of existing affordable housing stock, particularly in urban and core areas. This was in addition to $2 billion invested annually to support some 639,000 housing units. Despite the lack of a comprehensive national housing policy, the Government of Canada's commitment to affordable housing has been significant.

Just prior to the national election of 23 January 2006, the Liberal government had been considering collaborating with the private home-building sector to build more homes on reserves facing the most severe housing shortages. The Kelowna Accord announced by the Liberal government in November 2005 consisted of a $5.1 billion package to fight Native poverty; it included assistance in homeownership (but aimed at reserves, not cities) as well as programs to improve skills in the construction trades such as carpentry, in collaboration with the Assembly of First Nations (AFN), the Metis National Council, Inuit Tapirit Kanatami, the Congress of Aboriginal Peoples (CAP), and the National Women's Association of Canada. Yet by 2006, financing for Native housing had not increased substantially for at least 15 years.

However, the government was defeated in the 2006 election and a new Conservative policy was initiated. That policy immediately made it clear that the Kelowna Accord would not be honoured. The federal budget tabled in March 2007 was criticized for excluding poor, homeless Aboriginals. For example, although the government announced that it would be spending $6 billion on new programs, only $70 million was now destined for such Aboriginal programs as job training, enhancing the Aboriginal Justice Strategy, and strengthening commercial fisheries. Reportedly $21 million a year was actually being spent; yet the finance minister argued that $9 billion was already being spent on Aboriginal programs. The AFN continued to press for First Nations skills development programs. In the wake of the Kelowna Accord, former Liberal Prime Minister Paul Martin launched a corporate-sponsored $50 million fund to assist Aboriginal entrepreneurs; the Martin Aboriginal Education Initiative includes a high school program aimed at teaching business skills.

By 2008 the federal government's contribution to affordable housing had reached $1 billion. It had also committed to invest another $1.8 billion in affordable housing, housing services for the homeless, and renovation of existing housing stock (CMHC 2005c). Then, in October 2008, a Conservative federal government was re-elected. This government did not initially think of itself as being in the social housing business, yet by 2009 it had promised to commit some $5 billion over the coming five years to provide shelter to the needy, as part of a massive financial package designed to stimulate the economy in a time of recession. Again, this funding would be administered through the provincial governments. Yet there was still no discussion of a national housing policy. Advocates for social housing have reportedly been deeply disappointed with the federal government's apparent lack of urgency and with the slow progress on housing at all levels of government (*Globe and Mail*, 5 December 2009).

The 2008 federal budget was also criticized for ignoring Aboriginal issues; indeed, the AFN claimed that its funding was decreasing. Finally, the 2009 budget did include $400 million for Aboriginal housing, in addition to another $515 million for other (non-housing) Aboriginal infrastructure projects, $305 million for Aboriginal health care delivery, and $200 million for skills training (with a goal of 6,000 new positions). However, the housing funding was for on-reserve housing rather than urban housing; it was to be divided nationally among 650 First Nations; it excluded Metis and urban Aboriginal people; and it was not annual but biannual, to be distributed over three years. In 2009 the federal Minister of Indian and Northern Affairs promised a $60 million fund for reserve housing, to be administered through CMHC, INAC, and the First Nations Housing Liaison Committee of the Assembly of First Nations (AFN); the intention was for reserves to apply for financing through this fund to support specific housing projects. When he met with the federal minister, the chief of the FSIN emphasized that more financing should allow seniors to stay on reserve instead of having to move into special care facilities in the city; and again, this new national funding would exempt urban First Nations people in need of adequate or improved housing.

The AFN has argued that the much-publicized federal apology for residential schools should now be followed by appropriate and sufficient funding, especially since the Conservative cancellation of the Kelowna Accord, which would have helped narrow the gap in Aboriginal housing, health, training, and skills development. The AFN has continued to press the federal government, now for $3 billion in 'stimulus funds' aimed in part at improving housing (yet again, only on reserve). Currently the federal government has promised to work with First Nations leaders in various respects, particularly aimed at improving the quality of life on reserves through placing sound education programs in place in reserve schools, eliminating obstacles to job creation, improving reserve governance, and identifying obstacles to economic growth on reserve. Yet though heralded as a major shift in policy and relations, this collaboration obviously does not directly affect First Nations residents in cities, nor Metis, much less urban Aboriginal housing. In fact, the federal budget actually *reduced* even reserve housing from $318 million in 2008–9 to $157 million in 2011–12 (*Globe and Mail*, 11 June 2011). Decreasing reserve finances have effectively caused reserves to fall further behind in delivery of basic services while provinces receive an average annual increase of 6% for statutory programs (Cuthand in *Saskatoon StarPhoenix*, 10 June 2011). Moreover, as the CRHA has pointed out in a news release (6 June 2011), 'with no new funding announcements [in the latest federal budget] for housing and homelessness, the situation of an estimated 1.5 million Canadians unable to afford adequate housing has not been improved.' It is now estimated that more than 20,000 housing units are urgently needed nationwide for First Nations on reserve. On one Alberta reserve, fully one-quarter of the 1,500 residents remaining on reserve are on a waiting list for housing, even though that reserve has made $115 million over the past five years from a casino (*Globe and Mail*, 11 June 2011).

At a summit held in January 2012, some 400 of the 630 First Nations chiefs in Canada met in Ottawa. Many of these chiefs had the impression that the summit was surprisingly disorganized and that opportunities to improve relations with the federal government were not effectively enough pursued. In fact, although this was the first meeting of the prime minister with such a large body of chiefs, he met with just 30 chiefs at a reportedly impromptu closed session. The primary focus of these discussions was on economic activity on First Nations lands – that is, on exploitation of natural resources, particularly on larger reserves with relatively higher employment. Strikingly, no specific attention seems to have been paid to improving housing, other than simply recognizing it as a crucial issue. The prime minister promised 'creative ways, collaborative ways, ways that involve consultation between our government, the provinces, and First Nations leadership and communities, ways that provide options within the [Indian] Act or outside of it for practical, incremental and real change.' More specifically than this elaborate and highly generalized statement, this means provision of multiyear funding to First Nations governments 'deemed to be functioning at a high level'; working towards self-sufficiency of First Nations and removing barriers to self-governance while respecting treaty relationships; reviewing the structure of financial arrangements between the federal government and First Nations; and creating an economic task force 'to look at ways to unlock the potential of Native communities.' In any case, the resulting Canada-First Nations Joint Action Plan has been rejected by the FSIN and other Western chiefs.

The Conservative federal government announced in March 2012 its 'intent to explore' with interested First Nations the option of proceeding with legislation extending property rights on reserve and privatization of reserve property and land; this became reinforced in August as the proposed First Nations Property Ownership Act (FNPOA). This concept had been advocated particularly by Tom Flanagan, a former research director of the Reform Party and adviser to the Conservative Party, and now a political science professor at the University of Calgary, who was the author of *First Nations? Second Thoughts* (2000) and co-author of *Beyond the Indian Act: Restoring Aboriginal Property Rights* (2010). However, the question of private ownership on reserve is fast becoming an increasingly contentious issue among First Nations. The AFN had already passed a resolution in 2010 rejecting the notion of private property ownership on reserve. At the time and subsequently, the AFN and most chiefs have argued that the FNPOA could allow non-Aboriginal interests to control, own, and exploit resource-rich Native land; impose a foreign conception of land value and offend traditional communal approaches to land and property ownership; erode traditional collective rights; negate constitutionally protected land and treaty rights; represent the federal government 'interfering with First Nations jurisdiction over our lands'; subvert First Nations' decision-making processes; and distract from the continuing work in First Nations to reform land management, in keeping with deconstruction of the colonial past. For its part, the FSIN was 'outraged and insulted' for not being properly consulted. Moreover, Aboriginal Affairs and Northern Development Canada (which has replaced INAC) collaborates with CMHC in the recently created First Nations Market Housing Fund to facilitate the development of market housing on reserves. The idea behind the Conservative government's First Nations property ownership and market housing initiatives is that First Nations residents cannot own their property on reserve (although they can off reserve), therefore cannot easily access a mortgage. Rather housing and property ownership are traditionally controlled by the First Nation, which is responsible for arranging the construction of new homes, repair and maintenance of existing homes, and distribution of housing, which penultimately requires federal government approval – too often a long drawn-out process. The proposed legislation would permit (not force) a First Nation to opt into the program and hold the legal 'fee simple' title to all or part of reserve property or land; however it would thereby render any 'fee simple' reserve property or land available to outside developers, 'eroding our collective rights in our reserved lands.' But how, exactly, this would relate to the question of private ownership of housing on reserves remains to be seen. Which reserves, exactly, would be able to access this Fund? To date, in Saskatchewan just two First Nations: La Ronge and Onion Lake, both large, populous, and enterprising First Nations. Whitecap First Nation has, of course, proceeded to develop its own market housing among several multimillion-dollar developments, but not in conjunction with the Fund. Smaller, less developed First Nations are not as likely to pursue market housing on reserve, nor as capable. And how, exactly, would all these initiatives impact urban First Nations people now representing virtually half the First Nations people of Canada, and their housing issues in particular (Anderson 2012)? There may be obvious implications of this potential movement towards privatization of reserve property – notably including housing – for urban Aboriginal housing, not only because this movement could affect migration between reserve and city with the possible improvement of housing and living conditions on reserve, but also because First Nations invest directly in urban housing, moreover housing may be developed on urban reserves.

The federal government anticipates cutting millions of dollars in funding to First Nations, particularly in Saskatchewan. The current core funding of the FSIN – an operating budget of $1.6 million – is slated to be reduced drastically by two-thirds – down to $500,000. The federal government said that these 'changes' were to help make First Nations 'healthier and self-sufficient.' Moreover, federal officials have suggested that funding is being reduced due to expected national interest rate increases; whereas financial experts have in fact predicted relatively stable and low interest rates in the foreseeable future. However, First Nations leaders in Saskatchewan and elsewhere in Canada argue that these cuts in funding will have a devastating effect on program delivery – not the least in housing. The shortage of reserve housing in Canada has most recently been estimated as at least 80,000 units, with 44,000 needing major repairs. These leaders had thought that the Attawapiskat housing crisis in northern Ontario would have led to a federal government increase in social housing funding as well as finally more explicit recognition of treaty right to shelter. Instead, a 30% reduction in CMHC funding for reserve housing construction and maintenance in Saskatchewan has been announced for the coming year: $18.7 million, down from $26.2 million the previous year. Although the province now has a shortage of at least 11,000 units on reserves, there are plans to build just 159 new homes on reserves through CMHC funding during the next two years.

It is becoming increasingly difficult for some smaller and poorer First Nations to qualify for CMHC/AANDC funding: of 74 First Nations, 27 qualified but only 14 received federal funding commitments. Unfortunately, the pressing need for reserve housing is rapidly increasing just as funding is being curtailed: many reserves now have occupancy rates that are double the provincial average. As Cuthand has observed, 'cutting back on housing in a time of crisis doesn't make sense. The federal government seems to have placed a low priority on improving living conditions in First Nations communities.' Meanwhile, the office of the minister of human resources and skills development points out that the government 'has made and will continue to make significant investments in First Nations housing' (*Saskatoon StarPhoenix*, 8, 9, 17 Aug., 7 Sept. 2012).

## 2. Canada Mortgage and Housing Corporation

To 'help[] Canadians in need,' CMHC provides 'financial assistance to maintain the quality of existing homes for low-income Canadians and support the creation of new affordable housing; technical and financial support to help housing providers develop affordable housing projects by and for their communities; funding for Aboriginal Canadians to build and renovate housing on- and off-reserve; and support for individuals and families whose needs are not being met through the marketplace' (CMHC 2008). CMHC coordinates these efforts through its Affordable Housing Centre.

Through CMHC the former Liberal government was committing approximately $2 billion a year to address the housing needs of lower-income residents living in some 636,000 units of existing housing stock (CMHC 2005d). The CMHC's policy of insuring 'risky' mortgages, announced in June 2006, has generated some apprehension (*Globe and Mail,* 17 July 2006); however, our experience in the Bridges and Foundations Project suggests that innovative measures must be taken in order to make truly affordable homeownership and even renting available to poorer residents, including most Aboriginal people living in cities. To its credit, CMHC has sponsored a variety of studies bearing directly on urban Aboriginal housing (e.g., Green 2001; CMHC 2004c, February 2005, May 2007).

CMHC offers a broad variety of programs to assist builders and residents in achieving affordable homeownership options and in solving the housing crisis facing Canadians. Specific affordable housing programs and initiatives now include these: Seed Funding; Proposal

Development Funding (PDF), which provides loans up to $100,000 to help with expenses incurred during the development of an affordable housing development proposal; the Residential Rehabilitation Assistance Program (RRAP); renovation programs; Smaller Scale Home Improvements; and Mortgage Loan Insurance (MLI), aimed at reducing the down payment required for a home. Aboriginal Capacity Development helps First Nations people work toward self-sufficiency in housing through training sessions for property management planning and home maintenance, healthy housing project development, and Aboriginal youth career fairs. With the slogan 'opening the door,' CMHC aims ideally at facilitating the supply of 'affordable, quality housing for all Canadians.' To encourage homeownership, CMHC offers 'innovative mortgage loan insurance products and tools that meet the needs of both lenders and consumers,' as well as 'Mortgage-Backed Securities and Canada Mortgage Bonds to help lower the overall cost of borrowing.' Yet CMHC also recognizes the need to assist rentals and renters, through 'flexible financing options to assist traditional and non-traditional borrowers in all parts of the country, including nursing homes, rental projects and other market segments not served by the private sector' (CMHC 2008). CMHC also provides counselling services aimed at generating community support. Specific examples of CMHC-backed affordable housing projects include the Housing Opportunity Partnership (HOP) in Winnipeg (aimed at west end rejuvenation); the Assisted Home Ownership Program (AHOP) in Ottawa, inclusive of the Multi-Faith Housing Initiative (homeowner and rental housing options for a range of income levels, all under one roof); and the Wave Project in Toronto (a private developer offering a purchase plan that brings homeownership within reach of first-time buyers and low- to moderate-income renters).

CMHC has long promoted small houses as a means of ensuring affordability. From 1947 to 1974, it published catalogues of designs for small houses by Canadian architects with the intention of addressing a housing shortage while improving living standards. Today, as part of its consultation process, the agency provides online information on how to select housing in keeping with lifestyle and finances. CMHC is by far the largest provider of default insurance on mortgages in Canada, with mortgage insurance now capped at $600 billion and assets of $345.3 billion in 2009 (*Globe and Mail*, 17 October 2009).

In early July 2011, CMHC created a $1.5 billion fund for assisted housing under a framework agreement with the federal government. Yet these funds were not new – rather, they were what remained from the federal–provincial agreement in 2008 to provide $1.9 billion over five years to assist poorer Canadians, including many urban Aboriginal residents, who were struggling to pay their rent or to find any shelter at all. While the CMHC cost-sharing program is intended to build new affordable homes and renovate older homes, rather than to provide direct grants or subsidies, it will be up to provincial governments, in collaboration with municipal governments identifying needs, to leverage sufficient financial resources from these national funds in order to achieve the goal of putting a roof over the heads of vulnerable residents at a more affordable cost (*Globe and Mail*,11 July 2011).

The Conservative federal government has most recently decided to scrutinize CMHC administration and operations through the national banking regulating agency, the Office of the Superintendent of Financial Institutions, arguing that more transparency and accountability are overdue. CMHC controls more than $500 billion worth of higher-risk mortgages, and has assets of $281 billion, more than the Bank of Canada, which has assets of $167 billion. The government intends to halt banks using mortgages insured by CMHC as collateral on covered bonds, on the grounds that this process exceeds CMHC's mandate. CMHC was originally established largely to provide social housing (initially to veterans) and insure mortgages to homeowners unable to meet down payments, so that more Canadians could be homeowners. However, the relationship between CMHC's mandate as a mortgage insurer and what has become its other main function, providing support for social housing for lower-income earners and, increasingly in collaboration with INAC/AANDC, on-reserve housing, has not been well defined; CMHC has become over-extended (*Globe and Mail*, 27 and 28 Apr. 2012).

3. National Non-Government Organizations

The Canadian Housing and Renewal Association (CHRA) was until recently heavily funded by the federal government. It has become the most comprehensive non-government organization to advocate for improved affordable housing, arguing that although 'Canadians hold access to decent housing to be a basic human right … still, growing numbers of our poorest citizens are denied access to adequate and affordable housing.' While applauding the Homeless Partnering Strategy announced in 2007, the CHRA points out that 'fixing homelessness alone does not address its root causes – among them a lack of affordable housing and the absence of a comprehensive and adequately-funded long-term national housing agency.' The CHRA appropriately questions the very notion and misuse of the term 'affordability': 'Low-income households cannot now and never will be able to afford the market cost of housing.' So in pressuring government, CHRA emphasizes that 'we cannot continue as we are now. The cost of inaction is too great' (*Saskatoon StarPhoenix*, 25 January 2008).

The Canadian Home Builders' Association (CHBA) unites provincial (e.g., the CHBA Saskatchewan) and local (e.g., the Saskatoon and Region Home Builders' Association – SRHBA) associations representing the homebuilding industry. The creation of the Affordability and Choice Today (ACT) initiative brought together the Federation of Canadian Municipalities, the CHBA, and the CHRA to share approaches to creating sustainable communities, preserving neighbourhood character, and making available more housing choices; however, it was not specific to the Saskatoon or prairie market and did not specifically address Aboriginal issues (Energy Pathways 1994).The Policy Research Initiative (PRI) also has addressed issues of housing policy. Housing policies particularly impact urban Aboriginal populations, so national, provincial, and local Aboriginal organizations have long been pressing for improved housing conditions. The most comprehensive organization specifically focused on Aboriginal housing issues is the National Aboriginal Housing Association (NAHA), which in turn encompasses provincial housing organizations such as the Metis Urban Housing Association of Saskatchewan (MUHAS).

*Provincial Policies and Initiatives*

Constitutionally, housing tends to be regarded primarily as a provincial responsibility: the provinces retain formal control over the design and delivery of both supply- and demand-side housing policies, although provincial governments can download this authority to municipal governments to facilitate community-based plans (PRI 2005, 21–2).

The Saskatchewan Housing Corporation (SHC), commonly known as Sask Housing, is an agency of the provincial Ministry of Social Services. The Director of Housing Development recently commented that the province takes a 'balanced approach' to affordable housing projects, meaning that the three levels of government should share the costs of these projects. He suggested that improvements in the vacancy rate have been a direct result of the province's commitment to funding affordable housing projects (*Saskatoon StarPhoenix*, 15 December 2010).

Despite the former NDP provincial government's intention to provide housing to at least 32,000 low- to modest-income households whose needs could not be met through the private market, there were still an estimated 56,000 households in Saskatchewan in 2002 lacking access to quality affordable housing (Government of Saskatchewan 2002). In 2004 the SHC maintained approximately 30,400 social housing units in 345 communities around the province. Of these, 18,400 were administered directly by SHC and targeted low-income seniors and families; another 11,100 were administered through agreements with not-for-profit groups and cooperatives for special-needs and low- to moderate-income families. However, SHC already appeared to be moving away from long-term funding commitments and more toward building self-sufficiency for clients. This was to be accomplished through the creation of 2,000 new homeownership and rental units and the repair and energy retrofit of existing homes. SHC was also focusing on converting family social housing units into owner-occupied units and on the disposal of marginal social housing units (Jones 2004). This would mean more options for low- to moderate-income families in Saskatoon; the challenge would be to find the land to build the units as well as builders to construct them (builders, after all, are business people concerned with profitable investments). The other challenge would be to ensure that the families chosen to enter into homeownership from rental housing were prepared for homeownership.

In 2005 the then-NDP provincial government announced three new home-upgrade programs to help low-income homeowners and tenants, including residents with disabilities, as well as landlords: first, a program for emergency repairs; second, a program called Adaptations for Independence that would allow people to make any necessary changes to their dwelling so that they could live independently, through a forgivable loan of $3,500; and third, a program that would allow landlords to bring their properties up to provincial standards by repairing and renovating rental units, through $6,000 to $9,000 forgivable loans.

HomeFirst was a strategy of the former NDP provincial government. This was a collection of programs targeting low- to medium-income families that involved housing supplements for special-needs groups as well as increased homeownership. This program provided forgivable loans of up to $20,000 and repayable low-interest mortgages of up to $30,000 for households making less than $50,000.

The Centenary Affordable Housing Program (CAHP) allows for the development of affordable housing for low- to medium-income families that will be available at or below market prices. The emphasis of this program is on creating additional affordable housing through new construction and on enabling lower- to moderate-income households to become successful homeowners. The CAHP provides one-time capital assistance to increase the supply of off-reserve affordable housing in Saskatchewan for low- to moderate-income households. Funding for this program is provided by all three levels of government: CMHC, SHC, and municipal governments. All housing that receives funding must be targeted to households with gross household incomes from all sources under the Maximum Income Limits set by SHC. For example, in June 2003, $3.2 million was received for four housing projects in Saskatoon through CAHP. At the time, CAHP expected to receive $45.8 million over the next five years from SHC, CMHC, municipalities, and other sources. Four hundred new homes had been given final funding under the CAHP Program. The plan was to deliver approximately 2,000 within five years. But while CAHP provides necessary funding toward affordable housing in Saskatoon, it qualifies a very narrow segment of the population.

The Neighbourhood Home Ownership Program (NHOP) has provided financial assistance to homeowner cooperatives for the down payment on a home. The home must be located in an inner-city area or a core neighbourhood in a major Saskatchewan urban centre. And lastly, Encouraging Community Housing Options has provided financial assistance for not-for-profit and private corporations, municipalities, and cooperatives to determine the feasibility of developing and investing in housing projects in communities where affordable housing is not available. Grants are available to eligible applicants who are interested in developing affordable housing for low- to medium-income families.

In November 2007, Saskatchewan's NDP government had announced that $100 million would be earmarked for the SHC, of which $60 million would go to the HomeFirst program and $22.8 million to support affordable housing projects in Saskatoon. Another $250,000 would help fund the Saskatoon Food Bank. The NDP also committed itself to be a major donor for the Station 20 West project in Saskatoon (*Saskatoon StarPhoenix*, 29 February and 21 April 2007). Also, it was contemplating an imposition of rent controls and a moratorium on condo conversions (contrary to the advice of Saskatoon civic officials). An existing city by-law already required two years for condo conversions, to give tenants adequate time to find new accommodations; also, tenants had the first option to buy the condominium (*StarPhoenix*, 11 August 2007). Then in October, just one month before the provincial election, the NDP announced $45 million for inner-city housing initiatives for low-income families (many of them Aboriginal), including $15.7 million for a variety of SHC projects in Saskatoon: 185 new housing units, a downtown supported-living residence, renovation of three apartment buildings to be managed by the province, construction of 19 Habitat for Humanity homes, a HomeFirst secondary suites program, expansion of the HomeFirst homeownership program, and deferred payments for low-interest mortgages (*StarPhoenix*, 6 October 2007).

When the Saskatchewan Party defeated the NDP in that election, the new provincial government wasted no time in cancelling the Station 20 West project, which would have developed a major community centre right in the middle of the two Saskatoon neighbourhoods with the greatest Aboriginal concentration. The 2008 provincial budget was sharply criticized for 'shortchanging' Saskatoon, for failing to fund a replacement for St Mary's school (the Catholic school with the highest Aboriginal enrolment, which was scheduled either for demolition or for preservation as a historic site), and for doing little to address the critical shortage of affordable housing. In September 2008 the SHC's HomeFirst program announced that it had run into financial difficulties, having used up its entire $22.5 million budget for two to five years in just eight months (*Saskatoon StarPhoenix*, 8 September 2008). In June 2008 a task force report titled *Affordable Housing: An Investment* suggested that the 'situation and solutions are complex, costly and difficult' and recommended that the province 'more aggressively seek immigrants who can help fill the shortages in the building trade.' But what about urban Aboriginals? The task force pointed out that there had been little or no rental apartment construction in Saskatchewan in more than 20 years. It also criticized the SHC for not being as effective as it should be – in fact, the task force called on the provincial government to overhaul the SHC in order to make it the lynchpin for the creation of affordable housing in the province. In January 2009, after what was billed as a 'historic meeting' between First Nations leaders and the provincial cabinet, the former commented that the two sides seemed to be 'poles apart' on key issues (*StarPhoenix*, 20 March and 7 and 26 June 2008; 27 January 2009).

Since the change in provincial government following the 2007 election, Sask Housing has spent $36 million to help build 412 units of affordable rental units in Saskatoon and has committed $40 million to another 590 units (400 of which will be in student residences at the University of Saskatchewan) (*Saskatoon StarPhoenix*, 15 December 2010).

The Saskatchewan government announced in March 2011 that it would be investing $1.7 million for two new housing initiatives to increase the supply of affordable housing, and that it would spend $252 million over the next five years to build at least 4,600 homes for people with modest incomes. Specifically, the HeadStart on a Home program will spend most of this amount on low-interest loans for property developers, covering 90% of construction costs (the remaining 10% paid by the developer), at a 4% interest rate. The construction or redevelopment project must be in the range of $180,000 to $300,000. Additionally, government grants of up to $5,000 per rental unit built are to be offered to construction companies to build new apartments and row housing, on a matching basis with municipalities (the Affordable New Home Development Foundation may also provide a $5,000 subsidy). First-time home buyers meeting 'certain income requirements' will be reimbursed the education portion of the municipal property tax. Habitat for Humanity will receive a $1.5 million subsidy to construct 30 new homes for low-income families.

A significant step in the right direction for a better-coordinated provincial housing strategy has been the first-ever comprehensive Saskatchewan Housing and Development Summit, called in April 2011 by the social services minister, where $6 million in provincial funding for creative affordable-housing proposals was announced. This will increase private-sector investment in housing, stimulate new affordable housing design, and finance those who are developing new types of housing. The summit brought together the SHC, the Saskatchewan Home Builders' Association, developers, low-income housing providers, shelter operators, not-for-profit community/housing organizations, financing agencies, and, not the least, First Nations and Metis organizations. The Summit Action Fund now supports eight housing projects receiving a total of $2,697,900 in government grants (*Saskatoon StarPhoenix*, 11 February 2012).

In August 2011 the provincial government declared that increasing housing supply and improving affordability are among its top priorities; the government claimed that it had put $263 million into housing in that one year, including an additional $5 million in new funding for the SHC homeownership and rental construction incentive program. Then an agreement signed in September with the federal government would see $55 million spent on affordable housing in Saskatchewan during the next three years, with each government contributing $9.27 million a year. The government is specifically encouraging construction of new homes and the development of rental units for families with low to moderate incomes in Saskatoon; home renovation, homeownership assistance, rent supplements, shelter allowances, and accommodations for victims of domestic abuse are to be included in this funding. On 16 October 2012 Saskatchewan Premier Brad Wall announced that a new Saskatchewan Plan for Growth will spend $2.5 billion over the next three budgets on 'infrastructure,' with $150 million coming out of the Growth and Financial Security Fund to create a new agency, SaskBuilds, which will invest $344 million in housing projects, including construction of 12,600 units for low- to moderate-income families. Moreover, both a home repair program and the Conversion Initiative will be redesigned. The former program combines ten repair and adaptation programs, and is aimed at assisting homeowners and rental property owners housing lower-income tenants to maintain repairs on their properties as a market asset; while the latter program will focus on development of new rental housing by private and non-profit groups converting non-residential properties into residential use.

However, the response of the NDP and some social agencies was less than enthusiastic in this election year. The NDP countered with a proposed policy of $250 million over four years (saved by increasing royalties paid by the potash industry), as well as a commitment to community-based organizations and cooperatives. It announced plans to build 2,500 affordable housing units and 1,000 units for students. It earmarked $20 million 'to fight homelessness'; and it declared its intention to defend rent controls. The party argued that 'the market simply is not taking care of the needs of families – and we intend to do something about it'. The Regina Anti-Poverty Ministry called these new provincial government initiatives 'a really limited response to the housing crisis' in Saskatchewan. In its view, the government needs to take steps to ensure that the costs for basic needs such as housing are actually affordable; a more significant government investment in terms of funding for both social housing and affordable housing initiatives is 'urgently needed'; and no real commitments to affordable social housing are to be found in the provincial budget (which is surprising, considering the massive resource wealth of the province). The province should be able to invest in income security programs and affordable housing. The NDP's housing and social services critic commented that when it came to housing, the 2011 provincial budget was 'an embarrassment … The government is completely unprepared to deal with the housing crisis we find ourselves in.' Housing is, after all, the highest-priority issue when it comes to affordable living in Saskatchewan. In the NDP's view, the provincial government could have done much more. The NDP suggested that the government's latest plan was undermining the affordable housing consultation process already under way and failing to address the real economic issues behind the housing crisis. The City of Saskatoon had already adopted a variety of affordable housing initiatives; why, critics wondered, had it taken the provincial government so long to follow suit and adopt a more aggressive approach to resolving the housing dilemma? (*Saskatoon StarPhoenix*, 24 and 29 March 2011, 23 April 2011).The NDP continued to criticize the provincial government's housing initiatives as lacking specific targets and benchmarks, and regarded the sudden and long overdue announcements of new housing initiatives as simply in anticipation of the provincial election. That election was held on 7 November 2011; the Saskatchewan Party overwhelmingly defeated the NDP.

The provincial policy of encouraging international immigration into Saskatchewan has raised some concern from an Aboriginal viewpoint. Increasing immigration and immigrant retention have clearly contributed to population and economic growth in Saskatchewan. However, to what extent has this trend been adding to the disadvantage faced by urban Aboriginal people? A recent editorial in the *Saskatoon StarPhoenix* (11 July 2011) commented: 'Whether it's immigrants or migrants from other provinces lured here to try to acquire a share of Saskatchewan's new wealth, or Aboriginal people moving to urban centres from reserves looking for opportunities sadly lacking in their economically and socially marginalized communities, the affordable housing they need to establish themselves is in short supply.' More specifically, political commentator Murray Mandryk has pointedly asked: 'Does a government need to spend valuable public resources on an immigration recruitment project that sounds as if it's mostly about meeting the niche needs of some construction companies? With First Nations unemployment far exceeding 14% in Saskatchewan, one might think the government needs a grander view of this issue. Shouldn't First Nations people with bleak employment prospects be its foremost priority?' (*Saskatoon StarPhoenix*, 6 Jan. 2012). Coincidentally, the provincial government intends to invest more than $200 million into the HeadStart on a Home program over the next five years to construct at least 1,000 new homes ranging in price from $180,000 to $300,000; not only is this cost well beyond any notion of affordability for most Aboriginal people, but these funds are tellingly to be derived from the Saskatchewan Immigrant Investor Fund.

*Municipal Policies and Initiatives*

1. The City of Saskatoon

Typically, to address shortcomings in the current housing system, municipalities and community housing organizations call for increased funding so that they can meet the responsibilities that provincial governments expect them to meet (PRI 2005, 23).

The City of Saskatoon has played an active role in affordable housing initiatives over the past several years. The City has made a strong commitment to affordable housing. To illustrate: it has hired a full-time Housing Facilitator, who works in the City Planning Branch; it has formed a Social Housing Advisory Committee (SHAC); it has established an Affordable Housing Reserve, which is dedicated to providing funding for housing initiatives; it has developed the Downtown Housing and Revitalization Action Plan as well as a housing database; it has strengthened enforcement of housing quality standards; and it has amended zoning by-laws to allow for secondary suites in all residential areas of the city (City of Saskatoon 2001). Also, the City regularly publishes *The Renters' Handbook* to help renters understand their rights and responsibilities, landlords' responsibilities, and health and safety standards.

The City of Saskatoon Development Plan was completed in 1998; this was followed by the City of Saskatoon Strategic Plan in 2004. City Council approved the Downtown Housing Incentives policy in August 2002, and updated it in May 2008 'to encourage residential development in the downtown area by providing financial and/or tax-based incentives to developers or owners of eligible residential properties.' In July 2007 the City announced a target of '500 affordable dwelling units annually, to be achieved with the participation and partnership of numerous sectors, including government-supported providers, financial institutions, developers, investors and faith-based groups.' To date the City has completed 1,200 units while another 1,000 are currently being constructed. However, a report to City Council in December 2011 estimated that at least 10,000 new homes would be needed over the next three years; of these, 81% would be in the suburbs, the remainder 'infill' housing in the inner city and in existing neighbourhoods (*Saskatoon StarPhoenix*, 3 December 2011). In short, very little of this new housing could possibly apply to poorer Aboriginal residents. Civic affairs columnist Gerry Klein has emphasized the need for 'managed growth' – but will the large and growing Aboriginal population be an important part of this management?

The City has developed comprehensive community business and housing plans and repeatedly revised them (e.g., City of Saskatoon 2001, 2002b, 2003c, 2006, 2007a, 2007b, 2008). The Housing Business Plan formulated in 2009 has as its vision 'to build a city where everyone can live in homes that provide a safe, stable, adequate, and affordable environment from which to participate in, and contribute to, the growth and development of stable neighbourhoods in our community.' The City's stated mission is to

> actively and creatively work with housing providers, community organizations, business, and all orders of government and other stakeholders to support the market through incentives, good planning, and collaboration in creative initiatives to increase the supply of affordable housing. The City will focus on creating a permanent supply of affordable housing and related supports for people who are at risk of homelessness, have special needs, are transitioning toward independence, or are simply low to moderate income earners … [According to the Plan,] the City understands that permanent, affordable, appropriate, safe, and secure housing is the necessary foundation for building healthy, well-educated, creative, and economically viable neighbourhoods. [Moreover,] the City, working with other levels of government, the private sector, and community organizations has chosen to focus its resources and efforts in the middle of the housing continuum – particularly on affordable and entry-level housing in both the rental and home ownership markets. [The focus of the Plan] is to encourage and support an environment where the market is more likely to supply housing that is inclusive, innovative, and integrated into all neighbourhoods.

The City intends to support housing that falls outside the conventional market and to work in a collaborative manner 'to ensure a range of suitable affordable housing is made available across the community in a choice of locations.' Moreover, 'the City also has a role in monitoring the condition of existing housing to ensure that homes throughout the city meet minimum health and safety standards' (City of Saskatoon 2008). The City is seeking community input into a comprehensive urban plan. A report from the City Manager tabled in December 2009 called for $400,000 to fund an ambitious two-year public engagement and planning process. Housing should be an important part of this process. The present mayor commented in 2009: 'I think one of the biggest things the Council has done is make a tremendous commitment to affordable housing, and rental as well. Over the next five years, $12.5 million is being allotted to affordable housing programs. The commitment at our end is to fund up to 2,000 units at the rate of 500 a year' (*Neighbourhood Express*, 16 December 2009). In October 2012, Mayor Don Atchison announced a renewed goal of constructing 2,500 affordable housing units over the next five years, adding to an equal number constructed during the past five years; specifically, assistance will be provided by the city (in conjunction with the provincial government) for 518 homes per year, particularly affordable entry-level housing and rentals. The new units are intended primarily for lower-income residents, seniors, and students.

The City has been utilizing and exploring several measures aimed at increasing affordable housing stock. In a land trust, a not-for-profit organization holds land for affordable housing, effectively relieving home buyers of the cost of land. Surplus land may be made available for affordable housing – for example, when the City acquires property due to the owner defaulting on tax payments. The City Land Development Program is managed by the Land Branch in partnership with other civic departments: the City, as the land developer, can directly influence the community's affordable housing agenda; the City can direct or hold parcels of land for affordable housing projects, and it can also direct revenue from this development activity into projects that ensure that all citizens benefit from land development growth in the city. Inclusionary zoning may require developers to construct a certain proportion of new affordable housing. In priority reviews, development proposals may be reviewed to see what they intend to contribute to affordable housing. And tax abatements allow owners or developers of new affordable housing to pay the current tax rate for a period of five years, even if substantial improvements may have increased the value of the property.

Civic Affairs columnist Gerry Klein observed recently that as far back as 1969, Saskatoon had a policy to ensure that affordable housing would be distributed throughout the city. Moreover, Saskatoon's involvement in the provision and marketing of housing is all but unprecedented in Canada – it is one of only a couple of Canadian cities to operate its own land bank and act as a major land developer. It does this by applying proceeds from the land bank to leverage a substantial supply of high-quality, affordable homes. Saskatoon has a history of using innovative techniques to address problems that come its way. 'Now is a time for innovation, rather than interference, to spur the marketplace into addressing the challenges of too few accommodations and too high prices.' Noting that CMHC had surveyed the city's approximately 13,000 apartments and found a vacancy rate of just 0.6% – lower than for any other major western city – he lauded the City for approving in principle a proposal to use $6 million of land reserve money for the construction of new rental units (which, however, would add only 1,000 units). In his view, 'while it's laudable that a provincial task force was established to look into affordable housing, if it creates delays … the pain mostly will be felt by those who are in greatest need.' Klein has suggested that the greatest challenge the city faces is living up to its original goal of ensuring that affordable homes are available right across the city. The tendency to build affordable homes on the cheapest land available tends to concentrate and isolate poorer residents, which in turn may damage urban social cohesion. City councillors will have a difficult task convincing voters of the need for more housing diversity in their neighbourhoods (*Saskatoon StarPhoenix*, 6 March and 11 April 2008; 10 March 2011).

City-sponsored incentive programs now include capital funding, property tax abatement, new rental construction land-cost rebates, and permit rebates for secondary suites. Policy-based programs include the direct sale of City-owned land for affordable housing projects and prioritized review of approved affordable housing projects. At the time of writing, a variety of new initiatives of the city's Neighbourhood Planning Section are being implemented. Under the First Home Ownership Program, Saskatoon is identifying City-owned sites for affordable entry-level housing, to be made available to housing providers through a Request for Proposals (RFP) process. The City is working toward establishing a new housing corporation to hold affordable housing units in trust; such a land trust will maintain a permanent stock of affordable housing in which tenants can accumulate equity in exchange for accepting typical homeowner responsibilities. The City is also exploring the creation of new zoning districts designed specifically for affordable and entry-level housing in both new and existing neighbourhoods, and will likely include provisions that constrain the size of dwellings in order to limit costs. The City is also undertaking consultations regarding a bonus provision in the zoning by-laws to encourage the inclusion of affordable entry-level housing in new housing developments. And during a review of the City Development Plan and zoning by-laws, the City is considering allowing the construction of 'granny,' 'garden,' garage, and carriage suites. The latter are self-contained small housing units built on a particular property, presumably to accommo-date elderly residents who need some degree of self-sufficiency yet also regular monitoring; this would have obvious implications for tradi-tional extended Aboriginal families moving into the city.

In December 2011 a City Council committee recommended curtailing financial incentives for new rental housing in inner-city neighbour-hoods, with the intention of spreading subsidized housing throughout the urban area and curbing its concentration in the inner city. According to Alan Wallace, a senior city planner, high concentrations of subsidized rental housing tend to create stigmatized communities. New affordable rental projects in particular neighbourhoods will not be supported by the city if three out of four conditions are met: if the average monthly rent is less than 90% of the city average; if the average rental price of a home is less than 70% of the city average; if the homeownership rate if less than half the city-wide rate of 64%; and if more than 5% of the homes are subsidized rentals. Another new city policy requires that landlords give 12 instead of 6 months' notice before increasing rents.

## 2.  Homebuilders and Developers

The Saskatoon Housing Initiatives Partnership (SHIP) is an organization founded in 1999 by a group of individuals from the private, public, and not-for-profit sectors who were concerned about affordable housing in Saskatoon. SHIP engages stakeholders from a cross-section of the com-munity to enhance housing affordability for low and moderate-income and special needs households. It facilitates financing for affordable housing projects; provides technical assistance and capacity building in the community; and fosters and supports partnerships. This coalition has accomplished quite a lot in recommending affordable housing solu-tions and in providing expertise and resources to builders, investors, home buyers, and renters. Most recently, it has focused on helping hous-ing providers develop project proposals for affordable housing. In 2008, SHIP organized and hosted a National Affordable Home Ownership Conference.

The Saskatoon and Region Home Builders' Association (SRHBA), a not-for-profit trade association organized in 1955 to represent the resi-dential construction industry, works proactively with governments, community groups, housing agencies, and its members to promote sound housing policy for the industry and for consumers. It promotes access to homeownership for all people in the Saskatoon area, as well as quality and innovation from the professional building industry. The SRHBA has been a key player in a multitude of affordable housing initiatives, some of which have been aimed specifically at urban Aboriginal residents. An interesting aspect of its work – one that has considerable potential – involves home improvement and renovation. Through Renoguide, the SRHBA is attempting to coordinate professional renovations at controlled cost.

The Affordable New Home Development Foundation (ANHDF) was established in 1999 'to help individuals and families with lower incomes become owners of affordable new homes.' The ANHDF, a registered not-for-profit organization, provides education and support to families and individuals who want to buy their first home but who, for various reasons, cannot access the traditional marketplace. It works closely with the professional homebuilding industry, the financial community, governments, and the community to design, finance, and build homes that are affordable and to develop alternative forms of homeownership. The foundation has helped more than 300 families buy new homes in various neighbourhoods throughout the city. All new homes are constructed by building members of the SRHBA and are backed by a New Home Warranty, which offers the maximum in quality construction and consumer protection. The ANHDF is based at Sun Ridge Group, which for several years has conducted home energy efficiency upgrades in Saskatoon through federal government programs; however, in January 2012 the federal government terminated new applications to its eco-ENERGY Retrofit program after paying out less than half the $400 million dedicated to this program in the last federal budget (*Globe and Mail*, 31 January 2012).

North Ridge Development Corporation, founded in 1981 and based in Saskatoon, has become one of the largest privately owned single-family homebuilding/development enterprises in the province. North Ridge's primary business is the construction of multiple-unit condominiums and residential housing. North Ridge has long been committed to community development and to providing new housing; however, as a private enterprise, most of this new housing is intended to be profitable and so is not really affordable to much of the Aboriginal population.

The City of Saskatoon and these organizations have long collaborated in developing affordable housing. In addition, the City meets on a regular basis with 'traditional non-profit housing providers,' including those providing housing to Aboriginal residents, such as Cress Housing Corporation, Habitat for Humanity, the Central Urban Metis Federation

Inc. (CUMFI), SaskNative Rentals, the Saskatchewan Housing Authority, and the Saskatoon Housing Coalition. These not-for-profit housing providers rely heavily on provincial and municipal support for capital assistance. In 2004 the ANHDF partnered with CAHP, CMHC, the City of Saskatoon, and SHC to build 50 new affordable homes. The SRHBA established a Business Initiatives Committee, which brought together key stakeholders from the housing industry, financial institutions, governments, and community-based organizations, to create appropriate and affordable housing opportunities that would be relevant to the community's needs. The committee conducted a review of Saskatoon's stock of affordable housing. This included examining the demand for housing and the opportunities to renovate existing units, as well as identifying the stakeholders that should be present in order to represent the interests of all individuals affected by affordable housing in Saskatoon. It found that housing was needed for 7,720 low-income families living below the poverty line; for 5,300 singles living on social assistance; for a fast-growing Aboriginal population, among which 40% of renters were in core housing need; for 6,620 new immigrants and 241 refugees who had arrived in the city; for 26,000 post-secondary students; and for 18,000 residents with special needs that affected the type of housing they required (*Saskatoon StarPhoenix*, 4 October 2006).

Affordable Housing Week, held every year, brings together the City of Saskatoon, SHC, CMHC, SHIP, and housing agencies to emphasize the need to provide a variety of housing options in the community. It recognizes that 'a community gets its character from both its people and the built environment citizens create for themselves.' Furthermore, 'investing in housing at the neighbourhood level' should be the goal of affordable housing. 'Whether they are homeless, have special needs, are transitioning out of a crisis situation, or simply have low to moderate incomes, people who cannot access housing in the marketplace on their own need affordable housing.'

This chapter includes two examples of Aboriginal housing organizations operating in Saskatoon: SaskNative Rentals and Cress Housing. Beyond Saskatoon, though, three other urban Aboriginal housing enterprises merit mention for their innovative practices: N'Amerind Housing Corporation in Regina, Vancouver Native Housing, and M'akala on Vancouver Island. N'Amerind, founded in 1977, has as its mission 'to provide safe, affordable, quality housing and economic development opportunities for Aboriginal people.' With a small staff of about 12, it now runs the Resting Place hospital patients' lodge, 19 condo units (in collaboration with SaskHousing, constituting about 15% of an extensive development), 23 units in an apartment building, as many as 300 houses (mostly single detached), and a small commercial mall, including a pharmacy, in a converted warehouse. N'Amerind now generates almost $1 million a year in revenue, which is reinvested back into affordable housing. The value of the converted warehouse housing the mall has doubled in just five years. The rental apartments are now valued at $100,000; several have recently been bought from N'Amerind. While it operates on a rental basis, homeownership is an option. Energy initiatives are impressive: solar power and electrical generators are used to reduce gas emissions. Properties are redeveloped, using trained contractors; 'spending smarter' is a goal in increasing the living standard by improving appliances and construction materials. Aboriginal control not only of housing but also of building supplies is intentionally sought, yet this implies developing good public relations, especially with government funding bodies. N'Amerind aims to have residents proud to call their properties home; improving relations between tenants and building a sense of community are emphasized. Derelict houses are sold or destroyed and replaced. N'Amerind is remarkably innovative, stressing the need to 'think outside the box' in every challenge.

The Vancouver Native Housing Society, developed by four host First Nations, has developed a wide range of innovatively designed buildings since the 1980s. The architecture incorporates traditional Aboriginal motifs: bas reliefs, wall murals, totem poles. Its priority is to house Aboriginal residents and services, including seniors' facilities, a medical clinic and healing lodge, and even an art gallery. The M'akala Group of Societies and M'akala Housing, with seven local branches on Vancouver Island, provides affordable, quality housing primarily for urban Aboriginal people. Established in 1984 and incorporated four years later as a not-for-profit society, it now provides services to both not-for-profit and for-profit organizations; in fact, entrepreneurialism is emphasized – business opportunities are actively pursued. In accordance with a comprehensive strategic plan, assets are leveraged back into affordable housing. M'akala operates a 50-unit home for persons with disabilities, a 60-unit elders assisted living building, a 40-unit family living complex, a condo tower, housing for youth, suburban land development, joint ventures with First Nations, and mixed residential/commercial development. Culturally sensitive design is employed in many of these properties and enterprises.

## 3. Local Community and Neighbourhood Organizations

Quint Development Corporation is a not-for-profit community economic development (CED) organization operating in Saskatoon's five core neighbourhoods: Riversdale, Caswell Hill, King George, Pleasant Hill, and Westmount. Quint has focused on community development in housing since its inception in 1995. Quint's vision statement reads in part: 'We see citizens who are caring and self-reliant in communities that are safe and stable, where all citizens can participate. We see a vital local economy that uses local resources, sustains jobs, business and community enterprises, with neighbourhoods that are prosperous, beautiful, and environmentally sustainable. We see the community initiating and supporting cultural, recreational, educational and social-economic opportunities for the good of all of us.' Quint's intention is to use affordable housing to foster broader economic and social development. It has worked hard to promote community partnerships; its involvement in housing has been extensive and recognized as highly successful. It has been a model community development agency in inner-city neighbourhoods, encouraging homeownership through its system of cooperative housing. Most recently, it has developed an apartment rental property in an area having the highest proportion of Native people in the city. Despite recent cutbacks, the provincial government continues to fund many Quint projects and programs; for example, it has provided $765,000 for Quint to operate the Male Youth Lodge and Pleasant Hill Place group homes (*Saskatoon StarPhoenix*, 30 March 2010). The Male Youth Lodge provides transitional accommodation for more than 40 homeless young men every year, while supporting them as they seek education, training, and employment opportunities. The Core Neighbourhoods at Work program helps over 300 individuals a year achieve their employment and training goals. Pleasant Hill Place provides supportive transitional housing that allows families to be reunited as an alternative for mothers who are 'at risk' or who have had their children placed into foster care.

Apart from these general initiatives, Aboriginal housing agencies have played a significant role in helping urban First Nations and Metis people access affordable housing. The Saskatoon Tribal Council (STC) operates Cress Housing, which oversees 225 rent-geared-to-income units, and which employs a Housing Coordinator to develop housing solutions for urban Aboriginals. SaskNative Rentals, originally created to address concerns about the lack of housing in the Metis community, now operates 290 rent-geared-to-income units throughout Saskatoon. And Camponi Trust has 73 affordable homes – a mix of detached and semidetached houses. In collaboration with the Bridges and Foundations Project, affordable housing manuals have been prepared by Quint (Keeling et al. 2004) as well as by the FSIN (Chhokar 2004) and CUMFI (Pruden 2004).

However, given the provincial government's re-evaluation of its housing programs, there is now considerable uncertainty over provincial (and thus municipal) funding of housing projects. For example, the City cancelled an entry-level housing project in April 2010 owing to a lack of proposals from housing developers. Wally Mah, president of North Ridge Developments, explained that an inherent problem had been encountered insofar as the city's land bank had a mandate to create a profit: 'maybe their policy has to change a bit to accommodate affordable housing.' Alan Thomarat, CEO of the SRHBA, added that this land was priced excessively at over $7 million ($590,000 an acre), when several years ago it had been valued at well under $300,000 an acre. He pointed out that the city now needed more than 5,000 units of affordable housing: 'People need a way to access home ownership ... You need starter homes.' Councillor Pat Lorje, representing Pleasant Hill, has suggested that a possible solution may be 'inclusionary zones' – that is, designating a certain proportion of housing stock in each neighbourhood for affordable housing. She contends that the City is working 'very aggressively' to increase the supply of affordable housing stock (*Saskatoon StarPhoenix*, 19 April 2010).

Quint has encountered a number of frustrations and setbacks. A successful housing program that has made 'the poorest of the poor' into homeowners has been forced to be abort projects because of soaring real estate prices. Through the Neighbourhood Home Ownership Program (NHOP), Quint had purchased and renovated 110 houses, then turned them over to cooperatives of low-income residents in a training program for responsible homeownership. Most of the families involved in the NHOP program earned incomes of around $18,000, whereas the HomeFirst program introduced by the provincial government in 2004 was targeting families earning between $32,000 and $52,000. At the time, Quint was assisting 65 families through its 'family-friendly' renovated rental housing program. Quint had played a major role in planning the Station 20 West project; but soon after being elected, the Saskatchewan Party provincial government withdrew its large share of funding for this comprehensive community project. The Minister of Social Services suggested that the NHOP program was already dying a natural death during the previous NDP government: 'It's very, very difficult to come up with a program that's going to work well in the market that Saskatoon is right now ... The $60,000 homes don't exist right now ... So it's very difficult to come up with a program to accommodate the poorest of the poor' (*Saskatoon StarPhoenix*, 25 July 2008). Was the minister implying that there was no point even trying? In March 2010, the social services ministry, which continued to provide substantial funding to not-for-profit community organizations, also cut $165,000 in funding to Quint, ostensibly because the organization's neighbourhood development had an undefined mandate and because the funds were being used for various causes such as community gardens. The provincial government still encourages community development and affordable housing, but Quint's capacity to carry out this work has been affected.

Aboriginal housing agencies, too, have recently been faced with increasing costs and taxes that have seriously undercut their operational capabilities. SaskNative Rentals contends that its taxes now amount to as much as $700,000 a year and that it cannot possibly keep up with housing demand.

*The Role of 'Slumlords'*

A great deal of the poorer inner-city rental housing in Saskatoon is controlled by 'property managers' who may well fit the connotation of 'slumlords.' Much of this poorer housing is occupied by Aboriginal residents. It is revealing to examine the recent history of one of the largest property holders (information compiled from reports in the *Saskatoon StarPhoenix* between 2006 and 2012). This one particular individual was reported in 2005 to have owned or managed 99 units in 33 properties – houses and apartment buildings – in the inner west side neighbourhoods. According to other reports the following year, he actually owned at least 64 rental properties with 192 tenants, besides managing two apartment buildings containing 33 suites, several four- and five-plexes, and 16 homes. Operating through five business names, these properties were collectively worth at least $2.7 million in 2005 (according to tax assessments). This one landlord collected an estimated $528,960 in 2001 (according to an investigating lawyer) or at least $325,000 (according to himself). Very little of this amount seems to have gone into maintenance; rather, his emphasis was always on buying more properties.

Living conditions in these properties have been extremely poor. Most of these properties have received warnings or been condemned for failing to comply with fire regulations. Landlords are legally required to check fire alarms every three months; yet many of the alarms in these accommodations have seldom if ever been checked and are non-operational. Deficiencies in these homes include broken stairs, exposed wires, uncovered light switches, ceilings full of holes, stored junk, damaged and cracked walls, boarded-up windows and missing panes, rotten window frames, damaged flooring, inadequate heating systems, leaking plumbing, walls, and house and garage roofs, outside doors that don't lock ... Overgrown yards are filled with discarded mattresses, appliances, auto parts, furniture, and other junk. Garages are used to store of dangerous and flammable goods. Tenants live in substandard conditions in these properties, which have not been approved by the Saskatchewan Rental Housing Industry Association. One building, recently deemed unfit for habitation due to 'structural deficiencies' and scheduled for demolition, now lacks water and power. The landlord argued that he had spent more than $40,000 upgrading this structure, which was estimated to be worth as much as $280,000.

These deplorable conditions constitute a real danger to neighbouring homes as well (some of which are owned by this same landlord). For example, one fatal fire in 2005 came close to destroying the neighbouring home, which recently was also lost to fire, as was a decrepit apartment building across the street. All of these properties were owned by this same landlord. Within just six years (2000 to 2005) at least 50 of these properties have had fires (and this does not include many other fires in dumpsters, vehicles, and yards). Some of these houses have had repeated fires: one apartment block had eight in just five years, and one home had six, while three neighbouring houses on a single block each had from two to five. That apartment block finally collapsed from a major fire on 17 April 2006, after having been vacated the previous October following yet another fire. Pirated electrical wiring in pooled water caused shocks to firefighters.

This one landlord has been charged with more than 200 violations and has been ticketed or convicted over a hundred times. He has been charged with (and sometimes convicted of) failing to maintain smoke alarms, obstructing firefighters, falsifying records, obstructing justice, and violating (variously) the Fire Prevention Act, the Fire and Protective Services By-Law, and the Property Maintenance By-Law, which sets minimum standards for buildings and yards. He has also received numerous improvement orders to remedy deficiencies in his properties. Within a five-year period he accumulated an incredible $58,537 in fines (of which $20,000 worth were still unpaid), in addition to court surcharges from 48 judgments. In a court decision in February 2003, the judge commented: 'There is a very alarming pattern emerging from [this property management company] style, which appears to be complaint-driven and court-remedied. It would appear that [this landlord] does not take any pre-emptive action or protective action on behalf of the health and safety of his tenants, which should be paramount in all consideration.' Yet repeatedly these charges and convictions have been appealed on the basis that the court charges are excessive and unreasonable, that he is being mistreated by inspectors and officials, and even that he is in ill health.

His victims have been many: in one fire in March 2005, two girls aged three years and nine months were burned to death (the three-year-old trying to shield her younger two-year-old brother from the flames). The younger brother and the mother were hospitalized with burns, along with a 22-year-old man who had been living in the basement and who was rescued unconscious by firefighters from a smoke-filled basement, 'permanently brain-damaged.' The landlord received a restraining order when he harassed the survivors in the hospital's intensive care unit in order to obtain signatures releasing him from any culpability. The Fire Department had rescued people from the landlord's houses a number of times before, including a three-generation Aboriginal family in January 2003; in that incident, four young children were left homeless. The landlord had already been fined $400 for the poor condition of this home.

Regarding the fatal fire in March 2005, the landlord was convicted in Saskatoon in June, but only for intentionally falsifying smoke detector records. He was sentenced in September to just a one-year term. The Crown prosecutor had said that he intended to 'send the message that you do not fool around with our justice system.' But this landlord has consistently taken pride in his ability to do exactly that. After he claimed poor health (an impending heart attack) and that he had not been aware that his handyman had not checked a smoke detector (and adding that the tenants could have checked it themselves), the Saskatchewan Court of Appeal overturned his conviction in December 2006. However, the Supreme Court countered this appeal in November 2007.

Then in January 2012 yet another home owned (and in this case occupied) by this notorious landlord burned, at the cost of another life and an estimated $300,000 damage. At the time, 11 people were home. The crowded fourplex house contained three bedrooms on each side of the main floor and five in the basement – 16 bedrooms in all.

The landlord's attitude is interesting. He does little to instil any sense of self-worth in his tenants, forcing them to live in substandard conditions that are often unlawful, yet he tends to view himself as doing poor residents a real favour by supplying inexpensive accommodation; in fact, he has pointed out that he sometimes lets them stay rent-free for months. His tenants, if not himself, view this service as a much-needed 'last resort' (his handyman seemed less enthusiastic about these tenants, referring to them as 'trash'). He calls himself a compassionate humanitarian providing affordable housing to people who can't afford high rents and who otherwise would have nowhere to live. However, the Crown prosecutor has not minced any words, calling the landlord's actions 'reprehensible ... Landlords have to understand that these rules aren't there for them. It's to protect the public.' He called the landlord's failure to maintain his properties 'nothing short of disgusting.'

In June 2009 the Saskatchewan Court of Appeal turned down an application by this same landlord that was his attempt to halt civic demolition of another of his properties, which he had owned since 1980, due to serious structural problems. This property, which housed five families, had been boarded up and vacated for a year. The city has become accustomed to his frequent claim that the requested work had been done; perhaps some had, but not to the standards expected by the city. When the landlord learned that another of his many properties would be purchased by the city as part of the Pleasant Hill revitalization project, he raised the selling price. Coincidentally, this extra amount covered the amount he owed the city for another 13 property maintenance violations. An evicted tenant of this property was a Native woman who reported that she had spent 10 years 'on the streets,' starting when she was a teenager: 'I slept in old cars, in bushes ... I'd eat from the garbage ... I don't want to do that again' (*Saskatoon StarPhoenix*, 26 September 2009).

There is overwhelming evidence that these properties and many others have been kept in a deplorable state by this and other landlords. Still, at the risk of 'blaming the victim,' the point should be made that many of the tenants have themselves been problematic. Homes, apartments, and yards have been unkept, uncleaned, and virtually destroyed. Electrical circuits have been overloaded, not infrequently with pirated power, and this has clearly contributed to house fires, often repeated fires at the same residence. Blame has often been placed not only on landlords but also on tenants, who have wilfully caused damage to property, often under the influence of alcohol and drugs. At one address – a property of the same landlord described – there were four fire calls in three years and 36 emergency medical calls in just a single year. Of course, unscrupulous landlords can and do use irresponsible tenants as an excuse for their own failure to maintain properties adequately. In the latest house fire, in the very home where the landlord himself lived, that landlord accused the tenant who died of tampering with a smoke detector, but the surviving tenants reported that the smoke detectors were not heard. Moreover, subsequently the city fire service concluded that at least three of four detectors were not functioning.

Often, the landlords of extremely poor lodgings inhabited mostly by Aboriginal tenants are themselves racial/ethnic minorities. In one recent example, the property was a seedy bar and grill in the remnants of Saskatoon's Chinatown, with apartments above and on the ground floor. (It served only the tenants, so it operated like a boarding house.) The owner, who had immigrated from Hong Kong in 1982, had repeatedly been charged with illegal trading in large volumes of prescription drugs, including morphine, from a back window. A police raid found numerous used needles in the restaurant washroom. Coincidentally, the owner herself lived in an affluent suburb (*Saskatoon StarPhoenix*, 10 July 2009). In another recent example, the apartments above a squalid former Chinese restaurant where the owner lived were finally closed down after yet another inspection found the property 'unsanitary and unfit for habitation' – to say the least: the units were dingy and mouldy, with exposed electrical wiring, and were littered with syringes; windows were broken, and walls were covered with gang graffiti; ceiling tiles had been torn apart, fire alarms ripped out, and wooden doors kicked in. The place had become a haven for reckless inebriation, abuse, and violence. The police had had to respond to as many as 20 calls a month, usually to protect medical personnel. Recently, a person with AIDS had been found dead on his toilet, while an inebriated man had fallen to his death from a third-floor balcony. In just three years, one man had been beaten to death and five other people had died, mostly from mixing lethal potions of hairspray, antifreeze, and anything else for a cheap fix. The owner — who, unbelievably, had once run for city mayor — simply claimed that he hadn't been able to deal with the gang members who frequented the place and driven out some tenants, and anyway, there was no point trying to fix anything because they were constantly trashing the place (*StarPhoenix*, 31 July 2009).

Rents in these poorer properties are paid largely by the taxpayer through provincial social assistance and shelter allowances. These payments are often by direct deposit, so in effect the province is paying the slumlord for substandard housing. Even though tax dollars keep slum-lords in business, the Department of Community Resources and Employment, which is responsible for housing, had done absolutely no screening of homes for social assistance clients in 2006. Newly instituted controls – such as tying housing supplements to quality of housing – may do a better of job of forcing landlords to better maintain their properties. To qualify for funding, the landlord will now have to permit random periodic checks by city inspectors. But there are some 10,000 social assistance households in the city, so inspecting a good number of them will be well-nigh impossible. Still, inspections could be made mandatory at the time new tenants move in. In an effort to encourage landlords to better maintain their properties, the last (NDP) provincial government announced a program that would have provided forgivable loans to bring housing up to standard. But governments change, and policies with them.

## Aboriginal Housing Needs: A Survey of SaskNative Rentals Clients

ALAN B. ANDERSON

*Introduction*

SaskNative Rentals Inc. (SNR) is a not-for-profit organization that assists with the Aboriginal housing needs of Saskatoon. The SaskNative Housing Society was founded in 1973; it later became the SaskNative Housing Corp.; 10 years later, SaskNative Rentals was incorporated. One of the earliest specifically Aboriginal housing providers, it has been kept very busy under the capable guidance of manager and CEO Jim Durocher, long an influential Metis political activist, and Executive Director Carole Gorgchuk, recently retired and recipient of the YWCA lifetime achievement award. The SNR's stated objective is to have Aboriginal families obtain a decent standard of living by offering clean, well-maintained units, with rents geared to family income. The SNR believes that when people are encouraged to live clean, healthy lifestyles, they find it easier to deal with other issues in their lives and go on to become productive citizens with renewed self-esteem and a sense of belonging in the Saskatoon community. The SNR's approach to housing is holistic: it views affordable, safe housing as a key element in helping Aboriginal people overcome life hurdles such as poverty, lack of education and training, unemployment, health issues, and physical and substance abuse. The SNR has served the community for over 30 years and today manages over 400 units, assisting both Metis and First Nations families. The may be as many as 1,200 people on its waiting list. The SNR is expanding its geared-to-income accommodation inventory in the short term, while developing an affordable homeownership program in the medium and long term for its Aboriginal clients.

The Bridges and Foundations Project conducted a survey in 2001–2 to gather data that would provide an accurate profile of all current SNR clients. This profile focused on demographic data (age, gender, occupation, educational attainment, monthly income of the principal respondent / household head), clients' housing needs (current cost of accommodation, number of dependents and bedrooms needed, special needs), and background information on clients (such as community of origin, previous urban experience ,and future intentions and ambitions).

*Research Methodology*

A researcher, an Aboriginal business student, was employed initially to access and review all available data on file on existing SaskNative Rentals clients, then to conduct personal interviews with tenants in order to obtain specific information not available in the files. While certain types of information could be derived from the files, the data collected were incomplete in many cases and it proved impossible to obtain adequate data for all current clients, which was our original goal. Moreover, these data had to be supplemented by more specific information acquired through personal interviews – a very time-consuming process. However, in the end, a significant amount of detailed information was successfully gathered, allowing us to construct an accurate and up-to-date profile of the typical clientele of this particular housing agency. The total completed sample was 336 respondents out of 695 applicants currently on file.

In the following analysis of findings, the data refer only to valid responses; incomplete responses are excluded.

*Demographic Data*

SaskNative renters tend to be quite young, in their twenties or thirties: 39.7% of respondents were between 30 and 39 years of age, 26.9% were under 30, 20% were between 40 and 49, and 13.4% were 50 or older. The very high proportion (72.5%) of female renters/household heads was striking.

The occupations of the respondents were varied: 22.3% identified themselves as students, 9.5% as 'stay-at-home' parents, 4.5% as labourers, and 3.9% as pensioners; 3.0% worked in management and administration, while others were housekeepers, health care and home care workers, teachers, social workers, office staff, and waiters. However, many did not identify an occupation and so may have been currently unemployed. Most respondents were relatively poor. Almost half of those who did report an occupation received income from it of less than $1,000 per month; over three-quarters under $1,500. However, more than one-quarter of the total sample did not report their income (they likely feared that doing so would affect their income-adjusted rent charged). An attempt was made to gather data on other sources of income, including transfer payments, and the results of this were extremely complicated: 42.6% reported other monthly income (other than their main occupation), typically well under $1,000 a month. While the addition of these other sources of income did substantially raise the household total income, almost three-quarters of respondents still received under $2,000 a month.

Of the respondents who provided data on their education, 43.3% had attained at least a high school education and another 30.7% at least some post-secondary education. The finding that a substantial proportion of respondents were well educated was not surprising, given the number of respondents who were students at the time. Renters' increasing levels of education are suggestive of improved potential entry into the Saskatchewan labour force and their eventual ability to afford better housing.

*Accommodation Needs*

SNR attempts to ensure that overcrowding is not an issue with its clients. It was found that 5.2% of respondents' households contained only a single person, 15.2% two people, 24.8% three people, 22.1% four people, 21.3% five people, and 12.4% six or more people. However, while 'official' renters had been carefully screened, they may have tended to add to the household other relatives or friends (such as from their original home community, who were newcomers to the city), in keeping with traditional Aboriginal hospitality. A very high proportion (94.3%) of the total sample reported dependents in the household. Approximately one-third of these reported more than three dependents, mostly younger than teenage. Also, 158 respondents reported teenaged dependents, and 101 of them reported adult dependents, most of whom were spouses but who also included such relatives as common law partner, son, daughter, mother, father, brother, or sister of the household head.

SNR has clearly emphasized accommodating clients in separate houses, although recently it has invested in apartment blocks. Not surprisingly, respondents most commonly lived in a house (67%), far fewer in a duplex (22.9%) or in an apartment (6.3%). Over three-quarters (77%) of respondents occupied a three-bedroom accommodation; the remainder had two bedrooms (16.1%), or just a single bedroom (2.1%), or they occupied units with four or more bedrooms (4.8%). We found that more than four-fifths of the homes (82.8%) included a refrigerator and stove and that about one in five had private use of a clothes washer and drier and/or dishwasher. This was to be expected, as SNR has its own upgrading shop to work on donated appliances. Most households were in neighbourhoods with substantial Aboriginal proportions.

The mean unit market value of these accommodations was between $500 and $550 per month; however, there was a considerable range: 19.4% of homes had a value of $1,000 per month or more. After the rental subsidy, 27.5% of renters were charged $100 to $199, 16.4% $200 to $299, 14.8% $300 to -$399, 25.3% $400 to $499, and 16% more than $500.

The largest number of respondents (43.3%) had lived in their present home for three to six years. Almost one-third of them had occupied their present accommodation for less than three years, whereas almost one-quarter had lived in their home for more than six years, and some more than fifteen years.

Very few respondents – only six – said they had needed special assistance for furnishings (although a far larger number of renters actually do have this need). Also, 29 respondents specified that they had 'special needs' to be met.

*Background of Applicants*

Although SNR was established by Metis (a Metis flag still hangs on the boardroom wall), it now serves First Nations and Metis impartially. Half the respondents (50.3%) reported that they were Registered Indian, compared to just over one-third (36.3%) who identified themselves as Metis. The rest either reported that they were Non-Status Indian, or would not respond to this question, or would not identify themselves as a particular type of Aboriginal. Nine-tenths (91.5%) of the respondents who specified the ethnicity of their spouse reported a Registered Indian or Metis spouse; few had married a non-Aboriginal.

In this study we were particularly interested in obtaining data on Aboriginal mobility. Yet it was extremely complicated to determine a 'community of origin' for most respondents. The largest numbers indicated Saskatoon and Prince Albert as their community of origin, while others referred to other cities in Saskatchewan. At least 30 reserves and 15 Metis communities were identified. A few respondents said they had come from out of province (not only the neighbouring provinces but also Ontario and as far away as Nova Scotia). Few respondents were able to state precisely the number of years they had lived in other urban centres prior to moving to Saskatoon. However, when questioned about their experience living in other urban centres, many respondents mentioned a wide variety of locations both within Saskatchewan and beyond.

Again, considerable variation was noted regarding length of residency in Saskatoon. A substantial proportion were long-term residents: 27% had resided in Saskatoon for five years or less, and another 20% between five and ten years, but a majority (53%) had lived here for more than ten years. Reasons given for remaining in Saskatoon included these: they had children in school; they were currently going to school, or had come here to start school; they were looking for work and better employment opportunities; they had business commitments; the housing was better; there was help in Saskatoon finding adequate housing; the community was more diverse; family members had moved here; and they were simply content with in Saskatoon as a place to live. Regarding intention to remain in Saskatoon, the largest number indicated that they planned to stay permanently; relatively few predicted transitional or short-term residence, or were unsure.

*Student Households Subsample*

Of the 695 household heads in the SNR database, 21.3% identified themselves as students. Also, 78% of student households acknowledged their community as Saskatoon, 16% identified a reserve or northern community, and 6% indicated another urban centre as permanent address. Of the student households surveyed, 76% were headed by a single parent. All of the student households declared dependents, ranging from one dependent (16.7%) to two (41.7%), three (27.8%), or four or more (13.6%). Of the students indicating post-secondary status, 34% relied on student loans or band funding for income.

*Conclusions*

This survey provided very useful insights into a broad cross-section of Aboriginal renters seeking both improved accommodation and better quality of life. Generally, it revealed a population that was quite well educated and that wanted to stay in Saskatoon to obtain a better education and employment. The rapidly increasing proportion of Aboriginal people seeking accommodation through SNR who are young students is noteworthy; it also portends a changing socio-economic profile for the urban Aboriginal population – these are the Aboriginal people most likely to succeed in the future. Also noteworthy was the increasing variety of employment in which Aboriginal residents are engaged. The Aboriginal population has been highly mobile, both within the city and between city and country, but this is becoming less so: those interviewed in this study tended to view themselves as relatively permanent urban residents, and many had lived at the same address for years. In this study we encountered few complaints about the city or about SNR; the prevalent view, rather, was that Saskatoon is a good place to live and that SNR is performing a much-needed service. The personnel at SNR pointed out that the Aboriginal demand for suitable and especially affordable housing far exceeds the available supply; moreover, the operations of SNR, which is the most experienced housing agency serving Aboriginal people, have been hindered by municipal taxation, making affordability increasingly difficult to maintain.

## First Nations Housing in Saskatoon:
## A Survey of Cress Housing Clients

ALAN B. ANDERSON

*Introduction*

The Bridges and Foundations Project contracted with the Saskatoon Tribal Council (STC) to conduct a survey of clients of Cress Housing Corporation, an affiliate of the STC that provides affordable homes to First Nations people in Saskatoon. An Aboriginal research assistant was employed to conduct interviews with as many Cress households as possible. Interviews were successfully conducted with 63 households. 'Respondent' refers to the principal householder who was interviewed, although data were also gathered on all other household occupants (thus on approximately 200 residents in all) in order to determine the size and relational complexity of each household.

*Data Analysis: Family Composition of Households*

The family composition of the Cress Housing households varied from three people within the household (15 households), to four occupants

(14), five (7), six (14), eight (1), and nine/more (1). Dependent children were found in a very high proportion of households (90.5%). One-third of these children were between 15 and 19 years of age, 27% were between 10 and 14, 9.5% were 25 or older, and the remaining 30% were under 15. A mother was identified in 46 of the households, typically aged between 30 and 39. A father was identified in 29 of the households, also typically aged between 30 and 39. Other household members identified included a grandmother, grandfather, aunt, nephew, niece, or grandchildren. This would suggest, then, that a relatively small number of families were of the extended rather than nuclear sort (i.e., including relatives other than father, mother, and their children).

## Migration and Mobility

The residents in Cress Housing have tended to be long-term residents of Saskatoon. Two-thirds (42) have lived in the city for over ten years; five for nine years, three for five or six years, four for three years, and only one for less than one year. Among those who are not originally from Saskatoon, almost half came to Saskatoon from a reserve, more than one-third moved here from another city, and several came from a smaller community off reserve. Of the 63 respondents interviewed, 26 indicated that they had previously lived in another city, whereas 17 said they have not had previous urban experience. Also, 24 suggested that they would not live in another city in the future, compared to 7 who thought they would.

More than one-third of the respondents (17) identified educational opportunities as their primary reason for migrating to Saskatoon. Other common responses included family considerations (12), employment opportunities (13), and health (8). Still other individual responses were more diverse, and included escaping from violence and alcohol/drug abuse on reserve, previous urban experience, the respondent 'always liked Saskatoon,' poor living conditions on reserve, and the proximity of Saskatoon to a reserve.

A majority of respondents (36) declared they would not return to the reserve to live, and 20 said they might return sometime; only 6 said they would definitely return to the reserve. Those who intended to return to the reserve commented that they would do so after retirement or when they were older, or if there was suitable housing, or if there were jobs on the reserve, or provided that they had a vehicle to travel. However, many respondents were cautious about the poor conditions and lower standard of living on the reserve.

Many respondents had lived in their present home for an extended period of time (13 for ten or more years, 15 for six to nine years); others had been more mobile (11 for three to five years, 16 for one to two years, 7 for less than one year). A majority of respondents (35) had lived in only one other home in Saskatoon prior to their current one, while 17 had lived in two to four other homes, and five had not lived in any other home in Saskatoon besides their present home.

*Satisfaction with Cress Housing*

When asked why they had chosen Cress Housing, a large majority of respondents (50) mentioned affordability. But a wide variety of reasons besides that one were given. Some examples: the housing was being supplied by an Aboriginal organization; the respondent had rented from Cress previously; Cress houses were well maintained; Cress houses had yards where children could play; there was enough room for families; they preferred a house to an apartment; and the reserve had helped them get a suitable house.

Satisfaction rates among occupants of Cress homes were high: of 63 respondents, 33 were very satisfied, 13 somewhat satisfied, 7 were not sure, and only 5 claimed that they were dissatisfied (5 did not respond). Maintenance was a key issue for residents, but just one respondent suggested that the house 'needs a lot of work.' Various individuals expressed preference for a bungalow, a garage, and/or a basement. When asked about the general condition of their home, 30 households were very satisfied, 13 somewhat satisfied, 4 neutral, 11 somewhat dissatisfied, and 4 very dissatisfied. Also, 19 households suggested that their home was in good condition, 13 that minor repairs were needed, and 6 that major repairs were needed. The repairs needed included to doors, windows, appliances, and heating systems. Also needing work, variously, were yards and basements (to prevent flooding). Some mentioned poor air circulation in the home, others that a new coat of paint was needed.

Cress Housing policy adjusts rent to the renter's income. Typically, renters are required to pay 25% of their income, which guarantees affordability. Given the wide variation in incomes, there was a corresponding variation in monthly rent paid, ranging from less than $100 (4 respondents), to $100 to $199 (14), to $400 to $499 (12), to $500 to $599 (8), to more than $600 (3). Despite this attempt to guarantee affordability, financial issues in general were the most commonly perceived barriers to homeownership. This factor was mentioned by over half the respondents (33). The down payment was cited as an obstacle by many respondents. Other obstacles mentioned included these: a bad credit rating; the lack of job opportunities; financial (and likely also domestic) instability; lack of familiarity with the procedures for purchasing a home; disagreement in the family over the type of home desired; indebtedness; not wanting to move children from the neighbourhood with which they had become familiar; and the amount of commitment required to buy a new home. When asked about the ideal home they would eventually like to purchase, almost all respondents wanted more bedrooms.

*The Neighbourhood Location*

The survey revealed somewhat conflicting results when it came to location. When asked whether they were satisfied with the neighbourhood, most respondents were: 36 said they were very satisfied, 13 were somewhat satisfied, 5 were neutral, 4 were somewhat dissatisfied, and 4 were very dissatisfied. When asked what they specifically liked or disliked about their neighbourhood, sources of satisfaction included good neighbours, quiet, proximity to schools, access to services, green space, little traffic, and safety. But a variety of negative factors were also mentioned: a high and increasing crime rate, gangs and kids 'hanging around,' racism, lack of services, proximity to train tracks or busy traffic arteries (especially dangerous to kids walking to school), noisy and obtrusive pets, distance from schools, and small yards. Some mentioned that their yards had been spoiled by drug users ('We can't even let the kids out in their own back yard.') Some respondents had disputes with their neighbours.

With regard to the ethnic composition of the neighbourhood, 30 said it did not really matter. A few respondents would have felt more comfortable with a higher proportion of Aboriginals in their neighbourhood; a larger number would have preferred a *lower* proportion of Aboriginal residents; the largest number felt that perhaps 'half and half' would be ideal (it is noteworthy that 'half and half' represented the actual proportion of Aboriginal population in Pleasant Hill at the time). Several respondents simply advocated a good mix of all races.

Local provision of services (shops, groceries, medical and cultural centres, and community activities and facilities) was important to most respondents.

*Problems with Homeownership*

In summarizing the problems they perceived with homeownership, respondents mentioned repair costs, inadequate space for the size of their family, the need to accommodate physical disabilities, the limited availability of Cress housing (especially given the long-term residence of many clients), and the need for more help to learn procedures for buying and maintaining a home.

## Chapter Eight

# Special Needs and Housing Design in Urban Aboriginal Housing

## Urban Aboriginal Populations in Special Need and Implications for Housing Design

### The Definition of 'Special Needs'

Housing for people with special needs could include quite a wide variety of 'needs.' Our concern is primarily with the urban Aboriginal population. In this chapter the focus is on the pressing need for student housing and seniors' housing. In this introduction, attention will also be drawn to housing for residents with disabilities and housing for released former inmates now being reintegrated into the community. After that, the implications of 'special needs' for housing design will be discussed, as well as the relationship between housing design and community design.

### Student Housing

It is estimated today that around 13,000 First Nations and Metis students are attending Saskatchewan's post-secondary institutions. Saskatoon is the location of several general and specifically Aboriginal institutions of higher education. These include the University of Saskatchewan, the Saskatchewan Institute of Applied Science and Technology (SIAST), the Saskatchewan Indian Institute of Technologies (SIIT), the Gabriel Dumont Institute (GDI), which includes the Dumont Technical Institute (DTI), and the former Saskatoon Campus of the First Nations University of Canada (FNUC). Almost 10% of the 20,000 students at the University of Saskatchewan are Aboriginal. Student housing in general has always been an issue in this city, but it has complex dimensions for Aboriginal students, many of whom have never lived in a city and have come from isolated communities. In fact, some university classes are larger than entire rural communities. So the potential for culture shock is considerable. Harder pressed to find adequate accommodation than the thousands of other university students who arrive in the city each fall, Aboriginal students too often end up in highly inadequate – but less expensive – housing in the poorest neighbourhoods, where Aboriginal residents have concentrated. Deplorable rental accommodations are occupied by students who represent the future hopes of their peoples and communities. Perhaps more fortunate are those who already live in the city (although they too may live in overcrowded inner-city homes that are hardly conducive to effective studying), or who have been provided housing by their bands investing in their welfare; or the relatively few who have been able to secure accommodation in university residences (assuming they are students at the University of Saskatchewan).

At the University of Saskatchewan, residences currently provide 1,190 beds. That is enough to house only about 6% of the 18,474 students. However, early in 2009 the provincial Minister of Advanced Education, Employment, and Labour announced that the provincial government would be contributing $15 million toward a fund of $34 million to initially construct an additional 400-bed student housing complex (the first such construction in three decades) as part of an ambitious large-scale project to extend the campus. The university president recognizes that 'the ability of the university to recruit students in a highly competitive education environment includes the ability to offer residence space' (*On Campus News*, 6 February 2009). A report by Shannon Dyck for the University of Saskatchewan Students Union (USSU) titled *Living Well, Learning Well* (2009) had recommended adequate funding of university projects to increase student housing on or near campus; taking steps to ensure landlord accountability and to increase awareness of landlord–tenant responsibilities; and the maintaining of communications among all levels of government. Realistically, though, given the competition for extremely limited accommodations for all university students not originally resident in Saskatoon, these developments will likely have very little effect on Aboriginal students entering the city, many of whom attend other institutions rather than the University of Saskatchewan.

An overview study of Aboriginal post-secondary student housing that focuses on the University of Saskatchewan is summarized in this chapter. Other studies of student housing commissioned by the Bridges and Foundations Project included a study of housing and day care on the former FNUC Saskatoon campus (Prokop and MacDonald 2004) and an extensive analysis of Metis student housing (Hammersmith, Littlejohn, and McCaslin 2004).

The FNUC study found that the typical student at FNUC-Saskatoon was between the ages of 20 and 30, was enrolled in a university credit program, and was living in rental accommodation. Many of these students were single parents and were experiencing difficulty balancing their academic endeavours with family commitments. Nearly 40% of the students surveyed indicated that they had dependent children living with them. Many of the students mentioned that family commitments and lack of proper care for their children were preventing them from complete success in school. Clearly, adequate child care is essential to many FNUC students.

Although Aboriginal student housing in Saskatoon has received considerable attention, little information has been available specifically on Metis post-secondary student housing needs and issues, in particular with regard to housing relevant to Metis practices, customs, and traditions. This study of Metis post-secondary students focused on those attending the Saskatchewan Urban Teacher Education Program (SUNTEP) based at the University of Saskatchewan; the Gabriel Dumont Institute (GDI); the Dumont Technical Institute (DTI); and the Saskatchewan Institute of Applied Science and Technology (SIAST), all in Saskatoon. The project clearly demonstrated that the needs of Metis students were not being adequately met. The challenge of achieving an inclusive, respectful approach in housing policies, development, and strategies requires the recognition that Metis students are not a homogeneous group. The research indicated there was a clear need for a variety of housing options for Saskatoon's Metis students; it also highlighted the lack of Metis-specific student housing models. The vast majority of housing occupied by these Metis students was not within the jurisdiction of an Aboriginal housing agency. For the most part, these students were not in low-income housing, nor were they in student residences; instead, they inhabited apartments that were in need of repair, that were in locations hardly conducive to studying, and that had safety and security issues. The few student respondents who had found accommodation through an Aboriginal housing delivery agency or a low-income agency had not been given priority when accommodations were being assigned. The researchers concluded that for Metis students in Saskatoon, housing was more than mere shelter; it was a place to study and raise children and a place to practise and share their culture.

Seniors Housing

By 2001 there were almost 4 million seniors in Canada, accounting for 13% of the total population. Senior households accounted for 20.8% of the 11.6 million private households in Canada, and almost half these senior households were maintained by a person aged 75 and over (CMHC 2005b). In 2007, Statistics Canada predicted that within a decade seniors would likely outnumber children in Canada. The 55 to 64 age cohort (the 'baby boom' generation) is by far the fastest growing and may account for as much as one-third of the total Canadian population. Moreover, the over-80 cohort is the second fastest growing and now exceeds 1 million people. One out of every seven Canadians is a senior, whereas the proportion of Canadians under 15 has declined to just 17.7% – the lowest level ever. Playing a significant role in this massive demographic shift have been increased life expectancy and a declining birth rate. Canada's median age has reached an all-time high of 39.5. The Aboriginal demographic profile differs markedly from this: there are proportionately far fewer seniors – especially in the oldest age cohorts – and far more youth under 15. Correspondingly, the median age is lower; and while life expectancy has been increasing steadily for decades as a result of improved health care, the birth rate remains high, especially on reserves, where the median age can be as low as 10.

Saskatchewan has the largest proportion of seniors of any province or territory in Canada. Saskatoon is home to increasing numbers of older residents. The number of senior residents is expected to increase by 83% over the next couple of decades, the number of seniors over 75 by 47%, and the number over 85 by 36%. Much larger numbers of seniors are staying healthier for longer, allowing more of them to continue to live independently. However, again, Aboriginal seniors in Saskatoon differ from the general population: not only are there proportionately far fewer of them, especially in older age cohorts, but also more tend to have serious health problems, and many do not live independently but in extended families sharing a domicile. While the proportion of senior residents in general seems to be highest in the relatively more affluent neighbourhoods to the east and north, the neighbourhoods having the highest proportions of Aboriginal residents do not exhibit higher proportions of Aboriginal seniors.

In 2001, 7% of seniors in Canada were living in collective dwellings (compared to only 0.7% of non-seniors); and 13% of seniors aged 75 and over. While the majority of seniors (58.5%) were living with a spouse or common law partner, more than one- quarter (28.9%) were living alone (compared to only 7.5% of non-seniors); and 38.9% of those aged 75 and over. Almost one-third (31%) of all senior households, and 37% of senior households maintained by a person 75 and over, occupied apartments (compared to 26.1% of non-senior households). Over three-quarters of senior households maintained by someone aged 65 to 74 owned a home, but the homeownership rate fell to two-thirds among households maintained by someone aged 75 and over. Also, 28.7% of senior households in Canada did not meet standards for adequate, suitable, or affordable dwellings as defined by CMHC, and 21.1% were in core housing need (compared to 14.4% of non-senior households). In fact, 73.4% of below-standard senior households were in core housing need (compared to 47.4% of non-senior households). However, senior households were far less likely to be overcrowded (CMHC 2005). Again, the contrast in certain respects with Aboriginal households is striking: there is a tendency for Aboriginal seniors to live with extended families rather than alone; there is a lower homeownership rate in cities; and there is far more prevalence of living in poor and overcrowded housing conditions.

Canadian researchers estimate that between 4% to 10% of seniors will experience some form of physical, emotional, or financial abuse (*Globe and Mail*, 29 July 2008). Given the crowded and poor conditions in which many Aboriginal seniors are obliged to live, such abuse is likely to be more prevalent in this population. Yet Aboriginal traditions promote more respect for elders than is found in general society. The report of the Royal Commission on Aboriginal Peoples (1996) documented the comprehensive role that elders play in preserving language, spirituality, oral traditions, cultural wisdom and values, traditional health and healing, and lands and resources. A group of some 50 *kokums* (grandmothers) has been meeting each month in Saskatoon since 1992. Called 'Strengthening the Circle,' it aims to improve elderly women's self-esteem and and strengthen their courage through discussions of spiritual and cultural needs, health issues, and feelings of isolation. A description of the Metis Elders Circle Housing Project is included in this chapter.

Housing for Residents with Disabilities

In 2001, almost half (49.7%) of all seniors in Canada reported a disability; the proportion was higher among those 75 and over (63.7%) but was much lower for those 65 to 74 (39.6%). In contrast, only 11.2% of non-seniors reported a disability (CMHC 2005). People with disabilities may need housing with special adaptations and features, and this can have an impact on their ability to find and afford suitable housing (Soles 2003). A study conducted by the Social Policy Research Unit at the University of Regina found that urban Aboriginal residents with disabilities encountered difficulty in finding housing and that what was available was substandard and of poor quality with regard to size, accessibility, and location; moreover, respondents reported that some landlords were taking advantage of renters with disabilities. Affordability was a problem, so there were limited choices as to where these people could reside. Most were concentrated in the core area, where rents were cheaper but housing conditions were much more unsuitable (Durst and Bluechardt 2001, 95–7).

Housing Former Inmates

Housing may be a problem for former prison inmates – a disproportion of whom are Aboriginal – who now must be reintegrated into the community. Deborah Drake conducted an extensive study of this problem in Saskatoon for the Bridges and Foundations Project (Drake 2003). This research investigated and documented the challenges faced by men upon their release from federal incarceration in Saskatchewan. Owing to the high number of Aboriginal people incarcerated in Saskatchewan, this research necessarily investigated the differences between Aboriginal and non-Aboriginal ex-prisoners. A qualitative approach was employed in order to understand post-incarceration from the perspectives of those who have experienced what it is like to return to the community after prison and those who work with men making this transition. The research described parole board hearings, the difficulties related to integrating into society as perceived by ex-prisoners, and the role of service providers and agencies in Saskatoon that assist former inmates. This research found that certain difficulties are common among all ex-prisoners, such as finding employment and housing and accessing appropriate support resources. That said, the difficulties experienced by all ex-prisoners appear to be amplified for Aboriginal ex-prisoners. Racism and the overall disadvantaged position of Aboriginal people in Canada are significant barriers for Aboriginal ex-prisoners who are attempting to integrate into the community.

A similar study of women offenders was later conducted in Vancouver (CMHC 2005c). This study examined the personal characteristics, housing, and housing-related needs of women offenders and the importance of post-prison transitional housing in helping them reintegrate into the community. This study concluded that 'safe, private, secure and stable transitional housing is critical for women who are leaving prison and re-entering the community ... Without the provision of stable and safe housing, it is doubtful whether their physical and mental health, addictions, relationships, and community reintegration issues can be addressed.' While Drake's research focused primarily on Aboriginal males, the Vancouver study focused on women who were not necessarily Aboriginal; nevertheless, there is much concurrence between these projects.

*The Importance of Housing Design to Urban Aboriginal Residents*

Many Aboriginal people live in seriously crowded conditions, both on reserves and in northern rural communities, and in cities. Obviously, these people need larger homes, but such homes are even less affordable for a generally poor Aboriginal population. Another aspect of this problem is that housing to accommodate larger Aboriginal families is unavailable. On reserves across Canada and certainly in Saskatchewan, with little exception, most homes are far too small, and so too are most of the houses and apartments occupied by Aboriginal tenants in cities. One attempt to increase space without sacrificing affordability has been the multilevel 'Shift home' constructed in Riversdale by Shift Development Inc.

This is not to suggest that all urban Aboriginal families are larger than non-Aboriginal ones. To the contrary – average family size tends to decrease with urbanization, not the least because such families are more expensive and thus more difficult to maintain in an urban than in a rural context. However, many families that have already grown large on reserve or in a rural community migrate into the city. Moreover, the Aboriginal tradition of extended families is still fairly common even in a crowded urban environment. Such households may include not just a conventional nuclear family but also other relatives and family members, and sometimes also friends of the family, other children from related families, or people from the same original community.

Of course, family size is only one consideration in housing design. The design of housing could also consider special features for physically challenged residents (such as wheelchair accessibility), students (e.g., quiet, well-lit study areas), elders (e.g., a comfortable setting for socializing), community services (meeting spaces), and so on (Mckinnon

2003). Well-designed family homes would include a spacious kitchen, sufficient bathrooms and bedrooms, and a finished basement. Energy efficiency is crucial and can be built into home design – for example through solar heating or more efficient furnaces.

What role might Aboriginal people play in housing design? Unique to Aboriginal homes and buildings could be specific cultural designs representing First Nations and Metis themes and traditions. Ray Gosselin, an Aboriginal architect and Manager of Planning at the University of Regina, has made a point of collecting traditional Native architectural designs and translating them into modern architecture, including housing. He was Project Coordinator for the striking FNUC building on the University of Regina campus (1990), designed by famous Canadian First Nations–Metis architect Douglas Joseph Cardinal, who also designed the Canadian Museum of Civilization in Ottawa (1989), the National Museum of the American Indian in the Smithsonian Institute in Washington, D.C. (1993), and the Kainai Cultural Resource Centre on the Blood Indian Reserve in Alberta (1996), always effectively combining Aboriginal philosophy with modern architecture.

In collaboration with the Bridges and Foundations Project, the Saskatoon and Region Home Builders' Association (SRHBA) issued a report titled *Community Housing and Design Options*, which emphasized the need for truly affordable housing to accommodate the growing and increasingly diverse Aboriginal population of Saskatoon (SRHBA 2004). A design charrette organized by the Bridges and Foundations Project (Johnson 2004) led to a large-scale inner-city redevelopment project. Yet another unique project involved several Aboriginal women learning alternative (straw bale) construction skills (Vandale 2004). The point to be made here is that there are ways to design new affordable housing that is functional and attractive without being costly. Now let us summarize each of these interesting projects.

Community Housing and Design Options

The SRHBA entered into an agreement with the Bridges and Foundations Project with the objective of developing sustainable relationships between Aboriginal and non-Aboriginal people and organizations that will result in the discovery of affordable housing options and the growth of culturally supportive communities. Included in this effort has been consideration of the design of homes and of the expertise required to build them. By building partnerships and encouraging open communication, trust has been developed between individuals and organizations and between Aboriginal and non-Aboriginal organizations. The focus of this working relationship has been on appropriate and affordable housing for the Aboriginal community. The methodology has included sharing information, technical knowledge, and expertise to generate Aboriginal housing that is relevant to the community.

In February 2004 the SRHBA hosted a Community Housing and Design Workshop, which was attended by a broad range of participants representing the residential construction industry, the financial sector, various community organizations, and various branches of government. Aboriginal participants represented the Federation of Saskatchewan Indian Nations (FSIN), the First Nations Bank, Oskayak High School, the Saskatoon Tribal Council (STC), Metis Employment and Training of Saskatchewan Inc. (METSI), and the Muskeg Lake Cree Nation. The workshop brought together Aboriginals and non-Aboriginals to discuss housing and community design issues facing Aboriginal populations in Saskatoon and the surrounding area. The workshop focused on two key areas: housing and community design, and the unique needs of urban Aboriginals. The project concluded that quality affordable housing needs to be made available for First Nations and Metis people in all Saskatoon communities. This housing needs to be energy-efficient and durable, and it must be modifiable to suit different lifestyles, including those of young families, elders, singles, and students. Initiatives must be developed that will help First Nations and Metis people access housing, and action must be taken to increase the amount of quality housing stock available. The project identified a need to provide education and mentorship programs to ease people into their first homeownership experience. Finally, input from First Nations and Metis communities must serve as the basis for proceeding with the design of any housing or communities built, with the goal of creating culturally supportive communities.

## An Urban Aboriginal Housing Design Charrette

A 'charrette' is a focused and collaborative design forum that leads toward specific proposals. The Affordable New Home Development Foundation (ANHDF) coordinated and facilitated this design charrette, whose purpose was to provide an opportunity for stakeholders to explore together the issue of urban Aboriginal housing and to seek solutions. The goals were to identify appropriate housing styles and types on identified pieces of city land. Ray Gosselin was contracted to devise a program for the charrette and to help coordinate and facilitate it. The ANHDF worked directly with the City of Saskatoon Land Branch to identify pieces of land available that might be sites for the charrette to consider. The participants in the charrette represented a broad range of Aboriginal organizations, homebuilders, financiers, academics, civic departments, and community members, as well as CMHC. Among the pertinent conclusions reached were the following: There is an unnecessary shortage of affordable housing for Aboriginal people in Saskatoon. Affordable housing may not be ideal, but it is a first step in building equity and improving the quality of available housing. People want communities and neighbourhoods that are safe and affordable and that provide a multitude of services and schools. Housing developments should be accessible and close to services. Suburban development is not helpful, since many individuals do not own a vehicle. Communities should include pedestrian walkways and should have 'friendliness' built into their design. Balanced development must occur across the city in order to avoid the clustering of income groups. Saskatoon should investigate successful housing programs in other communities to learn what is most effective. People's expectations in society can often be too high and may be unachievable in the short term, because it takes time to build equity and to inform individuals about the options available to help them buy a home. People must recognize that 'affordable' means *modest*, not *low in quality*. There are often misperceptions about what is affordable and what is available on the market. Housing is about far more than simply providing people with a place to live. Prioritizing and increasing housing affordability and providing quality rental accommodations will help improve standards of living in the city and also help individuals take greater pride in their homes and thus their communities.

Building Skills, Building Homes

The unique Building Skills, Building Homes project, directed by Carol Vandale, gave 11 young, unemployed urban Aboriginal women (selected by a resource officer from Human Resources and Skills Development Canada) the opportunity to work as apprentices with skilled teacher-builders from the alternative building industry. Besides gaining basic carpentry skills, the women were trained in ecologically sustainable construction designs, including vaults and various straw bale structures. The participants also learned about solar energy, water and waste management, cooperative landownership, and various alternative lifestyle practices. Throughout, they used materials and technologies particularly suited to the northern prairies. The women learned how to build a load-bearing straw-bale structure, as well as basic carpentry skills necessary for the mainstream construction industry. In addition to this, the project encouraged the women to focus on their individual talents, career goals, and training or education needs and desires. The whole project encouraged learning, growth, and reflection through participation in various workshops, gatherings, and teachings.

## Aboriginal Post-Secondary Student Housing

BRENDA WALLACE, BRENDA MAIRE, and ALLISON LACHANCE

*Introduction*

The Bridges and Foundations Project identified housing for Aboriginal post-secondary students as a priority need in Saskatoon. With this in mind, the Saskatoon Housing Initiatives Partnership (SHIP) undertook an assessment of housing issues among Aboriginal students in the city. Many factors affect housing affordability in Saskatoon. The cost of housing (i.e., rent or mortgage payments) is only a portion of total housing costs. Utility costs, insurance costs, and costs related to transportation when housing is not conveniently located all impact the total housing costs that students pay each month. In 2001, 13.8% of Saskatoon households were found to be in core housing need. Among these households, the average spent on shelter was 50% of income – the second-highest ratio among census metropolitan areas in Canada. Housing tenure can be a predictor of core housing need, and indeed, 5.9% of owners and 29.4% of renters in Saskatoon were found to be in core housing need in the same survey. Most striking within this, however, was the fact that 44.5% of Aboriginal renters, 45% of all Metis in Saskatoon, and 78% of Aboriginal lone-parent families were in core need.

Neighbourhoods with the sharpest decreases in value tended to be on the west side of the river where the housing stock was older; in these neighbourhoods, the average fair market values of properties are among the lowest. Dwellings that needed major repairs and that were overcrowded were increasing in number and were concentrated mostly in west side inner-city neighbourhoods. Furthermore, the residents most likely to find themselves living in crowded conditions were Aboriginal;

in 2001, for example, only 5% of all Saskatoon households fell short of Canadian National Occupancy Standards for crowding, but 18% of Aboriginal households were found to be in overcrowded conditions.

The availability of housing appropriate for Aboriginal students in Saskatoon is limited. The University of Saskatchewan is the only post-secondary institution in Saskatoon that provides student accommodation, and even that is limited; however, other organizations with links to the university also provide student accommodation. Community-based housing providers make available some subsidized housing units. The Saskatoon Housing Authority operates more than 2,000 social housing units in Saskatoon with an emphasis on housing families and seniors. Cress Housing, affiliated with the Saskatoon Tribal Council, managed 237 units of housing at the time of our research, while SaskNative Rentals, a Native (originally Metis) housing not-for-profit organization, operated 281 housing units, also with an emphasis on families. But the vast majority of the thousands of Aboriginal post-secondary students in Saskatoon are obliged to find accommodation completely on their own initiative.

*Research Methodology*

The Aboriginal Student Housing Assessment was not intended simply to gather information about Aboriginal students for outside organizations, but also to discuss housing issues within that group, validate their experiences, and inform students about how their challenges may link to Aboriginal as well as other organizations in developing housing solutions. Respect, relevance, and reciprocity were articulated within the study in two ways – through the establishment of a working group to guide the research, and through implementation of the research tools via partnerships.

The assessment had two objectives: first, to develop strong relationships between organizations serving Aboriginal students and those with the potential to improve housing conditions and availability for Aboriginal students; and second, to establish the components for an Aboriginal Student Housing Strategy, including critical market information inputs into business planning models for housing and service providers. Specific objectives were to determine the size and demographic composition of the Aboriginal post-secondary student population; to obtain general income information and other relevant information determining need for affordable housing; and to assess issues currently preventing access to appropriate housing for students.

The assessment developed implementation strategies based on the ethical best practices detailed by the Royal Commission on Aboriginal Peoples, as well as on standards set by the academic behavioural ethics review process. 'Talking circles' proved to be a crucial component of the research. Aboriginal students were provided with an opportunity to discuss with their peers the topic of housing and the housing barriers that affect students. In total there were seven talking circles with 91 participants. A survey completed by 215 Aboriginal students was designed specifically to capture market information. This survey consisted of questions that addressed demographic information, income information, information about current housing choices, and issues preventing access to appropriate and/or affordable housing.

*Characteristics of the Aboriginal Post-Secondary Student Population and Their Housing*

Results of the Aboriginal Student Housing Assessment found that the predominant segment is a family housing market: 64.7% of survey respondents had dependents, and the largest constituency of Aboriginal students is older and not 'fresh out of high school.' According to enrolment data provided by participating education institutions, the Aboriginal post-secondary student population is growing rapidly. The two largest institutions, the University of Saskatchewan and SIAST, are attracting growing numbers of students who identify themselves as Aboriginal. At the University of Saskatchewan, Aboriginal students are approaching 10% of the total student body. When planning for their housing needs, housing proponents can expect the Aboriginal student population to be at least 3,500 each year.

Given that nearly two-thirds of Aboriginal post-secondary students belong to the family market segment, their current housing choices are influenced by the needs of families. Smaller accommodations such as bachelor units and one-bedroom apartments are more affordable, but most of these students are in larger accommodations due to the needs of their families. In fact, 80.5% of survey respondents indicated that they live in suites larger than two bedrooms. The majority of students rented apartments (38%) or a suite in a house (15%). A small number of students rented (15%) or owned (7%) a house, townhouse, or duplex. Other housing situations identified by students included a low-income rental, a trailer, or a university residence. Some lived with family.

Because they desired larger accommodations in family-friendly neighbourhoods (i.e., safe, and with the necessary amenities), half the survey respondents were paying more than $500 per month. The amount they were paying for housing was evenly distributed: the largest number of Aboriginal students were paying between $500 and $599 per month; 14% over $700; and 14% less than $300.

Student respondents who had dependents indicated that their housing choices were guided by the following factors: affordability (45%), proximity to school (39%), to bus route (39%), to shopping (25%), to services for children (19%), 'took what was available – unfamiliar with the city' (16%), availability (7%), 'nice neighbourhood' (7%), close to family or friends (4%). The housing choices of students who did not have dependents tended to be guided by a somewhat different ordering of factors. For reasons of affordability, most students were in shared accommodation, ranging from two-bedroom units (24%) to three-bedroom (43%) or even four- or five-bedroom (28%).

*Student Housing Issues and Solutions*

Aboriginal post-secondary students face income shortages that prevent them from accessing affordable, appropriate, safe, and stable housing. Students have a variety of income sources, including wages and salaries, student loans, provincial training allowances, Metis or First Nations band funds, or social assistance.

According to the survey, Saskatoon's Aboriginal post-secondary student population includes both younger single students and students with dependents. Most of these students rent apartments or suites based on affordability and access to the school they are attending. Many (73%) said they faced housing issues. Among the students who identified themselves as having housing problems, the three most prevalent issues were high rent (65%), the high cost of utilities (45%), and housing that didn't suit their needs (40%).

Some important implications can be drawn from the detailed comments made during the talking circles. The students were having difficulties with the costs of rent, utilities, day care, and transportation, and these difficulties were affecting their academic performance. Students were highly dissatisfied with their landlords and with the rental programs available to them. Many had encountered discrimination when trying to find housing. They maintained that housing should reflect the size of their families. They voiced a preference for community housing. The opinions of students with families differed from those of students who were single; both groups, though, expressed interest in some type of communal arrangement for housing.

The students identified a number of key issues in terms of addressing Saskatoon's student housing problem. *First*, such housing should be affordable and family-friendly. Given that almost two-thirds of the Aboriginal post-secondary student population have dependents, housing should support healthy family living. Such supports would include a suitable number of bedrooms; spaces for children and adults to study and play; clean and safe kitchens, bathrooms, and living spaces; access to good light and fresh air; and soundproofing to minimize conflicts. Supports might also include convenient laundry facilities, playgrounds and open spaces, schools, convenient access to day cares, and proximity to shopping and transportation. *Second*, more choice should be available. The students felt that they were victims of prejudice because of their economic situation. Outside the inner-city neighbourhoods, Saskatoon offers little housing that students can afford, so they end up in locations that are experiencing disinvestment and increasing crime. *Third*, housing should be linked to support services. A more holistic approach to housing would go a long way to improve the chances of education success. Worth exploring in this regard are on-site child care, subsidized or cooperative transportation options, and links to employment and other community services. *Fourth*, the housing made available to these students should support their culture. This would include simple things like the provision of common space, opportunities for interaction with an elder, and ceremony space. All of these would improve students' connections to their culture and heritage and thereby build their confidence and self-esteem.

## The Metis Elders Circle Housing Research Project: A Study to Determine Respectful Sustainable Housing Options for Metis Elders

J. DUROCHER, J. HAMMERSMITH, C. LITTLEJOHN, and W. MCCASLIN

*Introduction*

All agree that there is a crisis in Aboriginal housing in Saskatoon, but very little information has been available on the housing needs specifically of Metis elders (*kehteyatis*). Part of the reason is that for many years, attention has focused on the growing young Aboriginal population. Moreover, the number of Aboriginal elders is, not surprisingly, small, although these numbers have been increasing steadily over the past few years. As a result, while Aboriginal housing authorities and governments grapple with the demands of a rapidly growing young Aboriginal population, the housing needs of Aboriginal elders continue to be overlooked or ignored. To address this issue with the hope of influencing public policy relating specifically to the housing needs of Aboriginal and in particular Metis elders, this project undertook a study through the eyes of stakeholders working in the field and, most important, through the voices of the Metis elders themselves. The research team took a multilevel approach, through community networking and information exchange. They organized a Metis elders gathering, conducted field research to document the housing situation of Metis elders, located and presented models of successful elder housing projects, and offered recommendations for Metis elders' housing in Saskatoon. The research project examined issues specific to Metis elder needs; it also looked for ways to develop or enhance established relationships and capacities. Most important, it suggested how to increase the effectiveness of housing stakeholders to serve the elder community. Although stakeholders have made some efforts to implement a respectful and meaningful approach to addressing elder housing needs, the reality is that this community's voices have not been heard. This project attempted to listen to their voices. The resulting report demonstrates that the needs of Metis elders are not being fully met.

Metis elders are not a homogenous group, and the research shows a clear need for a variety of housing options for them in Saskatoon. The research found that there are four basic divisions: those who live alone; those who live with a spouse; those who live with others; and those who are the primary caregivers for their grandchildren. These groups are further fragmented by the health of the individual or spouse and by the presence of other people in the household. There is evidence that the conditions of life of Metis elders can change very quickly and have an immediate effect on the housing situation. Service organizations are not prepared for these sudden changes of circumstance. Few Metis-specific elder housing models exist, and the ones that do are not highlighting the cultural traditions, practices, and customs of the residents.

For Metis elders in Saskatoon, housing is more than a shelter. It is a place to share with family and friends. It can be a place to bring up children. It is a place to carry on traditional activities. It is a place to connect and be a part of nature. It is a place to pray. The research shows that Metis elders housing should be the kind of space that supports not just the physical person but also the cultural aspects of Metis elders. The final report was shared with Metis elders, Aboriginal and non-Aboriginal housing organizations, community members and other interested parties, in the hope that the information gathered would be beneficial in creating meaningful housing options for Metis elders.

## Research Problem, Objectives, and Methodology

The project was undertaken through the eyes of Metis elders, describing their lives, perceptions, and beliefs. Although this qualitative approach has methodological limitations, it is critical if one hopes to hear and understand the voices of our Metis elders. The project focused on the following: policy visions and objectives for Aboriginal housing initiatives; the 'population being served' and 'expected population' forecast of Saskatoon Metis elders; the 'needs being served' and 'expected needs' forecast for Saskatoon Metis elders; the scope for Metis customs, practices, and traditions in current housing developments; the linkages between Aboriginal housing initiatives and other relevant agencies; factors at work in terms of enhancing housing options and community capacity; and suitable models for housing.

The primary research consisted of personal interviews conducted over several months. This was supplemented by secondary research of Aboriginal housing initiatives and processes and by dialogue with Metis elders. The research team administered the questionnaire in an ethical and respectful manner. Though time was short, it was possible to complete 97 questionnaires with Metis elders.

The project followed a Cree–Metis (*Ininiwi-Apihtawikosani*) ethical perspective. Accordingly, the research team organized an initial cultural gathering of Metis elders at Le Petite Ville, a Metis seniors home (*okehteyatisiwikamik*) in Saskatoon. Around 40 elders attended the gathering, during which the research team members described the project's framework and goals. Then the team formally asked the elders for permission to undertake the research and for their support – that is, for their personal input. The proper protocol having been followed, the elders approved the request. They had heard first-hand about the research that was being undertaken, and now they made it known that they wanted to be involved and that they were very pleased to learn their voices would have a platform from which to be heard. At the gathering, many elders introduced themselves to the research team and indicated not only their own interest but also names of other elders whom the research team should contact. The gathering, while not a time for conducting survey questionnaires, interviews, or eliciting specific information from the elders, was an important step in the research process. It was a time of traditional Metis music, feasting, and socializing.

The survey questionnaires followed established ethical protocols. The interviews were conducted in Cree (*Ininimowin*) or Michif where appropriate. The questionnaire was conducted through personal, door-to-door visits. A research team resource member who spoke Cree–Michif fluently oversaw all aspects of this phase of the project. In developing the questionnaire, this resource member, who was well versed in Cree–Metis protocol, examined the suggested questions for their appropriateness. Some questions were intended to help determine which policies were currently available or were needed to support Metis elders' housing needs. Other questions were intended to ascertain the physical health of respondents, and again, the resource member was consulted regarding these questions' appropriateness. The project did not want to intrude on elders' privacy.

During interviews, each Metis elder was asked whether he or she was familiar with other Metis elders who might be interested in participating in the survey. One Metis woman who had worked extensively over the years with Metis elders conducted all the interviews. This maintained consistency and ensured the quality of the data. This interviewer was well versed in Metis customs, practices, traditions, and protocols. She was also very familiar with Aboriginal housing in Saskatoon and knew the available support services in the city.

Regarding dissemination procedures, a gathering of Metis elders was held during which the final report was presented, using the conventional oral tradition in the Cree, Michif, and English languages.

*Demographics*

The total population of Metis in Saskatoon in 2001 (the most recent census before this project was initiated) was 8,305 (NAHA 2004). According to Statistics Canada, of the 920 total Aboriginal elders aged 55 and over in Saskatoon, there would have been 374 Metis. In other words, around 40% of the Aboriginal elders in Saskatoon are Metis. The national proportion of Metis elders is 4% of the total Metis population (according to Statistics Canada). So the proportion of Metis elders in Saskatoon is obviously higher than the national average. Moreover, our estimate of Metis elder population, based on our own knowledge of the Metis community, would be much higher than official numbers or expectations. In any case, if we accept the official demographic data, we may surmise that approximately one- quarter of all Metis elders in Saskatoon participated in this project.

*Results*

The 97 Metis elders who shared their experiences with us represented 74 separate households. The respondents were between 55 and 89 years of age. Over two-thirds of the respondents (69%) were in their sixties, while 12% were between 55 and 60 and 18% were in their seventies. Also, 43% of the interviewees were male and 57% were female. These figures were almost identical to the percentage by gender (males, 42%; females, 58%) reported for Saskatoon's Aboriginal elders in the 2001 Census.

Around half of all households had a single resident. Of those living with others, couples made up 32% of households, living together either by themselves or with others. Half the elders living with others lived with their own or foster children, while the remaining half were living with grandchildren The survey found that 36% of these elders did not have their grandchildren's parents living in the same household – in other words, these grandparents were the primary caregivers of young children. Yet when asked who they would like to live in the home, 69% of all respondents said they preferred to live alone. Most of the Metis elders who wanted to have people living with them (15%) commented that they enjoyed living with their grandchildren.

The Metis elders reported income from various sources: Canadian Pension Plan (CPP) (46%), Old Age Security (OAS) (42%), wages from employment and providing services (about 31%), another form of pension (21%), Social Assistance (8%), Disability Pension (7%), OAS Supplement (6%), and Family Allowance (1%). Monthly income was highly variable, ranging from none at all (1%), to less than $500 (8%), $501 to $1,000 (26%), $1,001 to $1,500 (48%), $1,501 to $2,000 (15%), $2,001 and above (3%).

Affordability is a vital consideration in housing options for Metis elders. 'Affordable' should mean that rent is geared to income level and that tenants should have some flexibility with regard to such things as damage deposits. However, the research showed that few Metis elders with these monthly incomes would be able to afford $600 to $900 per month for housing, using the standard level of 30% of income to spend on housing.

Twelve per cent of the respondents had lived in Saskatoon their whole lives, 19% for more than 40 years, 52% between 20 and 39 years, 9%

between 10 and 19 years, 7% for less than 10 years, and 1% for less than one year. Almost half of our informants (46%) had come to Saskatoon from one of the recognized Metis communities in Saskatchewan (Beauval, St-Louis, Cumberland House, Lebret, Batoche, St-Laurent, Ile-à-la-Crosse, Gabriel Crossing, Duck Lake, Green Lake). Prince Albert had been the home community of 18% of respondents. Other Saskatchewan locations accounted for 18%, while 7% had come from out of province. The rest reported that Saskatoon was their home community. Also, 80% of Metis elders in this study had moved to Saskatoon when they were under 40 years of age; 18% had moved here during their forties, fifties, or sixties; and only 2% had moved to Saskatoon as seniors. Most of the respondents (60%) had come to Saskatoon for employment. Family already living in the city had brought 20% to Saskatoon; 7% had come for their or a family member's health or for medical reasons. Other individual reasons for relocation accounted for 13% of elders' moving: these included to be close to the children; for better housing; for retirement; for 'adventure'; and 'just for a change.'

Most elders and their spouses reported health conditions. Almost all were living with some chronic condition. 'Chronic conditions,' as defined by Statistics Canada, are 'health conditions that have been diagnosed by a health-care professional and have lasted or are expected to last, at least six months.' Regarding the relationship between health and housing, it has been stated that 'many studies have established that living in appropriate, affordable, and safe housing of good quality contributes to seniors' quality of life.' 'Appropriate housing' is defined as 'housing that is designed and supported as per the specifications of those who live in it.' Moreover, adequate, affordable, and appropriate housing is a prerequisite for good health' (CHRA 2003, 16) The research found that arthritis and failing eyesight were the most prevalent health conditions among Saskatoon's Metis elders. Arthritis affected 52% of individuals but 68% of households. Failing eyesight affected 51% of individuals but 66% of households. High blood pressure affected 28% (almost one in three Metis seniors) and was present in 36% of households. Slightly over one in four (26%) suffered from diabetes, which was found in 35% of households. Poor hearing was a problem for 23% of Metis elders sampled and affected 30% of all elder households. Heart problems existed for 16% of Metis elders and affected 22% of the elder residences. Fifteen per cent of individual respondents and one in five households were affected by respiratory/asthma conditions. Stomach and bowel conditions affected 11% of elders and 15% of households. Cancer was a factor in the lives of 5% of the sample and affected 7% of households.

Four per cent of respondents had hip/knee replacements; this affected 5% of households. Another 1% of the sample and households had amputations, and 1% had osteoporosis. Compared to other Aboriginal people, the Metis elders had a higher level of medical access; Metis contact with health professionals was greater than that reported by other urban Aboriginal people (Statistics Canada 2003). However, when it comes to traditional medicines, healing, and wellness practices in their community, Metis elders have a lower rate of access (16%) than do other urban Aboriginal people (31%). Yet contact between Metis elders and nurses seems to be less common than among other urban Aboriginal people; only 11% of Metis elder households were attended by a nurse. Compared to all Aboriginal households, around 23% of Aboriginal people had contact with a nurse (Aboriginal Peoples Survey 2001). Metis elders, particularly those living alone, want and could benefit from more contact with a health professional, particularly in regard to diet and medication. Having a nurse employed, perhaps part-time, in a Metis elder facility would be highly beneficial. It would be advisable, then, for housing authorities to work with health districts to create a position specifically geared to the health and housing issues of Metis elders. Such a program could be structured much like the one for Community Health Representatives, who for many years have served First Nations communities. These people would teach and advise Metis elders regarding their individual health situations in a culturally appropriate way.

The survey asked a number of questions related to services needed and received by elders. It was found that 97% of households had regular contact with a doctor; that 29% reported seeing a specialist; that 80% reported seeing an optometrist; and that 61% regularly saw a dentist. When asked who prepared their meals, almost all (94%) said they prepared their own. Almost two-thirds of households (64%) reported that there was no one to help with home maintenance and repairs. Over half of Metis elder households had no help with lawn care and snow removal. Only 31% of households had access to traditional foods and 16% to traditional medicines. Of the respondents, 69% claimed that they could drive a car, whereas 84% reported that they had access to a vehicle. Less than half the respondents or their spouses ever took the bus. More than half reported that they had someone to drive them to appointments and to get groceries for them. But four out of ten did not have anyone to accompany them to appointments.

The survey found that Metis elders remain very active. Cultural activities dominate their time. Metis culture is grounded in social activities. Metis songs, stories, history, and cultural ways are passed on at gatherings. These gatherings very often centre on food, which is cooked out of doors. Food is especially important to Metis elders, many of whom come from communities where people still camp out. Barbecues are an urban adaptation of this cultural activity (a large majority of respondents said that they barbecue). Metis cultures are oral cultures, which means that the history, culture, and social norms of the Metis peoples are passed on to the next generation through person-to-person contact. Visiting is more than getting together. It is how the culture maintains and transmits itself. It is an opportunity to pass on the traditional songs, stories, skills, foods, and medicines. This research found that 81% of the Metis elders liked to go visiting in other parts of the city.

Spirituality is very important to Metis elders. Dual traditions are not uncommon, for Metis spirituality is inclusive. This research found that 72% of the Metis elders attended church and that 35% participated in Aboriginal spiritual ceremonies.

Metis women have long been recognized as talented seamstresses. Since the time of the Red River Settlement, coats, moccasins, and other articles sewn and decorated by Metis women have been much sought after. Metis women create articles of clothing that combine European with First Nations designs and materials. They have passed their design skills on to their children through the years, and this is reflected in the fact that 68% of the Metis elder women in this survey sewed, although only 12% reported producing Metis traditional crafts. Another 7% said that they do woodworking. Food being the centre of Metis cultural activities, 65% of the Metis elders in the sample were still doing baking. Some Metis elders in Saskatoon still enjoyed traditional fishing and hunting activities, even though they now lived in the city. Much of Metis culture revolves around music, and the Metis elders of Saskatoon were continuing that tradition: 43% sang; 41% went to dances; and 30% played a musical instrument.

*Housing*

When asked which items they would want to see in Metis elders' homes if they were planning for future elders, the respondents mentioned a variety of facilities and appliances. The research found that many Metis elders living with chronic diseases could be accommodated by such changes in their homes. Housing planning committees need to tap the expertise of groups for the disabled and the Canadian Arthritis Society, the Saskatchewan Institute for the Prevention of Handicaps, and other resource centres to formulate appropriate designs for particular medical conditions.

The research found that over half the Metis elders in Saskatoon were living alone and that more women than men were living in single-person households. Also, 39% of the total sample had grade eight or less; another 40% had some high school; 17% have completed grade twelve; and just 3% had some post-secondary training. Educational attainment was somewhat lower for elders living alone: a significant number (63%) had less than grade nine; and for men in this category, 73% had less than grade nine. Given, then, that grade nine is universally accepted as the level of functional literacy, many of the Metis elders living alone were not functionally literate to follow instructions on such things as medicine bottles, pharmacy medical materials, and other materials given to them by doctors to help them cope with a medical condition.

A large number of Metis elders living alone survive on a very low fixed income: 30% of female and 27% of male Metis elders living alone had a monthly income of less than $1,000. Only one male Metis elder and two female Metis elders living alone did not have health problems.

Of those Metis elders who were living with others, almost all were living with family members; very few were living in a seniors home. The survey found that 11% of Metis elder households were comprised of three generations. Also, that many Metis elders were living with others out of necessity. Even when people were living with them, many Metis elders had no one to help them maintain the house, or to go with them for appointments or to do other chores.

Metis elder households that are responsible full-time for their grandchildren are referred to as 'grandfamilies.' A representative of GIFT (Grandparents Involved Full Time) explained: 'The role of grandparents in society is being redefined as new extended family members are added, which opens up family boundaries to new members as these families change and evolve. Instead of playing a peripheral role in the lives of their natural grandchildren, many grandparents find themselves becoming responsible for raising them and/or other children from "new extended family."' These families present the designer of Metis elder housing with a different set of issues. For example, for these Metis elders it may be of utmost importance to live near a school and playground. Moreover, the house may need safety precautions to protect toddlers.

The inventory of Metis elders housing stock in Saskatoon is limited at present. There is a much larger representation of family households in the urban Metis population than in the non-Aboriginal population. This holds important implications for the types of housing units funded and built. Urban Metis renter households live in lower-quality dwellings: 16.5% dwellings are in need of major repair, compared to 9% of non-Aboriginal dwellings. Metis households encounter more affordability problems than do non-Aboriginal households, with 37% spending more than 30% of family income for housing and 15% (one in every six) facing a severe rent burden, paying half their income for rent. Non-family households are a smaller proportion of Aboriginal households, but they experience a greater incidence of severe rent cost burden: 20% of non-family Aboriginal renter households spend 50% of income for rent. The average income of Aboriginal households is 87% that of non-Aboriginal households (NAHA 2004). The current Centenary Affordable Housing Program framework, which makes average market rent the basis for grant eligibility, specifies a maximum federal grant of $25,000 per unit, to be matched by provincial and/or local sources. Research by the National Aboriginal Housing Association (NAHA) has demonstrated that the current criteria cannot provide affordable housing for Aboriginal people in Saskatoon. The program criteria (average market rent and a maximum of $50,000 grants) are incapable of supporting the production of rental units that would be affordable to low-income Saskatoon Metis households. A more realistic amount would be in the order of $70,000 to $75,000.

One Metis-specific elder housing model exists in Saskatoon: La Petite Ville, which was home to some of the Saskatoon Metis elders interviewed for this study. Many lessons have been learned from the experience of designing, building, and operating Saskatoon's first and currently only Metis elders' residence. It is time to build on the strengths of La Petite Ville to develop a holistic model that incorporates the voices of Metis elders. The primary and secondary data collected by the Metis Elders Circle Housing Research Project has led to the development of a model of Metis Holistic Housing for Elders, which encompasses many features of community area development and design development.

*Conclusions and Recommendations*

The research indicates that Metis elder housing options are not just about shelter; they must also support Metis elders in their quest for independent living in a culturally appropriate manner. When Metis elders are approached according to traditional protocols, they have much to say about their lives and their living conditions. It is essential that stake-holders respect the contributions and voices of the Metis elders by tak-ing the knowledge shared and translating it into respectful Metis elder housing options. There are obviously severe problems relating to the provision of Metis elder housing options in Saskatoon. Recently, as a result of this research project, Aboriginal and non-Aboriginal stakehold-ers have expressed an interest in partnering to develop a Metis elder housing project that would capture the best practices discussed in this report.

Specific recommendations include the following: Housing stake-holders should implement a housing strategy that is culturally appro-priate as well as representative of Metis elders. Government housing agencies should involve Metis elders when developing and imple-menting strategies, and that process should be collaborative and re-spectful of the diversity in the Metis elder community. At every stage of housing development, from planning to completion, there must be Metis elders. Housing stakeholders should refine their current housing strategies to better meet the housing needs of Metis elders; this might include reviewing current strategies and, where appropriate, engaging government, Aboriginal housing authorities, elders, and partner stake-holders in an advisory capacity. Governments' housing strategies for Metis elders should include partners from the various health, social services, security, and disability agencies. Government stakeholders should establish a communications strategy for partnerships among Aboriginal and non-Aboriginal housing stakeholders. Protocols should be developed to be engaged around housing initiatives targeting Metis elders. Housing development initiatives under which Aboriginal and non-Aboriginal stakeholders could partner should be better promoted. Establishing personal relationships between Aboriginal and non-Aboriginal stakeholders is one approach to overcoming the barriers to achieving culturally inclusive partnerships between the parties, and in that regard, there is a pressing need for an Aboriginal housing initia-tive officer who would foster these relationships. A database of Aboriginal and non-Aboriginal housing stakeholders should be de-veloped and maintained to encourage communication between the parties. A list of Aboriginal linkages (one that includes Aboriginal stakeholders, Aboriginal media, and community organizations that could be utilized to advertise successful partnerships between Aboriginal and non-Aboriginal housing stakeholders) should be de-veloped. Aboriginal internships with housing stakeholders could be established as a step toward relationship building between the parties; this might include job rotations among the stakeholders, job shadowing, and mentoring programs. Finally, housing stakeholders' awareness of the Aboriginal peoples of Canada should be improved and enhanced; moreover, it is recommended that stakeholders increase the numbers of staff who have participated in learning and improving their understanding of Aboriginal people. A core theme found throughout the research project was that no housing initiatives or relationship-building exercises among stakeholders will be effective unless those stakeholders take a holistic and culturally appropriate approach.

## Chapter Nine

# Aboriginal Participation in Economic and Community Development and Homebuilding

## Involving Aboriginal People in Economic and Community Development and the Homebuilding Industry

Aboriginal people are becoming increasingly involved in economic and community development in Saskatoon; but they have quite a long way to go, given their sizeable proportion of the city's population. Aboriginal participation in businesses of all sorts has become more obvious in recent years. So, too, has Aboriginal participation in community development, although the poorest inner west side neighbourhoods most in need of development – which happen to be the area of the city with the highest concentration of Aboriginal residents – could use more proactive Aboriginal leadership. Aboriginal participation in the homebuilding industry should also be increased, and this is being ensured through apprenticeships intended specifically to train more Aboriginal young people in the homebuilding skills that will be increasingly needed.

### *Aboriginal Economic Development*

Back in 1991, the national chair of the Canadian Aboriginal Economic Development Strategy observed that First Nations were going to have to pay more attention to the demographic shift. Specifically, he pointed out, more and more of the First Nations population was living off reserve, and they would need help in developing their own businesses in the cities, as well as their housing. Aboriginal people in urban areas had higher labour force participation and employment rates than those living in non-urban areas; moreover, those who found work were earning more income and were more likely to have steady, full-time work. But at the same time, unemployment rates for the urban Aboriginal labour force were more than double those for the non-Aboriginal population, even though the labour force participation rates were almost the same. Rates of poverty among urban Aboriginal people were still far higher than among other urban residents. A further impediment to the development of distinct Aboriginal economic and cultural communities in urban areas was a perceived lack of urban Aboriginal governing structures and institutional development. Moreover, governments tended not to recognize urban Aboriginal communities when it came to important policies and programs. Provincial governments across Canada had been open to developing policies aimed at addressing the distinct needs and circumstances of some sectors of the population, such as immigrants; yet they were reluctant to do so for Aboriginal people. Educational attainment and training among Aboriginal people tended to be higher in urban areas than in rural areas or reserves but still remained substantially lower than among non-Aboriginal urban residents. Racism, felt most strongly in urban areas, was also inhibiting Aboriginal economic prospects. Lack of accessible child care was yet another barrier: Aboriginal women living in cities did not have the same support, in the form of extended family and community networks, as women in rural or reserve communities.

Much of this sounds familiar today. But two decades later, what *has* changed markedly is urban Aboriginal economic development. A 1996 report by the Micro-Economic Policy Analysis Branch and Aboriginal Business Canada, *Aboriginal Entrepreneurs in Canada: Progress and Prospects*, found that Aboriginal entrepreneurs were already playing an increasingly important role in the Canadian economy. The number of Aboriginal people who were self-employed had grown 170% in just 15 years – more than two-and-a-half times faster than the national increase in self-employment of Canadians in general (65%). Aboriginal business entrepreneurs were now found in virtually every sector of the Canadian economy. Two out of three Aboriginal businesses were out west, and more than half were in cities. Many Aboriginal businesses had both Aboriginal and non-Aboriginal employees and in this respect as well were contributing to economic growth. According to data from that Aboriginal business survey, 12,710 new Aboriginal businesses were added during this period, generating 48,502 new jobs, of which 30,444 had been taken up by Aboriginals.

The Royal Commission on Aboriginal Peoples (1996) had forecast that the Aboriginal population of Canada would be growing more than twice as quickly as the non-Aboriginal population. Because of this rapid growth and the need to address high Aboriginal unemployment, half a million jobs for Aboriginal people would be needed by 2016. This young Aboriginal population would have an enormous contribution to make to the labour force. Aboriginal youth were making significant strides in their education and qualifications and, like adults, were steadily increasing their competencies.

By 1996, the proportion of Aboriginal workers aged 15 to 24 who were self-employed was actually higher than the Canadian average. Yet despite its rapid growth, Aboriginal business ownership remained well below the national average: only 3.9% of all Aboriginal adults aged 15 and over owned a business, compared to the Canadian average of 7.9%. Aboriginal women, too, were establishing their own businesses in significant numbers. However, a lower proportion of Aboriginal businesses (62%) were profitable, relative to the percentage for Canada as a whole (71%). Also noteworthy is that Aboriginal people were underrepresented in business services, finance, insurance, and real estate. In addition, Aboriginal businesses seemed to be less well positioned for the future by not being more strongly a part of the burgeoning knowledge-based industries. A Statistics Canada survey of more than 1,000 Aboriginal businesses concluded that the priorities for business success were management skills, improving productivity, innovation, financing and access to capital, employee training and skill development, and broader marketing. The same survey found that even urban Aboriginal people can feel isolated and marginalized – hence the perceived importance of self-reliance, mutual support, and Aboriginal 'connectedness.' And hence, too, the importance of peer models and of information specifically tailored to the needs and experiences of young and aspiring Aboriginal entrepreneurs.

Lorne Sully emphasizes that the city has been well served for 20 years by a municipal policy that invites Aboriginal businesses to locate and develop here; the city's strategic and business plans were the first in Canada to explicitly invite partnerships between the City and Aboriginal organizations (*Saskatoon StarPhoenix*, 27 December 2010). In 2010 the First Nations Bank of Canada, headquartered in Saskatoon, had a net income of $10.2 million and was growing by 12% a year. This Aboriginal-controlled bank's stated 'primary objective is to serve the financial service needs of Aboriginal people, business and governments.'

Partnerships have been developing between Aboriginal and non-Aboriginal businesses, and between the former and the provincial government, although the present provincial government has been criticized for terminating partnership agreements that had the potential to increase Aboriginal employment. Dozens of partnership agreements among employers, unions, and the Ministry of First Nations and Metis Relations had been forged under the Aboriginal Employment Development initiative, only to have the provincial government cut this $786,000 program. The provincial minister has pointed out, however, that eliminating this program has actually *freed* his ministry to increase funding for Aboriginal post-secondary education, including skills training programs (see in particular the section in this chapter on Aboriginal participation in apprenticeship programs).

Meanwhile, during 2009–10 the federal government gave Westcap Management Ltd. (a private venture capital and equity fund management firm based in Saskatoon, founded in 1991) a total of $7.6 million to develop the BRIDG initiative for the advancement of First Nations and Metis business opportunities in Saskatchewan. Twenty First Nations and Metis communities now participate in this program (*Saskatoon StarPhoenix*, 21 April 2010, 3 February 2011). The federal government has also contributed $5 million to the Clarence Campeau Development Fund (CCDF) to establish the Metis Energy and Resource Program, which aims to increase the participation of Metis businesses in the resource and energy sectors in Saskatchewan. CCDF was established in 1997 through an agreement between the NDP provincial government and the Metis Nation of Saskatchewan, as a response to the obvious lack of equity capital available to the Metis community. It provides funding for business development, community economic development, and management skills development, as well as other assistance to new and existing businesses owned and run by Metis. Specifically, the new Equity Contribution Program will provide support to independent Metis entrepreneurs, and the Community Infrastructure Program will create and build Metis-owned businesses. Since its founding, CCDF has approved more than $33 million in funding and leveraged another $110 million from conventional lenders, thereby injecting more than $143 million into the Saskatchewan economy. The federal government's investment in the Metis Energy and Resource Program comes through a major resource and energy development initiative designed to help Aboriginal businesses partner in major economic developments and energy projects (*Regina Leader-Post*, 23 April 2010; *Saskatoon StarPhoenix*, 25 May 2010). In March 2011, CCDF established the Metis Economic Development Sector to act as an information broker and coordinator of Metis business opportunities in Saskatchewan (*Saskatoon StarPhoenix*, 8 March 2011).

A report of the National Aboriginal Economic Development Board (NAEDB), released in July 2012, indicated that while progress is being made in Aboriginal economic development, a gap between Aboriginal and general Canadian economic development persists; significant strides need to be made if there is to be any chance of closing this gap. This report was intended to track progress towards the vision of the Federal Framework for Aboriginal Economic Development announced in 2009, which focussed on the income, employment, and well-being of Aboriginal people, and towards overcoming existing barriers including land and resources, entrepreneurship and business development and infrastructure. In the process, the NAEDB intended to collect comparative information on the economic standing of Aboriginal and non-Aboriginal people, identify variations among 'Aboriginal heritage groups,' and where possible identify differences between on- and off-reserve First Nations, inform policy and program direction, and provide a baseline and set goals so that trends and progress can be measured over time (*Globe and Mail*, 3 July 2012).

Aboriginal populations have often been seen as a possible solution to Saskatchewan's labour shortage. The CEO of the Regina and District Chamber of Commerce has commented: 'The importance of Aboriginal people to Saskatchewan cannot be underestimated ... Aboriginal people will become a dominant force in Saskatchewan's economy' (*Saskatoon StarPhoenix*, 28 April 2009). However, Aboriginal people have continued to face challenges entering the workforce. A study released in July 2000 by the Saskatoon Labour Market Committee indicated that only 17% of Saskatoon's private-sector employers were actively recruiting Aboriginal employees. First Nations communities have just over half the level of economic development of non-First Nation communities, measured by average earnings from employment (CMHC 2004). Aboriginal unemployment in Saskatchewan remains disturbingly high: in 2005, Saskatchewan Aboriginal people had the lowest employment rate in the western provinces at 50.7%, while their unemployment rate stood at 15.9%, compared to 4.5% for all non-Aboriginal people in the province (*Saskatoon StarPhoenix*, 15 June 2005). The income gap between Aboriginals and others continues to be a major concern. A University of Ottawa study released by Statistics Canada in June 2008 found that in Saskatoon, male Registered Indians resident off-reserve were earning 63% less than non-Aboriginal men, while

Aboriginal women were earning 44% less than other women. Even when we compare people of the same age and educational level, Aboriginal people come out far poorer. The income of Aboriginal men with Registered status who live on reserve is 50% lower than that of non-Aboriginals; for women, the equivalent figure is 21% lower.

Currently, despite an international economic recession, Saskatchewan has the highest economic growth rate of any Canadian province; indeed, that rate is accelerating. The CIBC World Markets ranking of 24 Canadian cities places Regina and Saskatoon first and third respectively for 'economic momentum.' So opportunities abound. So do solutions to the problems of economic integration and advancement of Aboriginal people in the province, especially in the larger cities. For example, the Aboriginal Skilled Workers Association (ASWA) was established in Regina in November 2005 to deal with persistent Aboriginal unemployment and limited recruitment. The File Hills–Qu'Appelle Tribal Council has been creating partnerships and entering into discussions with businesses; it has also been working with the FSIN and the Regina Chamber of Commerce to develop a mentorship program aimed at encouraging potential employers to hire Aboriginal people. The Saskatoon and Region Home Builders' Association (SRHBA), with the collaboration of the Saskatchewan Apprenticeship and Trade Certification Commission (SATCC) and the Bridges and Foundations Project, has established a bursary for careers in residential construction, particularly for Aboriginals. The SRHBA has also formed the Bridges and Foundations Career Development Corporation, which is described later in this chapter. Also in Saskatoon, an information technology program at the Saskatchewan Indian Institute of Technologies (SIIT) is collaborating with SaskPower to offer guaranteed summer employment as well as scholarships to Aboriginal students. The federal government has established a $33.1 million program called the Northern Career Quest Partnership to help Aboriginal workers develop skills and gain experience in the mining, mineral, and oil and gas industries. Recent First Nations partnerships include McNair Business Development Inc. The Saskatoon Community Service Village has been a beneficiary of the Saskatchewan Indian Gaming Authority (SIGA). There is great potential for Aboriginal participation in cooperatives, including in the home-building industry. Yet an extensive report on *The Social and Economic Importance of the Co-operative Sector in Saskatchewan* (Ketilson et al. 1998) did not specifically single out Aboriginal participation.

Everywhere in Saskatchewan there are large-scale economic developments on or near reserves. An example is Dakota Dunes, a golf course, casino, hotel, and housing complex on Whitecap Dakota First Nation just south of Saskatoon (see Chapter 3). Others include CTK Plastics Ltd. on Carry-the-Kettle First Nation, and Kihiw Construction and Trucking, based on Cowessess First Nation. Still other recent examples of Aboriginal economic development in Saskatchewan have centred on mining and resource development: the Indigenous Potash Group has secured an estimated $25 billion to strengthen a competitive bid for the Potash Corporation of Saskatchewan; Muskowekwan First Nation signed an agreement with Encanto Potash Corporation in November 2010 for the development and operation of a mine on their reserve; and Kitsaki Management, based in the La Ronge First Nation, is collaborating with Golden Band Resources, a northern mining company (Kitsaki Management has been operating for three decades and currently has about 800 employees).

A business development corporation at Onion Lake Cree First Nation oversees an economic boom in this community of 4,000, contributing to long-term planning with an emphasis on education and training and aggressive economic diversification. Oil and natural gas production began during the 1970s; today 7,500 barrels of oil are produced daily, which is expected to double when a thermal steam capture project is completed. Black Pearl Resources provides this First Nation with a 34.5% royalty for each barrel extracted, while Calgary-based Fogo Energy provides a recently negotiated 50% royalty with an option for company control. Natural gas is produced by the Onion Lake Natural Gas Co-operative. Assets from these projects contribute to a band trust or are reinvested in business development, which now includes more than 40 trucks to service the extractive businesses, sheet metal and glass manufacturing, retail growth, construction supplies, and housing and a home-ownership program. This First Nation has its own force of 22 trained 'peacekeepers' who work with the RCMP, as well as its own medical services including a clinic, ambulance, pharmacy, and dental school program (*Saskatoon StarPhoenix*, 11 Sept. 2012).

And the Meadow Lake Tribal Council owns 50% of Mistik Management, which possesses 1.8 million hectares of forest, harvested by NorSask and other forestry companies owned by MLTC; NorSask produces 150 million feet of lumber a year. Wood waste from this production will be converted into enough energy to power 30,000 homes by a

$150-million Bioenergy Centre currently being constructed by MLTC; this centre is expected to employ more than 300 people by 2014. An estimated 2,500 people already work for MLTC enterprises, which collectively gross $300 million annually; besides forestry, these companies also include home and business construction, trucking, fertilizer, hotels, and airlines (*Saskatoon StarPhoenix*, 12 Sept. 2012).

There is an Aboriginal Tourism Association of Saskatchewan (ATASI). The Saskatchewan Indian Equity Foundation (SIEF) is controlled by the province's 74 First Nations. A very significant recent development has been First Nations participation in corporate farming in Alberta and Saskatchewan. A single recent contract with One Earth involves 17 Saskatchewan First Nations with over a million acres of agricultural land, as well as $1 million contributed to the University of Saskatchewan to establish a scholarship fund for Aboriginal students to study agriculture.

To an appreciable extent, this economic development on reserves could stem the flow of First Nations people into the cities. Yet Aboriginal businesses in Saskatoon have become highly diverse. Most are independent, but many are supported by bands, and some are located on urban reserves or on land purchased by First Nations (see chapter 10).

*Community Development*

The Definition of 'Community'

The Centre for the Study of Cooperatives at the University of Saskatchewan has provided useful discussions of 'community,' 'community engagement,' and 'community economic development.' The word 'community' (*kapesiwin* in Cree) usually makes us think about where we live, play, or work, about the groups we belong to, and about how we are connected to other members of that community. It gives us a sense of belonging – community must be 'realized' (Findlay and Findlay 1995). Is it possible to build community? How does that happen? What does it take? Communities celebrate diversity; they motivate people and get them involved. We want to feel that we belong, that our needs are recognized, that we have the ability to contribute. We want to be proud to say 'this is my community.' So how do we make the dreams for our community become a reality? Building inclusive communities ensures respect, equality, and justice for all and allows communities to grow increasingly strong, vibrant, and healthy. Central to this building process is community engagement – people working collaboratively, through inspired action and learning, to create and realize bold visions for their common future ( Centre for the Study of Cooperatives 2010).

Citizen engagement is vital to a healthy and democratic society. Engagement is about connections and interactions. It is about building relationships among people working together toward a common objective. It is about encouraging participation – determining local priorities and then getting everyone involved in developing policy and making decisions. It is about acknowledging local expertise and acting on it. It is as much about the process as the results. And overall, it is about making one's community a better place to live. Ideally in an engaged community, people work together to solve complex issues. They define local priorities and create a common vision. They are concerned and committed, and they participate in community events. They value local knowledge and expertise; volunteer their time for the benefit of the community; recognize and value cultural diversity; listen to and respect others' opinions; and participate in local events and initiatives.

Community economic development (CED) focuses on the needs of the whole community and uses internal resources to create sustainable results. CED emphasizes local solutions to local problems, with communities using their own resources, skills, and abilities; it involves the entire community in creating a long-term strategy inclusive of environmental, economic, and social outcomes; and it promotes local ownership and local capacity building so that the benefits of economic growth remain within the community.

A recent study of social enterprise in Saskatoon's inner-city neighbourhoods by the Community-University Institute for Social Research (CUISR) and the Centre for the Study of Cooperatives (Diamantopoulos and Findlay 2007) suggested that social enterprises – autonomous not-for-profit community organizations such as Quint and CHEP – are more effective at improving conditions in these poorer core neighbourhoods than governments or private concerns. It follows that social enterprises need more financial and community support. Yet there are significant obstacles, such as competition among community organizations for scarce funding, a lack of coordination and unified political stance, and the availability only of short-term funding when effective community economic development requires long-range vision and commitment. Other research conducted by CUISR on community economic development has included studies of community resilience, community economic development and economic development (Radloff 2006), and poverty elimination strategies (CUISR 2006).

Riversdale

In discussing community development, first let us profile the two inner west side neighbourhoods in Saskatoon that have the highest concentrations of Aboriginal people: Riversdale and Pleasant Hill. Riversdale, immediately west of the city centre, is the second poorest neighbourhood in the city. The overall population has seemed stable, although there is considerable mobility into and out of the area. At least one-quarter of the residents aged 15 and over have less than a high school education. Enrolment at the public school, Princess Alexandra, has fluctuated in recent years, with some periods of rapid increases; enrolment is now largely Aboriginal. Average family income has remained low. The proportion of single-parent families increased very rapidly with the influx of Aboriginal people. The housing in this area has been among the least expensive in the city – around three times more affordable than the city average, according to the housing affordability index. However, this has recently been changing. Average gross rent has been increasing, while the number of households has been substantially decreasing. Homeownership has slowly been increasing, renting correspondingly decreasing. (Riversdale is one of five inner west side neighbourhoods where Quint Development Corporation has been actively promoting homeownership cooperatives.) Riversdale is one of the oldest neighbourhoods in Saskatoon; most of the houses there were constructed before 1945, and a high proportion (over 80%) before 1960, so they are now over half a century old and in general represent the oldest housing in the city.

Riversdale merges west into the West Industrial Area, the front line of extreme conflict between residential areas and industrial storage yards. Inevitably, this has resulted in many violations of city zoning regulations. The concentration of pawnshops along the neighbourhood's main artery has been an issue – 13 of the 17 pawnshops on the inner west side were once located here; however, since the province gave the city the regulatory tool to implement separation distances for pawnshops in 2001, the number in this area has declined from 17 to 6. A Local Area Plan has been produced by the Riversdale Local Area Planning Committee (LAPC), consisting of more than 150 residents,

business and property owners, community groups, and other stakeholders. Its specific recommendations deal with housing, land use,
parks and recreation, traffic circulation, municipal services, economic
development, heritage and culture, neighbourhood perception, and
safety. The plan recommends the creation of a 'vacant lot registry'
to encourage development on vacant residential and commercial sites,
of which there were 45 at the time the plan was drafted, 16 of them
residential. The Riversdale Business Improvement District aims to encourage businesses to locate in the area. The recent sale of land designated for a park to a chain discount variety store upset many residents
and community interest groups; in any case, such a store hardly re-
solves the pressing need for a supermarket. With safety increasingly an
issue, the LAPC has recommended regular 'safety audits' and the elimination of 'hiding spaces' between buildings and especially near school
grounds, as well as improved lighting, better pedestrian pathways, and
an easing of traffic congestion (children going to the one public school
have to cross major thoroughfares from residential areas, one of them
six lanes wide, the other four). Riversdale, incorporated in 1905, has
long been a working-class area. Increasing numbers of Aboriginal people have settled here in recent years, adding to an older mix of
Ukrainians, Chinese, and Vietnamese.

Riversdale has been changing. Property values in Riversdale, both
commercial and residential, have recently been increasing at a faster rate
than in most areas of the city. For example, houses south of 20th Street
(the main commercial thoroughfare) used to sell for around $35,000, but
some now sell in the $150,000 to $200,000 range. Commercial properties
are now attracting small business owners seeking to purchase property
for less than they would have paid elsewhere in the city, and there has
been a recent influx of young entrepreneurs. The recently redeveloped
and expanded Farmers Market is a major attraction. The Riversdale
Community Association and Riversdale Business Improvement District
are active community organizations. The highly reputable Saskatchewan
Native Theatre and Roxy Theatre (for genre films) are located here,
while the major riverfront development of River Landing, home to the
Persephone Theatre, is just a short walk away.

There is a growing sense of community. Safety issues are lessening,
and residents comment that they can now walk the streets without feeling harassed or endangered. In fact, neighbourhood walking tours
(named 'Jane's Walks' in hundreds of participating cities internationally,
after crusading urban planner Jane Jacobs) have been held here as well

as in other inner-city neighbourhoods of Saskatoon. A police substation was established in what had once been the Little Chief service station.

Yet all of these positive changes have not necessarily increased affordable housing. Now that the 'gentrification' of Riversdale seems to have begun, homes have become even less affordable. As city columnist Charles Hamilton explained in his annual City Report (*Planet S*, 12–16 December 2010), gentrification is a process by which a poorer neighbourhood is slowly made more prosperous as businesses and relatively more affluent people choose to settle there. The neighbourhood then starts to become a destination, and rents and housing prices increase. Sooner or later, the lower-income people who had predominated in the area are forced to move. While the City and developers see opportunity in this demographic shift, low-income residents inevitably pay the price of this development and find themselves increasingly at risk of homelessness. According to senior planner Alan Wallace, displacement cannot be prevented: 'that is just the way the market economy works.' To which Hamilton responds: 'That's probably true ... but if it is, shouldn't there be a counter-balance to make sure the market economy works for everyone, not just those with enough money to partipate? As property and housing prices go higher and higher, that's something worth thinking about.' The vacancy rate in Riversdale, close to 40% just 10 years ago, has declined markedly to the present 8.3%. Clearly, then, housing availability has become far more limited.

City councillor Pat Lorje has expressed her concern about what she views as the overabundance of support agencies for poor and homeless people in Riversdale and has advocated what she calls 'solution by dilution.' In her view, the area's poverty is being perpetuated by the large number of social support agencies there (including church-based services); as a consequence, poor residents become trapped in their negative lifestyle and fail to resolve their poverty, homelessness, and addiction issues. According to Lorje, the issue is not simply poverty – it is the *concentration* of poverty, and this concentration prevents residents from rising out of the lifestyle to which they have become accustomed. This concentration in turn diminishes the potential strength of the community. So Lorje recommends that services and support agencies should be spread throughout the city (an alternative would be a moratorium on social organizations, which she has suggested has been done in other impoverished neighbourhoods in Canada and the United States).

There are, however, other opinions on this issue: it is not simply coincidental that these agencies and services have concentrated in Riversdale

– they are responding to a need. Attempts to clean up the area may amount simply to getting rid of the street people – that is, driving them away to make room for more 'respectable' people. And a significant proportion of the neighbourhood's residents are Aboriginal – Riversdale contains the second highest proportion of Aboriginal residents of any neighbourhood (after Pleasant Hill). What, then, do the residents themselves think?

## Pleasant Hill

Pleasant Hill, immediately to the west of Riversdale, has the highest proportion of Aboriginal residents of any Saskatoon neighbourhood (now at least half the residents and continuing to increase), and coincidentally is the poorest neighbourhood in the city. Its population has been relatively stable. The education levels attained by residents have been comparatively low (estimates are that around one-quarter of the residents aged 15 and over have less than high school education). Public and Catholic school enrolment, now largely Aboriginal, has rapidly increased at times in recent years. Average family income, persistently the lowest of any city neighbourhood, has been gradually increasing. The proportion of single-parent families has been steadily increasing. The housing affordability index indicates that housing is almost three times more affordable in this area that in the city in general. Average gross rent has been slowly increasing but is still the lowest in the city. The total number of households has been slowly decreasing; three-quarters of households are now rented, one-quarter owned. Housing in this area is generally not as old as in Riversdale (just 14.5% of houses were constructed before 1945, 41.4% before 1960). The average selling price for a home has increased substantially in recent years, mainly as a result of speculation by developers, as in Riversdale.

The Final Report of the Pleasant Hill Local Area Plan (City of Saskatoon 2002a) provided a great deal of information on pressing issues in the community along with recommendations for actions to address these issues. That report included an extensive discussion of housing. It specified a number of approaches to improving residential land use: encouraging compatible redevelopment in the neighbourhood; providing incentives for property owners to preserve and enhance existing housing; strengthening opportunities for renters to become owners; encouraging infill housing development on vacant properties; encouraging land development that would address the housing needs of all residents; acknowledging and promoting redevelopment that would foster cooperative relationships among developers, businesses, and residents; strengthening the coordination and further development of housing policies among governments, developers, and the community; and encouraging people to take pride in their home and community. Many older and poorer houses in Pleasant Hill had begun to deteriorate; many had been abandoned and boarded up. Between 10% and 15% of housing units were in need of major repair. So the community plan called for property owners to enhance and preserve existing housing, which could in turn improve residential stability and investor confidence.

At the same time that the community's population was increasing, the number of good-quality housing units was decreasing. The emerging problem was that property maintenance costs were rising and that owners were becoming less willing to pay them. Many rental properties were now owned by landlords (often absentee), who viewed themselves as investors rather than as property managers and who were doing little to maintain their properties. The Residential Rehabilitation Assistance Program (RRAP) was available to help homeowners pay for housing improvements, but this program relied on the willingness of owners to renovate their homes. At the time of the report, Saskatoon's core neighbourhoods were receiving approximately $17 million a year in Shelter Allowance to pay for accommodation; from this, owners were expected to cover all operating costs, including maintenance. Fully one-quarter of Pleasant Hill's population was receiving Social Assistance. One of the more notorious stretches of dilapidated apartment buildings, with houses sandwiched between, along a main thoroughfare, had more than its fair share of fires and crimes (even murders). That stretch has recently been completely replaced by a new Metis housing complex.

Homeownership in Pleasant Hill decreased during the 1990s, then stabilized, and more recently has been slowly increasing. The planning group felt that owner-occupancy rates had fallen too low for long-term neighbourhood stability (in this regard, the neighbourhood's northern section has far lower owner-occupancy rates than the southern). The group recognized that families would be more stable if they owned their own homes; that neighbourhoods are more stable when there are more homeowners, who are less likely to move; and that homeowners have a vested interest in maintaining and improving their properties. The work carried out by Quint and SHIP in promoting homeownership in the community has been recognized.

In recent years, several interrelated trends have compounded the difficulties faced by the residents of Pleasant Hill in their efforts to find and keep well-maintained, affordable housing: rising maintenance and renovation costs; increases in house prices; and steadily increasing taxation. While the cost of accommodation continues to be lower in Pleasant Hill than anywhere else in Saskatoon, it has still climbed out of reach of a great many residents in this area, most of whom are relatively poor. The price increases have in turn increased the potential of relative or virtual homelessness; they have also made it increasingly difficult for agencies like Quint to operate their programs.

Pleasant Hill and other inner west side neighbourhoods have the highest vacancy rates in the city, yet affordability has become more of a problem. At the time of the report, there were at least 40 large vacant lots in Pleasant Hill, and many more smaller ones. This suggested that land was being underutilized, that properties were being abandoned, that investor confidence was waning, that properties were being poorly maintained, and that security problems were increasing (in fact, the vacant lots were contributing to crime). Consequently, the community plan called for more infill housing and commercial development.

The Pleasant Hill Revitalization Project

A major housing and urban renovation development in Pleasant Hill has evolved from the original housing charrette organized by the Bridges and Foundations Project (briefly described in the previous chapter). In what has become the Pleasant Hill Revitalization Project – the largest inner-city renewal project in the province – two city blocks have been demolished to make way for a massive redevelopment in the very centre of Pleasant Hill. A multifamily housing plan was proposed that would provide low-cost housing in Pleasant Hill and would serve as a training ground for local young people to learn the construction trades under the supervision of senior builders.

The City of Saskatoon contributed $3.7 million to purchase the land – part of $6.3 million in government contributions. Thirty-three family homes, all of them rental properties in poor condition, were demolished; all but three were owned by a single landlord who was one of the largest landholders in the area. This landlord collected over $1.8 million ($1.4 million for the destroyed houses plus a 25% 'land assembly premium' that he negotiated). The property owners were paid far more than the actual property values – for example, $470,000 just for one beauty salon and bungalow whose real worth was estimated at $103,700 (*Saskatoon StarPhoenix*, 13 February 2007, 17 July 2007). Residents of these houses complained about not being sufficiently informed and about a lack of assistance in moving to new accommodations. It must be said, though, that they had been invited to give their opinions on the project at an early meeting held at the Catholic school; few of them attended, and they were far outnumbered by officials and planners who were already committed to the project. As part of the redevelopment project, St Mary's Community School, the oldest Catholic school in the city, now virtually completely Aboriginal, was replaced by a new school.

The original Pleasant Hill Concept Plan, approved by City Council early in 2007, intended to create a mixed housing development and a new school; a seniors' complex, park and recreational space, and community centre were also discussed. The plan called for higher-density apartments or condos above ground-level retail and office space along the main thoroughfare. But only three potential developers submitted plans, and in the end, the housing part of the project was divided between two entities: the Affordable New Home Development Foundation (ANHDF), a partner in the Bridges and Foundations Project, which contracted with River Ridge Homes and Ehrenburg Homes to build two 'big house' structures – stacked townhouses of twelve units each – on its site; and Cenith Energy Corporation, which contracted to build 16 two-storey townhouse units. The Saskatchewan Housing Corporation (SHC) contributed $8 million to the construction of this affordable housing (another $8 million has since been announced for other affordable housing developments in Pleasant Hill). What is now being called Pleasant Hill Village consists of 96 multi-unit homes, including the 24 comprising Parkview Green (the medium-density ANHDF housing project), and 75 seniors housing units. There are also several small pockets of low-density housing, a mixed-use commercial and high-density housing complex, and the community-based Affinity Credit Union along the main traffic corridor (20th Strett). This is in addition to a medium-density mixed-use area, the new school, a Metis apartment block, and 466 acres of green space, including Grace Adam Metawewinihk Park and an archaeological site (the housing will be concentrated on just 13 acres). The seniors complex was expected to cost $14 million, other housing $15 million.

It is anticipated that Pleasant Hill Village, besides providing affordable housing, will make the neighbourhood safer and more attractive. The units in Parkview Green are of different sizes, costing between

$193,470 and $241,034. Half the units were reserved by Cress Housing and Quint; the rest will be available on the open market. It is expected that Aboriginal tenants will occupy at least half the units. The City of Saskatoon agreed to purchase any units not sold within five months of the opening in June 2010.

Energy efficiency has been built into these technologically advanced units. For example, they have high-efficiency furnaces, increased insulation (e.g., around windows), and heat recovery ventilation. All of this will ensure maintenance costs around 25% lower than for conventionally built homes. These units have private and secure entrances, ample closet space, recessed lighting, resistant materials (e.g., in doors and cabinets), water-saving toilets, and wheelchair accessibility (in ground-floor units). Rents will be controlled, with subsidized financing available from both the province and the city, and 'rent to own' will be made possible. Financial assistance for occupants of Parkview Green will include down payment assistance from the city, a new housing rebate program, an energy-efficient rebate for new homes, the Energy Star refund on a mortgage loan insurance premium, and the SHC homeownership program.

Schools (*kiskinohamatowikamik*) can be vital to Aboriginal life in the city. Today about one in five students in Saskatoon's Catholic school system are Aboriginal, and the Catholic School Board collaborates with the Saskatoon Tribal Council and the Central Urban Metis Federation in planning and delivering an increasing range of Aboriginal programs and services. The provincial government contributed $8.3 million toward a new $15 million St Mary's School, which will offer day care, community space, and a wellness centre with an optometry clinic.

Station 20 West

Another major community development project in Pleasant Hill, hailed as a stellar example of urban renewal and community participation, is Station 20 West. Originally conceived in 2005, this planned complex on one of the two main thoroughfares running through Pleasant Hill was intended to enhance community services and amenities; to create a public space in the urban core; to revitalize inner-city neighbourhoods; and to be a showcase for green building design. Specifically, it would have facilitated access to the following: affordable housing (through the Quint Development Corporation); nutritious food (through CHEP Good Food Inc. and Good Food Junction Co-op); health care (provided by the West Side Community Clinic along with dental, pediatric, mental health, addiction, and family support and maternal services and AIDS Saskatchewan); legal and restitutive consultation (the Elizabeth Fry Society); cross-cultural organizations (the Saskatchewan Intercultural Association and International Women of Saskatchewan); and education and literacy (an Outreach and Engagement Centre of the University of Saskatchewan, and a community library). The centre would also have fostered business development, employment opportunities, and community engagement. The offices of all these organizations would have been centrally located in the Community Enterprise Centre, separated by attractive green space from a community library and an affordable housing development of 55 units managed by Sask Housing. Central location and accessibility to local residents would have been key. The project would have 'epitomize[d] the intelligent approach to sustainable design' and would have featured renewable energy from a solar wall, the capture of waste heat given off by large coolers in the Good Food Junction, and a biowall to enhance internal air quality.

Work commenced in 2006 when the municipal, provincial, and federal governments shared the cost of demolishing existing buildings and cleaning up contaminated soil on the site. To its credit, the municipal government donated the land for the development for a token dollar. The provincial government was to contribute $8 million to the project, with private donors adding another $12 to $14 million. However, all of this development ground to a halt after the provincial election of 7 November 2007. The new Saskatchewan Party government cancelled the essential provincial contribution outright. This resulted in a protest march of around 2,500 irate residents and other concerned citizens. The City Council now became divided on its support of the project, concerned that it would be forced to contribute more financially, and public pressure on the council increased. The West Side Clinic, which was to be given new quarters in the complex, reluctantly decided to consider relocating elsewhere. One of its doctors, who had been very vocal in promoting the project, ran with considerable support for the provincial NDP leadership the next year.

The project had always been controversial, however. For example, its costs were high at a time when there were other health priorities, and the support of the Aboriginal community was not solid – the Saskatoon Tribal Council initially had refused to support the project because of a lack of appropriate First Nations consultation. Health columnist Mark Lemstra noted that 'in the ultimate act of irony, $8 million for a project that was designed to prevent complex and expensive health problems among low-income residents was used to pay for an $8.7 million budget shortfall of the Saskatoon Health Region to provide medical treatments' (*Saskatoon StarPhoenix*, 22 April 2010).

The end result of all this: the project has been scaled down to half its original size and the number of tenants reduced. Construction was repeatedly delayed; it finally recommenced in July 2011 at a revised cost of $5 million. Not the least because of the provincial government has withdrawn its backing, the project received widespread community support: more than $2.75 million was raised from over 2,000 individual donors and 150 businesses and organizations, with an equal amount to be covered in mortgages. A local columnist has commented that 'in a neighbourhood described as a "food desert" for its lack of ready access to fresh produce, meat and other nutritious staples by poor people with limited means of transportation, it was absurd for [the provincial premier] to suggest that a co-operative food store at Station 20 West would be unfair competition for other grocers' (*Saskatoon StarPhoenix*, 17 June 2011). In response, the major church denominations in the city have agreed to raise funds for the Good Food Junction Co-op. Meanwhile, the Affordable Housing Development (of 55 units) connected with the overall project was completed, with a regional branch of the Saskatoon Library on the main floor. The entire Station 20 West project officially opened Oct. 17 2012.

## Other Community Development Issues

Besides specific housing issues, a number of other community development issues and initiatives merit mention. The Core Neighbourhood Development Council (CNDC) was an attempt to pull together inner west side community organizations with a vested interest in community development, with a particular emphasis on First Nations and Metis involvement. Charlie Clark (now a city councillor), in his analysis of the CNDC in a report prepared for the Bridges and Foundations Project (Clark 2003), observed that politicized competition for scarce community development funding could explain the cautious involvement of First Nations and Metis organizations. Despite a rapidly increasing Aboriginal presence in west side neighbourhoods, Aboriginal participation in community meetings has too often been minimal.

Through the CNDC, Pleasant Hill and other inner west side communities would comprise an 'enterprise zone,' which would be offered incentives relating to economic activities and particular types of services (City of Saskatoon 2002). These communities have been described as a 'food desert' lacking adequate sources of healthier, inexpensive nutrition. A report of the Saskatoon Health Region in 2008 observed that residents living in the core neighbourhoods were 13 times more likely than other residents to develop diabetes and that a lack of grocery stores in these neighbourhoods was to blame. 'Food deserts' develop when food stores leave communities where there are not enough customers. For those left behind – the poor and elderly, who often lack their own means of transportation – living in a food desert can have a major impact on health and finances; they may be forced to shop mainly at smaller-scale convenience stores that don't offer a variety of healthier foods.

In the Local Area Plan, a need was perceived to change the poor perception of Pleasant Hill by eliminating prostitution, improving relations with the city police, improving the physical appearance of the community, promoting more of a sense of community, and of course improving the housing situation. Many Aboriginal residents have stressed the importance of a community centre (*mawawihitowikamik*). An ad hoc group that included residents, police, Habitat for Humanity, the Saskatoon Tribal Council, and the Saskatchewan Indian Gaming Authority (SIGA) raised funds in 2004 to purchase a house that would be turned into a community centre for youth, as a supplement to the White Buffalo Youth Lodge (an active Aboriginal youth centre in the community). And a residence offering free programs for both youth and adults was opened several years later farther west in the community, managed by the STC.

The City of Saskatoon intended to show that it was listening to the concerns of community residents and that it was willing to help make relevant changes. But as Saskatoon civic affairs columnist Gerry Klein commented: 'People who are crammed into inadequate housing, threatened by sex-trade workers or their pimps, harassed by johns, left feeling helpless by landlords or subjected to direct or systemic racism have difficulty believing they can actually effect change just by complaining that they feel unsafe walking home at night' (*Saskatoon StarPhoenix*, 17 May 2006). *Exit Routes: A Street Survival Guide,* which is distributed in Saskatoon, covers such wide-ranging topics as safety, the sexual exploitation of youth, needle safety, peer counselling, where to find community resources, youth involvement and volunteering opportunities, food and shelter basics, life skills, health services, legal services, schools, and alternative programs.

In June 2009, following the lead taken by the Bridges and Foundations Project charrette, which eventually contributed to the

Pleasant Hill Village development, the City held a community design workshop in Caswell Hill, the neighbourhood to the immediate north, to gather residents' ideas for a block of city land on which had been located city transit sheds and a bus repair garage. The participants proposed a medium-density townhouse development, park space, and a pedestrian mall.

Recent Canadian research has drawn some interesting conclusions. A Statistics Canada report in 2008 referred to 'social incivility,' ranging from noisy neighbours to drunkenness, drug use, and homelessness, and 'physical incivility,' which included excessive litter, abandoned buildings, graffiti, vandalism, and vacant lots. Another study found that in ethnically diverse cities, each ethnocultural group tends to blame others for irritations. Perhaps, though, there is a more communal spirit in poorer neighbourhoods. In Regina this has been reflected in the depressed North Central neighbourhood, where the previous diverse immigrant working-class population has been largely replaced by Aboriginal people; the residents there organized a public demonstration in November 2005, during which hundreds of residents participated in what has since become an annual 'smudge walk' led by the File Hills–Qu'Appelle Tribal Council, meant to symbolically link reserve and urban First Nations people and to cleanse the neighbourhood.

The present chapter includes a concise description of Quint Development Corporation's affordable housing program, which has involved many Native families. This description is excerpted from a Quint housing manual produced under the auspices of the Bridges and Foundations Project (Keeling, Szejvolt, and Untereiner 2004). The authors who compiled this manual included Laverne Szejvolt, Assistant Manager of Quint, who has extensive experience with affordable homeownership in inner-city neighbourhoods, and Julie Untereiner, one of the first homeowners in the Quint homeownership program, who went on to become a housing coordinator for Quint, then Manager of Project Development and Community Liaison at the Saskatchewan Housing Corporation.

*The Need for Aboriginal Collaboration and Training
in the Homebuilding Industry*

Partnerships between Aboriginal governments and their federal, provincial, and municipal counterparts have proliferated over the past couple of decades. Indian and Northern Affairs Canada has emphasized that partnerships are crucial to Aboriginal economic development.

Intergovernmental partnerships are of particular importance in Saskatchewan, where there are more partnership arrangements between Aboriginal and provincial governments than in the rest of Canada. Many such partnerships have been developed as a response to the disadvantageous socio-economic realities faced by Aboriginal communities – realities that include inadequate urban housing, higher incidence of poverty, and marginalization. Strategies to resolve inadequate housing include developing collaborative partnerships among various sectors. Research conducted under the auspices of the Bridges and Foundations Project by Cathy Nilson (2004) developed a theoretical framework that could be used to establish partnerships for Aboriginal housing projects, based on lessons learned from this author's extensive study of partnerships between the FSIN – through SIGA – and the Government of Saskatchewan, and on the application of these lessons to urban Aboriginal housing partnerships.

Recent researchers and commentators have pointed out that demographic and economic circumstances in Saskatchewan – including a shortage of labour, an active construction business, increasing numbers of Aboriginal entrepreneurs, Aboriginal urbanization, improving education of Aboriginal people, and a disproportion of youth in the fast-increasing Aboriginal population – are such that opportunities abound for meaningful Aboriginal participation in the Saskatchewan labour force. The construction trades are a prime example of such opportunity. The Construction Sector Council reports that an additional 7,000 construction workers will be needed in 2011 and 2012, obliging the industry to recruit outside the province (*Saskatoon StarPhoenix*, 18 March 2011). While more and more Aboriginal people are working in the homebuilding industry and related trades (it takes at least 40 separate trades to build a new home), they are employed primarily as common labourers, so getting more Aboriginal young people to qualify for specialized trades has become a priority of the Saskatchewan Apprenticeship and Trade Certification Commission (SATCC). To encourage women and equity groups to view skilled trades as viable careers, SATCC created the Saskatchewan Youth Apprenticeship Program in 2005. The program has since grown from an original 49 students at two high schools into 4,400 apprentices in 242 schools; 1,138 students have now graduated from the program, with certification. Saskatoon hosted a national conference on Aboriginal careers and employment in March 2011. The provincial government's Career and Employment Services centres play an important role in counselling Aboriginal people on employment and training opportunities; in 2010–11, 41% of clients were Aboriginal (*Saskatoon StarPhoenix*, 18 March 2011).

In 2010, Statistics Canada reported an unemployment rate of 13.9% for Aboriginal people aged 15 and older in Canada (compared to 8.1% for non-Aboriginal people); the Aboriginal youth employment rate was 45.1% (compared to 55.6% for non-Aboriginals). Also, employment of Aboriginal people in the construction industry had decreased by 16% during 2009 (compared to a 5% decrease among non-Aboriginal workers) (*Globe and Mail*, 14 July 2010). However, with the homebuilding industry expanding in Saskatchewan, construction trades seem to be an excellent way for Aboriginal people to enter the labour force and develop careers.

CMHC's 'Building Communities' program provides internships in the building trades to youth aged 17 to 29 who are residents of a First Nations reserve or Inuit community, are currently out of school and unemployed, and (preferably) are a single parent, illiterate, or disabled. While commendable, this initiative seems highly restrictive and if carried out literally would exclude well-educated urban Aboriginal youth, especially Metis.

We should be looking to a future where almost *any* homebuilding work would be done by Aboriginal people, from common labour to specialized trades, project supervision, and administration and management (and, ultimately, company ownership). But not necessarily *every* sort of work, insofar as homebuilding and construction more generally are complex endeavours involving so many diverse types of work, management, and financing. So it would make more sense to promote collaboration rather than exclusivity, although theoretically a particular building project could be carried out entirely by Aboriginal people.

In 2004 the Bridges and Foundations Project completed a study of Aboriginal involvement in apprenticeships related to residential construction in Saskatoon, under the direction of Val Sutton, Program Manager of the Sun Ridge Group) (Sutton 2004). It was not known how many Aboriginal people were currently working in the residential construction industry in Saskatoon, or how many were currently enrolled in all apprenticeship programs, much less how many might be interested in apprenticing to a residential construction trade. So the objectives of Sutton's study were to estimate these numbers and to learn the attitudes of potential employers – particularly owners and managers of residential construction companies – toward employing Aboriginal people.

The Bridges and Foundations Project, through initiatives of the Saskatoon and Region Home Builders' Association (SRHBA) and the

SATCC, has developed apprenticeships and bursaries for young First Nations and Metis people to learn construction trades. These initiatives, described later in this chapter by Alan Thomarat, currently CEO of both the local SRHBA and provincial Canadian Home Builders' Association, are among the most concrete and sustainable achievements of the Bridges and Foundations Project and have evolved into the Bridges and Foundations Career Development Corporation.

## More Than Four Walls and a Roof:
### QUINT DEVELOPMENT CORPORATION

*Community Economic Development*

Community Economic Development (CED) is a planned, community-controlled process of social change by which communities – in particular, disempowered ones – acquire through new institutions the control over the economic resources they need to ensure individual and collective fulfilment. CED is a more holistic approach than traditional models of economic development. It integrates economic, social, ecological, political, and cultural development as part of a strategy, and it has the revitalizing and reclaiming of community as its primary aim. CED focuses on developing community organizations that will enable minority or low-income groups to pool their resources and talents to create community ownership, jobs, training, and income for community members.

CED strives to be inclusive of marginalized groups and individuals, who are often excluded from full participation in the economy; to undertake economic development in a manner that is in keeping with community culture and values; to combine the development of an 'enterprising culture,' based on a philosophy of self-reliance, creativity, and innovation, with a belief in, and commitment to, cooperation, equity, and equal opportunity; to develop community capacity, skills, and resources; to ensure that social and economic resources remain in the community; to promote local ownership, community control over capital and resources, and local reinvestment to guarantee long-term development; and to develop enterprises and meet 'multiple bottom lines' – economic efficiency as well as enhanced social and environmental conditions and healthier communities. Central to each of these objectives is the belief that community representation in, and control of, the economic development process will result in greater ultimate benefits than a strategy that lacks community involvement. Only with such a community focus will the jobs and opportunities offered by economic development be advantageous to both the workers and the residents. Profits generated or assets acquired by the CED organization are then used for further development of programs, training, job creation, and employment development initiatives in the core neighbourhoods.

*CED and Affordable Housing*

In Saskatoon, Quint Development Corporation's Affordable Housing Program (AHP) was developed because community members identified improved and more affordable housing as one of the highest priorities for residents of the city's core communities. Affordable housing options for low-income families in marginalized neighbourhoods were seen as a powerful engine for social and economic development. The AHP has the following community economic development objectives: improved and stabilized family living situations within the community; decreased social costs related to poor and unstable housing conditions; reduced poverty and hunger through the creation of affordable housing alternatives; healthier communities created by increasing residents' stability, pride, and commitment to their communities; housing co-ops that provide support for and building the capacity of families and new homeowners; a sense of community developed by families working together in housing co-ops; the building of equity by low-income families; a stemming of the outflow of income from the core communities; the purchase, renovation, and improvement of the aging housing stock in the core communities; and the creation of employment, training, and economic development opportunities for community residents and businesses through the restoration and improvement of the houses.

In some core neighbourhoods the population has increased significantly, but with very little development of additional affordable housing. The core neighbourhoods are some of the oldest neighbourhoods in Saskatoon, with an aging housing stock increasingly owned by absentee landlords. The effect of this has been rising rents (in many cases for substandard housing), a growing demand for existing housing, and more instability and greater transience for renters. Recent statistics indicate that the annual mobility rate in these neighbourhoods is half again as high as the city average. In fact, Pleasant Hill has the highest annual mobility rate in the province (34.8%). High mobility rates can significantly affect the social fabric and stability of neighbourhoods. Creating homeownership opportunities for low-income residents of

Saskatoon's core neighbourhoods will result in more stability and commitment in those communities. It will also begin to reverse the trend toward rental housing in those communities.

There are significant social costs related to poor and unstable rental housing. A community's schools are a good barometer of the negative consequences of high mobility rates and substandard housing. Educators are beginning to understand the connection between housing and children's ability to learn and grow. Many classrooms in core neighbourhood schools experience annual turnover rates of 100% to 200%. Principals and teachers attribute this directly to the unstable housing that the children's families are experiencing. Low vacancy rates, combined with high rents, have meant that families are being forced to move frequently, and this has a direct impact on their children's education. The AHP is seeking to reverse this trend by promoting the stability and pride that traditionally accompany homeownership. More stable housing alternatives would help children succeed in school.

Around one-quarter of the families in the core neighbourhoods depend on social assistance, and about 40% of the families have an annual income of less than $20,000. As rents rise, the pressure on low-income families to meet their rent payments increases. In almost all cases, the social assistance housing allowance is significantly less than the actual cost of rent in Saskatoon. This means that many families have to use their food budget to pay for part of their rent. In the AHP almost all families pay less for their monthly mortgage than they used to for rent.

Community members also recognize that affordable homeownership addresses other critical social problems. Owner-occupied housing is seen as essential to encouraging a neighbourhood's stability and pride. Once families realize that they own their home and won't be forced to move, they take a more active interest in their communities, participating in local politics, associations, schools, and other community-based endeavours. Stable housing is a prerequisite for family members to become more independent. They can make long-term plans instead of worrying where they are going to be living next month. Many family members have gone back to school or achieved full-time employment since becoming members of a Quint co-op. Homeownership has been a turning point for many families.

Becoming a homeowner is a daunting endeavour that entails major responsibilities and commitments. This is true for most new homeowners, but especially true for many low-income families (most of whom are Aboriginal), and it takes a period of adjustment and support to understand and appreciate this reality. The housing co-op model allows 10 families to learn from and support one another through this adjustment period. The co-op members learn how to develop and administer policies as well as how to make collective decisions. The experience and learning related to making a co-op work over a five-year period significantly builds the capacity of the members of the co-op. Housing co-ops also allow low-income families to obtain mortgage financing when they would not be able to do so individually. Financial institutions see co-ops as a sites where the members can mentor and support one another, thereby reducing the risk to the lender.

Families who work together in co-ops also find their sense of isolation reduced. The co-ops meet at least once a month (and usually more often for committee meetings) to work collectively on issues that are common to all of the members. This can be a very empowering experience, especially since most people have had to deal with their problems in isolation. The co-ops also create opportunities for their members to socialize among themselves. Co-ops often organize themselves politically around housing and other community issues.

Building assets and equity is increasingly being recognized as a principal route for families to exit poverty. Recent studies indicate that homeowners are economically better off than renters because they are building significant assets. The average annual income of the 90 families in homeownership co-ops (at the time) was typically been less than $17,000. Through Quint's housing program, these families would have more than a 30% equity position in their house after the five-year co-op membership period. They would continue to build their equity as they make their monthly mortgage payments. Had they continued paying rent each month, they would have spent more each month, and they would have no equity in their home now. In addition, the program has co-op members paying an additional $50 per month into a pooled capital reserve fund during their five years in the co-op. If unused during this period, this results in another $3,000 of savings for each of the new homeowners. Their combined equity and savings translate into a solid foundation for further credit if required. Credit opportunities for most low-income families are usually non-existent.

The transition from renting to homeownership in core neighbourhoods can stem the outflow or leakage of income from the local economy. We view the outflow of rent as one of the largest holes in the 'rusty bucket' of the core neighbourhoods' local economies. Every year, the Department of Social Services (DSS) spends around $40 million on rent

in Saskatoon. We conservatively estimate that in the core neighbourhoods, between $4 and $5 million annually of DSS shelter allowance
flows out in the form of rents to landlords and thus does not stay to
stimulate the local economy. With co-op homes, by contrast, mortgage
dollars remain in the community either as equity in homes or as interest
to local credit unions. Credit unions are reinvesting their returns to provide more opportunities to low-income families. Programs that prevent
further income leakage from local economies are key to successful community economic development.

Moreover, the AHP provides a means to revitalize and improve existing housing stock in the core neighbourhoods. Quint renovates the
houses it purchases. We only have to look at the low-income neighbourhoods in other Canadian cities to see the immense negative impact of
allowing the stock of older homes to deteriorate. Quint provides opportunities to proactively address this problem while improving the
quality of affordable housing in the community. The restoration and
improvement of the housing stock has the added benefit of generating
employment and training opportunities for community residents in
various trades; it also stimulates the local economy through purchases
of building materials and equipment. Quint's CED approach also leads
to a concerted effort to strengthen economic linkages within the core
neighbourhoods, through the production and purchase of local goods
and services relating to housing construction and renovation.

*The Model: Quint's Affordable Housing Program*

Quint developed the following model for its Affordable Housing
Program in 2004: Eligibility to become a homeowner and a co-op member is based on several criteria: the family must have at least one child
under 19 years of age; their combined income must be less than $30,000;
and they must be willing to participate in a co-op. Applicants with past
credit problems and recipients of social assistance are encouraged to
apply. Other assets include a demonstrated commitment to the community and various practical skills. Community meetings are held in
each of the five neighbourhoods, where information about the program
is provided. Quint staff look for all potentially suitable homes for sale
in the neighbourhood, then provide lists of potential homes to successful applicants.

The City of Saskatoon provides grant funding toward the total cost of
the program, including equity, renovations, and support. Under the

Neighbourhood Home Ownership Program (NHOP), the Saskatchewan Housing Corporation provides forgivable equity loans of the house's assessed post-renovation value, up to a maximum home value of $64,000. These two government sources make down payments possible by providing up to 35% of the homes' equity; they also provide a $2,000 emergency repair fund to each co-op. Mortgages are arranged through a neighbourhood credit union. Only through the development of many partnerships has the program been possible; the program relies on the collaboration of local financial institutions and businesses.

To undertake the house renovations within a limited budget, Quint has developed a training program in which local residents learn carpentry and renovation skills and gain on-the-job experience, and thus opportunities for entering the workforce. The renovation crew works to ensure that the purchased homes are liveable and that they surpass health and safety standards. The Bent Nail Tool Co-operative was established to provide assistance to members who wished to access tools at little or no cost; this co-operative also provides workshops – for example, on how to install flooring.

The shift from tenant to homeowner can be intimidating. Within their cooperatives, members share skills, organize and direct the co-op's business, get to know their neighbours, and make the transition to homeownership. The co-op is the nominal 'owner' of the ten homes comprising each cooperative; actually, though, individual families pay mortgages on their own homes, so they are the real legal owners. At the end of five years, the SHC equity loan is forgiven and families have the option of assuming their mortgage and taking the title of their home; or, they may remain with the cooperative for longer if they wish. Quint's position is that it takes more than just the provision of four walls to meet the goals of the AHP. The co-op members require support as they develop policies and direction for their co-operative, so Quint staff regularly attend co-op meetings in advisory roles; however, each co-op develops its own policies.

*The Family-Friendly Housing Initiative (FFHI)*

While the primary focus of the Quint Development Corporation has been on homeownership, Quint has more recently become involved in rental housing and the need for an innovative approach to the challenges people face in renting in the core neighbourhoods, through the Family Friendly Housing Initiative (FFHI). The FFHI is guided by certain values, standards, and principles: first, safe, clean, and affordable rentals; second, a good relationship between landlords and tenants; and third, building community through the property they share. Initially, there was a strategy to start community discussion by forming a Tenant–Landlord Cooperation (TLC) Group; the intention was to discuss the negative experiences that tenants had with landlords and property managers and the possibilities for positive change. Community is being built through developing partnerships. Positive tenant–landlord relationships have been built through monthly meetings in an apartment building and the management's open-door policy for tenants to contact the landlord. These meetings have helped create a sense of communalism in the building; they have also provided an opportunity for tenants to establish positive relationships with one another and with the landlord. In turn, the building's status has improved the neighbourhood's reputation.

*Conclusions*

As a whole, the FFHI has been a success and has had a positive impact on the neighbourhood. The FFHI concept has generated ideas and alternatives for providing better rental housing. It has helped increase interest and initiative for the community, and it has allowed community members to bring improved rental housing to the forefront of the community's consciousness. The most successful part of the FFHI has been an initial apartment project. It made a significant difference in people's lives and in the community, and it provided a clear example of how housing can improve for low-income renters. This project brought about better discussion and an interest in incorporating these concepts on a larger scale. Quint now implements the FFHI concept in all five core neighbourhoods, taking on the role of facilitator in addressing housing issues and assisting in the creation of innovative community-led solutions.

We continue to see benefits of stable affordable homeownership and the transmission and sharing of the skills that are necessary as families make the transition to living in and caring for their own homes. We also can see that the housing cooperatives are doing more: with mentorship, their members are growing as individuals (they are learning to take charge and make decisions and have confidence – they are not simply 'clients' or 'tenants' but collective owners) and as good neighbours (they want to be able to influence their neighbourhoods to become better places to live, for themselves, for their children, and for others – they envision themselves as making a contribution to the long-term betterment of the neighbourhood). By learning cooperative approaches, members are gaining valuable experience in setting up an organization, running meetings, giving and receiving help, and working collectively toward common goals. They are developing as citizens, gaining a broader understanding of how communities work, and advocating for change and improvements in their neighbourhoods.

## Urban Aboriginal Homebuilding Apprenticeships

ALAN THOMARAT

*Introduction*

The residential construction industry is being challenged with chronic shortages of skilled labour. The issue is generally not the number of applicants but the skills available. New technologies, building systems, and materials have created skill gaps between those with experience and those attempting to enter the industry (Construction Sector Council 2004). This situation will only grow worse now that large numbers of tradespeople and residential construction professionals are nearing retirement age. Back in 2004, Statistics Canada noted that nearly 58% of Saskatoon's workers will be reaching retirement age in the next 10 to 15 years. Clearly, then, positive steps must be taken in the interests of housing and sustainability of the industry. Moreover, *SaskTrends Monitor* predicted at the time that at least 50,000 and possibly 100,000 people would be leaving the Saskatchewan labour force in the next 10 to 15 years; but concurrently, 30,000 to 40,000 young First Nations and Metis people would be entering the labour force age group. And in addition to the skilled labour shortage, there is a shortage of entrepreneurs to own and operate the corporations and small businesses that comprise the residential construction industry in the Saskatoon region. According to Statistics Canada, 80% of all organizations operating within the residential construction industry in Canada have four employees or fewer, and many owners of these businesses are within 10 years of retirement age. Much of the residential construction industry is built on small business; it is estimated that around two-thirds of all start-up businesses fail within the first five years (Ibrahim and Soufani 2002). So it is of utmost importance to build a skilled and knowledgeable workforce – both skilled workers and entrepreneurs – in order that the province that can continue its economic growth.

The SRHBA entered into two agreements with the Bridges and Foundations Project in June 2003. The first agreement, 'Aboriginal

Apprenticeship Consultations in Residential Construction Trades,' was designed to help achieve the goal of increased First Nations and Metis involvement and recognition in careers and trades in the residential construction industry. The SRHBA's expertise in trades training and residential construction, and its strong willingness to work with Aboriginal organizations to realize affordable housing options and strong cross-cultural relationships, coincided well with the overall objectives of the Bridges and Foundations Project.

The second agreement, 'Management and Coordination of Apprenticeship Training Opportunities for Aboriginal Students in Residential Construction,' focused on partnerships and bursary administration. The initial objective was to develop working relationships with a number of Aboriginal organizations. Doing so would help the SRHBA identify Aboriginal students who were enrolled in apprenticeship programs in residential construction trades. The second phase of the agreement involved disbursing financial support to these students. The association selected these apprentices and coordinated the resources allocated to them.

*Aboriginal Apprentice Consultations in Residential Construction Trades*

To achieve the objective of increased First Nations and Metis involvement and recognition in the residential construction industry, a collaborative strategy had to be employed. The strategy was to educate First Nations and Metis people, as well as employers in the residential construction industry, about engaging in mutually beneficial partnerships for building careers and homes. Employers in the residential construction industry had to be made aware of the benefits of hiring First Nations and Metis employees. The SRHBA's approach included conducting demographic and labour market analyses, encouraging companies to participate in the Saskatoon Tribal Council's Employers' Circle program, and promoting employment opportunities through the Industry Development Coordinator at the SRHBA office as well as through the Residential Construction Job Coach at Construction Careers Saskatoon. The association developed partnerships with First Nations and Metis communities in part by communicating with youth, parents, educators, and career counsellors. All stakeholders were brought into this process because many parties have an influence on the career-planning decisions of youth; inclusiveness was considered the best way to achieve long-term success. Work was also done with adults who were thinking of a new career direction and who were seeking information about opportunities and requirements. Information must be made available about careers in the residential construction industry and about the resources that are available to help enter those careers; the pressing need is to place this information in the hands of youth, parents, individuals, teachers, and counsellors. This approach helps reach those who have not considered a career in residential construction either because information is hard to find or because of negative perceptions of the industry in terms of the pay and the nature of the employment. Many perceive incorrectly that residential construction is not steady employment.

The SRHBA is pursuing a variety of initiatives aimed at encouraging and facilitating Aboriginal involvement in residential construction. These include participating in employer orientation sessions in the Employers Circle Job Fair of the Saskatoon Tribal Council (STC); hosting Employers' Forums in order to encourage employers to partner in recruitment efforts, promote subtrade initiatives, and attract more people; establishing a Women's Council in order to encourage a greater role for women in the residential construction trades and professions; establishing the Home Builders' Trades Training Project, through which First Nations and Metis employees – including recipients of social assistance and employment insurance – can access trades training, employment opportunities, and personal and financial support; and applying to the Saskatchewan Apprenticeship and Trade Certification Commission (SATCC) for the designation of particular subtrades, in order to attract more Aboriginal young people to the residential construction industry and to facilitate a more expeditious process for entry into the trades. The SRHBA also participates in the following: the steering committee of Construction Careers Saskatoon (CCS) (through the SRHBA's Executive Director); the Home Builders' SchoolsPlus partnership, a cooperative program that allows students (including Aboriginal) to gain experience in trades through work-based training in addition to classroom content; the Home Builders' Work Education Program, which allows high school students to gain experience in the trades through a combination of curriculum and work-based training; HomeStyles, an annual homebuilding trade show; 'See Your Future, Build Your Future,' the association's annual youth-oriented career symposium; and tours of construction work sites and show homes, which allow students to watch the process of building a home and gain exposure to various trade opportunities. Finally, the SRHBA has created the positions of Residential Construction Job Coach and Industry Development Coordinator.

*Management and Coordination of Apprenticeship Training Opportunities*
*for Aboriginal Youth in Residential Construction*

The SRHBA began recruiting for bursaries in February 2004. These bursaries covered not only tuition payments but also (where applicable) living expenses, tools, and equipment. The base living allowance allocated per candidate was $1,200. That was the amount received by candidates who were single and without children; individuals with children received an additional $250 per dependent child per payment.

The bursary program has succeeded, and deserving recipients have been chosen. It did, though, encounter some challenges. One was to find ideal candidates – that is, candidates who were committed to the construction industry *and* who truly needed funding. Another was that many applicants felt overwhelmed (and perhaps unprepared) for the challenges of an apprenticeship program despite the resources available to help them. These people knew about the job coaches at Construction Careers Saskatoon, and about other available counsellors, but they lacked the confidence or the motivation to approach them for help. While many employers in the SRHBA applauded the bursary program, some had a poor reputation in the First Nations and Metis communities, and some had a negative impression of Aboriginal workers. When approached about hiring First Nations or Metis candidates, some employers were hesitant, based on negative experiences in the past. These employers often cited a lack of work ethic and work readiness as well as consistent tardiness in arriving to the work sites (or not arriving to work at all). Candidates had a strong desire to enter the housing industry, yet they found it difficult to find steady employment that offered enough hours for them to continue their education. There is merit in helping selected candidates enter the residential construction trades, but a lack of certainty regarding the availability of assistance can discourage them from pursuing further training. Some of the candidates interviewed were not pursuing further education because they did not have the necessary financial resources. Financial support is vital to the success of any trades training program, but so too are guidance and mentorship.

The number of spots available for training, upgrading, and programs must be increased in Saskatoon. Individuals should not have to wait for years to improve their education and quality of life. As of this writing, the province's largest city with the most jobs and the largest workforce is unable to train its own workforce in the trades. This is encouraging youth to leave the province. The need to relocate to continue education can place unnecessary financial and emotional stress on a family.

Many candidates expressed an interest in starting their own business and working for themselves. Such initiatives should be encouraged, and the proper resources should be made available to help them achieve their dreams. These resources might include management and entrepreneurship training. Small business loans and the ability to increase capital are important resources to make available. If individuals encounter difficulties accessing funding through traditional means, alternative funding sources should be made available.

Many individuals lack confidence in their ability to succeed in school. When they see friends and peers succeed, they will believe they can too. Many of the people the association interviewed are capable of achieving a great deal, and we must encourage and support them in their efforts to do so.

Finally, youth, educators, and parents must learn to accept and encourage the career opportunities that are offered by the residential construction industry. The industry must market itself better and improve its training programs; otherwise, misperceptions about it will not be overcome. At the same time, cultural sensitivity training must be conducted in order to change the negative perceptions that some employers still hold about First Nations and Metis employees. Such training, and good references, will increase employers' willingness to hire First Nations and Metis people as equal and fully capable members of the labour force.

## Further Developments: The Bridges and Foundations Career Development Corporation

After the Bridges and Foundations Project completed the two research projects, 'Aboriginal Apprenticeship Consultations in Residential Construction Trades' and 'Management and Coordination of Apprenticeship Training Opportunities for Aboriginal Youth in Residential Construction,' the SRHBA applied successfully to the federal government (through the Aboriginal Skills and Employment Partnership [ASEP] program of Human Resources and Skills Development Canada [HRSDC]) and the provincial government (through the Ministry of Advanced Education, Employment and Labour and the Saskatchewan Housing Corporation) for funding of the Bridges and Foundations Career Development Corporation, which was established in March 2009. Between June 2009 and April 2010, ASEP contributed $743,000 to the corporation in three stages. This new initiative has as its vision 'to empower and inspire a new generation of Aboriginal workers, including First Nations and Metis people, by facilitating partnership between the construction industry, learning institutions, government and communities.'

The corporation seeks to improve access to training and career opportunities in the residential construction industry, with a focus on improving the quality of housing in Saskatchewan. Through collaborative partnerships (which include many of the partners in the original Bridges and Foundations research project: the SRHBA, the Saskatoon Tribal Council (STC), the Affordable New Home Development Foundation (ANHDF), the Saskatchewan Indian Institute of Technologies (SIIT), and the Saskatoon Housing Initiatives Partnership (SHIP), as well as a broad variety of government bodies, career development and employment agencies, and applied trades institutions), the corporation offers pre-employment and construction-specific trades training to provide a foundation for careers in the residential construction industry. Training in at least 24 trades is currently being offered through the First Nations and Metis technical institutes, respectively SIIT and Dumont Technical Institute (DTI), as well as through the Saskatchewan Institute of Applied Science and Technology (SIAST). On-the-job training allowances of up to $5,000 are extended to employers when applicable.

The success of this new initiative, which grew out of the earlier research conducted within the Bridges and Foundations Project, can hardly be overstated. This program currently provides around 400 First Nations and Metis people with training and work experience related to the construction of affordable housing. To date, 269 participants have found work and more than 1,500 have completed essential skills-training courses. Within just a few years, strides have been made toward addressing the shortage of skilled workers in Saskatchewan's residential construction industry, and Aboriginal young people have begun to enter the provincial labour force as workers in great demand.

Add to this the latest initiative: collaboration between the SRHBA (and thereby also the CHBA – Saskatchewan), the corporation, and Whitecap Dakota First Nation in an Aboriginal Housing and Career Development Model. This is a pilot project to encourage Aboriginal trades training and apprenticeship opportunities in conjunction with the current developments on Whitecap First Nation. The residential development, alongside commercial developments, will consist of 49 single-family homes and three 12-suite apartment buildings for a total of 85 housing units. Over the next five years, around $40 million worth of construction and development is planned. This should provide a great opportunity to increase Aboriginal access to skills training leading to careers in the residential construction industry.

## Chapter Ten

# Urban Reserves

## The Development of Urban Reserves

In recent years, urban reserves have been extensively debated. Criticisms and concerns that have been expressed are that urban reserves are unfair tax havens, free from property taxes, income taxes, provincial sales, gas, alcohol, and tobacco taxes, and federal GST; that Aboriginal self-government in urban areas would make urban reserves exempt from municipal control; that Native control of schools would set them apart from school divisions; that urban reserves would promote segregation, especially if used for residential development; and even that urban reserves would become havens for 'lawlessness.' Yet for all of these accusations, there have been clarifications. Status First Nations people pay the same taxes, unless they are working or purchasing on a reserve, in which case they are subject to Section 87 of the Indian Act providing an exemption (a 5% refund on provincial gas and tobacco taxes). Still, consumer taxes may be charged by First Nations governments. First Nations owning land within or near a city have to apply for recognition as urban reserves, which is not readily granted; First Nations have to negotiate financial agreements, service agreements, and agreements with the City, school boards, and police and fire protection services before receiving urban reserve status. Sales taxes are exempted only for goods sold to Status First Nations people on reserve. Once that status has been granted, First Nations owning urban reserve land are obliged to pay for services provided by the City, in the same amount as they would pay in property taxes – for example, by 2003 Muskeg Lake Cree First Nation was paying over $100,000 to the City of Saskatoon for services each year (*Saskatoon StarPhoenix*, 12 June 12 2003).

Cooperation between First Nations and municipal governments has been key to the establishment of urban reserves. Moreover, urban reserves have opened a new era of cooperation and partnerships between First Nations and corporate Canada, making for economic integration without assimilation. In the process, though, tax exemptions have become complicated with joint ventures between First Nations and outside enterprises (Melting Tallow 2001).

Urban reserves have become very successful in economic terms. Lorne Sully, a former senior planner for the city, has commented: 'Saskatoon, among cities, is a leader in Canada in establishing new working relationships with Aboriginal people. Urban reserve creation in Saskatoon to foster First Nations economic development has set a new and positive standard for other cities across the country' (*Saskatoon StarPhoenix*, 27 December 2010). The first and most developed reserve within Saskatoon has become a model for similar developments throughout the province and across Canada. In 1988, Muskeg Lake Cree Nation began developing the Asimakanisekan-Askiy reserve on 35 contiguous acres in Sutherland, an outlying industrial and residential suburb of Saskatoon. Over the past 20 years this reserve has built up $20 million in building assets, which include the McKnight Business Centre and the Cattail Centre (home of the Saskatoon Tribal Council). More than 400 people now work on this urban reserve. Kocsis Transport grew in just four years from two drivers to more than 80 driving 65 trucks and 90 trailers; this one company was earning $6.6 million a year by 2000 (*StarPhoenix*, 29 September 2000). The more than 40 other businesses, offices, and services located here represent remarkable diversity. These include First Nations organizations (the head offices of the FSIN, the STC, the Saskatchewan Indian Gaming Authority [SIGA], and the First Nations Agricultural Council of Saskatchewan); banks and financial institutions (Peace Hills Trust, SIEF, First Nations Trust); dental and medical clinics; and a wide variety of other businesses, including a café, a dry cleaner, sports venues, fine arts and framing shops, a gas station (Cree Way Gas), Via Tech Solutions, and RBK Place, 'a gathering-place for success' (*'kamiyopayak otay nikan mamaopaaiwin'*).

Since then, other urban reserves have been developed in and around Saskatoon. In 1995, Red Pheasant First Nation purchased 80 rural acres just northwest of Saskatoon for $65,000 with the intention of turning this land into an urban reserve. While seeking approval, the scheme ran into opposition from the Northern Saskatoon Business Association. Nonetheless, the land was rezoned in 1999, by which time three commercial properties had been purchased with the city's approval to turn them into reserves. This was done under the 1992 Treaty Land Entitlement, which provided 27 bands with $450 million from provincial and federal governments to buy land (*Saskatoon StarPhoenix*, 12 December 1998, 4 January 1999; 10 November 1999). Similarly, the English River First Nation from northern Saskatchewan purchased land at Grasswood, on the main highway to Regina just south of Saskatoon. So far, this urban reserve – billed as 'an English River enterprise' – includes the Office of the Treaty Commissioner, the University of Saskatchewan Office of Aboriginal Initiatives, an office of the Saskatchewan Indian Cultural Centre, a SIGA office, a travel centre, a picnic area and rest park with an Aboriginal theme, a gas station (tax-free for Status Indians), a car and recreational vehicle wash, Tron Power, a restaurant, a Subway fast food outlet, Pots of Clay, and Eagleye Security Systems. Other properties that have achieved urban reserve status are owned by One Arrow First Nation, Battlefords Tribal Council, and Yellow Quill First Nation. Pending are the Avord Tower and Canterbury Tower, both in downtown Saskatoon. One Arrow First Nation now operates the Firecreek service station; another service station, Cree Way West, on a main traffic artery in the west end, opened in January 2012. Both have received the city's approval to be designated as urban reserves.

Besides urban reserves, a variety of Aboriginal centres have been established in the city. For example, the FSIN opened a downtown information and resource centre in 1991. In January 1995, Beardy's and Okemasis First Nation opened an urban office to serve band members living in the city; however, this office was phased out within a couple of years because the band couldn't afford the $120,000 needed to operate it (*Free Press*, 29 November 1996, 1 December 1996). The Urban First Nations Healing Initiative was developing a spiritual centre in 1996. By 1998, the STC's Urban First Nations Services Inc. had incorporated the following programs: Employment and Employer Services, Urban Pathways, Community Justice, First Nations Parents as Teachers, Children First, and Aboriginal Court Workers. The Building a Nation Centre opened in November 1999, funded partly by the Aboriginal Healing Foundation.

The Asimakanisekan-Askiy reserve in Saskatoon, the first urban reserve (*kihci-ihtawin iskonikan*) in Canada created specifically for commercial development, has become the economic prototype for other urban reserves in Saskatchewan and throughout Canada. By 2005 there were 28 urban reserves in Saskatchewan (Western Economic Diversification Canada 2009). Almost all of these reserves have been created for commercial and institutional purposes rather than residential ones. If urban reserves become residential, this of course will raise the interesting dilemma of First Nations self-segregation within urban places. In this chapter Joseph Garcea thoroughly explores the rationale for and uses of residential urban reserves.

## Residential Urban Reserves: Issues and Options for Providing Adequate and Affordable Housing

JOSEPH GARCEA

*Introduction*

The challenges of providing adequate and affordable housing for low- and moderate-income Aboriginal households in urban areas across Canada is a major concern for all orders of government in this country (Hanselmann 2001, 2002a, 2002b). This concern was articulated in the reports of the Royal Commission on Aboriginal Peoples (1996); the then-Liberal federal government's response to the RCAP report echoed that concern and acknowledged the importance of continuing to implement the policy introduced in 1996 designed to deal with the housing needs of Aboriginals both on and off reserve across the country (INAC 1997a). That document also explained that the federal government had committed itself to providing support for off-reserve Aboriginal housing through various types of programs managed by CMHC; it also noted that CMHC would continue to work with Aboriginal and non-Aboriginal stakeholders to facilitate the acquisition of housing by Aboriginals through the private housing market, using resources from on-reserve and urban Native housing programs. Within three years, the federal government had entered into a formal cooperative arrangement with the Saskatchewan government to deal with issues affecting Metis and off-reserve First Nations people in the province. At the same time, the Saskatchewan government adopted its *Framework for Cooperation*, which was designed to foster consultation and cooperation among governmental and non-governmental stakeholders to deal with problems that Metis and off-reserve First Nations families and individuals faced in urban areas (Saskatchewan 1999). The consultation process produced a strategy that included the objective 'to increase the proportion of Metis and off-reserve First Nations people living in adequate, affordable housing over 20 years' (Saskatchewan 2001, 2004). The success of that strategy will depend on exploring the potential of a wide range of feasible and sustainable housing options.

This paper explores one such option: the creation of residential urban reserves for the purpose of providing adequate and affordable housing for Aboriginals (and possibly also for non-Aboriginals) with housing needs within culturally supportive communities. Here, 'residential urban reserves' refers to First Nations reserves consisting of least one residential subdivision located very close to major urban centres; 'culturally supportive communities' refers to those in which Aboriginal culture is valued, celebrated, and promoted. To date, two urban reserves have been established in Saskatoon; neither has a residential subdivision. But in addition to those two reserves, First Nations own developed and undeveloped lands either within or immediately adjacent to Saskatoon that have the potential be designated as urban reserves (WEDC 2004). Later sections of this paper will discuss the following: the policies and procedures for creating and operating residential urban reserves; models for configuring and operating residential urban reserves; decisions for creating residential urban reserves; challenges in creating residential urban reserves; the value and viability of residential urban reserves; suggestions for further analysis of urban reserves; and strategic initiatives related to the creation and operation of residential urban reserves.

*Policies and Procedures for Residential Urban Reserves*

Several key policies and procedures exist for creating residential urban reserves as well as for developing residential subdivisions, allotting residential lots, and allotting housing stock within such reserves. The policies and procedures for creating residential urban reserves are the same as those for the creation of reserves that are to be used either exclusively for institutional, commercial, or industrial purposes, or for any combination of those purposes. Federal policies and procedures for creating residential urban reserves as well as other types of reserves are found mainly in the Additions to Reserves policy (ATR) contained in INAC's Land Management Manual (INAC 2001, 2003), and in the Treaty Land Entitlement Framework Agreement (TLEFA). The former is the federal government's national policy (outlined in INAC's Land Management Manual) and applies to lands that have been acquired by bands (whether through land claims agreements or any other means) and that have been targeted for conversion to reserve status (INAC 2001b). The latter is a special regional policy that applies to all First Nations acquiring land and creating reserves, and is pursuant to a province-wide land claims agreement signed in 1992 by the federal government, the Saskatchewan provincial government, and 26 treaty land entitlement bands in the province (Saskatchewan 1992; Justice Canada 1993).

The policies and procedures contained in the ATR and TLEFA continue to apply to reserve creation even if First Nations opt to operate under the First Nations Land Management Act (FNLMA). This is because the FNLMA does not deal with the creation of reserves or additions to existing reserves per se; it only deals with the management of reserve lands either on an existing reserve or on any reserve that may be created in the future (Government of Canada 1998, 1999). The creation of reserves is also subject – albeit very indirectly – to provisions contained in a provincial statute: the Saskatchewan Treaty Land Implementation Act (S.S. 1993, c. T-20.1), which contains provisions relating to consequential amendments to municipal, education, and Crown minerals acts designed to sanction negotiations and agreements between TLEFA entitlement bands on the one hand and municipalities, school boards, or some Crown corporations on the other as these relate to certain matters of importance for each stemming from the setting aside of any land as reserve land (Martin-McGuire 1999; Miller 1999; Barron and Garcea 1999, 2000). The procedures for creating residential urban reserves in Saskatchewan under both the ATR and the TLEFA involve the band councils and either the federal minister responsible for Indian Affairs or the federal governor in council (i.e., the cabinet), or both. Although provincial and municipal governments are granted a consultative role related to some issues that arise when reserves are being created and operated the reserve, they do not have an authoritative role in such matters. The involvement of the band councils and their members stems from the fact that both the creation of new reserves and additions to existing reserves require a request from, and the consent of, band councils and their members.

Setting aside differences in detail, the reserve creation processes outlined in the ATR and the TLEFA entail three major phases: documentation; consultation and negotiation; and the granting or rejection of reserve status. The *documentation* phase requires the band to produce documentation on an array of matters, including the policy justification, the land use, the legal description of the land being considered for reserve status, the anticipated contentious issues, the communication plan, and the band council resolution endorsing the proposed conversion of the property to reserve land. The *consultation and negotiation* phase requires First Nations band councils to undertake consultations and negotiations with the provincial and municipal governments, and possibly also with school boards if they deem it necessary. The first step in this particular phase requires the First Nations band council to inform the provincial government and any affected municipal government in writing of the proposed land acquisition, the intended use of that land, and any other relevant matters. Moreover, where appropriate, that band council must also undertake negotiations for one or more agreements with any affected neighbouring municipality on several key issues, including these: (1) whether compensation will be paid for the loss of municipal and school taxes once the land acquires reserve status; (2) the types of municipal services to be delivered to the new reserve, and how they will be financed; (3) by-law compatibility between the municipality and the reserve, particularly where reserve development has the potential to affect neighbouring municipal lands and residents; and (4) a joint consultative process, especially a dispute resolution mechanism, for addressing matters of mutual concern (Tota 2002). The *granting or rejection of reserve status* phase entails a series of successive deliberations on the part of federal officials regarding the proposal submitted by a band council.

Slightly different policies and procedures apply when residential urban reserves are being created, depending on whether the First Nation undertaking the initiative already has land that is designated as a reserve in Saskatoon, or owns a property that has not yet been designated as reserve land, or does not yet own land in Saskatoon. When a First Nation already has an urban reserve in Saskatoon, to establish a residential reserve it need only adopt a band council resolution to create one or more residential subdivisions and then seek ministerial approval. When a First Nation has land or buildings in Saskatoon that have not been converted to a reserve, to establish a residential reserve it must adopt band council resolutions both to create the reserve and to develop residential subdivisions on it, and then seek ministerial approval. When a First Nation does not have land or buildings in Saskatoon, creating a residential reserve requires them to adopt band council resolutions related to acquiring land, converting that land to a reserve, and developing any residential subdivisions, and then to seek ministerial approval. A few Saskatchewan First Nations fall within the first and second categories; the vast majority, though, fall within the third – they do not own any property in Saskatoon.

A reserve can be created either for one band or for several. There is nothing that prevents two or more bands from collaborating on creating a reserve for their mutual benefit. Moreover, even if reserves are set aside only for one band, there is nothing that prohibits several band councils, tribal councils, or any other Aboriginal governance bodies from consulting and collaborating with one another in establishing residential subdivisions designed to meet the housing needs of members of several bands and anyone else whom they allow to live there (INAC 2001).

The *creation* of residential urban reserves and the actual *development* of one or more residential subdivisions therein are not one and the same. The development of residential subdivisions is a relatively distinct process with its own set of policies and procedures based in the Indian Act or FNLMA. For the majority of First Nations the decision-making process for developing residential subdivisions is governed by at least three sets of provisions contained in the Indian Act: first, provisions that deal with the powers and processes for using designated reserve land that has not been allocated for creating residential subdivisions (FNALM 2003c); second, provisions that deal with the process for creating residential subdivisions using land that is held by band members through either a certificate of possession or a 'locatee ticket'; and third, provisions whereby band councils can be authorized to control and manage their designated lands (Adkin 2003).

For some band councils the decision-making process related to the creation of residential subdivisions is now governed by the FNLMA. Although only a few bands are currently operating under this statutory regime, the probability that many more will be doing so in the future is relatively high, given the penchant for increased authority and autonomy as part of the self-governance movement that is becoming quite pervasive among First Nations (FNALM, 2003b). The key provisions in the FNLMA related to the creation of subdivisions are contained in subsections that deal with the power of band councils operating under that statute to enact laws in accordance with their land code regarding matters related to the development, management, and zoning of lands.

The creation of a residential subdivision is essentially a decision of designating a parcel of reserve land for the specified use of providing lots primarily for housing purposes and to some extent also for a limited number of institutional or commercial purposes deemed to be integral and essential to that residential subdivision. A residential subdivision can be developed by any one or more of the following four potential developers: the band council itself; a property development agency of the band council; a property development company owned by one or more band members; or a property development company owned by someone who is not a band member. The development of a residential subdivision could involve a special business partnership between any such potential developers.

Although individual band councils are generally the ones responsible for making various types of land management decisions, including those regarding the development of residential subdivisions, they may appoint tribal councils to manage their lands. The process for developing residential subdivisions is similar to the one for creating new reserves or additions to existing reserves. It is essentially a two-phase process (i.e., the land designation phase, then the lease and agreements negotiations phase). To a varying extent, this two-phase process involves the band council, its members, federal officials, any property developers who may be participating in developing the land for residential purposes, and in many cases also municipal governments, which are likely to be involved in providing some municipal services to such subdivisions (FNALM 2003d).

The allotment or reallotment of reserve lands either to band members or to non-band members is guided by special statutory provisions and regulations under the Indian Act. The general process for allocating or reallocating land to band and non-band members has two major stages: first, a band council resolution on the lot allotment; and second, ministerial approval. Besides the two principal modes of allotting lands to members of First Nations bands (certificate of possession and certificate of occupation), there is one other way that lands can be allocated either to them or even to non-band members. The Indian Act allows the use of reserve land by a band member (or even by a non-band member) through leases or permits granted by a valid band council resolution that is approved by the minister (FNALM 2003b). But again, First Nations operating under the FNLMA do not need such ministerial approval.

Other important policies and processes relate to how various types of housing units (e.g., single dwellings, multiple-unit dwellings) will be allotted once they have been built on various types of reserve land (e.g., land held by the band, land held by band members, and land that has been designated for leasing to developers). This allotting can involve selling or renting. Such policies and processes have important implications for any First Nation that is considering using a residential urban reserve to provide adequate and affordable housing for Aboriginals and non-Aboriginals.

The allotment of housing units on reserves is contingent on the nature of ownership of the housing units as well as on the nature of the land-holding on which the housing unit is located. In the case of the owner-ship of housing units, the allotment is contingent on whether they are owned by the band council, by a band member, by a non-band member, or by a property development or management corporation. In the case of the landholding, the allotment is contingent on whether the housing units are located on land held by the band, on land held by band members by various means, on land held by non-band members under a lease, on land held by a developer under a head lease, or on land held by a band member (or someone who is not) under a sublease.

The right to allot housing units owned by the band council on its reserve rests either with that band council or with any housing authority/committee that it establishes. In such instances the band council or its housing authority/committee has substantial authority to determine the precise terms and conditions (e.g., the selling price, rent, use, etc.) of such an allotment to any individual or corporate entity.

Band councils have substantial authority and autonomy regarding housing matters. Arguably, there are no major insurmountable jurisdictional obstacles for First Nations in providing adequate and affordable housing units for band members (and even non-band members). More specifically, they have extensive authority and autonomy for, among other things: deciding the number and types of privately owned units that they will permit to be built on reserve; the number and types of housing units they will construct and operate for families and any special needs group (e.g., the elderly and persons with disabilities); and the type of housing supports or subsidies they will provide for band members. For many band councils, therefore, the major obstacles for providing adequate and affordable housing for their members on reserve are not jurisdictional; instead, they tend to be largely financial. Such financial obstacles stem from the dual effect of the lack of adequate financial capital within the community and the reluctance of financial institutions to provide mortgages for housing on reserves without the standard level of down payment, security for repayment of the mortgage, or repossession rights.

In summary, the creation of residential reserves, the establishment of subdivisions, and the allocation of lands and housing therein are subject to a complex set of policies and processes that are embodied largely in the Indian Act, the FNLMA, the TLEFA for First Nations in Saskatchewan, the ATR policy in INAC's Land Management Manual, and the policies and by-laws of band councils. The major governmental actors involved in decisions related to those three matters are the following: the band councils; the band members; either or both the federal minister and the governor in council; and to a much lesser extent the provincial and municipal governments. Regarding the latter, First Nations are obliged to consult and possibly also enter into agreements with them related to various aspects of the creation of such reserves and of residential sub-divisions therein (O'Neill 1997). The trend in recent years has been to-ward increasing the level of authority and autonomy of First Nations band councils and their members for dealing with land management matters. This is occurring largely as part of the self-government initia-tive as manifested in the FNLMA. There has been increased use of sec-tions of the Indian Act that may be used to transfer decision-making authority for many land management matters from the minister to the band councils (FNALM 2003c).

*Models for Configuring Residential Urban Reserves*

First Nations that are considering establishing a residential urban re-serve in Saskatoon, or in any other major urban centre in Saskatchewan, should be aware of several aspects of existing residential urban reserves and subdivisions therein in several other provinces. This includes the configuration of residential urban reserves; of residential subdivisions, landholdings, and housing stock on such reserves; and of reserve–municipal agreements and reserve–municipal relations.

In examining the configuration of residential urban reserves it is use-ful to focus on four major types of configurations: geographic, struc-tural, demographic, and functional. Geographically, residential urban reserves are located in one of three ways vis-à-vis the neighbouring urban municipality: first, entirely within the boundaries of a major ur-ban centre; second, immediately adjacent to a major urban centre; and third, within a very short commuting distance from such a major urban centre. Structurally, there are at least three general models of urban re-serves: (a) reserves that consist only of a single apartment block or tower; (b) reserves that consist only of fully developed residential sub-divisions without any other types of developments; and (c) reserves that consist of fully developed residential subdivisions as well as commer-cial and industrial developments. Two other general models of urban reserves are based on the level of 'institutional completeness.' One model consists only of residences; the other consists of an extensive institutional or organizational infrastructure needed for governance, management, and service delivery in the community. Demographically, the population of residential urban reserves is configured in one of two ways in terms of the Aboriginal status of the residents: whereas on some reserves the population consists only of First Nations band members, on other reserves it consists of a mixture of First Nations band members, Aboriginal non-band members, and non-Aboriginals. And finally, functionally, residential urban reserves are configured in two general ways: some are configured so that land is used exclusively for residential purposes, while others are configured so that the land is used for institutional, commercial, or industrial purposes as well as residential purposes. In the case of First Nations that have multiple parcels of land in an urban setting, there is a tendency to use some parcels either exclusively or primarily for residential purposes and others for commercial or industrial purposes. One factor that seems to affect the functional configuration of residential urban reserves is the size of the reserve population. Generally, the pattern seems to be that the larger the population on the reserve, the greater the likelihood that it will have a combination of residential, institutional, commercial, and industrial developments. Moreover, indications are that the larger the population, the greater the likelihood that there will be a high degree of 'institutional completeness,' characterized by a wide array of governmental, community, and commercial services available on reserve.

The configuration of residential subdivisions on urban residential reserves is varied. There are four basic models of residential subdivisions: first, a single residential subdivision with a housing stock that is relatively uniform in size, quality, and price; second, a single residential subdivision with a housing stock that is relatively diverse in size, quality, and price; third, multiple residential subdivisions with housing stocks that are essentially the same in size, quality, and price across the subdivisions. The fourth model consists of multiple residential subdivisions, each of which contains housing stock that is relatively uniform in size, quality and price within the subdivision, but different than that of one or more of the other subdivisions. The configuration and scale of the residential subdivisions are correlated to the size of the reserve population and its socio-economic stratification. Reserves with smaller populations that are relatively homogenous socio-economically, and that do not sublease lots to Aboriginals and non-Aboriginals who are not band members, are more likely to have a single residential subdivision in which the housing stock is relatively homogenous. Reserves with larger populations that are relatively heterogeneous socio-economically, and which lease lots to Aboriginals and non-Aboriginals who are not band members, are more likely to have either of the following: one subdivision with a housing stock that is not uniform in size, quality, and price; or two or more residential subdivisions each of which consists of a housing stock that is relatively homogenous in size, quality, and price but differs in size, quality, and price from the housing stock of at least some, if not all, of the other subdivisions. In sum, the overview of the extant urban residential reserves suggests that homogeneity and heterogeneity in housing stock is a function of homogeneity and heterogeneity in the socio-economic stratification among band members as well as non-band members living on reserve.

Two major categories of landholdings have been established within residential subdivisions on existing residential urban reserves. In one category, land is assigned to band members through the following three legal instruments: a 'certificate of possession,' which authorizes them to use the land on a long-term basis for the designated purpose; a 'certificate of occupation,' which authorizes them to use the land on a short-term basis while any unresolved issues related to that particular parcel of land are resolved; and a 'locatee ticket,' which is a unique form of landholding on some reserves comparable to a 'certificate of possession' granted to holders until 1951 pursuant to a historic entitlement based largely on a family's use of the land prior to the creation of the reserve. In the other category, land is assigned through head leases and subleases. Head leases, which authorize holders to develop and manage an entire subdivision, are assigned to the following three general categories of property developers acting individually or in partnership: a band council's own property development corporation; a property development corporation owned privately by one or more entrepreneurial band members; and a property development corporation that is owned privately by non-band members. In all three of these cases, residential lots can be subleased either to band members or to non-band members as specified in the head lease. Again, for band councils managing their lands pursuant to the Indian Act, the assignment of the head leases must be approved by a band council resolution and by the minister, whereas for band councils managing their lands pursuant to the FNLMA, the approval of the minister is not required.

The configuration of the type, value, quality, and forms of ownership of the housing stock on residential reserves is similarly varied. Although the bulk of the housing stock consists of single-unit dwellings, there are some multiple-unit dwellings (condominiums, apartment blocks, and special residences). Multiple dwelling units are less common and tend to be used primarily for social housing to meet the health and personal care needs of disabled and aged band members. The value of the housing stock covers the full cost spectrum from the lowest to the highest range within their respective regions. The quality of the housing stock is generally comparable to that of the surrounding residential subdivisions in the neighbouring municipalities. Regardless of its age, the housing stock is generally in relatively good shape; clusters of a large number of 'rundown' or 'slum' houses are not very common. This is perhaps because band councils and band members from urban residential reserves may have the requisite amount of financial resources and community pride to maintain the housing stock in relatively good condition. The housing stock on urban residential reserves is owned by three categories of owners: band members, Aboriginal and non-Aboriginal persons who are not band members, and the band council.

The precise configuration of agreements between reserve governments and neighbouring municipal governments is quite varied (FSIN/SUMA 1993; Redl 1996; Townsend 1997; Sully and Emmons 2004; Dalhousie University 2000, 2002; Manitoba 2004). There are at least three major types of agreements between them: by-law compatibility agreements; land use, land development, and land taxation agreements; and service agreements. Most of the existing residential urban reserves in Canada have agreements related to the provision of basic municipal services such as water and wastewater management, waste collection and recycling, street maintenance, fire suppression, policing, animal control, recreation, library, and emergency planning. However, some First Nations do not enter into agreements with municipalities for the provision of those services; instead, they either choose or are constrained to provide some of those services themselves or, alternatively, they do not provide them at all.

Moreover, the configurations of relations between neighbouring reserve and municipal councils are complex and highly varied (Molgat 1998; UBCM 1994, 2000, 2003a, 2003b, 2004a, 2004b; Adams, 1999). The climate of such relations varies on a continuum from highly positive to highly negative on a consistent basis (Irwin 1994; Hughes 1997; Larbi 1998; Mountjoy 1999; Lafond 1999; CMAR 2002; Alberta et al. 2002; FNALM 2003a). The positive relationships between reserve and municipal officials were attributed to the following factors: a shared attitude between them that reserve and municipal communities are essentially two parts of the same community that are involved in an interdependent and symbiotic relationship; a shared set of goals between them for developing a strong and sustainable local or regional economy and a healthy and harmonious local or regional community; a high degree of familiarity and trust between them; and a set of ongoing, regularized, formal and informal meetings and communications between them to discuss matters of mutual interest and concern. The negative relationships between band and municipal officials were attributed to disagreements on the precise nature, scope, and causes of problems between them; disagreements on the best means to deal with those problems; different visions and interests related to economic and community development matters; different views regarding their respective rights and responsibilities related to governance and service delivery; lingering trust issues based on past interactions between them or their predecessors on various matters; public statements by both sides that reflected a lack of sensitivity and understanding; an unwillingness to meet and work in concert to advance the needs and goals of their respective communities; the negative interpersonal relations between such representatives; an obsession with protecting and exercising their respective jurisdictional authority in matters related to planning, development, user fees, taxation, and commercial operations such as casinos and bingo halls; a belief that consulting with each other is unnecessary, inconvenient, counterproductive, and prone to cause costly delays; and negative attitudes about each other.

Band and municipal officials identified several sets of benefits and problems generated for their respective governments and communities by the proximity of residential urban reserves and the neighbouring urban centres. These included housing, land use planning and development, finances, social conditions, and social relations. In the case of housing, band and municipal officials noted that the existence of residential urban reserves made a contribution toward meeting some of the housing needs of Aboriginal residents. However, rapid population growth has also placed some pressures on the ability of First Nations to provide housing to their members on reserves near large urban centres with high or rapidly escalating housing costs. In the case of land use planning and development, band and municipal officials pointed both to benefits and problems: some pointed to the benefits that such proximity had for improving both land use and land development in the case of some subdivisions when they were able to collaborate, while others pointed to the problems that existed and persisted when they were unable to collaborate. Both band and municipal officials also noted that the proximity of urban reserves to major urban municipalities contributed to the finances of their respective communities and, by extension, to the finances of their respective councils. Financial benefits related to the level of federal government funding for infrastructure, community development, health, and social services targeted for the reserve community; increased consumer choice and convenience offered by on- and off-reserve businesses, and in some instances also increased tourism and convention draws; substantial revenue streams derived from land leasing, house rentals, user fees for local services and programs, and band taxes imposed on businesses operating on the reserve; and financial benefits for band members in their capacity as workers, entrepreneurs, and consumers, including increased access to a large and highly diversified labour market, opportunities for economic and business partnerships, and a large consumer base that likely would not have existed for First Nations businesses on a reserve located in a remote or isolated rural area.

Some band officials added that such benefits could be even greater if certain practices and policies were improved. Beneficial in this regard would be the inclusion by municipal governments of band councils in various decision-making processes and potential development opportunities; better understanding by municipal officials and members of their communities of the potential advantages to on-reserve businesses provided by federal funding and tax exemption; less restrictive federal regulatory regimes regarding the financial management and economic development activities of band councils; and easier access to finances for residential and commercial developments by band councils and band members from agencies such as CMHC and banks. An obstacle to increased economic benefits for band councils and their members noted by some band officials related to the limited size and precise location of their existing reserves; they indicated that more land, either in their current location or in an even better location, would have substantial economic benefits for their respective councils and communities.

The most common financial problem identified by respondents concerned the nature of competition between reserve and non-reserve businesses. Some municipal officials pointed to concerns in their communities regarding the extent to which businesses located on the reserve had a competitive advantage by virtue of tax exemptions in selling gas, cigarettes, and other small consumer items; to this, band officials responded that small on-reserve businesses had difficulty competing with large businesses located in the neighbouring urban municipality.

In the matter of social conditions and social relations, the consensus among band and municipal officials was that the proximity of, and interactions among, the two communities generally tended to contribute to greater access to education, health, and recreational services; greater accessibility to various other types of social and cultural activities that raise the quality of life both for reserve and municipal communities; and increased intercultural awareness and appreciation.

However, not all band and municipal officials perceived the existence of the aforementioned benefits to social conditions and social relations; in fact, some band and municipal officials stated that *no* such benefits existed. Indeed, some indicated that there were no differences either in the social conditions or in the social relations of urban residential reserves compared to reserves located in remote rural parts of their province. In commenting on the social distance that persists between reserve and municipal residents, some band officials noted that the majority of residents in the neighbouring municipality would not know anything about the urban reserve. Similarly, some municipal officials noted that the proximity of residential urban reserves to the urban municipal centre contributed to tensions and even to altercations between reserve and municipal residents.

In sum, although there are many similarities among them, existing residential urban reserves in various provinces are by no means configured in a uniform manner. There are substantial differences among them in their geographic, demographic, and functional configurations. Differences among them also exist in the configuration of residential subdivisions, landholdings, and housing stock, and in the configuration of the agreements and relations between band and municipal councils. Some differences among them also exist regarding the perceived benefits and problems they generate related to housing, land use, the local economy, the finances of individuals, the finances of band and municipal councils, and local social conditions and relations. Despite any such differences, however, the consensus among band and municipal officials is that the benefits outweigh the problems. The existing urban residential reserves across Canada offer a range of models that may be used for any First Nations band council that is interested in creating either a new residential urban reserve or a residential subdivision on an existing urban reserve.

## Decisions for Creating Residential Urban Reserves

First Nations that are considering establishing residential urban reserves face several important and interrelated decisions (Dion et al. 1997). First, band councils must decide whether they should create, manage, and operate the residential urban reserve. Second, the precise geographic location for the reserve must be determined. There are three basic options: locate it on land within the existing municipality of Saskatoon; on land immediately adjacent to Saskatoon; or on land that is a very short distance from Saskatoon. Third, they must decide on the precise purpose of a reserve: whether it will serve only residential purposes and therefore consist only of housing units; or whether it will also serve commercial and institutional purposes and therefore also consist of buildings devoted to governance, management, and community service agencies. In effect, the First Nation must decide on the level of institutional completeness that will exist within the reserve community. Fourth, they must decide whose housing needs will be addressed within each residential subdivision established on the reserve: will it be only their band members, or only Aboriginal and non-Aboriginal non-band members, or some combination of the two? The other choice for them is whether to address the housing needs only of persons with low- or moderate-incomes experiencing homelessness, relative homelessness, and core-housing needs, or also those of people with relatively high incomes who are not experiencing those housing challenges. Fifth, they must decide who will develop and manage the residential subdivision. The project will need to be developed and managed; the question then is by whom, and the choices are among the following: an agency owned and controlled by the band council; a private company owned and controlled by band members; a private development agency owned by non-band members; or a partnership comprising any two or more of those (Koschinsky 1998). Sixth, a decision must be made about how to allocate housing lots, and to whom: Should lots be allocated to band members using certificates of possession, to band and non-band members using leases or subleases, or to band and non-band members using a mix of certificates of possession, leases, and subleases? Seventh, the design, ownership, management, and price of the housing stock that will be developed on the residential urban reserve must be determined. The design of the housing stock might be only single dwellings; only multiple dwellings; or a mix of single and multiple dwelling. The options for ownership of the housing stock are as follows: ownership by individual homeowners, ownership by band councils, and ownership by private developers. Concerning the management of the rental housing stock, it could be managed by a band housing management agency, a community-based housing management agency, or a private housing management agency. Regarding the price of housing stock, the options are to develop only low-priced housing stock, only medium-priced housing stock, only high-priced housing stock, or a mix of low-, medium-, and high-priced housing stock. And the eighth decision relates to the demographic profile and Aboriginal status of homeowners and renters who will be allowed to live on any residential subdivision that is developed: whether to allow band members from only one band, band members from more than one band, band members and Aboriginal non-band members, band members and Aboriginal and non-Aboriginal non-band members, Aboriginal and non-Aboriginal non-band members, Aboriginal non-band members, or non-Aboriginal non-band members. Decisions involving these particular choices will become increasingly important and complicated in the future as a result of the fragmentation of citizenship within First Nations (INAC 2004b).

*Challenges of Creating Residential Urban Reserves*

Any First Nation wishing to create a residential urban reserve faces several major challenges: limited fiscal capacity; uncertainties about the precise costs and benefits of creating residential urban reserves; the magnitude of housing needs; the lack of consensus among the First Nations leadership and membership regarding the value of creating residential urban reserves, either in Saskatoon or in any other major urban centre; the dilemma of how to deal equitably with all band members in terms of setting residency criteria for living on a residential urban reserve; and the negative views espoused by many residents in urban centres. Such views include the perception that a residential urban reserve would create a 'segregated urban ghetto' within the city, resulting in an 'uneven playing field' for those living, working, or operating businesses on reserves vis-à-vis their counterparts in the city, as well as obstacles to social cohesion insofar as a 'we' versus 'them' mentality would prevail between those living on reserve and those living in the municipality. First Nations need to consider the effects of this perception not only on the short-term dynamics surrounding the creation of urban residential reserves, but also on the long-term dynamics and relations between those living in residential subdivisions on reserve and those living in neighbouring municipal residential subdivisions.

The challenges posed by the lack of broad consensus both among members of the urban community and within First Nations themselves (i.e., their leaders *and* members) should not be surprising. After all, broad consensus is very difficult to achieve regarding much of what governments and markets do in urban areas either to urban communities or to the urban landscape. Even when there is relatively strong consensus on goals, there is not likely to be a comparable degree of consensus on means. Thus, a widespread consensus may exist on the *goal* of providing adequate and affordable housing, but not on whether creating residential urban reserves is the best means to achieve it (Melting Tallow 2001; Simard 2003; Black and Silver 2003; Wilmont 2003; Winnipeg Social Planning Council, 2004; Niigonwedom 2003).

*Value and Viability of Residential Urban Reserves*

The potential value and viability of residential urban reserves for providing adequate and affordable housing for low-income households generates debates from time to time. First Nations that are considering creating residential urban reserves should be fully aware of the key points raised in those debates and should evaluate the arguments and evidence very carefully in light of their respective circumstances, which can be quite challenging because the value and viability of such reserves is highly contingent on an array of factors.

The experience of First Nations in other provinces with residential urban reserves suggests that they are of potential value both for band members and for band councils. The potential value for band members rests on the benefits that would accrue to them as a result of living or working on the reserve (WEDC 2004). These include tax exemptions, as well as access to loans or grants for First Nations members living or working on reserve (the extent to which this particular benefit exists depends in part on whether the band council has chosen to impose any taxes or user fees of its own on people working or living on reserve). Other benefits can include the opportunity to acquire affordable and adequate housing and to live in a subdivision or neighbourhood that potentially is safer, healthier, and more appreciative and supportive of Aboriginal culture.

For First Nations band councils, creating residential urban reserves can have two major benefits. First, it can enable them to exercise their authority related to planning, development, and management matters outlined in some sections of the Indian Act in ways that ensure that such a reserve yields benefits both for them and for their members. Second, the proper management of residential urban reserves can generate financial returns on investment – depending, of course, on whether the focus is on providing housing for those with lower incomes or for those with higher incomes. The few residential urban reserve developments that have been contemplated by some First Nations band councils either in the Saskatoon region or in other urban regions of the province in recent years have tended to focus on the housing needs of relatively affluent people who can afford to lease land or housing units from the band council's property development and management agency, rather than on affordable housing. For example, on Whitecap First Nation, one development project has involved constructing housing around a golf course on existing reserve land.

Any First Nations thinking of developing residential urban reserves as a revenue-generating venture should be mindful that such reserves are not a panacea for revenue generation. While they have some potential benefits, they also entail substantial financial risks that would be too great for most First Nations to bear if the development failed. They should also be mindful that if they merely want to generate revenue through real estate developments, creating residential urban reserves is not the only way to do it; revenue-generation opportunities are also available through investments in residential and commercial real estate off reserve. That option, which can indirectly assist band members living in urban areas with their housing needs, has this advantage over reserve housing: it does not require ministerial or cabinet approval for sales.

A major objective for First Nations creating residential urban reserves is to ensure that such reserves are viable and sustainable both financially and socially. Financially, they will want to ensure that the reserve either generates revenue or at least does not *lose* revenue to the point that it becomes a financial drain. Socially, they will want to ensure that the reserve has a high degree of social development, cohesion, and harmony. The experience of First Nations operating residential urban reserves in other provinces suggests that such reserves can be financially and socially viable in various urban centres (including Saskatoon); however, their viability is contingent on such factors as the policy and program frameworks of the federal and provincial governments, the configuration of the governance and management framework of reserves, the number of residential urban reserves that exist in particular urban areas, the geographic location of the residential urban reserve, the functional configuration of the reserve, the demographic profile of the reserve, the mix of owner-occupied properties and rental properties, and the quality of life in the residential urban reserve community.

Although certain types of communitarian-based housing projects for the affluent are readily accepted (e.g., 'gated communities'), the same is not always true of projects designed either for the less affluent or for members of Aboriginal and ethnocultural groups regardless of their degree of affluence. This would seem to suggest that in Canadian cities, as in cities in other countries, there is a hierarchy of acceptable and unacceptable forms of group-based communitarianism (Bennett 1998). The Frontier Centre for Public Policy (FCPP) has cogently pointed out, in relation to proposals for urban reserves in Winnipeg:

> The City of Winnipeg's endorsement of urban reserves has racist overtones, but so do existing laws that harm Aboriginal economies ... Diversified centres of wealth creation have great potential for lifting Native populations out of poverty. Urban reserves are not the final answer, but a temporary expedient until other harmful laws are reformed ... Arguably Indian reserves represent the most deficient public policy model in Canadian history, so the idea that we should replicate that model in our cities seems distasteful. The ultimate answer is to bring this community back into the economic mainstream by ending all special reserves. In the interim, to people who are fleeing a framework biased in favour of poverty and failure, the urban reserve is a temporary leg up, in the other direction. (FCPP 2003)

*Conclusion*

This paper has provided an overview of several important issues and options for creating, managing, and financing residential urban reserves for the purpose of providing adequate and affordable housing for Aboriginal people generally having relatively low incomes. The central objective has been to explain that residential urban reserves are a potentially valuable and viable option for that purpose, but that it is neither the only option nor a panacea; other options are available to achieving key financial and housing goals. This paper has also underscored the fact that many factors have to be dealt with effectively and efficiently to ensure that residential urban reserves are valuable and viable. All stakeholders should be encouraged to engage in serious and systematic thinking before making any decisions related to the creation and operation of residential urban reserves, and to ensure that any potentially positive residential urban reserve initiatives are not negatively impacted by prejudicial presuppositions that such reserves represent the creation of segregated and impoverished 'urban ghettos' leading to inevitable social conflict. The experiences of existing residential urban reserves suggest that if they are established and managed properly, the prospects that they will raise problems or concerns will be reduced substantially.

## Chapter Eleven

# Race Relations and Crime

## Being Aboriginal in Saskatoon

Negative attitudes toward Aboriginal people unfortunately remain common among other residents of Saskatoon, and quite often these attitudes have been influenced by perceptions about Aboriginal people's responsibility for an increasing crime rate. One recent Member of Parliament (originally a Reform MP, then Canadian Alliance, and finally independent) who represented many thousands of Saskatoon residents claimed to be combating 'race-based inequality' – for example, 'segregationist policies of the Indian Act which isolate and divide society ... race-based hiring quotas for Indians ... two-tier Criminal Code sentencing provisions that give lenient sentences to Indian criminals ... special privileges ... Indians exempted from paying taxes.' He intended to contrast 'myth' versus 'fact,' to 'tell it like it is on behalf of constituents' (*Saskatoon StarPhoenix*, 5 February 2010).

Doubtless there has been in recent years in Saskatoon disproportionate Aboriginal involvement in certain types of criminal behaviour, which will be summarized in the second paper within this chapter. However, while recognizing problems in this city, our intention will be not to perpetuate negative generalizations founded on and contributing to racism, but to seek solutions based on clear understanding. It should hardly merit emphasizing the obvious point that the vast majority of Aboriginal residents not only do not in any sense participate in any sorts of criminal activities, but also abhor and fear crime in the city. It is they, not the general public, who are most often victimized by crime.

A variety of recent studies have revealed that racism and negative attitudes have continued to be directed against Aboriginal people in

Saskatoon, and have been quite pervasive. Back in 1991, a City Planning Department report on 20th Street (the main commercial artery running through Riversdale and Pleasant Hill) generated a lot of reaction for pejorative comments made by some businesspeople, who referred to 'crime and safety' issues caused by a growing Native population, and 'potential customers fearing to come here because of all the filth and garbage that walk around and annoy people' (*Saskatoon StarPhoenix*, 10 and 12 July 1991). In an article published in the *Globe and Mail* (3 November 2001), dramatically titled 'Welcome to Harlem on the Prairies: Canada's Apartheid,' journalist John Stackhouse described the rough conditions and constant police pursuit of Aboriginal people in these inner-city neighbourhoods (Proulx 2012).

Two surveys completed in 2002 – one by the *Saskatoon StarPhoenix* with the Department of Sociology at the University of Saskatchewan, the other by the City of Saskatoon Race Relations Committee with Fast Consulting – both suggested that awareness of racism and negative attitudes seems to be increasing, that most Saskatoon residents recognize that Aboriginal people are forced to overcome racial prejudice to survive in the city, and that there should be specific programs to help them. The university study also found that younger people seem to be more open to finding solutions for past injustices than older; moreover, there seemed to be considerable distrust of Aboriginal organizations, leadership, and accountability (*Saskatoon StarPhoenix*, 20 November 2002).

The following year, a study conducted by the Saskatchewan Population Health and Research Unit (SPHERU) at the University of Saskatchewan provided detail on the problem of transiency in inner-city schools with high Aboriginal enrolments; even children from relatively low-income Aboriginal families with home stability tended to succeed despite their economic circumstances, compared to children from more frequently mobile families.

A persistent common perception of Native people in the city is that they are transitory and ill equipped to settle on a longer-term basis. As Native columnist Ken Noskiye has commented, First Nations and Metis in the city are accustomed to derisive comments made by other residents, and young women to being approached on the street (*Saskatoon Sun*, 21 March 2004). In 2005 a telephone survey conducted by the City with Fast Consulting found an increasing number of residents reporting that they had experienced racial discrimination and a declining proportion of respondents believing that relations between different cultures and ethnic groups are good to very good; 28% of all 500 adult respondents had personally experienced racial discrimination and 72% had witnessed an act of racism or discrimination (*Saskatoon StarPhoenix*, 4 and 20 May 2006).

A CanWest poll conducted in 2006 found that at least one in five people in the province believe that 'racial and ethnic intolerance is a serious problem in the community'; also, that Aboriginal people find Saskatchewan 'to be a very racist place to live … We still live in some pretty tough conditions …We shouldn't [have to] face the discrimination and the racism that we do. If nobody knows that, then nothing changes.' The mayor of Regina commented: 'Does racism exist? I think that is pretty evident. I think we see it every day' (*Leader-Post*, 8 March 2006). In yet another telephone survey conducted by the City of Saskatoon Cultural Diversity and Race Relations Office with Fast Consulting in 2007, young people interviewed (302 students aged 14 to 20) in general tended to think that ethnic/cultural relationships are positive (51%), but also that Aboriginal young people (70 students) were 'less enthusiastic' (37%) (*Saskatoon StarPhoenix*, 21 January 2008).

A Saskatchewan Anti-Racism Network survey conducted in 2007 suggested that public perceptions that race relations were recently improving in Saskatchewan contradicted reality: 76% of 675 people interviewed in this telephone survey (301 of whom were Aboriginal) said that race relations had either improved or stayed the same during the past five years. However, one in five respondents (and two in five Aboriginal) reported that they themselves had experienced racial discrimination just in the past year alone. The survey also found that Aboriginal people are far more likely to be targets of racial discrimination than any other ethnic group (including non-Whites or so-called 'visible minorities') (*Saskatoon StarPhoenix*, 16 May 2008).

The nationwide Urban Aboriginal Peoples Study (2010, 72–85) learned that urban Aboriginal people believe they are consistently viewed in negative ways by non-Aboriginal people; in fact, the study revealed 'almost unanimous belief' that Aboriginal people are subjected to discrimination. Negative stereotyping continues to be prevalent. A high proportion of Aboriginal respondents reported personal experience with negative behaviour or unfair treatment by others. Moreover, there is some evidence that in certain cities non-Aboriginal perceptions of Aboriginal people are worsening, largely due to media reports of increasing crime, gangs, addictions, prostitution, and a failure of urban Aboriginal residents to take advantage of opportunities to better their lives and to integrate into the urban environment. However, concerning

Aboriginal respondents' sense of acceptance by non-Aboriginal people, responses varied: 36% strongly disagreed that they were not being accepted, 26% disagreed somewhat, 28% agreed somewhat, and just 8% strongly agreed. The survey probed into non-Aboriginal perspectives as well; the information gathered was based on telephone (rather than personal) interviews conducted during April and May 2009 of a sample of only 250 non-Aboriginal residents in each of the ten cities studied (UAPS 2010, 141–72). These non-Aboriginal respondents seemed to have generally quite positive impressions of Aboriginal people; however, impressions seem to have been slow to change, so negative stereotypes persist. Finally, the study found that regardless of the extent to which they actually use general or non-Aboriginal services, or whether these experiences have been positive or negative, a large majority of urban Aboriginal people think it is important to also have distinctly Aboriginal services.

The City of Saskatoon Cultural Diversity and Race Relations Committee has issued the following ambitious policy vision: 'The City of Saskatoon will work with community organizations, business and labour, all orders of government, and other stakeholders to create an inclusive community, where cultural diversity is welcomed and valued, and where everyone can live with dignity and to their full potential, without facing racism or discrimination.' The same statement identified four basic policy outcomes: 'The workforce will be representative of the population of Saskatoon; there will be zero tolerance for racism and discrimination in Saskatoon; community decision-making bodies will be representative of the whole community of Saskatoon; and there will be awareness and understanding in the community regarding the issues, and acceptance of the various cultures that make up Saskatoon's population.' The committee has been working to increase women's participation in municipal consultation processes, in concert with the Saskatoon Tribal Council (STC) and the Metis Employment and Training Institute of Saskatoon. Mention should also be made of Equal Justice for All, a Saskatoon-based social advocacy organization, founded in 1985, that helps low-income people – many of whom are Aboriginal – to obtain 'appropriate benefits and rights.'

The first paper in this chapter provides a critical analysis of race relations in Saskatoon with the housing needs of Aboriginal residents in mind. One focus for combating racism in this city – and in many others across Canada – has to be on helping Aboriginal people find suitable housing and ensuring that they are treated impartially and without discrimination by landlords. CMHC has recently sponsored research specifically on housing discrimination affecting Aboriginal people in Winnipeg and in the northern mining centre of Thompson, Manitoba (CMHC 2003). Among the many problems identified in that study were discrimination in the housing market (fewer choices available); landlords discriminating by failing to provide adequate maintenance; limited choice in neighbourhood location; being forced to pay higher rent; a need to search longer for a place to live; being forced to move frequently; being subjected to overcrowding; being denied tenancy unfairly; being asked stereotypical and irrelevant questions; and being subjected to health issues. Virtually all of these findings from a neighbouring province would apply to Saskatoon.

## Race Relations and Housing

CARA J.A. SPENCE

*Introduction*

This report had its genesis in a race relations internship contracted by the Bridges and Foundations Project on Urban Aboriginal Housing to explore the fundamental racial inequalities facing the Aboriginal community and how those inequalities are connected to Saskatoon's housing industry. This internship served the mandate of the Bridges and Foundations Project in that it was an attempt to generate research, policies, and partnerships that might establish affordable housing options for Aboriginal people, as well as improve discourse in the city. All of this was part of an effort to reduce the discrimination that Aboriginal people currently face in the housing sector. Some neighbourhoods of Saskatoon have obvious concentrations of poverty, severely decaying housing stocks, hungry children with poor school achievements, and increasing crime. While there are significant differences in average income levels among Saskatoon neighbourhoods, these communities are segregated not only by economics but also by race. This report also examines the issue of racial inequality outside congested inner-city neighbourhoods. While the revitalization of inner-city communities is important, housing options and opportunities need to be expanded for Aboriginal people outside their 'traditional' neighbourhoods. Improved housing options and community development would also improve opportunities for the growing Aboriginal population in Saskatoon, and with this, do much to reduce racial tensions.

*Neighbourhood Differentiation*

A neighbourhood is not simply a geographical territory; it also represents a matrix of social relations with wider symbolic and ideological
meanings. The physical form of housing and community design literally
represents the social structures and values of the society that produces
it (Valentine 2001). The term 'community' is often intrinsically linked to
'neighbourhood'; community members shape community identity
through their values and capabilities. The differentiations between
Saskatoon neighbourhoods reflect the social differentiations within our
society as a whole.

Research supports the fact that income polarization and economic inequalities are growing across Canadian cities (RCAP 1996; Pendakur and
Pendakur 1998; Maxim, White, and Beavon 2003). In a study of income
differentials, the Federation of Canadian Municipalities (2003) pointed
to Saskatoon as a prominent example of a pattern developing among
urban centres in Canada: the concentration of low- and high-income sectors contained largely within specific neighbourhoods. Saskatoon's large
and steadily increasing Aboriginal population makes up a disproportionate share of low-income families in Saskatoon. That population has
the largest representation within the lowest sectors of the economy and
is seriously underrepresented in the highest sectors. The median total
income of Aboriginal persons 15 years of age and older is little more than
half that of the non-Aboriginal population. This differentiation has been
devastating to Aboriginal people and to relations with and perceptions
of them within the Saskatoon community as a whole.

The income differentials of Saskatoon's neighbourhoods are spatially
evident. The five highest-income neighbourhoods are found east of the
river; the five poorest are found in the inner west side. When we compare the average income of these five most affluent neighbourhoods
with the average income of the five poorest, we find that the most affluent neighbourhoods have an average income about six times that of the
lowest. Pleasant Hill, the poorest neighbourhood in the entire city, has
the largest concentration of Aboriginal people; whereas not a single
Aboriginal family lives in the most affluent neighbourhood.

Academic and community researchers have been developing quality-
of-life indicators. These indicators include the following: adequate physical well-being, perceptions of well-being, basic level of satisfaction,
sense of self-worth, and social, environmental, economic, and political
opportunities and positions. Quality-of-life research conducted by the

Community–University Institute for Social Research has pointed to a positive relationship between income and quality of life: as income increases, so does quality of life. Furthermore, as quality of life increases, so does one's satisfaction with neighbourhood, housing, income, health, and services. The study found that all quality-of-life indicators registered 'satisfactory' within the medium- to high-income neighbourhoods. In low-income neighbourhoods, the opposite was found: residents considered housing, safety, security, and self-perception all detrimental to quality of life.

In recent years Saskatoon has registered the country's sharpest increases in average home selling prices, concomitant with the lowest vacancy rates. Furthermore, failure to continually upgrade existing housing stock has led to disinvestment in some neighbourhoods; this disinvestment, particularly within older inner-city neighbourhoods, is creating a crisis situation where families – an increasing number of them Aboriginal – are occupying substandard housing.

The City of Saskatoon report *Keeping the Plan Alive* (2002b) indicated that 16.5% of all Saskatoon households were in core need. But within the Aboriginal population, 37.4% were in core need, which translated into more than 8,000 residents. In Pleasant Hill, where almost half the residents were Aboriginal, little more than one-quarter of the residents owned their own home; in contrast, Briarwood, with no Aboriginal population, had the highest homeownership rate in the city, with an average home selling price more than quadruple that of Pleasant Hill. In general, the higher the Aboriginal concentration, the fewer the homeowners and the less new construction or development.

With market prices steadily increasing, high-end housing developments are flourishing; at the same time, disinvestment in some neighbourhoods is creating substandard living conditions. This is contributing to a growing crisis in the availability of quality, affordable housing. The lack of investment and homeownership is a concern for inner-city communities. Homeownership contributes to community stability and cohesion as well as to a sense of belonging. It also encourages political, social, and economic participation while contributing to a higher quality of life for the community's stakeholders. Social cohesion increases as people develop local connections, relationships, and supports that stabilize communities and their residents.

High income inequality tends to generate racial tensions and stereotypes. A rising proportion of economically disadvantaged people translates into higher taxes and poor people's dependence on government transfers; it also contributes to class and racial tensions. Furthermore, maintaining a sector of the population below the poverty level creates even greater social problems. If Aboriginal people had a stronger social position and were able to make a greater economic contribution to the city, it is probable that resentments and tensions among communities would be reduced.

The existing residential trend is creating further divisions and is heightening race and class polarities. Allowing substandard housing to continue in the city's lower-income neighbourhoods is fostering the impression that Saskatoon is encouraging residential differentials. Graham and Peters (2002) warn us of the dangers of split populations. They confirm that as inequalities among communities perpetuate themselves, the resulting lack of social and political cohesion creates a tense environment. Such an environment increases the susceptibility to crime, violence, and threats to public safety; it also silences important minority issues, including poverty and inequalities. The current inequalities in Saskatoon are compounded by spatial inequalities, further encouraging such dangers.

*Residential Segregation*

As suburban housing opportunities increase, more affluent people are moving farther out to suburban communities, particularly in the eastern and southeastern areas of Saskatoon. At the same time, core-need neighbourhoods with high concentrations of Aboriginal people are increasing in population as a result of the steady in-migration of Aboriginal people. This trend separates communities, not only by race but also by class. Moreover, this tendency can be expected to increase, along with the demand for more affordable housing options in the core neighbourhoods as the Aboriginal population grows relatively more quickly than the non-Aboriginal population.

The growing residential differentiation makes a discussion of residential segregation inevitable. Urban centres are increasingly applying exclusionary policies; suburbs are characteristically separating and isolating people based on economics, race, or other status differences (Dasgupta 2000). The separation of communities encourages community conflict, unequal access to resources, misconceptions, and other social consequences. The lack of affordable housing options throughout the City of Saskatoon has created social isolation and residential segregation. Segregation of communities is widespread, indeed predominant, within developing urban centres; segregated residential patterns in turn create poorer life chances and opportunities for residents.

The rising demand for affordable housing further suggests that the gaps among communities are increasing. The politics of exclusion has created a bad image of 'affordable housing.' Some residents resist integrated or affordable housing in their neighbourhoods for fear of demographic change, downward pressure on property values, and an invasion of the poor. What escapes the minds of many is the fundamental right to decent and affordable housing, as well as the gross injustice being meted out to a growing number of people by not providing them with affordable housing and quality services. Diversifying neighbourhoods would, perhaps, foster a greater social consciousness.

There is a widely held perception that poverty is the problem of the poor. One result is that poor people are forced to bear responsibility for the fundamental failings of our modern social structure. There is not the remotest chance that poverty will be abolished under our current social arrangements (Seabrook 2003, 21). Rather, trends indicated in this discussion seem to suggest that the degree of poverty will actually *increase*. The segregation of poverty pushes the overwhelming imagery of the poor out of sight, which in turn allows the pressures for major changes in social and housing policies to be resisted or ignored.

The segregation of poverty creates misconceptions and stereotypes. Mostly, though, segregation exacerbates other social problems such as crime, poor education, lack of municipal services, obstacles to job opportunities, disempowerment, and withdrawal from community involvement, including political participation. Furthermore, poverty-related social problems, such as crime, dramatically increase when poverty is concentrated in one place. These grossly unequal living conditions, and the subsequent lower quality of life and restriction of life choices, create a culture of dependency among communities, with all the ensuing tensions.

Quality and security of housing are inextricably linked to educational success. Several studies have demonstrated a direct link between inadequate housing or homelessness and the lack of educational achievement (Haven and Wolfe 1992). Children simply cannot be expected to fulfil their potential while dealing with concerns connected to substandard housing or lack of housing. When continuity of education is disrupted by excessive residential mobility, academic performance significantly decreases. This process can be particularly damaging when relocation occurs during adolescence, as a result of peer group pressures, the development of identity, and social isolation. Moreover, mobility affecting student turnover is detrimental to teaching strategies as it may create discontinuity, instability, and disruption within the classroom (Kerbow 2002).

Inner-city school administrators and academic experts agree that the vast majority of school mobility, with its corresponding academic failure, is the result of housing instability. The community-based organization Community Solutions for Children Not in School has reported that elementary school children living in the inner city (a high proportion of them Aboriginal) switch schools an average of three times per school year, with inadequate housing being the major reason. Stability and security are necessary in order for a developing child to thrive, so policy and development plans must focus on stabilization of housing.

Resident surveys conducted in inner-city neighbourhoods have demonstrated the serious situation that people face with respect to crime in deteriorating neighbourhoods (SIIT 2004). Race, poverty, and crime have long been linked together. The general assumption is that a higher concentration of poverty equates to a higher degree of criminal activity. There is a high degree of poverty among Saskatoon's Aboriginal population; racial segregation concentrates poverty and therefore crime.

When communities with high crime rates also exhibit significant Aboriginal concentration, stereotypes form that link criminality to the Aboriginal population. However, deviant behaviour and crime are not inherent properties of the individual; rather, they are a result of a series of internal and external forces. Simply put, Aboriginal people are not by nature more deviant or criminal than mainstream Whites. Criminality has much more to do with environmental factors, such as poverty, or internal factors, such as necessary or expected behaviour to ensure survival in a competitive setting. Crime is largely rooted not in race but in structural differences among communities.

The crime rate itself is a source of residential segregation. As people who can afford to move to escape crime, do so, economic segregation increases as crime increases. It should not be a surprise that Saskatoon's crime rate varies by neighbourhood. Data compiled by the Saskatoon Police Service point to concentrations of certain types of criminal offences within the most impoverished areas of the inner city. It is clear that the inner-city neighbourhoods are exposed to higher levels of violent crime than other neighborhoods in Saskatoon. Exposure to and tolerance of crime is certainly part of the process that spatially separates people and leads to disparate residential outcomes.

In turn, the social conditions and economic struggles that residents of the inner city encounter contribute to weakened social norms of the sort that could control crime effectively. The police suggest that they cannot completely control crime and that a reduction in crime must come from the will of the community. In short, the differentials and inequalities that exist among individuals and communities can be expected to continue in high-poverty neighbourhoods, resulting in increased levels of criminal activity.

The concentration of poverty ensures that inner-city neighbourhoods do not have the economic strength to support a sufficient retail sector, with the result that goods within the inner city are either unavailable or overpriced. The focus of inner-city development needs to be on encouraging and growing inner-city-based businesses, as well as nearby employment opportunities for inner-city residents. A sustainable economic base can be created in the inner city, but that will require governments, Aboriginal agencies, and local authorities to provide incentives for investment. To build healthy and sustainable inner-city communities, healthy economies must be created in and near those communities. Naturally, as job opportunities increase, Aboriginal people will be better able to achieve the necessities of life such as wealth, power, prestige, education, health care, and respect. In turn, they will be better able to contribute more to the urban community as a whole.

High unemployment rates and segregation of poverty create perceptions that economic success is unattainable, weakening traditional societal norms. Unemployment is highly correlated to juvenile delinquency and to the spread of the informal market. An increased misfortune to the future of young residents of these neighborhoods would be the progression toward ghetto formation. An urban ghetto is commonly defined as an area where 40% or more of residents are poor (Jargowsky and Bane 2004). Some Saskatoon neighbourhoods are near this level of poverty and show signs of ghettoization. The subculture that develops to respond to these impoverished conditions promises few life chances for the residents of such communities. Economic development plays an intrinsic role in reducing segregation and the formation of an urban ghetto.

Residents living in poverty are both realistically and symbolically isolated from political spheres. The political isolation of poor inner-city residents, and the resultant apathy toward municipal affairs, together lead to a loss of power by the minority group as well as to a diminishing of the share of local public services it can command (Pascal 1989). Poorer neighbourhoods are shortchanged in public services such as sanitation, recreation, transportation, education, and fire and police protection (Dasgupta 2000).

Yet to some extent the propensity toward voluntary segregation is both natural and understandable. Minority cultures can often be expected to create separate communities to a degree. Homogeneous communities become cohesive when people share a culture, common experiences, histories, kinship ties, and socio-economic level. Community 'sameness' also permits easier communication and understandings, which encourages the establishment of support and services for the population. Segregation is not necessarily harmful; its outcome depends on the condition and attitudinal factors of the community. The already established Aboriginal communities provide an opportunity for Saskatoon to develop and support Aboriginal residents by focusing on rebuilding these neighbourhoods.

Saskatoon segregates many of its poor in core-need neighbourhoods. When the effects of segregation or the motives underlying it are damaging, segregation negatively affects racial perceptions across the whole community, fostering stereotypes and stigmas. Although voluntary segregation plays some role in residential choice, the race prejudice of non-Aboriginals toward Aboriginals (and of Aboriginals toward non-Aboriginals), combined with the intolerance of the rich toward the poor (and vice versa), bears substantial responsibility for the observed segregation in housing (Pascal 1989). It is noteworthy that when asked, only a very low proportion of the surveyed members of the Aboriginal community expressed a preference for living in neighbourhoods with a high Aboriginal proportion.

The future of racial segregation in housing will depend on a number of factors, including changing racial attitudes and perceptions, the strength of the tendency toward increasing socio-economic disparities between Aboriginal and non-Aboriginal people, the relative rates of population growth in the two populations, and importantly, housing policies. Racial segregation involves depriving people of opportunity. The fundamental hypocrisy is to suggest that people have the choice and the right to live where they want and that Aboriginals want to live with other Aboriginals. In a structure that maintains poverty, those who are disadvantaged, whether by race or by other factors, do not have the same opportunities as those who can *gain* from our society. People – particularly Aboriginals on low incomes – cannot choose where they

live. Suggesting that Aboriginals want to live in poor inner-city neighbourhoods simply to be with other Aboriginals may negate their desire
for respect, for self and from others.

## Right to Housing

Housing is indispensable to human dignity, equality, and respect and is
essential for normal, healthy living. It fulfils deep-seated psychological
needs for privacy and personal space; physical needs for security and
protection; and social needs by creating a basic gathering point where
important relationships can be shaped and nurtured. It needs to be ensured for all persons, irrespective of income, ethnicity, or any other form
of discrimination. Perhaps the irony here is that housing has been confirmed as a basic human right at an international level, yet that right has
not been realized for those in the most marginalized positions in our
Canadian cities, including Saskatoon. This is an embarrassment to our
social values.

The right to adequate housing is founded and recognized under international law. It has been enunciated in the Universal Declaration of
Human Rights and codified in other major international human rights
treaties, including the International Covenant on Economic, Social, and
Cultural Rights (1976). The right to housing touches on affordability,
habitability, location and accessibility, legal security of tenure, availability of services, and cultural adequacy (Walker 2010). That housing is a
human right does not mean that governments are required to provide
free housing; rather, it means that governments must ensure, through
their policies, that affordable and acceptable housing is available to the
entire population. The right to adequate housing therefore provides a
unique opportunity for our leaders to take steps toward ensuring it,
when citizens demand that this basic human right be fulfilled.

Adequate housing is not simply a fundamental social right; shelter
(which includes housing, renovations, and related infrastructure) is also
a First Nations treaty right and a responsibility of Canadian governments. (This derives from the special Indian–Crown relationship that
dates back to the Royal Proclamation of 1763, as enhanced by the
Constitution Acts of 1867 and 1982.) In its brief to the Royal Commission
on Aboriginal Peoples, the National Aboriginal Housing Committee
stated that 'the federal government has a moral, ethical and legal
responsibility to continue funding Native housing both on- and off-
reserve, until at least such time as parity in living conditions between

Natives and non-Natives is achieved' (AFN 1992). The adoption of a clear housing strategy to fulfil basic rights would be an important step toward this equal social and economic position.

## Community Rejuvenation

Community rejuvenation is key to stability and growth in inner-city neighbourhoods. The efficient use of Saskatoon urban space would include converting declining inner-city neighbourhoods into communities where homes are affordable, diversity is respected, and services are available. All of this would create places where people want to live. Adequate housing builds the foundation for a community to grow.

These neighbourhoods are valuable urban spaces, and the people who reside in them are important members of the community. Development of the inner city through financial assistance, incentives, and grants would do much to encourage working families to stay there; this in turn would promote conventional values and responsibilities among the residents. A stabilized community would then encourage further new growth and investment. Improvements in inner-city neighbourhoods in general, and in the perceptions of Aboriginal residents in particular, would reduce tensions among and within communities.

## Views of Non-Aboriginal Residents

Many of Saskatoon's more affluent neighbourhoods, especially on the east side, contain few if any Aboriginal residents. Apparently, many residents in these neighbourhoods feel threatened by the growth of their city's Aboriginal population and perpetuate highly negative stereotypes of Aboriginal people. To gain a clearer understanding of race relations and residential patterns in Saskatoon, the discussion must venture beyond inner-city neighbourhoods and into the communities whose populations are largely non-Aboriginal. To document and understand the pereptions of east-side residents regarding affordable housing for Aboriginal people in their neighbourhood, randomly selected households were interviewed.

In response to the question 'Would you support the development of Aboriginal affordable housing in your neighbourhood?' the results were predictably split. Two-thirds of the residents interviewed supported or held little objection to the idea; however, most of these respondents acknowledged unequal relations or discrimination directed toward

Aboriginal people. Others pointed to a need to 'balance' poverty and to create more housing options for Aboriginal people. One respondent commented that it was a 'matter of respect.' Others supported the idea but wanted to know how 'affordable' would be defined and suggested that such a development be appropriately priced in order to prevent the creation of a future 'slum.' The remaining third of respondents generally resisted the idea. Most of their concerns related to assumptions about falling property values and rising crime. Others argued that for equality's sake, such developments should not be directed specifically toward Aboriginal people. One distraught respondent suggested that 'they' (presumably Aboriginals) should 'go back to where they came from' (a statement usually directed at immigrants).

When residents were asked how race relations between Aboriginal and non-Aboriginal people could be improved in Saskatoon, most called for improved education and awareness. Many suggested that neighbourhoods be diversified. Again, an argument of equal rights emerged, mainly referring to equality in taxes and benefits. Others suggested that Aboriginal people needed to participate economically in society; one respondent, though, suggested that 'they' stay within their own communities. Most respondents saw race relations in Saskatoon as poor and in need of improvement.

Throughout these interviews, a subtle (and sometimes not so subtle) racism was consistently observed. Many respondents viewed themselves as racially and culturally neutral, yet they did not recognize their racial and cultural privilege, nor did they acknowledge what it means to be part of the dominant group. McIntosh (1998) clarifies this dominant perspective when she points out that 'Whites are taught to think of their lives as morally neutral, normative, and average, and also ideal, so that when we work to benefit others, this is seen as work which will allow "them" to be more like "us."' Discussions of relations among races need to include understandings of various types of advantages that reinforce our present hierarchies. Without the awareness that opportunities are not unconnected to race, misconceptions will permeate the dominant perspective.

*Conclusion*

Social change often meets resistance; however, the willingness to change creates the foundation for change. More education about and understanding of Aboriginal people and their history is necessary. With change in community structure, this awareness may develop through increased social interactions. Community spaces evolve in ways that come to represent the social structures and values of the societies that produce them. Racial difference may be a sustained feature of Canadian cities; this feature also predicts how the city is experienced differently by different people. However, racisms as social constructs become normalized in and through spatial configurations, just as social spaces are made to seem natural and defined in racial terms (Razack 2002). The residential separation of Saskatoon's diverse population continues to perpetuate the inequalities of history. Little can be done to relieve poverty without corresponding economic development. However, policy and responsible leadership can reduce the effects that develop when poverty is concentrated. Alleviating the stress and poor social conditions that permeate impoverished neighbourhoods is important for the progressive development of society as well as necessary to reduce racial tensions. Creating partnerships and multidimensional collaborations among stakeholders in Saskatoon and its Aboriginal communities is essential. The need for Aboriginal affordable housing in Saskatoon serves in this sense as an opportunity for Aboriginal leaders, bands, and individuals to work with community developers, policy makers, and agencies to meet the growing needs of the community. Addressing racial tensions and inequalities is a complex task with no simple solution. Continued dialogue and renewed commitments are essential.

## Life in the Inner City: Crime and Policing

ALAN B. ANDERSON

### Crime Rates

In assessing Aboriginal involvement in criminal behaviour, and determining trends, let us examine national, provincial (Saskatchewan), and particularly city (Saskatoon) and neighbourhood data for the past couple of decades and especially for the past several years (drawing primarily from Statistics Canada, provincial, and Saskatoon Police Service data). Crime rates can be viewed both from a positive and from a negative perspective.

First, the 'good news': The overall provincial crime rate has decreased for the seventh consecutive year. In Saskatoon the overall crime rate has now reached its lowest level in 15 years. The overall crime rate for Saskatoon has decreased 30% during the past ten years (2003–12).

Violent crimes have decreased by 10% (21% in a single year, 2007–8, representing the fastest decline in any major Canadian city), property crime by 40%. Currently (in 2012) the annual decrease in overall crime varies between 3–8%; in the past year homicides have decreased by 50%, motor vehicle thefts 21%, robberies 3%, break and enters 2%. The overall number of crimes committed in Saskatoon over a five-year period was 31,340, according to the most recent data; assaults, sexual violations, robberies, and armed robberies were all below the five-year average for each category. Data on categories of crimes against the person (including assaults, robberies, attempted murder, and other physical attacks) show a slight decline. Similarly, the number of complaints received by police has lessened. Saskatoon has a fairly good record nationally for its crime clearance rate weighted by seriousness of offences. Nationally, the overall Canadian crime rate has decreased by 17% during the past decade, and is now decreasing approximately 6% a year, although the most significant decreases have been in non-violent crimes. In fact, the crime rate in Regina has actually been falling during this period at twice the national rate. During the past decade both the provincial and national crime severity indices have been decreasing (by about 22%).

Now for the bad news. Provincial data indicate that in 2004, Saskatchewan had the highest rate *per capita* for violent crimes, as well as for household crimes, of any province (a 57% increase since 1999); and again in 2006, Saskatchewan had the highest crime rate per capita of any province (over 14,000 incidents per 100,000 population, which was twice the national average). In 2008, Saskatchewan still had the highest crime rate per capita of any Canadian province, for the tenth consecutive year; it also had the highest rate of violent crime (2,551 reported incidents per year per 100,000 population) and the highest youth crime rate (20,371 reported incidents per 100,000 population), according to data from the Canadian Centre for Justice Statistics (CCJS). Despite the aforementioned decreases in provincial crime rates, currently Saskatchewan and Manitoba have approximately double the rate of major assaults compared to most other provinces; Saskatchewan is second only to Alberta for the provincial homicide rate; and Saskatchewan still reports the highest rate of break-ins and motor-vehicle theft. Data released by Statistics Canada in July 2010 indicated that despite having the highest per capita crime severity index in Canada, Saskatchewan offenders are actually sentenced less often than in most other provinces: 26% compared to a national 34%; however, the sentencing rate for Aboriginal people remains much higher.

As for Saskatoon in particular, the Bridges and Foundations Project, comparing data for 1993 and 2003 in order to discern trends, noted extremely high increases in reported criminal harassment or stalking (5,425.0%), armed robbery (511.9%), and 'other' break and entry (364.3%); as well as substantial increases in general robbery (206.6%), arson (77.2%), drug and substance abuse (133.4%), and vehicle theft (128.8%); and slower increases in general 'mischief' or vandalism (67.0%), business break and entry (48.2%), general assaults (47.2%), and violations causing death (33.3%) in those ten years. By 1997 there were already somewhere between 500 to 1,000 solvent-abusing addicts in the city (*Saskatoon StarPhoenix*, 10 May 1997). By 2004, Saskatoon was reporting the highest rate in Canada per capita for break-ins, robberies, and violent crimes; the city now had 15,164 Criminal Code offences per 100,000 population (according to data from a CCJS report in July 2004). There were numerous incidents of knife stabbings: 401 in 2005 alone, 47 just in January and early February 2006 (*Saskatoon StarPhoenix*, 16 February 2006). Although certain types of crime were starting to decrease (break and enter, minor theft, property crimes, prostitution), other types were increasing (especially robbery and arson). Saskatoon now had the highest crime rate of any Canadian metropolitan city, as well as the highest per capita rate of violent crime, even though this rate had been decreasing for several years (CCJS data, July 2008). Much controversy was generated over a survey published in *Maclean's* (24 March 2008) suggesting that Saskatoon and Regina were Canada's 'most dangerous cities.' In general, the survey pointed out, Saskatoon's crime rate was 146% above the national rate for Canadian cities; regarding specific crimes, it was 243% above the national rate for robbery and 93% above for sex assault (the highest rates for these particular crimes in Canada), 204% above for aggravated assault (second only to Regina), 113% above for murder, and 70% above for break and enter. According to the police-reported Crime Severity Index, Canadian cities averaged 90.0, whereas Saskatoon had an index of 137.8 and Regina 163.1 (the highest of any city) in 2008.

Saskatoon is currently ranked second among all Canadian metropolitan areas for all police-reported crime (after Regina), and also second for violent crimes (after Winnipeg). The latest data indicate that Saskatoon is even with Regina per capita for top ranking in Canada for break-and-entry; and both break-and-entry and vehicle theft have shown increases during the most recent statistical year (vehicle theft increased from 1,210 in 2010 to 1,474 in 2011). For all Canadian cities over 10,000 population, Saskatoon drops to 26th; but two smaller cities in the province, North

Battleford and Prince Albert, respectively rank 2nd and 7th, while Regina ranks 19th. The national police-reported Crime Severity Index, which gives greater weight to more serious offences, ranked Regina highest in all of Canada and Saskatoon second as recently as 2010. Yet these rates are per capita; in absolute numbers, of course, there are far fewer of these crimes in Saskatoon than in a large metropolis such as Toronto. In certain categories of criminal offences – including property crimes – rates have most recently continued to increase. Intentionally set home fires are occasionally investigated – in one recent case, fourteen members of a single family living in Riversdale were displaced by suspected arsonists (this home had been the target of several attacks). It may be misleading simply to count assaults – city police records show that they have become increasingly vicious, with knives being used more often and injuries more serious. Specifically, aggravated assaults have been steadily increasing. At the same time, assaults with a weapon causing bodily harm seem to have fluctuated .

These armed assaults have been occurring all over the city, but according to police, they are concentrated most heavily in inner west side neighbourhoods, particularly Riversdale and Pleasant Hill, which are the areas with the greatest poverty, racism, and substance abuse. These neighbourhoods continue to see a disproportionate amount of violence. While Saskatoon homicide rates have most recently been declining, all five murders during the past year (2012) – half the number the previous year – have been Aboriginal and on the west side. Among the general population of Saskatoon, concern is growing about increasing crime rates in the poorer inner-city neighbourhoods where Aboriginal people are most concentrated; in fact, it is Aboriginal residents of those neighbourhoods who are *most* concerned. It is in these neighborhoods that Aboriginal youth gangs, as well as violent assaults, armed robberies, residential and business break and entries, vehicle thefts, petty thefts, and prostitution, are most prevalent. For example, in 2000 the Pleasant Hill planning report indicated that the 355 incidents of wilful damage that single year represented an annual increase of 15% a year, the 32 business break and enter an increase of 10% a year, and the 394 violent assaults an increase of 6% a year (City of Saskatoon 2002, 80). Violent crimes and property crimes had become very heavily concentrated in the rectangular corridor between the two main thoroughfares running east-to-west through the area (20th and 22nd Streets), where much of the poorest housing was found and where the most vicious gang activity seemed to be occurring. In a single year (2003), in Pleasant Hill, there were 477 reported assaults, 472 incidents of public mischief, 449 of theft under $5,000, 431 of break and enter, 324 of residential theft, 182 of vehicle theft, 61 of armed robbery, and 72 of other robberies reported, apart from 59 businesses robbed, 60 charges for prostitution, 60 for drug or substance abuse, 36 for sexual assaults, 23 for arson, and 14 for stalking. That year, Pleasant Hill was the site of the majority of sex trade violations in the city, as 'the stroll' was situated in this area. Meanwhile, in neighbouring Riversdale, crimes reported were, in order of frequency, 236 thefts under $5,000, 185 assaults, 161 public mischief, 159 break and entry, 98 residential robberies, 74 vehicle thefts, 49 general robberies, 48 business break and entry, 35 armed robberies, 11 prostitution, and 10 sexual assaults. In the quieter King George neighbourhood to the south, reported crimes were less frequent; nevertheless, that year there were significant problems with break and entry (142 reported incidents), minor theft (138), residential robberies (111), public mischief (80), and assaults (80). Caswell Hill to the north had the most problems with minor theft (376), mischief (288), break and entry (269), residential robberies (196), and assaults (108). Westmount to the west was concerned with minor theft (181), break and entry (139), residential robberies (104), and assaults (82).

Especially troubling to residents of these and other inner west side neighbourhoods was that almost all of these crimes were on the increase, some of them (vehicle thefts, arson, armed robberies) very rapidly. Yet there are indications that in Pleasant Hill, some criminal activities have been abating or at least may be variable. For example, between 2002 and 2006, property crimes decreased by 17%, break and enters by 21%, and minor thefts by 26%. A CanWest survey released in May 2007 interviewed 3,500 people in seven western cities and Toronto (but just 500 in Saskatoon) and found that over two-thirds (68.3%) of the Saskatoon respondents said they were afraid to set foot in certain neighbourhoods (however, this was less than in Regina, Winnipeg, Edmonton, or Vancouver). The Pleasant Hill planning report specified a number of socio-economic indicators associated with criminal activity in the neighbourhood, including these: poverty and unemployment deriving from social exclusion, especially for youth; dysfunctional (including violent) families with uncaring and inconsistent parental attitudes; social valuation of a culture of violence; the presence of facilitators such as weapons and drugs; discrimination and exclusion deriving from sexist, racist, and other forms of oppression; degradation of urban environments and social bonds; and inadequate surveillance and maintenance of security.

Saskatoon residents consider crime and policing to be the most important local issues for the city, according to the Civic Services Survey conducted by Insightrix, released in December 2009. Coincidentally, these respondents ranked housing fourth; however, in such a general random sample (of only 501 residents aged 18 and over), in which over 90% of the respondents reported that Saskatoon's quality of life was good to very good, we have to assume that very few of the residents encountering housing problems would have been interviewed.

## The Aboriginal Factor

According to a Statistics Canada study released in June 2006, across Canada, Aboriginals were far more likely to be both victims and perpetrators of crimes. That study reported that Aboriginals were twice as likely as others to have consumed an intoxicant before a violent attack – for example, 89% of Aboriginal accused murderers. Also, 94% of Aboriginal women and 66% of men accused of homicide were believed to be abusers of alcohol, drugs, or other intoxicants. Moreover, Aboriginal victims were almost twice as likely to have consumed an intoxicant. Crime rates on reserves were far higher than elsewhere: eight times higher for assaults, seven times for sex assaults, six times for homicides. Aboriginal youths on reserves were being charged with murder at a rate eleven times higher than for youths elsewhere. Despite being just 3.3% of Canada's population, Aboriginals were 22% of admissions to federal and provincial custody. Almost 40% of Aboriginal respondents reported having been victimized at least once in the past year; 17% of all homicide victims were Aboriginal. A high proportion of homicide victims in Saskatoon have been Aboriginal (in fact, all victims and perpetrators during the past year).

Aboriginal people in Saskatchewan currently have the highest provincial incarceration rate in Canada – 81% of all sentenced adults in custody – though they represent just 11% of the total provincial population. Aboriginals are an even higher proportion (over 90%) of women incarcerated in provincial facilities. This has been explained in part by the circumstance that proportionately more Aboriginal people are young, poor, less educated, underemployed, and poorly housed, although we have noted changes in all of these respects. The Saskatoon police chief is optimistic that a cohort of well-educated young Aboriginal people is developing who are positive in their outlook and who have ample potential to help build their city (literally, if they opt for training in the construction trades). A senior city planner has stated that it may be very misleading to view young Native people as primarily responsible for the city's crime.

The Urban Aboriginal Peoples Study gathered some interesting information on urban Aboriginal residents' views of the justice system (UAPS 2010, 96–102). Half the Aboriginal respondents to that survey had been in contact with the justice system as either a witness to or a victim of crime, or had been arrested or charged (First Nations more likely than Metis). Also, half of those who reported 'serious involvement' with the criminal justice system felt that they had definitely been treated unfairly, and another quarter probably unfairly. On the whole, urban Aboriginal people lack confidence in the justice system (22% of the sample expressed no confidence, 33% little, and 37% some); consequently, they endorse the concepts of a separate Aboriginal justice system and alternative approaches to justice.

*The Problem of Aboriginal Youth Gangs*

Saskatchewan has the highest youth crime rate of any province in Canada (20,371 incidents per 100,000 population) (CCJS, July 2008). Not only that, but it has a rate far above the national average for firearms-related violent crime. In addition, Saskatoon has one of the highest rates of gun incidents involving youth: 91.6 per 100,000, an increase of 32% since 2002, comparable to what is found in Toronto (96.2), and far above the national average (55.5). In absolute numbers, of course, Saskatoon (19 incidents a year) pales in comparison to Toronto (363) (CCJS, February 2008). In the extensive neighbourhood surveys conducted for the Bridges and Foundations Project, residents often expressed concerns about increasing youth gang crime. Crime seems to be a fundamental part of these gangs' activities. Just to become a gang member, the prospect has to engage in a crime; a criminal record is usually a prerequisite for membership, and those wishing to be accepted by a gang must prove themselves worthy through random acts of violence.

There is ample evidence that youth gang violence has been increasing all across Canada (*Globe and Mail*, 17 October 2005; *La Presse*, 24 October 2008; Buddle 2012). This has drawn the attention even of mental health researchers (CIHI 2008a). In 2002, the Canadian Police Survey on Youth Gangs reported that Saskatchewan had the most youth gang members per capita in Canada (cited in *Saskatoon StarPhoenix*, 4 June 2004); the same survey estimated that 96% of these gang members were Aboriginal.

By 2003, Saskatoon police had identified 280 known youth in the city with street gang ties (*Saskatoon StarPhoenix*, 3 April 2003). Gang members were estimated to number about 1,500 in Saskatchewan. Actually, fewer than 30% were under the age of eighteen, although gangs had been recruiting in city schools with high Aboriginal proportions. Some gangs operating in Saskatoon are quite widespread: the Indian Posse also has a presence in Prince Albert, and the Native Syndicate in Regina and Prince Albert, while the Terror Squad was formed in Saskatoon five years ago but has recently been spreading to northern communities. Terror Squad members (not exclusively Aboriginal) recently arrested for drug trafficking have ranged in age from 17 to 45. Other gangs are more localized in Saskatoon (the Crazy Cree, West Side Boyz, and West Side Crips), Regina (Redd Alert), or Prince Albert (Tribal Warriors). Some have connections beyond Saskatchewan; the Alberta Warriors have moved into Prince Albert. There are also various associate gangs: Baby Blue Crew, Brown Premise, Native Pride, Young Bloods. There is ample evidence that problems with Aboriginal gangs are not restricted to the cities: youth may have been familiar with gangs long before moving to the city. For example, in the predominantly Aboriginal northern community of La Loche, a gang-related murder took place recently in broad daylight on the main street. This incident was widely seen as a revenge killing by the Scorpions, a gang that had been formed in prison by inmates of Dene descent to defend themselves against the dominant Cree-based gangs. When former prisoners return to their home communities, they bring their gang affiliations with them.

The Saskatoon Police Service now estimates that at least half the near-record number of homicides in the city are gang-related. Aboriginal gang members have often been charged with assault causing bodily harm (*notinikewin*), battery (*wanitotamakewin*), aggravated assault (*sehkeniwi notinikewin*), causing a disturbance (*manenihcikewin*), destructive behaviour (*kwespanatisiwin*), break and enter (*pikonikewin akwa kimohci pihtikwewin*), and vehicle theft (*kimotin otapanaskwa*).

These gangs have generated a lot of critical attention, including recommendations for solutions. In Winnipeg back in 1992, a streetwise 'peacekeeping force' called the Bear Clan was formed as a counter-gang by members of the Ma Mawi Wi Chi Itata Centre youth program. Saskatoon columnist Doug Cuthand has often written about the gangs, suggesting that the marginalization of urban Aboriginal youth has led these young people to join gangs as a survival mechanism and as a means to find self-worth. 'There is a lot of hate out there and it's boiling over with mindless violence, crimes against our own people ... We are losing a large part of our Indian Nation to a new culture of urban crime and poverty' (*Saskatoon StarPhoenix*, 12 April 1996). He has argued that Natives must solve their own problems and that elders should play more of a role to 'broaden the cultural and social revival [of urban Aboriginal people] into a moral and ethical revolution. We must work to eliminate the reasons our young people turn to gangs and then we must work with the law enforcement agencies to clean up our communities. Failure means turning over our communities to internal terrorism, resulting in good folks moving away in fear' (2 May 2008). Cuthand quoted from a recent RCMP report: 'If the status quo of Aboriginal economic and educational initiatives continues, street gangs and violent activity will increase and already marginalized Aboriginal population will experience a diminishing quality of life' (22 August 2008). Other commentators have recommended increased policing as well as enhanced programs for 'at risk' youth. Still others has stated that Aboriginal leaders, including those back on reserve, must take far more responsibility for youth. Meanwhile, police across Canada are seeking more creative, community-based approaches to combat gang activity. Saskatoon's strategy includes a leadership development program, in which the city and the community are working together to provide alternatives to gang involvement. However, a local priest working with gang members has suggested that such programs will not be as successful at reaching gang members as individual contacts and perhaps a 'gang strategy forum' aimed at persuading gang members to change their lifestyle.

The police have reported that gang activity in Saskatoon has recently been fairly stable, not the least due to an increase in police assigned to gang control. They suggest that the public and the media tend to overstate the involvement of gangs in assaults on city streets. Gang initiations are often cited as the impetus behind seemingly random attacks. The police admit that this happens – just not as often as people think. While gangs are clearly responsible for some attacks (e.g., for retaliations against rival gangs), most assaults are not gang-related. The police emphasize that gangs operate all over the city, not just on the inner west side, and that members (even of Aboriginal gangs) are not limited to a particular ethnic group. The fear factor is very real – neighbours are afraid to go out at night, and the prospect of gang retaliation often accounts for residents' refusal to cooperate with the police. In one recent incident of overt gang violence, a Native victim was viciously beaten by five gang members armed with metal pipes and baseball bats in broad daylight right on the main street in Riversdale (*Saskatoon StarPhoenix*, 6 Sept. 2012).

*Policing Aboriginal People in Saskatoon*

Unfortunately, the ability of Saskatoon police to relate constructively to Aboriginal residents has been greatly diminished by several tragic cases of police misconduct in recent years (see, for example, Desjarlais 2002; Reber and Renaud 2005; Comack 2012). On 24 November 1990, a First Nation youth named Neil Stonechild was found frozen in a field in a northern industrial area far from the city centre. Subsequently, Constables Hartwig and Senger were implicated, as they had made the last known contact with him; however, the case was soon closed following an inconclusive police investigation. But this case garnered renewed attention ten years later when two more Aboriginal men, inadequately clothed for the bitter cold winter weather, were found in fields far to the south of the city beyond an industrial area: Rodney Naistus on 29 January 2000 and Lawrence Wegner the very next day. Then another Aboriginal man, Darrell Night, reported that he too had been dropped off in the same specific area by a couple of police officers, Constables Hatchen and Munson, on 18 January; he had survived by seeking help at a nearby power station. These two officers were sentenced to short jail terms for 'unlawful confinement.' Finally, in May 2004, Hartwig and Senger were found guilty of last being in possession of Stonechild and suspended for 'negligence of duty.' In March 2007, Hatchen and Munson, still protesting their innocence, countered with their own documentary film, *When Police Become Prey*. On 19 June 2008 the Saskatchewan Court of Appeal heard a formal appeal by Hartwig and Senger; this appeal would eventually go all the way to the Supreme Court, which on 18 December 2008 declined to hear the case.

In March 2006, the Saskatoon Police Commission released its final report on improving race relations between the police and the Aboriginal community. This was done without inviting the city's First Nations and Metis leaders. Notwithstanding that oversight, a number of actions have been taken to improve relations. A police substation (*simakanisiwikamik*) was established in Riversdale; police street patrols have been increased by almost one-third; the Saskatoon Police Service has been honoured in the annual city and university powwows; the police, and especially the new chief, are making sincere efforts to change the prevalent Aboriginal view of them as 'outsiders'; attempts are being made to recruit more Aboriginal police officers; the chief is moving more quickly to control and reprimand the 'inappropriate behaviour' of police officers; a blend of 'soft' and 'hard' policing is being developed; and above all, communication has been increased between police and Aboriginal and neighbourhood organizations. It is absolutely essential that the Saskatoon Police Service establish its credibility with Aboriginal residents; that it be seen as helping local neighbourhoods restore safety and security; and that it work hard to change the all-too-prevalent 'us versus them' relationship with Aboriginal people. There are many well-intentioned and empathetic police officers in Saskatoon (not the least the present chief); unfortunately, the recent behaviour of some police officers toward Aboriginal people – which has been at the very least suspicious and what many residents (both Aboriginal and non-Aboriginal) would view as racist – has not helped race relations. Even if most police are 'not like that' – as this author has been told – *none* of them should engage in racist or questionable behaviour if they are meant to serve the public peace (Anderson 1990, 1992). It has taken fully 10 years for the police service to lay a charge in one particular stabbing death; both the accused and victim were Aboriginal.

The police (*simakani*) continue to be accused of brutality and harassment by Aboriginal residents. In one recent case, an officer dealt what the police called 'distraction blows' to a young Metis man while attempting to handcuff him in a back alley. The arrested individual was allegedly intoxicated, and when the police arrived they were accosted by pipe-wielding residents. A complaint was filed with the police service with the assistance of the Metis Nation of Saskatchewan (*Saskatoon StarPhoenix*, 14 May 2009). In another case, police raided a house looking for firearms (in vain) after cordoning off the area. The Aboriginal occupants later said that the police 'tore our house apart.' This family was well-known to police; it had previously accused them of using excessive force (i.e., they had shot the family dog in the backyard). On this raid, the occupants were charged with illegal possession of prohibited weaponry (a Taser) and careless storage of ammunition (*Saskatoon StarPhoenix*, 29 April 2010). One home in a sad state of disrepair in Riversdale that had been the scene of fire department charges for maintenance violations, an armed standoff with police, and the arrest of a 15-year-old boy on a murder charge (a shooting incident that took place just down the block) in July 2011 was demolished in November.

*Toward Solutions*

According to the CCJS, for the past ten years Saskatchewan has had the highest ratio of police officers to population of any province: 220 per

100,000 people (the nationwide ratio is 198 per 100,000). Moreover the ratio is currently increasing by 6.1% a year (the nationwide increase is 1.6% a year). In Saskatchewan, 17.3% of officers are women, compared to about 19% across Canada. The present city police chief has credited a reduction in certain types of crimes with a variety of factors: greater visibility of officers on the street and in the neighbourhoods, especially in the most crime-prone areas; partnerships with community and particularly Aboriginal groups; and more Aboriginal police men and women in the service. He has emphasized that more policing has to be supplemented with effective social change – that is, with improved housing and reductions in poverty, racism, and substance abuse.

Unless social conditions change, increased numbers of police will not have much of an effect on crime rates. Improving the education of Aboriginal young people seems crucial; this will open the door to more meaningful employment and improved living conditions, which in turn reduce the crime rate. Initiatives such as the redevelopment of Pleasant Hill and other inner west side neighbourhoods will play an important role in crime reduction. The City of Saskatoon has plans to prevent crime through environmental design and urban renewal. This is expected to have a real impact on communities by reducing racism, promoting community solidarity and pride, and increasing residents' resolve to drive out criminal elements. Police have been educating landlords about the need for improved building maintenance and more careful screening of prospective tenants and have been supporting them in their efforts to evict undesirable tenants. The Saskatoon Police Service distributes pamphlets: *How Safe Is Your Rental Property?* (advising residents what is expected in proper property maintenance, and who to contact in the new Crime-Free Multi-Housing Program) and *Community Connections Guide* (providing residents with a large diversity of contacts in emergency services, shelters, health, justice, and family wellness). The Saskatoon Police Service now has a 'crime-free multi-housing coordinator' as well as a full-time race relations coordinator (an Aboriginal woman who until recently headed the City Race Relations Committee). This housing initiative is based on a program that originated in Arizona in 1992 and was first tried in Saskatoon in 2004. It involves three phases: first, teaching property managers and owners how to deal with crime and undesirable tenants; second, building inspections and upgrading assistance; and third, community-building events that bring tenants together with owners to discuss relevant issues. In apartment buildings run by the Central Urban Metis Federation Inc. (CUMFI), police calls have dropped 70% in the past three years as the result of a zero-tolerance policy for alcohol and drugs, security camera surveillance, and community-building initiatives – in other words, a combination of controls with community incentives.

Community associations are playing an increasingly important role in community betterment and in emphasizing the need for attitude change – not only among residents but also among outsiders. In the view of police, city planners, and community representatives, it is counterproductive to make generalized assumptions about neighbourhood, age, race, and gang affiliation. The police chief suggests that 'getting tough on crime' has to be supplemented by comprehensive solutions to social problems. A multi-jurisdictional approach is needed that incorporates the ministries of health, social services, housing, and education. In short, what is needed is a far broader strategy than simply targeting particular types of crime with more policing.

A recent report for the Saskatchewan Ministry of Corrections, *The Road Ahead: Towards a Safer Correctional System* (2009), notes that the province's detention centres contain only 833 cells, whereas the average number of inmates through 2009 came to 1,498. So the FSIN is currently working with the provincial government to develop a unique $90 million remand centre (*kanawenimikowikamik*) for Aboriginal people awaiting trial in Saskatoon (*Saskatoon StarPhoenix*, 16 December 2010).

Clearly, Saskatoon continues to be seriously challenged by disproportionate Aboriginal involvement in criminal activities, some of it committed by youth gangs. However, it bears repeating that a great many of our neighbourhood survey respondents – indeed the vast majority of Aboriginal residents – have expressed their mounting concern over safety issues, over the pressing need for improved family and cultural values in the urban context, and over the need for more effective police collaboration with the community.

*Chapter Twelve*

# Conclusion

Throughout this book we have emphasized that the Aboriginal population of Canada, of Saskatchewan, and specifically of Saskatoon, has been changing. While our focus has been on housing and living conditions, just how First Nations and Metis people will fit into the emerging social economy of the 'new Saskatchewan' is drawing increasing attention (Seymour 2011; McGrane 2011; Settee 2011; Beatty 2011). Housing policies and initiatives at the federal, provincial, and municipal levels were described in Chapter 7; in this concluding chapter a more theoretical overview and rethinking of housing policies will be provided, as well as a description of planning concepts and local community involvement. The chapter then returns to a discussion of urban Aboriginal housing and politicization; again, we are particularly concerned with how housing policies affect urban Aboriginal people, so attention will be drawn to Aboriginal critiques of these policies. Finally, we take a retrospective look at the Bridges and Foundation Project – on what exactly this unique project has or should have accomplished, especially from an Aboriginal perspective.

**Housing Policies: An Overview**

*Public Policy and Housing Policies*

If a good society is one that combines a market economy with a goal-oriented approach to fixing market failures in order to build and sustain resilient communities, then the housing sector is in need of sustained public policy intervention, as Walker (2010) has observed. Housing is central to social policies: to social, economic and community development; to health care; to labour force stability and mobility as well as income security; and to education (Myers 2008). Housing is simply good social policy: affordable and adequate housing is necessary in itself; it also facilitates the success of initiatives taken in other, interrelated policy sectors (Carter and Polevychok 2004).

Public policy has been defined as the set of rules or principles that guide government action on particular issues. Policy can evolve over time and is usually influenced by relevant stakeholders; however, it can sometimes unintentionally produce barriers to community development. Housing policies often conform to this rather narrow definition, insofar as they tend to be primarily (albeit not necessarily) driven by government. Even if the localized community could be considered a 'relevant stakeholder,' this definition seems to miss the very important point that policies affecting the public may increasingly originate in the local community.

The Urban Aboriginal Economic Development (UAED) Network raises some fundamental questions about the direction of policy: Who are the key decision makers? What are the main blocks to effective policy? Policy matters ... but whose policy? And *how* does it matter? Policy may not actually be what it needs to be. It involves assumptions – for example, both Aboriginal and non-Aboriginal. In whose view is policy determined, and who is affected by policy? What really makes a difference on the ground? What is the real impact of programmatic intervention? How do policies relate to capacities? Housing policy may often reflect particular vested interests of government and the private home-building business. To what extent do governments and businesses really intend to benefit communities rather than just profiting from them? How may effective relationships be built among major players, if policies are to be developed not simply from the top down but (more important) from the bottom up, from the community 'grassroots'? This raises the whole question of governance. Are strategies just short-term or are they aimed at becoming longer-term? An important role may be played by financing, not simply of projects but also (most important) of residents – for example, through homeownership education and personal finance workshops. There is a huge body of knowledge that could inform public policy. The Community Research Hub in the Spence neighbourhood in Winnipeg has further pointed out that research informs public policy, government activities, legislation, and consumer services. But how are research data used, if at all? There is a pressing need to develop a capability to consolidate research findings into meaningful recommendations and concise policy briefs so that they will have the greatest impact on government and business. Ultimately, policy should be aimed at change, which may first depend on critical evaluation. Policy seeks a way forward (i.e., progress), and this implies guidance – and *that* is where academic and community research collaboration becomes so vital.

The Policy Research Initiative (PRI) based in Ottawa has provided a useful theoretical framework for summarizing Canadian housing policy. This report, *Housing Policy and Practice in the Context of Poverty and Exclusion* (PRI 2005), emphasizes that the provision of adequate housing is increasingly being viewed as a core issue that must be addressed if poverty and exclusion are ever to be effectively reduced. Simply put, a house is a home, a space that allows individuals to introduce a sense of order into their lives (Daly 1996, 149). Yet the PRI report comments that 'unfortunately, despite the extent to which scholars, activists, and policy analysts increasingly recognize this logic, a policy disconnect persists between those focused on housing challenges and those working on issues of social policy more generally' (PRI 2005, 2). While the vast majority of Canadians seem to be served quite well by their housing – in fact, this country's standards are comparable to or better than those in any other country – Canadian housing fails to address the needs of *all* Canadians: one in every six households lives in core housing need (as defined by CMHC). According to the PRI, housing exclusion is a result of complex circumstances and tends to reflect poor or inadequate urban planning and policies. Thus effective policy should respond to housing challenges found in particular communities.

The PRI report outlines a multidimensional model of factors associated with housing stress, consisting of three basic dimensions: first, the private market accounting for micro- and macro-economic realities (e.g., employment and housing markets); second, the state dimension centring on policies for social welfare and housing (e.g., rent control and regulation of onerous practices); and third, civil society, which through the social economy and not-for-profit and non-governmental organizations is an important service provider capable of mobilizing community resources. Add to this a fourth dimension: relevant household or personal characteristics, possibly including ethnicity, age, socio-economic status, and disabilities. Thus financial affordability is only one consideration, although undoubtedly the most important one. A multitude of factors may contribute to individuals and families being excluded from acceptable housing; moreover, these social and economic forces tend to disproportionately affect vulnerable groups, including urban Aboriginal people, who have to confront other social and economic integration challenges.

So according to the PRI, all of this suggests that housing policy should not be formulated in a vacuum, isolated from other social and economic policies targeting long-term poverty; any efforts to improve the socio-economic integration of Aboriginal people, as well as effectively reduce child poverty, will require that this be recognized. The PRI concludes: 'The self-reinforcing nature of these connections also suggests that housing policy can be made more effective if social supports are incorporated into housing policy. As a result, identifying effective approaches for addressing housing stress and exclusion is vital if progress is to be made on an array of socio-economic policy issues and returns on housing investments are to be maximized' (PRI 2005, 12–13).

The PRI has outlined what it considers to be effective approaches to addressing housing issues. *Supply side approaches* argue that the supply of housing is naturally determined by demand and cost. But to whom? The housing market typically functions better for those above certain income levels, while few adjustments occur naturally to address the needs of poorer residents. One major challenge associated with this approach, when represented in large-scale construction projects, is that relatively more affluent communities surrounding poorer neighbourhoods have often expressed hostility toward the concentrated presence of lower-income residents and the services and supports they require (coincidentally, this is exactly the view currently expressed by both a city councillor and a business development advocate in Riversdale; see chapter 9). Challenges such as these have resulted in large-scale social housing projects falling out of favour; policy makers may be understandably reluctant to direct resources toward the development of large-scale projects that may reinforce the existing character of a community. Increasingly, initiatives aimed at the supply of affordable housing tend to be driven more from the bottom up. This approach is more responsive to the inherent strengths and assets already existing in the local community. Cities that wish to increase affordable housing stocks through urban planning may require the inclusion of affordable housing units in new development, or they may offer incentives to accomplish this. This is currently being tried in the Pleasant Hill neighbourhood in Saskatoon. However, this approach can encounter problems in cities having land shortages, high construction costs, and an inflated housing market – all of which can also be said to apply to Saskatoon. Finally, also with reference to housing supply, there have been advocates of reform of housing stocks; in other words, the Canadian homebuilding industry has tended to favour certain types of housing that are only affordable to relatively well-off earners at the expense of others.

*Demand-side policy approaches* attempt to increase the purchasing power of individuals and families. The problem with these approaches is obviously that housing costs tend to increase far more rapidly than any sort of financial assistance. The effectiveness of housing assistance programs based on housing allowances is itself highly dependent on prevailing market conditions. Further restricting the effectiveness of housing allowances in a tight market is the problem that when rents increase, so do subsidies. Therefore the PRI recommends that housing allowances be restricted primarily to markets where vacancy rates are relatively high and a good supply of affordable housing is available.

The *integrated approach* merits acknowledgment. This third, more mixed approach has been exemplified by the Saskatoon Housing Initiatives Partnership (SHIP), which, as the PRI concisely explains, has

> combined supply side initiatives that engaged private sector resources within a forward-looking urban plan, with demand-side supports in the area of consumer financing, to restructure effectively the bottom end of the city's housing market ... In Saskatoon it is apparent that housing issues are indeed being integrated within the broader social agenda and that the federal government, province and other actors, particularly the private sector, are being effectively engaged. Evidently local governments and community actors need to be integrated into developing and delivering effective housing policy and practice in the context of poverty and exclusion. (PRI 2005, 18, 27)

As Russell Mawby (2004), the former Housing Director for the City of Saskatoon, has explained: SHIP facilitates social and economic investment in the community by engaging private sector resources and actors in the construction of low-income community-based housing. Using a systematic approach that targets all aspects of the housing system (including financing, construction, social supports, regulations, and urban planning), this program effectively addresses both the supply- and demand-side issues with the goal of supporting the entry of lower-income homeowners into the market. Homebuilders, who are ultimately business people most interested in making or ensuring profits, have been innovatively engaged through initiatives that emphasize market opportunities and reduced construction costs to allow for more afford-able housing. The overall effect, according to Mawby, has been a trans-formation of the Saskatoon housing market: where once the bottom fifth of income earners were very poorly served, housing affordable to fami-lies with incomes under $33,000 is now being constructed by the private sector. He has suggested that this success in Saskatoon is worthy of fur-ther study and potentially wider application to other Canadian cities. The PRI has agreed, commenting that 'if implemented in a manner re-sponsive to specific community needs, such an integrated approach is capable of fundamentally adjusting the parameters within which a hous-ing market operates' (PRI 2005, 18–19). However, these appreciative comments were made just before the economic recession and a rapid escalation in housing costs along with a marked decline in vacancies.

But before we get too immersed in evaluating the intricacies of supply and demand and integrated approaches, it hardly needs to be pointed out that government financial support of affordable housing has to compete with other pressing social issues, including health care and child poverty, as a recent editorial in the *Globe and Mail* (27 May 2010) reminds us. In response, we would emphasize that housing policy should not be viewed exclusively as a government responsibility. Moreover, improvements in affordable housing are not intended to be at the expense of other social programs; rather, they need to be integrated closely with them, as the PRI has clearly recognized in the above summary of housing policies.

*Planning Concepts and Localized Community Involvement*

Several concepts relating to affordable housing should be clarified: en-try-level housing, filtering, inner-city infill, and cooperative housing, including co-housing.

*Entry-level housing* refers to housing offered at prices near the low end of the market without subsidies. Such homes are typically purchased by young families, individuals with new jobs, recent immigrants, and others (including increasing numbers of Aboriginal residents) who can-not yet afford the home they would prefer but who want to enjoy the benefits of homeownership. An entry-level home can be a relatively low-cost first step in homeownership. Entry-level houses are typically found on the resale market and tend to be relatively smaller (City of Saskatoon 2008).

*Filtering* (or 'welfare filtering') refers to the movement of housing stock from higher-income to lower-income households as housing deteriorates and becomes less expensive. This movement can actually improve the living conditions of lower-income households by making homeownership attainable. Several conditions are required for such filtering to occur: the metropolitan area has to function as an integrated market; households must be mobile, able to change neighbourhoods and make substitutions between housing and neighbourhood attributes; new units have to be added at a rate exceeding household formation and in-migration; disequilibrium has to be created as a result of oversupply; and buildings must be depreciating at a rate commensurate with the reduction of maintenance expenditures (CMHC December 2004a).

*Inner-city infill* occurs either when vacant lots are purchased by developers for new housing or when existing housing – typically in dilapidated condition – is bought for demolition and replacement. The advantage here is that such housing is considerably less expensive than if the housing was constructed on new suburban lots. Also, proximity to the urban core, with its businesses, shopping, and entertainment, may seem attractive. But there are also obvious disadvantages. This process could lead to further Aboriginal concentration in the poorest neighbourhoods, assuming that the housing filling in such empty spaces is indeed kept inexpensive. However, homebuilders and developers, of course, realize that inner-city infill can be more profitable when designed for more affluent households than for the poor; as a result, the inner-city neighbourhood may be upgraded and given more aesthetic appeal but poorer residents are driven out. Quint's philosophy was that renovation should be a realistic option; also, that when entire rows or blocks of dilapidated housing are demolished, they can be replaced with attractive affordable housing that includes relevant institutional services. Rezoning goes on constantly in any city (CMHC April 2005a). In March 2011 the City of Saskatoon approved an ambitious program to promote affordable housing construction on the more than 400 vacant lots and buildings occupying 115 acres within the former city limits. This program's long-term goal is the revitalization of areas that have been rendered unsightly by vacant properties and that are beset with security and public health problems. The program offers developers the option of five years without property taxes or an equivalent cash grant. Quint has been quick to collaborate with Shift Development to take advantage of this incentive; together they will be constructing 12 units of affordable row housing on a vacant lot in Riversdale dubbed The Flats (*Saskatoon StarPhoenix*, 5 March 2011).

There continues to be extensive debate in Canada over the economics of urban land (Skaburskis and Moss 2011), inner-city transformation (Bain 2011; Walker 2011), and housing and neighbourhood transformation (Walker and Carter 2011). In Saskatoon, one transformation has been the 'gentrification' of Riversdale, the closest inner west side neighbourhood to the city core (see Chapter 9). Another has been the current plan to develop sufficient housing in the urban core to accommodate as many as 10,000 residents. These two processes could be interrelated, and both could diminish the strong and growing Aboriginal presence near the city centre as property values rise at the expense of affordable housing.

A form of cooperative housing is the Quint model, with several subsidized homes forming a co-op; another would be rental apartment buildings operating on a cooperative basis. A unique housing concept being explored in Saskatoon is *co-housing*, a concept which originated in Denmark. This is based on private ownership of self-contained homes centred around shared facilities. The shared common space may include living room, lounge, kitchen, laundry facilities, exercise room, workshop, art room, and 'multi-purpose' rooms. This effectively cuts down on individual home size, yet would seem more appropriate for seniors than large families with young children, exemplified by the Wolf Willow Co-housing Community for seniors, a $6 million 21-unit complex currently being constructed in Riversdale.

Professors Ryan Walker and Bob Patrick, of the Regional and Urban Planning Program at the University of Saskatchewan, have observed that much has changed since the inception of Plan Saskatoon, a community planning vision, more than ten years ago. Planning is concerned with 'future seeking,' which should be quite different from remaining a spectator in urban development. 'Good urban design, in its esthetic sense, can create attractive and interactive public spaces, bring together a streetscape and express the diversity of our civic identity' (*Saskatoon StarPhoenix*, 20 February 2009). David Hulchanski, who occupies the Endowed Chair in Housing Studies at the University of Toronto, has suggested that in the end, the debate over whether and how to address housing need and homelessness comes down to a set of ethical questions. Will those in a position to make the necessary decisions actually do so? This is a political problem, and there is no objective way to arrive at an answer to a political problem. Yet the nature of the problem is well enough understood;

moreover, solutions are not really complicated or even particularly expensive for a wealthy country like Canada (Hulchanski 2002).

The conceptualization of localized community governance is closely related to community economic development (Clark and Stewart 1998; Stoker 2004; Totikidis et al. 2005; Shah and Shah 2007; Edge and McAllister 2009). Currently research is being planned by the Community–University Institute for Social Research (CUISR) to explore the potential of localized community governance to build sustainable and culturally appropriate responses to community needs. The central research question is how to create local community governance models that are comprehensive, representative, responsive, culturally appropriate, and sustainable. A wide variety of community organizations in Saskatoon are involved in planning this research; many of them participated in the Bridges and Foundations Project, which established a strong basis for intersectoral collaboration.

The PRI has suggested that local control over both supply- and demand-side housing programs aligns with the more effective community-based solutions that emanate from a bottom-up approach to policy development (PRI 2005, 22). In Winnipeg, Carter (2000, 21) has explained that 'if housing challenges are to be effectively addressed, then the return on current investments must be maximized through an approach that packages housing as part of a broader suit of social and economic development initiatives intended to address the range of needs of individuals and their communities.' And Silver et al. (2006, 4) have referred to 'people themselves identifying the problems that they want to solve and the ways they want to solve them, and this does not imply the adoption of the attributes of the dominant culture.' It is a question less of what is being done *for* the community as more of what is to be done *with* the community. In Saskatoon there is much local community interest in localized governance, with many implications for housing policy. The ideal intention is 'to work together to reconstruct a community where the capacities and contributions of all citizens count' (Findlay and Wuttunee 2007). Involved in this process would be a reimagining of ways to actively engage residents in localized partnerships to 'deliberate, plan, and manage the diverse community resources impacting quality of life' (Melo and Baiocchi 2006).

Residents are increasingly demanding participation in localized decision making; this is informed by a growing literature on 'community-based governance,' 'place-based governance,' 'networked governance,'and 'multi-sectoral governance' (Clarke and Stewart

1998; Bache and Flinders 2004; Stoker 2004; Bradford 2005; Edge and McAllister 2009). Saskatoon has an established record of community partnerships, exemplified in the work of the Bridges and Foundations Project as well as other projects led particularly by CUISR; these have included neighbourhood and localized community-based organizations, businesses, all levels of government, academic institutions, and Aboriginal organizations.

## Urban Aboriginal Housing and Politicization

Extensive research has emphasized that urban Aboriginal households are at a much higher risk of experiencing a wide variety of social challenges and exclusion, including in housing; urban Aboriginal households are still more likely than non-Aboriginal ones to be classified as in core housing need – as high a proportion as two in five Aboriginal households renting accommodations in Saskatoon, Regina, Winnipeg, and Vancouver. The concentration of Aboriginal housing stress adds another layer of complexity to the social and economic challenges being faced in these cities (PRI 2005, 10, 12).

The provision of Aboriginal housing on reserve has long been a contentious political issue; in fact this is increasingly the case. But what about housing of urban Aboriginal people? Much attention has been devoted in recent years to urban Aboriginal politicization in Saskatoon and across Canada. Already back in 1993, the Royal Commission on Aboriginal Peoples heard that urban Aboriginal people desire a greater say in running their own affairs. The president of the Native Council of Canada recommended four possible models for urban Aboriginal governance: first, a neighbourhood model, in which Native residents would form a localized majority and run their own housing programs, schools, policing, and other services; second, pan-Aboriginal government, in which a city-wide Aboriginal body would set rules for services such as housing, education, health, and policing; third, autonomous Aboriginal agencies, in which diverse Native service agencies would report to government funders, with little or no accountability to the local Aboriginal community; and fourth, urban reserves, which would be satellites of existing rural reserves, established through municipal and provincial government agreements but subject to federal jurisdiction through Indian Affairs.

During the 1990s there seemed to be a prevalent feeling that more attention would be paid to Aboriginal concerns in Saskatoon, including housing, if Aboriginal representation in municipal government could be prioritized. The dearth of Native representation on City Council was noted in a report as early as 1981; that year, only ten of Saskatoon's 2,080 municipal employees were Aboriginal. Since then, the need for more Natives in City Hall, on crucial decision-making boards, on City Council, and running in civic elections has been repeatedly emphasized. At the time of writing, no Aboriginal person has yet been elected to municipal government in Saskatoon. However, Aboriginal candidates have run in recent municipal elections, and several Aboriginal candidates in Saskatoon and Regina have recently been elected to the province's Legislative Assembly (both in the Saskatchewan Party government and in the NDP opposition). The UAPS probed into urban Aboriginal politicization across Canada and found that 41% of Aboriginal respondents do not identify with any particular political party that they feel might best represent their interests.

Yet a dilemma has gradually arisen regarding who actually represents urban Aboriginal people. The Saskatoon Tribal Council (STC) transcends tribal affiliations within the city; yet the Federation of Saskatchewan Indian Nations (FSIN), historically based on those tribal affiliations (as the name implies), claims that it represents First Nations people whether they are on reserve or not; while the successor to the Native Council of Canada (NCC), the Congress of Aboriginal Peoples (CAP), purports to be a national organization representing all Aboriginal people, both First Nations and Metis, living off reserve and especially in cities. CAP has an extensive urban housing program (CAP 2002); so too does the National Aboriginal Housing Association (NAHA).

But let us return to a point made in chapter 9: Aboriginal participation in community development too often is minimal. This can be seen as troubling insofar as a strong Aboriginal voice is needed in community planning. To their credit, the present mayor and police chief and some city councillors have made a point of attending events that are significant to Aboriginal residents. But a lot more is needed: specific policies must be developed with Aboriginal input.

Native affairs columnist Doug Cuthand has pointed out that in the urban areas

> our people are on their own ... There is no political organization, no social network ... But the long-term answer will come from within our urban people. There needs to be a serious push to organize politically. At present there is a vacuum in leadership ... While the chiefs and the FSIN can create

a climate [for change], the answers must come from within our own people
... We need a strong urban voice to move the city councils on side and to
bring in the resources ... There is no doubt the new battleground is the
cities. We are at an important time in history ... Political organizing is the
way to bring pride to our people and address the serious issues all citizens
face.' (*Saskatoon StarPhoenix*, 2 April 2004)

Aboriginal housing has continued to be strongly criticized by
Aboriginal commentators. A feature article in *Aboriginal Times* (July–
August 2004) commented that the First Nations housing crisis is moving
'beyond ridiculous and up to wilful incompetence.' And Cuthand has
added:

Without a doubt, one of the biggest social problems on any First Nation is
housing. Good housing is the bedrock of any community. It means healthy
living, a good place to study, and family stability. An overcrowded, substandard house leads to conflict, disease, poor educational opportunities and
an overall lack of stability and safety. Yet this is where many of our people
find themselves. The federal government for years has followed a policy of
warehousing our people on welfare and poor housing in the vain hope that
we would simply go away. It has never had any developmental policy for
First Nations. The sense at the colonial office was that we would move away
and assimilate, and then there would be no 'Indian problem.' But that's not
what has happened. Our population continues to grow. Despite the fact that
more than half our people have migrated to the cities for employment,
housing and better health services – items that successive federal governments have failed to develop or provide – even the on-reserve population
continues to increase. (*Saskatoon StarPhoenix*, 17 Aug. 2012)

A member of the Mistawasis First Nation living in Saskatoon blamed
both Native leaders and politicians for ignoring 'homeless hordes,' commenting that 'I don't want the FSIN telling me that this is a federal area
of jurisdiction. If we are to proceed to Native self-government, the FSIN
should take some initiative and show responsibility for its jurisdiction
in these areas' (*Saskatoon StarPhoenix*, 26 June 2008). As Cuthand has
explained,

First Nations people who live off-reserve in urban areas have very few
treaty rights. The federal government assumes that we are a provincial
responsibility once we leave the reserve. There is no basis in law for this.

The British North America Act states that the federal government has jurisdiction for 'Indians and land reserved for Indians.' It doesn't state that we have to live on a reserve ... It is therefore not much of a stretch to assume that treaty rights exist off-reserve too ... The new Treaty Commissioner (George Lafond, the first Aboriginal Treaty Commissioner in Saskatchewan) should see that the funds to support our treaty rights are not subject to cutbacks and the whims of the government of the day. (*Saskatoon StarPhoenix*, 1 June 2012)

Current leaders of the FSIN and the Metis Nation of Saskatchewan have continued to make statements emphasizing economic development, while paying less attention to urban Aboriginal housing. A Treaty Right to Shelter Conference was held in Saskatoon in September 2000, but it emphasized on-reserve housing (as have subsequent conferences); similarly, Indian and Northern Affairs Canada (INAC) reports, such as *Good Public Works Management in First Nations Communities* (2002), have focused on reserves. Yet substantial First Nations commercial development has been occurring in cities. For example, a sale of commercial properties (hotels, restaurants, and office buildings) in Prince Albert and Saskatoon recently netted the Prince Albert Grand Council some $20 million (*StarPhoenix*, 23 January 2009).

Commenting on Aboriginal policy, John Richards has stated:

Many Aboriginals are trapped between rural poverty and life in "very poor" urban neighbourhoods. Something dramatic needs to be done to render the urban environment more hospitable. No single policy will resolve the problems at hand. Solutions must seek to reinforce a sense of shared citizenship and provide for economic incentives. Solutions will require blunt, sometimes contentious, discussion between the "races." None of this will be easy. Overcoming historical injustice never is.' (*Globe and Mail*, 19 June 2001; Richards 2006)

To this, the president of the National Association of Friendship Centres, Vera Pavis Tabobondung, has pointedly added:

To close the opportunity gap between Aboriginal peoples and other Canadians, governments must put in place urban Aboriginal strategies that are concrete and adequately resourced. These must involve a partnership of federal, provincial, territorial and municipal governments as well as Aboriginal governments and Native organizations ... These Aboriginal organizations must take the lead role so the essence of people's needs, and not just the perception of their needs, is addressed by specific and effective programs and services ... Without concerted intervention in urban centres, Canada's dismal record for addressing Aboriginal poverty will continue to fail the basic standard of a civil and prosperous nation. (*Saskatoon StarPhoenix*, 10 April 2006)

The debate continues as to whether housing constitutes an inherent treaty right for First Nations. While the federal government is of the opinion that this has not been challenged in court, it does assume responsibility for financing reserve housing, in view of the fact that housing is fundamental to healthy living conditions. Yet the collective definition of reserve property remains a problem: the lack of individual or family land title makes it difficult to obtain mortgages and therefore to build on an individual family basis. This dilemma may be resolved by the First Nations Market Housing Fund, but perhaps only the most populous, economically developed, and best managed reserves will be able to afford to buy into this scheme (Anderson 2012). If First Nations are to become more empowered to develop their own housing projects on reserve, this will imply improving their financial capabilities, strengthening their governance and management, helping them gain expertise in construction standards, and increasing their training in necessary construction trades. The same could apply to First Nations and Metis housing in cities. The Acting Chief Commissioner of the Canadian Human Rights Commission has argued that the Canadian Human Rights Act should be used to challenge chronic disparities in funding for basic services and needs on reserve, calling the failure to do so a 'collective failure' that 'no one will forgive.' However, the Office of the Attorney General disagrees (*Globe and Mail*, 24 June 2011). But again, what about urban Aboriginal residents? We have seen that in many ways, potentially the best educated, employed, and indeed housed Aboriginal people – especially the emerging generation – are living in cities rather than on reserves (or in traditional communities in the Metis case). And these urban Aboriginal people now constitute the majority of Canada's Aboriginal population.

## The Bridges and Foundations Project on Urban Aboriginal Housing in Retrospect

The central vision of the Bridges and Foundations Project on Urban Aboriginal Housing was 'to build functional, sustainable relationships between Aboriginal and non-Aboriginal organizations to design and develop culturally supportive communities and quality, affordable housing options in Saskatoon.' In the process this project sought to develop a better understanding of how to establish and sustain culturally inclusive partnerships between Aboriginal and non-Aboriginal organizations, working to improve the quality of life by providing housing options. With its emphasis on collaboration between Aboriginal and non-Aboriginal partners, the Project intended to pay particular attention to evaluating processes of building not just houses but more importantly relationships between the Aboriginal and general communities in the urban setting. Thus, much of the specific research undertaken under the Project's auspices intentionally included descriptions and analyses of the processes that work (or do not work) when building relationships between the Aboriginal and non-Aboriginal communities in an urban setting.

A central goal of the Project was to determine the difference between what was available in housing and community services in Saskatoon and what was most needed by its Aboriginal community. Learning to build stable liaisons between those organizations, both Aboriginal and non-Aboriginal, that are trying to develop accessible housing was a very important component of this project. The aim was to understand the gap between the housing options and community amenities available and what was needed to meet the cultural and social expectations of the Aboriginal community. Throughout the Project, and long after the completion of the immediate component research projects, policy recommendations affecting all three levels of government as well as Aboriginal, community, and homebuilding organizations would be made. It was originally hoped that the Project would result in specific changes, such as more Aboriginal training and involvement in the building trades, and increased attention paid by homebuilders to the need for affordable housing to accommodate urban Aboriginal residents. Furthermore, most important, the many lessons learned in Saskatoon could then be applied to other Canadian cities as well as urban indigenous populations in other countries.

Doubtless the Bridges and Foundations Project has succeeded in gathering more and better-quality information on urban Aboriginal housing, living conditions, and quality of life in Saskatoon. A very large volume of pertinent information has been accumulated, to the extent that this city may well have a more detailed knowledge of its Aboriginal population than any other city in Canada. An extremely wide variety of information was collected, covering the extraordinary diversity of the urban

Aboriginal experience, yet there is also more information that would have been useful and pertinent to collect. The broad variety of research projects conducted under the Bridges and Foundation Project is represented, albeit selectively, in the diverse research projects and topics described in the present book.

Concerning partnerships, it is our conviction that considerable progress was made in building relations of trust among the Aboriginal communities, the universities, the city, local community organizations, and homebuilders. While admittedly there had been some collaboration before between some of these sectors (such as between the city and the homebuilders, notably evidenced in the Saskatoon Housing Initiatives Partnership), the more comprehensive cooperation characterized by the Project was quite innovative, perhaps not only in Saskatoon but also other Canadian cities. The University of Saskatchewan, like other universities across Canada, has quickly become far better attuned to the need for – and methodologies of – community-based research. We initially found it somewhat problematic, though, that university academics and graduate students tended to prioritize neither community research nor housing research. This obliged us to put substantial efforts into recruiting and developing interest, despite the community's interest in receiving assistance and expertise from the university. The Aboriginal institutions of higher education that collaborated in the Project – notably the First Nations University of Canada, the Saskatchewan Institute of Indian Technologies, and the Gabriel Dumont Institute – professed interest in university–community research alliances yet by their own admission possessed limited research expertise.

A most important outcome of the Bridges and Foundations Project has been to empower Aboriginal people – provincial and city organizations, institutions, and not the least local residents – to gain increased control over their destiny through participation in decision making and by being heard. It is important that the Project not be seen simply as yet another research project using Aboriginal people as subjects without involving them in original decisions on what and who should be studied and why, in developing research plans, in carrying out the actual research, and in translating research into effective policy and action. This project has thus been a beneficial mutual learning experience between our Aboriginal and other partners. The enthusiasm, openness, and sincerity of the many hundreds of Aboriginal residents who so generously contributed to the project were more than appreciated; they were absolutely essential.

The indigenous Maori people of New Zealand/Aotearoa emphasize what they call 'the Maori way,' which involves a strategy *for*, *with*, and *by* Maori people. It is instructive to apply this agenda to an evaluation of the Aboriginal role in the Bridges and Foundations Project. Reviewing what has been accomplished, and how, first it is clear that the project as a whole has been intended *for* Aboriginal people, by its very title and definition. Virtually all of the surveys and many of the other specific research projects have been aimed at giving voice to local Aboriginal residents in order to make recommendations for improving their living conditions – hence the enthusiastic support shown by so many residents. Second, from the outset, the Project was intended to be done *with* Aboriginal partners. We have enjoyed and profited from close collaboration on particular research projects with First Nations and Metis organizations, academic institutions, and housing agencies. Yet it did take time to achieve this degree of collaboration between Aboriginal and non-Aboriginal partners, and even between First Nations and Metis communities; trust and confidence had to be built. Aboriginal people tended to feel that they and their own organizations should and could deal with their own problems, including an acute shortage of quality affordable housing. Yet our research into, for example, the minimal Aboriginal participation in the homebuilding industry, problems faced by Aboriginal people in financing (necessary for improved housing), and the general level of pervasive poverty in the urban Aboriginal population, implied that far more could be accomplished on a cooperative basis. Third, it is important to review the extent to which this research has been done *by* Aboriginal people. Our emphasis has consistently been on building partnerships *between* Aboriginal and other organizations, rather than to have all of the work done exclusively by Aboriginal people. Any particular home construction may involve as many as forty different trades working together, so while the Bridges and Foundations Project has led directly to the encouragement of Aboriginal participation in the homebuilding trades, collaboration between Aboriginal and non-Aboriginal tradespeople and business people would seem both necessary and inevitable. Nevertheless, Aboriginal personnel have in many ways played very significant roles in the project. They have included a co-director, the Project Coordinator, Conference Coordinator, several board members (representing Aboriginal organizations, institutions, and housing agencies), almost all administrative assistants, research assistants and interviewers, the directors of several projects, many workshop participants, and not the least more than 2,000 survey respondents were Aboriginal. Aboriginal people played a significant role in planning and directing particular research projects.

The penultimate question must be whether the Bridges and Foundations Project will result in improved housing and living conditions for the Aboriginal population. The many reports of the Project have suggested numerous policy recommendations. In the final analysis, it is up to our partners and governments to create meaningful changes. For example, Aboriginal organizations should continue to collaborate in diverse ways with non-Aboriginal organizations, especially the city and homebuilders, to develop improved housing and quality of life for First Nations and Metis residents; to play a more proactive role in developing meaningful research with the universities; to stimulate the learning of research and managerial skills; to develop policies and programs aimed at possible incentives for Aboriginal youth (the collaboration of Whitecap Dakota First Nation with the Bridges and Foundations Career Development Corporation in its residential construction projects is a good example). Homebuilders need to continue to collaborate with Aboriginal people and organizations in order to work toward providing quality affordable housing options for the rapidly growing urban Aboriginal population; to promote more Aboriginal involvement in home construction in every trade and at every level (exemplified in the creation of the Bridges and Foundations Career Development Corporation from the original apprenticeships research in the Bridges and Foundations Project); and to reconsider how financial options and affordability may apply to the unique situation of urban Aboriginal residents. Moreover, general Canadian universities such as the University of Saskatchewan should not only prioritize Aboriginal education in every college, but also research project development with Aboriginal organizations and higher education institutions. Universities could promote the increased involvement of faculty in research with the community. Policies and programs should be developed aimed at the full integration of better-educated Aboriginal students into the labour force. Universities should play a far more significant part in assisting students with affordable housing; while Aboriginal and general technical institutes could collaborate with the homebuilding industry to provide training to qualified Aboriginal young people. Canadian cities – in this case the City of Saskatoon – should implement policy recommendations from the city housing plan, particularly as these may relate to Aboriginal residents. Cities should continue to promote improved race and community relations involving Aboriginal residents; and should continue to provide detailed demographic and socio-economic data on the Aboriginal population in the city. Local community and neighbourhood organizations could work more effectively together and with the City to help Aboriginal residents find better quality of life and affordable homes in neighbourhoods of choice; to improve landlord responsibilities; to promote improved race relations in the community; and to ensure better recreational facilities and green space, safer neighbourhoods, and shops and services.

With so many urban Aboriginal people in need of acceptable and affordable housing, it stands to reason that these residents should be far more involved in community decision making that could play a significant role in the creation of new housing and in the rehabilitation of existing housing. Moreover, with so many urban Aboriginal young people entering the labour force, their education is of utmost importance to career development and opportunities, which would in turn better their living conditions and thus their social and geographical mobility in the city, countering their concentration and effective ghettoization within the poorest neighbourhoods. While all of the accumulated research findings have laid a firm foundation for policies that should result in improved housing and living conditions for Aboriginal residents, it is perhaps the very collaboration that has developed in this project that is most important in the long term. Continuing to work together can only prove highly beneficial to our common effort to improve the situation of Aboriginal residents. Saskatoon has made significant advances in establishing broad-based cooperation between Aboriginal and non-Aboriginal organizations as well as between university and community. Partnerships that have developed, and that continue to develop, among Aboriginal and non-Aboriginal people, businesses, community organizations and services, and governance are mutually beneficial in many ways, not the least in improving the housing situation, if not most importantly in improving the rightful expectations and empowerment of Aboriginal residents. It is entirely possible to construct truly affordable housing, accessible to urban First Nations and Metis residents, in attractive, well-planned neighbourhood communities – housing that is energy-efficient and sustainable, that incorporates the latest technological features, and that is appropriate to Aboriginal needs, traditional culture including the extended family, and mobility. Ideally, skilled Aboriginal construction workers will play an increasingly significant role in the design and building of this housing in every capacity. A vital legacy of the Bridges and Foundations Project is that this is already being accomplished in

Saskatoon through such initiatives as progressive partnerships among the private homebuilding sector, all three levels of government and local community organizations, and specifically the Pleasant Hill Revitalization Project and Bridges and Foundations Career Development Corporation.

This book has focused primarily on Saskatoon, while placing the experience of this particular western Canadian city in a provincial, regional, national, and even international context. It is our hope that the diverse community-based research and ensuing initiatives attained in Saskatoon may benefit not only our own urban Aboriginal residents but also, through example, indigenous people in other urban areas of Canada and in other countries.

# Home in the City: A Photographic Essay

KIRSTEN ANDERSON

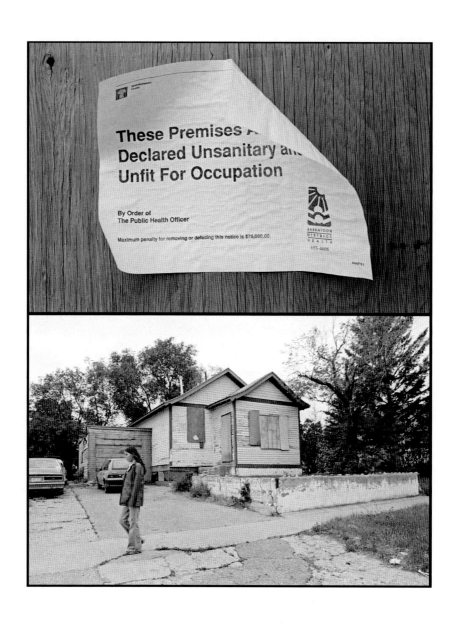

# Bibliography

**Books**

Armitage, Andrew. 1995. *Comparing the Politics of Aboriginal Assimilation: Australia, Canada, and New Zealand.* Vancouver: UBC Press.

Bache, I., and M. Flinders. 2004. *Multi-level Governance.* Oxford: Oxford University Press.

Barron, F. Laurie, and Joseph Garcea, eds. 1999. *Urban Indian Reserves: Forging New Relationships in Saskatchewan.* Saskatoon: Purich Publishing.

Bernard, Russell H. 1995. *Research Methods in Anthropology: Qualitative and Quantitative Approaches.* Walnut Creek, CA: Altamira Press.

Buckley, Helen. 1992. *From Wooden Ploughs to Welfare: Why Indian Policy Failed in the Prairie Provinces.* Montreal and Kingston: McGill–Queen's University Press.

Carter, Novia. 1981. *Housing.* Scarborough, ON: Nelson Canada.

Comack, Elizabeth. 2012. *Racialized Policing: Aboriginal People's Encounters with the Police.* Halifax and Winnipeg: Fernwood.

Daly, G. 1996. *Homeless: Policies, Strategies, and Lives on the Street.* New York: Routledge.

Desjarlais, Joy. 2002. *The Right to Remain Silent: A Night to Remember.* Moose Jaw, SK: Eagle Publishing.

Dosman, Edgar J. 1972. *Indians: The Urban Dilemma.* Toronto: McClelland and Stewart.

Driedger, Leo. 2010. *At the Forks: Mennonites in Winnipeg.* Kitchener, ON: Pandora Press.

Durst, Douglas, and Mary Bluechardt. 2001. *Urban Aboriginal Persons with Disabilities: Triple Jeopardy!* Regina: University of Regina.

Findlay, L.M., and I.M. Findlay, eds. 1995. *Realizing Community: Multidisciplinary Perspectives*. Saskatoon: Humanities Research Unit and Centre for the Study of Cooperatives, University of Saskatchewan.

Fixico, Donald L. 2000. *The Urban Indian Experience in America*. Albuquerque, NM: University of New Mexico Press.

Flanagan, Tom. 2000, 2nd edition 2008. *First Nations? Second Thoughts*. Montreal and Kingston: McGill-Queen's University Press.

Flanagan, T., C. Alcantara, A. Le Dressay. 2011. *Beyond the Indian Act: Restoring Aboriginal Property Rights*. Montreal and Kingston: McGill-Queen's University Press.

Friesen, J.W., and V.L. Friesen 2008. *Western Canadian Native Destiny*. Calgary: Detselig Enterprises.

Guillemin, Jeanne. 1975. *Urban Renegades: The Cultural Strategy of American Indians*. New York, NY: Columbia University Press.

Haven, Robert, and Barbara Wolfe. 1992. *The Window Problem in Studies of Children's Attainments: A Methodological Exploration*. Madison: University of Wisconsin Press.

Hawthorn, H.B., C. Belshaw, and S. Jamieson. 1960. *The Indians of British Columbia: A Study of Contemporary Adjustment*. Toronto: University of Toronto Press and Vancouver: UBC Press.

Hodge, G., and D. Gordon. 2008. *Planning Canadian Communities: An Introduction to the Principles, Practice, and Participants*. 5th edition. Toronto: Nelson Education.

Hopkins, R.L. 1994. *Narrative Schooling: Experiential Learning and the Transformation of American Education*. New York, NY: Teacher's College Press.

Howard, Heather A., and Craig Proulx. 2011. *Aboriginal Peoples in Canadian Cities: Transformations and Continuities*. Waterloo: Wilfrid Laurier University Press.

Jargowsky, Paul A., and Mary Jo Bane. 2004. *Ghetto Poverty: Basic Questions*. Washington: National Academy Press.

Johnston, Basil. 1976. *Ojibway Heritage: The Ceremonies, Rituals, Songs, Dances, Prayers, and Legends of the Ojibway*. Toronto: McClelland and Stewart.

Krotz, Larry. 1980. *Urban Indians: The Strangers in Canada's Cities*. Edmonton: Hurtig Publishers.

Kymlicka, Will. 1998. *Finding Our Way – Rethinking Ethnocultural Relations in Canada*. Toronto: Oxford University Press.

Labonte, R., et al. 2009. *Healthy Populations*. Toronto: Institute of Wellbeing.

Layton, Jack. 2000. *Homelessness: The Making and Unmaking of a Crisis*. Toronto: Penguin Books Canada. Revised 2008 as *Homelessness: How to End the National Crisis*. Toronto: Penguin Canada.

Lemstra, Mark. 2012. *Saskatchewan Health*. Saskatoon: Benchmark Press.

Maaka, Roger, and Augie Fleras. 2005. *The Politics of Indigeneity: Challenging the State in Canada and Aotearoa/New Zealand*. Dunedin: University of Otago Press.

Mariasy, Judith, and Laura Thomas. 1990. *Triple Jeopardy: Women and AIDS*. London: Panos.

McGrane, David P., ed. 2011. *New Directions in Saskatchewan Public Policy*. Regina: Canadian Plains Research Center.

Meili, Ryan. 2012. *A Healthy Society*. Saskatoon: Purich Publishing.

Merriam, S.B. 1999. *Qualitative Research and Case Study Applications in Education*. San Francisco: Jossey-Bass Publishers.

Nagler, Mark. 1970. *Indians in the City: A Study of the Urbanization of Indians in Toronto*. Ottawa, ON: St Paul University Press.

Nagler, Mark, ed. 1972. *Perspectives on the North American Indians*. Toronto: McClelland and Stewart.

Nagler, Mark. 1975. *Natives Without a Home*. Toronto: Longman Canada.

Newhouse, David R., and Evelyn Peters, eds. 2003. *Not Strangers in These Parts: Urban Aboriginal Peoples*. Ottawa: Policy Research Initiative.

Pascal, A.H. 1989. *The Analysis of Residential Segregation*. Santa Monica, CA: RAND Corporation.

Ponting, J. Rick. 1986. *Arduous Journey: Canadian Indians and Decolonization*. Toronto: McClelland and Stewart.

Price, John A. 1979. *Indians of Canada: Cultural Dynamics*. Toronto: Prentice-Hall Canada.

Reber, Susanne, and Robert Renaud. 2005. *Starlight Tour: The Last, Lonely Night of Neil Stonechild*. Toronto: Random House Canada.

Richards, John. 2006. *Creating Choices: Rethinking Aboriginal Policy*. Toronto: C.D. Howe Institute.

Rose, Albert. 1980. *Canadian Housing Policies: 1935–1980*. Toronto: Butterworths.

Ryan, Joan. 1978. *Wall of Words: The Betrayal of the Urban Indian*. Toronto: Peter Martin Associates.

Seabrook, J. 2003. *The No-Nonsense Guide to World Poverty*. Toronto: New Internationalist Publications.

Sealey, D. Bruce, and Antoine S. Lussier. 1975. *The Metis: Canada's Forgotten People*. Winnipeg: Manitoba Metis Federation Press.

Settee, Priscilla, ed. 2011. *The Strength of Women: Ahkameyimowak*. Regina: Coteau Books.

Seymour, David Breen. 2011. *Birth of a Boom: Saskatchewan's Dawning Golden Age*. Regina: Frontier Centre for Public Policy with Indie Ink Publishing.

Silver, Jim, et al. 2006. *In Their Own Voices: Building Urban Aboriginal Communities.* Halifax: Fernwood Publishing.

Sorkin, Alan L. 1978. *The Urban American Indian.* Lexington, MA: Lexington Books.

Stanbury, W.T. 1975. *Success and Failure: Indians in Urban Society.* Vancouver: UBC Press.

Stoker, G. 2004. *Transforming Local Governance: From Thatcherism to New Labour.* New York: Palgrave Macmillan.

Valentine, Gill. 2001. *Social Geographies: Space and Society.* London: Pearson Education.

Walsh, Gerald. 1971. *Indians in Transition.* Toronto: McClelland and Stewart.

Webel-Orlando, Joan. 1991. *Indian Country, L.A.: Maintaining Ethnic Community in Complex Society.* Urbana: University of Illinois Press.

White, Jerry P., Paul S. Maxim, and Dan Beavon, eds. 2003. *Aboriginal Conditions: Research as a Foundation for Public Policy.* Vancouver and Toronto: UBC Press.

## Chapters

Andersen, C. 2005. Residual Tensions of Empire: Contemporary Metis Communities and the Canadian Judicial Imagination. In *Reconfiguring Aboriginal–State Relations*, ed. M. Murphy. Montreal and Kingston: McGill–Queen's University Press.

Anderson, Alan B. 1992. Policing Native People: Native Militancy and Canadian Militarism. In *Deconstructing a Nation: Immigration, Multiculturalism, and Racism in '90s Canada*, ed. V. Satzewich. Halifax: Fernwood Publishing.

Anderson, Alan B. 2005. Aboriginal Population Trends; Urban Aboriginal Population. In *Encyclopaedia of Saskatchewan*. Regina: Canadian Plains Research Centre.

Bain, A. 2011. Re-imaging, Re-elevation, and Re-placing the Urban: The Cultural Transformation of the Inner City in the Twenty-First Century. In *Canadian Cities in Transition*, eds. T. Bunting, P. Filion, and R. Walker. 4th edition. Toronto, ON: Oxford University Press.

Barron, F.L., and Joseph Garcea. 1999. The Genesis of Urban Reserves and Role of Governmental Self-interest. In *Urban Indian Reserves: Forging New Relationships in Saskatchewan*, eds. F.L. Barron and J. Garcea. Saskatoon: Purich Publishing.

Barron, F.L., and Joseph Garcea. 2000. Reflections in Urban Satellite Reserves in Saskatchewan. In *Expressions in Canadian Native Studies*, eds. R.F. Laliberte et al. Saskatoon: University of Saskatchewan Extension Press.

Barter, Ken. 1996. Collaboration: A Framework for Social Work Practice. In *Issues in Northern Social Work Practice,* eds. R. Delaney, K. Brownlee, and M.K. Zapf (pp. 72–94). Thunder Bay: Centre for Northern Studies, Lakehead University.

Beatty, Bonita. 2011. Beyond Advising: Aboriginal Peoples and Social Policy Making in Saskatchewan. In *New Directions in Saskatchewan Public Policy,* ed. D.P. McGrane. Regina: Canadian Plains Research Center.

Clatworthy, S.J. 2003. Impacts of the 1985 Amendments to the Indian Act on First Nations Populations. In *Aboriginal Conditions: Research Foundations for Public Policy,* eds. J.P. White, P.S. Maxim, and D. Beavon. Vancouver: UBC Press.

Clatworthy, S.J., and M.J. Norris. 2007. Aboriginal Mobility and Migration in Canada: Trends, Recent Patterns, and Implications. In *Aboriginal Policy Research: Moving Forward, Making a Difference,* eds. J.P. White, S. Wingert, D. Beavon, and P. Maxim. Toronto: Nelson Education.

Darnell, Regna. 2011. Nomadic Legacies and Contemporary Decision-Making Strategies between Reserve and City. In *Aboriginal Peoples in Canadian Cities,* ed. H.A. Howard and C. Proulx. Waterloo: Wilfrid Laurier University Press.

Davis, Arthur K. 1965. Edging into Mainstream: Urban Indians in Saskatchewan. In *A Northern Dilemma,* eds. A.K. Davis et al. Bellingham, WA: Western Washington State College.

Falconer, P. 1990. The Overlooked of the Neglected: Native Single Mothers in Major Cities in the Prairies. In *The Political Economy of Manitoba,* eds. J. Silver and J. Hull. Regina: Canadian Plains Research Centre.

Finkel, Alan. 2006. Housing and State Policy, 1945–1980. In *Social Policy and Practice in Canada: A History.* Waterloo, ON: Wilfrid Laurier University Press.

Guimond, Eric. 2003a. Changing Ethnicity: The Concept of Ethnic Drifters. In *Aboriginal Conditions: Research as a Foundation for Public Policy,* eds. J.P. White, P.S. Maxim, and D. Beavon. Vancouver: UBC Press.

Guimond, Eric. 2003b. Fuzzy Definitions and Population Explosion: Changing Identities of Aboriginal Groups in Canada. In *Not Strangers in These Parts: Urban Aboriginal Peoples,* eds. D. Newhouse and E. Peters. Ottawa: Policy Research Initiative.

Hanselmann, C. 2003. Ensuring the Urban Dream: Shared Responsibility and Effective Urban Aboriginal Voices. In *Not Strangers in These Parts: Urban Aboriginal Peoples,* eds. D. Newhouse and E. Peters. Ottawa: Policy Research Initiative.

Ignace, Marianne. 2011. 'Why Is My People Sleeping?' First Nations Hip Hop between the Rez and the City. In *Aboriginal Peoples in Canadian Cities,* ed. H.A. Howard and C. Proulx. Waterloo: Wilfrid Laurier University Press.

Irwin, Marty. 1994. A City's Experience with Urban Aboriginal Issues. In
    *Continuing Poundmaker and Riel's Quest*, eds. R. Gosse et al. Saskatoon:
    Purich Publishing.

Jorgenson, Joseph G. 1971. Indians and the Metropolis. In *The American Indian
    in Urban Society*, eds. Jack O. Waddell and O. Michael Watson. Boston: Little,
    Brown.

Jules, Mary. 1997. First Nations and taxation. In *Aboriginal Issues Today: A Legal
    and Business Guide*, eds. S.B. Smart and M. Coyle (pp. 157–67). North
    Vancouver: International Self-Counsel Press.

Kerr, Don, Eric Guimond, and Mary Jane Norris. 2003. Perils and Pitfalls of
    Aboriginal Demography: Lessons Learned from the RCAP Projections. In
    *Aboriginal Conditions: Research as a Foundation for Public Policy*, eds. J.P. White,
    P.S. Maxim, and D. Beavon. Vancouver: UBC Press.

Lafond, Lester. 1999. Creation, Governance, and Management of the McKnight
    Commercial Centre in Saskatoon. In *Urban Indian Reserves: Forging New
    Relationships in Saskatchewan*, eds. L.F. Barron and J. Garcea. Saskatoon:
    Purich Publishing.

LaPrairie, Carol, and Philip Stenning. 2003. Exile on Main Street: Some Thoughts
    on Aboriginal Over-Representation in the Criminal Justice System. In *Not
    Strangers in These Parts: Urban Aboriginal Peoples*, eds. D. Newhouse and
    E. Peters. Ottawa: Policy Research Initiative.

Loxley, John, and Fred Wien. 2003. Urban Aboriginal Economic Development.
    In *Not Strangers in These Parts: Urban Aboriginal Peoples*, eds. D. Newhouse
    and E. Peters. Ottawa: Policy Research Initiative.

Martin-McGuire, Peggy. 1999. Treaty Land Entitlement in Saskatchewan:
    A Context for the Creation of Urban Reserves. In *Urban Indian Reserves:
    Forging New Relationships in Saskatchewan*, eds. L.F. Barron and J.Garcea.
    Saskatoon: Purich Publishing.

Maxim, Paul S., Carl Keane, and Jerry White. 2003. Urban Residential Patterns
    of Aboriginal People in Canada. In *Not Strangers in These Parts: Urban
    Aboriginal Peoples. Ottawa: Policy Research Initiative*, eds. D. Newhouse and
    E. Peters. Ottawa: Policy Research Initiative.

Maxim, P.S., and J.P. White. 2003. Toward an Index of Community Capacity:
    Predicting Community Potential for Successful Program Transfer. In
    *Aboriginal Conditions: Research as a Foundation for Public Policy*, eds. J.P.
    White, P.S. Maxim, and D. Beavon. Vancouver: UBC Press.

Maxim, Paul S., Jerry P. White, and Dan Beavon. 2003. Dispersion and
    Polarization of Income among Aboriginal and Non-Aboriginal Canadians.
    In *Aboriginal Conditions: Research as a Foundation for Public Policy*, eds. J.P.
    White, P.S. Maxim, and D. Beavon. Vancouver: UBC Press.

McIntosh, P. 1998. White Privilege: Unpacking the Invisible Knapsack. In *Race, Class, and Gender in the United States: An Integrated Study*, 4th edition, ed. Paula Rothenberg. New York, NY: St Martin's Press.

Mihesuah, D.A. 2003. Finding a Modern American Indigenous Female Identity. In *Indigenous American Women: Decolonization, Empowerment, Activism* (pp. 81–112). Lincoln, NE: University of Nebraska Press.

Miller, David R. 1999. Textual Analysis of First Nation–Municipal Agreements. In *Urban Indian Reserves: Forging New Relationships in Saskatchewan*, eds. L.F. Barron and J. Garcea. Saskatoon: Purich Publishing.

Mountjoy, Terry. 1999. Municipal Government Perspectives on Aboriginal Self-Government. In *Aboriginal Self-Government in Canada*, ed. John Hylton. Saskatoon: Purich Publishing.

Mulvale, J.P., and K. Englot. 2011. Shaping a Poverty-Free Saskatchewan: Thinking Strategically. In *New Directions in Saskatchewan Public Policy*, ed. D.P. McGrane. Regina: Canadian Plains Research Center.

Nagler, Mark. 1972. Status and Identification Groupings among Urban Indians, and Minority Values and Economic Achievement: The Case of the North American Indian. In *Perspectives on the North American Indians*, ed. Mark Nagler. Toronto: McClelland and Stewart, Carleton Library no. 60.

Newhouse, D.R. 2003. The Invisible Infrastructure: Urban Aboriginal Institutions and Organizations. In *Not Strangers in These Parts: Urban Aboriginal Peoples*, eds. D. Newhouse and E. Peters. Ottawa: Policy Research Initiative.

Newhouse, David R., and Evelyn Peters. 2003a. Introduction. In *Not Strangers in These Parts: Urban Aboriginal Peoples*, eds. D. Newhouse and E. Peters. Ottawa: Policy Research Initiative.

Newhouse, David R., and Evelyn Peters. 2003b. The Invisible Infrastructure: Urban Aboriginal Institutions and Organizations. In *Not Strangers in These Parts: Urban Aboriginal Peoples*, eds. D. Newhouse and E. Peters. Ottawa: Policy Research Initiative.

Newhouse, David R. 2011. Urban Life: Reflections of a Middle-Class Indian. In *Aboriginal Peoples in Canadian Cities*, ed. H.A. Howard and C. Proulx. Waterloo: Wilfrid Laurier University Press.

Norris, Mary Jane. 2000. Aboriginal Peoples in Canada: Demographic and Linguistic Perspectives. In *Visions of the Heart: Canadian Aboriginal Issues*, 2nd edition, eds. D. Long and O.P. Dickason. Toronto: Harcourt Canada.

Norris, Mary Jane, and Stewart Clatworthy. 2003. Aboriginal Mobility and Migration within Urban Canada: Outcomes, Factors, and Implications. In *Not Strangers in These Parts: Urban Aboriginal Peoples*, eds. D. Newhouse and E. Peters. Ottawa: Policy Research Initiative.

Norris, Mary Jane, Martin Cooke, and Stewart Clatworthy. 2003. Aboriginal
    Mobility and Migration Patterns and the Policy Implications. In *Aboriginal
    Conditions: Research as a Foundation for Public Policy*, eds. J.P. White, P.S.
    Maxim, and D. Beavon. Vancouver: UBC Press.
Norris, M.J., M. Cooke, E. Guimond, D. Beavon, and S. Clatworthy. 2004.
    Registered Indian Mobility and Migration in Canada: Patterns and
    Implications. In *Population Mobility and Indigenous Peoples in Australasia and
    North America*, eds. J. Taylor and M. Bell. London: Routledge.
Norris, Mary Jane, and L. Jantzen. 2003. Aboriginal Languages in Canada's
    Urban Areas: Characteristics, Considerations, and Implications. In *Not
    Strangers in These Parts: Urban Aboriginal Peoples*, eds. D. Newhouse and
    E. Peters. Ottawa: Policy Research Initiative.
Norris, Mary Jane, and Karen MacCon. 2003. Aboriginal Language Transmis-
    sion and Maintenance in Families: Results of an Intergenerational and Gen-
    der-Based Analysis for Canada, 1996. In *Aboriginal Conditions: Research as a
    Foundation for Public Policy*, eds. J.P. White, P.S. Maxim, and D. Beavon. Van-
    couver: UBC Press.
O'Neill, Stephen. 1997. Decision-Making on Reserves – The Current Situation.
    In *Aboriginal Issues Today: A Legal and Business Guide*, eds. S.B. Smart and
    M. Coyle. North Vancouver: Self-Counsel Press.
O'Sullivan, Erin. 2003. Aboriginal Language Retention and Socio-economic
    Development: Theory and Practice. In *Aboriginal Conditions: Research as a
    Foundation for Public Policy*, eds. J.P. White, P.S. Maxim, and D. Beavon.
    Vancouver: UBC Press.
Peters, Evelyn. 1994. Geographies of Self-Government. In *Implementing Aboriginal
    Self-Government in Canada*, ed. J. Hylton. Saskatoon: Purich Publishers.
Peters, Evelyn. 1995. *Self-Government for Aboriginal Peoples in Urban Areas*, ed.
    E. Peters. Kingston, ON: Institute of Intergovernmental Relations, Queen's
    University.
Peters, Evelyn. 1996. 'Urban' and 'Aboriginal': An Impossible Contradiction?
    In *City Lives and City Forms: Critical Research and Canadian Urbanism*, eds.
    J. Caulfield and L. Peake. Toronto: University of Toronto Press.
Peters, Evelyn. 2000. Aboriginal People in Urban Areas. In *Visions of the Heart:
    Canadian Aboriginal Issues*, eds. D. Long and O.P. Dickason. Toronto:
    Harcourt Canada.
Peters, Evelyn. 2007a. Are Aboriginal People in Regina and Saskatoon Forming
    Ghettos? In *Saskatchewan: Geographical Perspectives*, eds. B.D. Thraves, M.L.
    Lewry, J.E. Dale, and H. Schlichtmann. Regina: Canadian Plains Research
    Centre.
Peters, Evelyn. 2007b. First Nations and Metis People and Diversity in
    Canadian Cities. In *Belonging? Diversity, Recognition, and Shared Citizenship*

*in Canada*, eds. K. Banding, T.J. Courchene, and F.L. Seidle. Ottawa: Institute for Research on Public Policy.

Peters, Evelyn, and V. Robillard. 2007. Urban Hidden Homelessness and Reserve Housing. In *Aboriginal Policy Research*, eds. J.P. White, P. Maxim, and D. Beavon. Toronto: Nelson Education.

Peters, E.J. 2011. Aboriginal People in Canadian Cities. In *Canadian Cities in Transition*, eds. T. Bunting, P. Filion, and R. Walker, 4th edition. Toronto: Oxford University Press.

Proulx, Craig. 2011. A Critical Discourse Analysis of John Stackhouse's 'Welcome to Harlem on the Prairies.' In *Aboriginal Peoples in Canadian Cities*, ed. H.A. Howard and C. Proulx. Waterloo: Wilfrid Laurier University Press.

Razack, Sherene H. 2002. When Place Becomes Race. In *Race, Space, and the Law*. Winnipeg: Between the Lines Press.

Settee, Priscilla. 2011. Indigenous Perspectives on Building the Social Economy of Saskatchewan. In *New Directions in Saskatchewan Public Policy*, ed. D.P. McGrane. Regina: Canadian Plains Research Center.

Siggner, Andrew. 2003a. Urban Aboriginal Populations: An Update Using the 2001 Census Results; and The Challenge of Measuring the Demographic and Socio-economic Conditions of the Urban Aboriginal Population. In *Not Strangers in These Parts: Urban Aboriginal Peoples*, eds. D. Newhouse and E. Peters. Ottawa: Policy Research Initiative.

Skaburskis, A., and M. Moss. 2011. The Economics of Urban Land. In *Canadian Cities in Transition*, eds. T. Bunting, P. Filion, and R. Walker, 4th edition. Toronto: Oxford University Press.

Smale, G.G. 1995. Integrating Community and Individual Practice: A New Paradigm for Practice. In *Reinventing Human Services: Community and Family-Centred Practice*, eds. P. Adams and K. Nelson (pp. 59–80). New York, NY: Aldine de Gruyter.

Snyder, P.Z. 1971. The Social Environment of the Urban Indian. In *The American Indian in Urban Society*, eds. J.O. Waddell and O.M. Watson. Boston: Little, Brown.

Todd, Roy. 2003. Urban Aboriginal Governance: Developments and Issues. In *Not Strangers in These Parts: Urban Aboriginal Peoples*, eds. D. Newhouse and E. Peters. Ottawa: Policy Research Initiative.

Townsend, Roger. 1997. First Nations and Municipalities. In *Aboriginal Issues Today: A Legal and Business Guide*, eds. Stephen B. Smart and Michael Coyle. North Vancouver: Self Counsel Press.

Walker, Ryan. 2007. The Historical Development of the Canadian Urban Native Housing Program, from Winnipeg to Vancouver. In *Past Matters: Heritage and Planning History – Case Studies from the Pacific Rim*, eds. Caroline Miller and Mike Roche. Cambridge, UK: Cambridge Scholars Press.

Walker, R., and T. Carter. 2011. At Home in the City: Housing and Neighbourhood Transformation. In *Canadian Cities in Transition*, eds. T. Bunting,
P. Filion, and R. Walker, 4th edition. Oxford University Press.

Walker, Ryan. 2011. Equitable Urbanism in Saskatchewan's Large Cities: Balancing Environmental Design, Society, and Our Concept of Place. In *New Directions in Saskatchewan Public Policy*. Regina: Canadian Plains Research Center.

White, J.P., and P.S. Maxim. 2003. Social Capital, Social Cohesion, and Population Outcomes in Canada's First Nations Communities. In *Aboriginal Conditions: Research as a Foundation for Public Policy*, eds. J.P. White, P.S. Maxim,
and D. Beavon. Vancouver: UBC Press.

Wotherspoon, Terry. 2003. Prospects for a New Middle Class among Urban
Aboriginal People. In *Not Strangers in These Parts: Urban Aboriginal Peoples*,
eds. D. Newhouse and E. Peters. Ottawa: Policy Research Initiative.

**Journal and Newsletter Articles**

Andersen, C. 2008. From Nation to Population: The Racialization of 'Metis' in
the Canadian Census. *Nations and Nationalism* 14(2): 347–68.

Anderson, Alan B. 1981. Urban Native Study. *Canadian Ethnic Studies Association
Bulletin* 8(1), Spring.

Anderson, Alan B., and Cara Spence. 2008. Social Indicators in Surveys of
Urban Aboriginal Residents in Saskatoon. *Social Indicators Research* 85: 39–52.

Anderson, R. 2002. Entrepreneurship and Aboriginal Canadians: A Case Study
in Economic Development. *Journal of Developmental Entrepreneurship* 7(1).

Armstrong, Robin. 1999. Mapping the Conditions of First Nations Communities.
*Canadian Social Trends*, Winter: 14–18.

Bennett, Larry. 1998. Do We Really Wish to Live in a Communitarian City?
Communitarian Thinking and the Redevelopment of Chicago's Cabrini-
Green Public Housing Complex. *Journal of Urban Affairs* 20(2).

Black, Errol, and Jim Silver. 2003. Urban Reserves Have a Place in Winnipeg's
Aboriginal Strategy. *New Winnipeg Magazine Online*.

Carter, Tom, and Anita Friesen, eds. 2006. Winnipeg Inner City Research
Alliance. *Canadian Journal of Urban Research* 15(1), special issue.

Centres of Excellence for Women's Health. 2003. *Research Bulletin* 4(1).

Dasgupta, Partha. 2000. Population and Resources: An Exploration of Repro-
ductive and Environmental Externalities. *Population and Development Review*
26(4).

Davis, Arthur K. 1968. Urban Indians in Western Canada: Implications for Social
Theory and Social Policy. *Transactions of the Royal Society of Canada* 6, series 4.

Denton, Trevor. 1972. Migration from a Canadian Indian Reserve. *Journal of
Canadian Studies*.

Dyck, Roland. 2010. Epidemiology of Diabetes Mellitus among First Nations and Non-First Nations Adults. *Canadian Medical Association Journal*, February.

Easton, Beth. 1992. Women and AIDS. *Healthsharing*, 12–19.

Edge, S., and M.L. McAllister. 2009. Place-Based Local Governance and Sustainable Communities: Lessons from Canadian Biosphere Reserves. *Journal of Environmental Planning and Management* 52(3): 279–95.

Fiedler, R., N. Schuurman, and J. Hyndman. 2006. Hidden Homelessness: An Indicator-Based Approach for Examining the Geographies of Recent Immigrants at-Risk of Homelessness in Greater Vancouver. *Cities* 23(3): 205–16.

FNALM (First Nations Alliance for Land Management). 2003a. Nineteen First Nations Sign Framework Agreement to First Nations Land Management Initiative. *FNALM Newsletter* 2(5), Spring.

FNALM. 2003b. RLAP – 53/60 Evaluation. *FNALM Newsletter* 2(5), Spring.

FNALM. 2003d. Six General Stages of the Designation Process, *FNALM Newsletter* 2(6), Summer.

Hill, R.P. 1994. The Public Policy Issue of Homelessness: A Review and Synthesis of Existing Research. *Journal of Business Research* 30: 5–12.

Jamieson, Roberta. 2004. *Aboriginal Times*, July–August.

Kelly, William H. 1957. The Economic Basis of Indian Life. *Annals of the American Academy of Political and Social Science*, May; reprinted in *Perspectives on the North American Indians*, ed. M. Nagler. 1972. Toronto: McClelland and Stewart.

Kitchen, P., and N. Mahajarine. 2008. Quality of Life Research: New Challenges and New Opportunities. *Social Indicators Research* 85(1), January.

Koschinsky, Julia. 1998. Challenging the Third Sector Housing Approach: The Impact of Federal Policies (1980–1996). *Journal of Urban Affairs* 20(2).

Lemstra, Mark. 2009a. Report in *Canadian Journal of Public Health*, January–February, cited in *Saskatoon StarPhoenix*, 7 February.

Lemstra, Mark. 2009b. Report in *Paediatric Child Health*, cited in *Saskatoon StarPhoenix*, 2 April.

Luffman, J., and D. Sussman. 2007. The Aboriginal Labour Force in Western Canada. *Perspectives on Labour and Income* 8(1): 13–27.

McCaskill, D.N. 1981. The Urbanization of Indians in Winnipeg, Toronto, Edmonton, and Vancouver: A Comparative Analysis. *Culture* 1(1).

McMurtry, Alyssa. 2009. Meetings Held to Find Beds for Homeless. *Community Speaks* 1(1), 15 June, 3.

Melo, A.M., and G. Baiocchi. 2006. Deliberative Democracy and Local Governance: Towards a New Agenda. *International Journal of Urban and Regional Research* 30(3): 587–600.

Melting Tallow, Paul. 2001. Urban Reserves: Canada's Changing Landscape. *Aboriginal Times* 5(6): 16–28.

Myers, D. 2008. Failed Urban Policy: Tear Down HUD. http://www.planetizen
.com.

NHRC (National Housing Research Committee). 2008. The Dynamics of
Housing Affordability in Canada. *NHRC Newsletter*, Spring.

NHRC. 2009. Trends in Acceptable Housing and Core Housing Need: 2006
Census. *NHRC Newsletter*, Spring.

NHRC. 2010. Housing Conditions of Off-Reserve Status Indian Households:
2006 Census. *NHRC Newsletter*, Spring.

Niigonwedom. 2003. Scared Off the Urban Reserve? Why? *New Winnipeg
Magazine Online*.

Norris, M.J. 1998. Canada's Aboriginal Languages. *Canadian Social Trends*,
Winter: 8–16.

Panet-Raymond, J. 1992. Partnership: Myth or Reality. *Community Development
Journal* 27(2): 156–65.

Pendakur, Krishna, and Ravi Pendakur. 1998. The Color of Money: Earning Differentials among Ethnic Groups in Canada. *Canadian Journal of Economics* 31(3).

Peters, Evelyn. 1998. Subversive Spaces: First Nations Women and the City.
*Environment and Planning: Society and Space* 16.

Peters, Evelyn. 2001. Geographies of Aboriginal People in Canada. *Canadian
Geographer* 45(1), Spring.

Peters, Evelyn. 2002. Our City Indians: Negotiating the Meaning of First
Nations Urbanization in Canada, 1945–75. *Historical Geography* 30.

Peters, Evelyn, and Ryan Walker. 2005. Introducing a Framework. In E. Peter,
ed., Indigeneity and Marginalization: Planning for and with Urban
Aboriginal Communities in Canada. *Progress in Planning* 63(4).

Policy Research Initiative. 2004. Poverty and Exclusion: New Perspectives,
New Approaches. *Horizons* 7(2), December.

Price, John A., and D.N. McCaskill. 1974. The Urban Integration of Canadian
Indians. *Western Canadian Journal of Anthropology* 4(2).

Randall, J., P. Kitchen, and A. Williams. 2008. Mobility, Perceptions of Quality
of Life, and Neighbourhood Stability in Saskatoon. *Social Indicators Research*
85(1), January.

Séguin, Louise. 2009. Report published in the *Journal of Epidemiology and
Community Health*, cited in *Globe and Mail*, 20 January.

Shah, A., and F. Shah. 2007. Citizen-Centred Local Governance: Strategies to
Combat Democratic Deficits. *Development* 50(1): 72–80.

Simard, Colleen. 2003. Urban Rez Issue Reveals Public Reservations. *Uniter
Newspaper Online* (Winnipeg).

Springer, S. 2000. Homelessness: A Proposal for a Global Definition and
Classification. *Habitat International* 24: 475–84.

Starchenko, O., and E.J. Peters. Forthcoming 2010. Aboriginal Settlement
    Patterns in Canadian Cities: Does the Classic Index-based Approach Apply?
    *Environment and Planning* A 39.
Stokes, Janice. 2004. More Than Bricks and Mortar: The Consequences of Poor
    Housing Conditions in Regina's Aboriginal Community. Regina:
    Saskatchewan Institute of Public Policy *Briefing Notes* 8.
Tait, Heather. 1999. Educational Achievement of Young Aboriginal Adults.
    *Canadian Social Trends*, Spring: 6–10.
Williams, A.M. 2002. Establishing and Sustaining Community–University
    Partnerships: A Case Study of Quality of Life Research. Draft of paper for
    special Population Health issue, *Critical Public Health*.
Williams, A., et al. 2008. Changes in Quality of Life Perceptions in Saskatoon,
    Saskatchewan: Comparing Survey Results from 2001 and 2004. *Social
    Indicators Research* 85(1).
Wilmont, Sheila. 2003. Urban reserves. *New Socialist Online Magazine*,
    November–December.
Wouters, S.L., and E.J. Peters. Forthcoming 2010. Urban Aboriginal Settlement
    Patterns and the Distribution of Housing Characteristics in Prairie Cities,
    2001. *Prairie Perspectives*.

**Research Reports, Resource Guides, and Data Sources**

Aboriginal Peoples Survey. 2001, 2006, 2008. Ottawa: Statistics Canada.
ANC (Action for Neighbourhood Change). 2004. *Housing Research, Policy, and
    Practice in the Context of Poverty and Exclusion.* Ottawa, ON: Policy Research
    Initiative and SSHRC.
Adams, Peter. 1999. *Approaches and Options for Treaties in Urban Areas: A
    Discussion Paper.* Prepared for the Union of British Columbia Municipali-
    ties, the Ministry of Aboriginal Affairs, and the Ministry of Municipal
    Affairs.
Adkin, Robert. 2003. *Setting Up a Business on a Reserve.* Continuing Legal
    Education Society of British Columbia.
Alberta, Manitoba, and British Columbia. 2002. *Report Concerning Relations
    between Local Governments and First Nation Governments.* Submitted to the
    Provincial/Territorial Senior Officials of Local Government Committee.
Amnesty International. 2010. *No More Stolen Sisters: The Need for a
    Comprehensive Response to Discrimination and Violence against Indigenous
    Women in Canada.* London: Amnesty International.
Anderson, Alan B., with AMNSIS. 1979. *Preliminary Socio-economic Survey
    of Metis and Non-Status Indian People in Saskatoon.* Association of Metis

and Non-Status Indians of Saskatchewan with the Employment Development Branch, Canada Employment and Immigration Commission.

Anderson, Alan B., R.J. Devrome, and A.R. Guy. 1991. *Saskatchewan Indian
Demographic Study*. Saskatoon: Office of the Treaty Commissioner.

Anderson, Alan B. 2012. *Final Report: Literature Review for the Evaluation of the
First Nations Market Housing Fund*. Ottawa: Aboriginal Affairs and Northern
Development Canada.

AFN (Assembly of First Nations). 1992. *First Nations' Housing*. Presentation to
the Standing Committee on Aboriginal Affairs, 18 February, Ottawa.

Association of Canadian Studies. 2004. Report cited in *Saskatoon StarPhoenix*,
6 August.

AHURI (Australian Housing and Urban Research Institute). 2006. *An
Audit and Review of Australian Indigenous Housing Research*. Melbourne:
AHURI.

AHURI. 2009. *Indigenous Homelessness: A Comparative Approach*. Melbourne:
AHURI.

Beavis, M.A., N. Klos, T. Carter, and C. Douchant. 1997. *Literature Review:
Aboriginal Peoples and Homelessness*. Ottawa.

Beavon, D., and M.J. Norris. 1999. *Dimensions of Geographic Mobility and Churn
in Social Cohesion: The Case of Aboriginal Peoples*. Ottawa: Research and
Analysis Directorate, Indian and Northern Affairs Canada.

Bidonde, J. 2006. *Experiencing the Saskatoon YWCA Crisis Shelter: Residents' Views*.
Saskatoon: Community–University Institute for Social Research (CUISR).

Bowditch, J. 2003. *Inventory of Hunger Programs in Saskatoon*. Saskatoon: CUISR.

Bradford, N. 2005. *Place-Based Public Policy: Towards a New Urban and
Community Agenda for Canada*. Ottawa: Canadian Policy Research Networks.

Brody, Hugh. 1971. *Indians on Skid Row*. Ottawa: Northern Science Research
Group, Department of Indian Affairs and Northern Development.

Burk, E. 2004. *Community Voices: Assessing Capacity and Needs within Inner-City
Neighbourhoods*. Saskatoon: Bridges and Foundations Project on Urban
Aboriginal Housing.

CMHC (Canada Mortgage and Housing Corporation). 1996. *Effects of Urban
Aboriginal Residential Mobility*. Ottawa: CMHC.

CMHC. 2000. *Measuring Residential Mobility of Urban Aboriginal People*. Ottawa:
CMHC.

CMHC. 2002 (March). *Evaluating Housing Stability for People with Serious
Mental Illness at Risk for Homelessness*. Socio-economic Series 100. Ottawa:
CMHC.

CMHC. 2002 (December). *Innovative Housing for Homeless Youth*. Socio-economic
Series 108. Ottawa: CMHC.

CMHC. 2003. *Housing Discrimination and Aboriginal People in Winnipeg and Thompson, Manitoba.* Ottawa: CMHC.

CMHC. 2003 (February). *Housing, Long-Term Care Facilities, and Services for Homeless and Low-Income Urban Aboriginal Peoples Living with HIV/AIDS.* Ottawa: CMHC.

CMHC. 2003 (May). *A Study of Tenant Exits from Housing for Homeless People.* Socio-economic Series 03-005. Ottawa: CMHC.

CMHC. 2004. *The State of Canada's Housing: An Overview.* Housing Observer.

CMHC. 2004 (February). *Transitional Housing: Objectives, Indicators of Success, and Outcomes.* Socio-economic Series 04-017. Ottawa: CMHC.

CMHC. 2004 (March). *Housing and Population Health – Research Framework.* Research Highlight 04-016. Ottawa: CMHC.

CMHC. 2004 (August). *Aboriginal Households, 2001 Census Housing Series.* Research Highlight 04-036. Ottawa: CMHC.

CMHC. 2004a. *2001 Census Housing Services Issue 6: Aboriginal Households.* Ottawa: CMHC.

CMHC. 2004a (April). *The Adequacy, Suitability, and Affordability of Canadian Housing.* 2001 Census Housing Series, Issue 3, Socio-economic Series 04-007.

CMHC. 2004a (December). *Filtering in Housing.* Socio-economic Series 04-040.

CMHC. 2004b. *Effects of Urban Aboriginal Residential Mobility.* Ottawa: CMHC.

CMHC. 2004b (April). *Assessment of the Outcomes for Habitat for Humanity Homebuyers.* Socio-economic Series 04-024.

CMHC. 2004b (December). *First Nation Economics: A Comparative Perspective.* Socio-economic Series 04-043. Ottawa: CMHC.

CMHC. 2004c. *Comprehensive Community Planning.* Ottawa: CMHC and INAC.

CMHC. 2004 (September). *Developing a Methodology for Tracking Homeless People over the Long Term.* Socio-economic Series 04-035. Ottawa: CMHC.

CMHC. 2005 (February). *Ideas That Work: Best Practices in Affordable Housing Management.* Socio-economic Series 04-037.

CMHC. 2005a. *Improving Quality and Affordability: More Affordable Housing for Canadians.* Ottawa: CMHC.

CMHC. 2005a (April). *The Impact of Zoning and Building Restrictions on Housing Affordability.* Socio-economic Series 05-012.

CMHC. 2005a (September). *Homelessness, Housing, and Harm Reduction: Stable Housing for Homeless People with Substance Abuse Issues.* Socio-economic Series 05-027. Ottawa: CMHC.

CMHC. 2005b. *The Housing Conditions of Canada's Seniors.* 2001 Census Housing Series, Issue 9, Socio-economic Series 05-006. Ottawa: CMHC.

CMHC. 2005b (April). *Homeless Applicants' Access to Social Housing.* Socio-economic Series 05-018. Ottawa: CMHC.

CMHC. 2005b (September). *Temporary Supportive Housing for Aboriginal People and Their Families.* Socio-economic Series 05-026.

CMHC. 2005c. *Women Offenders: Characteristics, Needs, and Impacts of Transitional Housing.* Socio-economic Series 05-002. Ottawa: CMHC.

CMHC. 2005d. *Programs and Financial Assistance: Residential Rehabilitation Assistance (RRAP).* Ottawa: CMHC.

CMHC. 2007. *Households Spending at Least 50% of Their Income on Shelter.* 2001 Census Housing Series. Research Highlight 05-004. Ottawa: CMHC.

CMHC. 2007 (May). *Equilibrium: Healthy Housing for a Healthy Environment: New Housing for a Changing World.* Ottawa: CMHC.

CMHC. 2008. *Advanced Affordable Housing Solutions: CMHC Affordable Housing Centre and Teaming Up with Experts.* Ottawa: CMHC.

Canadian Centre for Policy Alternatives, report cited in *Saskatoon StarPhoenix,* 20 November.

CCSD (Canadian Council on Social Development). 2003. *Aboriginal Children in Poverty in Urban Communities: Social Exclusion and the Growing Racialization of Poverty in Canada.* Subcommittee on Children and Youth at Risk.

CIHI (Canadian Institute for Health Information). 2006. *Improving the Health of Canadians: An Introduction to Health in Urban Places.* Toronto: CIHI.

CIHI. 2007 (August). *Improving the Health of Canadians: Mental Health and Homelessness.* Toronto: CIHI.

CIHI. 2008a. *Mental Health, Delinquency, and Criminal Activity.* Toronto: CIHI.

CIHI. 2008b. Report cited in *Saskatoon StarPhoenix,* 25 November.

CIHR (Canadian Institutes of Health Research), NSERC (Natural Sciences and Engineering Research Council of Canada), and SSHRC (Social Sciences and Humanities Research Council of Canada). 2005. *Ethical Conduct for Research Involving Humans.* Ottawa: Interagency Secretariat on Research Ethics.

Carter, Tom. 2000. *Canadian Housing Policy: Is the Glass Half Empty or Half Full?* Ottawa: Canadian Housing and Renewal Association.

Carter, T., and C. Polevychok. 2004. *Housing Is Good Social Policy.* Ottawa: CPRN.

Carter, T., C. Polevychok, and K. Sargent. 2005. *Canada's 25 Major Metropolitan Centres: A Comparison.* Ottawa: CMHC.

CMAR (Centre for Municipal–Aboriginal Relations). 2002. *Partnerships in Practice: Case Studies in Municipal and First Nations' Economic Development Co-operation.* Report prepared by the Municipal–Aboriginal Adjacent Community Cooperation Project through a partnership of the Federation of Canadian Municipalities, the Indian Taxation Advisory Board, and Indian and Northern Affairs Canada.

Chhokar, Jess. 2004. *Urban First Nation Residential Development Manual.* Saskatoon: FSIN (Federation of Saskatchewan Indian Nations) and Bridges and Foundations Project on Urban Aboriginal Housing.

Chopin, N.S., and J.S. Wormith. 2008. *Count of Saskatoon's Homeless Population: Research Findings.* Saskatoon: Community–University Institute for Social Research.

City of Saskatoon. 1998. *Neighbourhood Profiles,* 6th edition. Planning and Building Department, Community Planning Branch.

City of Saskatoon. 1999. *Neighborhood Profiles of the Aboriginal Population,* 2nd edition. Saskatoon: Planning and Building Department.

City of Saskatoon. 2001. *Saskatoon Community Plan for Homelessness and Housing.*

City of Saskatoon. 2002a. *Pleasant Hill Local Area Plan: Final Report.* Community Services Department, City Planning Branch.

City of Saskatoon. 2002b. *Keeping the Plan Alive.* Community Services Department.

City of Saskatoon. 2003a. *2003 Saskatchewan Health Population Estimates by Neighbourhood.* Community Services Department, City Planning Branch.

City of Saskatoon. 2003b. *Neighbourhood Profiles.* Community Services Department, City Planning Branch.

City of Saskatoon, 2003c. *Saskatoon Community Plan for Homelessness and Housing, 2003 Update.* Community Services Department, City Planning Branch.

City of Saskatoon. 2006. *The State of Saskatoon Housing: 2006 Update Report.*

City of Saskatoon. 2007a. *2007 Saskatoon Community Plan on Homelessness and Housing.*

City of Saskatoon. 2007b. *Community Plan 2007–2009: Homelessness Partnering Strategy Framework.*

City of Saskatoon. 2007c. *Housing Affordability 2008.*

City of Saskatoon. 2008. *Housing Business Plan.* Community Services Department.

Clark, Charlie. 2003. *Final Report: Core Neighbourhood Development Council.* Saskatoon: Bridges and Foundations Project on Urban Aboriginal Housing.

Clarke, M., and J. Stewart. 1998. *Community Governance, Community Leadership, and the New Local Government.* York Publishing Services.

Clatworthy, Stewart J. 1980. *The Demographic Composition and Economic Circumstances of Winnipeg's Native Population.* Winnipeg: Institute of Urban Studies, University of Winnipeg.

Clatworthy, S.J. 1995. *The Migration and Mobility Patterns of Canada's Aboriginal Population.* Ottawa: Royal Commission on Aboriginal Peoples.

Clatworthy, S.J. 2001. *Patterns of Registered Indian Migration between On- and Off-Reserve Locations.* Ottawa: Research and Analysis Directorate, Indian and Northern Affairs Canada.

Clatworthy, Stewart J., and J.P. Gunn. 1981. *The Economic Circumstances of Native People in Selected Metropolitan Centres in Western Canada.* Winnipeg: Institute of Urban Studies, University of Winnipeg.

Clatworthy, Stewart J., and Jeremy Hull. 1983. *Native Economic Conditions in Regina and Saskatoon*. Winnipeg: Institute of Urban Studies, University of Winnipeg.

Clatworthy, S.J., and M.J. Norris. 2003. *Aboriginal Mobility and Migration: Recent Patterns and Implications*. Ottawa: Strategic Research and Analysis Directorate, Indian and Northern Affairs Canada.

Clatworthy, Stewart J., A.J. Siggner, and D. Chamberland. 1996. *Migration and Mobility of the Aboriginal Population of Canada*. Ottawa: CMHC.

Clatworthy, S.J., and H. Stevens. 1987. *An Overview of the Housing Conditions of Registered Indians in Canada*. Ottawa: Indian and Northern Affairs Canada.

CUISR (Community–University Institute for Social Research). 2006. *Building a Caring Community Together: A Collaborative Poverty Elimination Strategy*. Saskatoon: CUISR.

CUISR. 2008. *Quality of Life in Saskatoon: Achieving a Healthy, Sustainable Community: Research Summary*. Saskatoon: CUISR.

*Compendium of Research on Family Violence and Offender Family Functioning*. 1993. Ottawa: Correctional Service of Canada.

CAP (Congress of Aboriginal Peoples). 2002. *Urban Native Housing Program*.

Cooper, Merrill. 2001. *Housing Affordability: A Children's Issue*. Discussion paper, Canadian Policy Research Networks, CPRN, Ottawa.

Dalhousie University. 2000. *First Nations Community Planning Model*. Halifax: Cities and Environment Unit and Joint Community Planning Committee, Faculty of Architecture.

Dalhousie University. 2002. *Case Studies: Volume 1, First Nations Community Planning Project*. Halifax: Cities and Environment Unit and Joint Community Planning Committee, Faculty of Architecture.

Daniel, B. 2006. *Evaluation of the YWCA Emergency Crisis Shelter: Staff and Stakeholder Perspectives*. Saskatoon: CUISR.

de Bruyn, Theodore. 1998. *HIV/AIDS and Discrimination: A Discussion Paper*. Montreal: Canadian HIV/AIDS Legal Network.

Deacon, P., with Turtle Island Association. 2001. *Urban Aboriginal People: Homes, Homelessness, and Residential Mobility*. Ottawa: CMHC.

Department of Families, Community Services, and Indigenous Affairs. 2006. *Community Housing and Infrastructure Program Review*. Canberra.

Diamantopoulos, Mitch, and Isobel Findlay. 2007. *Growing Pains: Social Enterprise in Saskatoon's Core Neighbourhoods*. Saskatoon: CUISR and Centre for the Study of Cooperatives, University of Saskatchewan.

Dion, Murray, J., et al. 1997. *Financing Self-Government: The Strategically Positioned First Nation*. Report prepared for Indian and Northern Affairs Canada, and the Indian Taxation Advisory Board (ITAB): National Research Project on Revenue Generation.

Distasio, J., G. Sylvestre, and S. Mulligan. 2005. *Home Is Where the Heart Is and Right Now That Is Nowhere ...: An Examination of Hidden Homelessness among Aboriginal Peoples in Prairie Cities.* Winnipeg, MB: Institute of Urban Studies.

Dressler, M.P. 2004. *Aboriginal Women Share Their Stories in an Outreach Diabetes Education Program.* Saskatoon: CUISR.

Drost, Helmar. 1995. Report of the C.D. Howe Institute cited in *Globe and Mail,* 27 December.

Dunning, H. 2004. *A Mixed-Method Approach to Quality of Life in Saskatoon.* Saskatoon: CUISR.

Dyck, Shannon. 2009. *Living Well, Learning Well.* A report of the University of Saskatchewan Students Union, cited in *Saskatoon StarPhoenix,* 3 February.

Energy Pathways. 1994. *Affordability and Choice Today – Case Study Project.* Community Support for Affordable Housing: A Public Education Package. Ottawa: Energy Pathways.

Engeland, J., et al. 1997. *Core Housing Need among Off-Reserve Aboriginal Lone Parents in Canada.* Ottawa: CMHC.

Engeland, J., et al. 1998. *Core Housing Need among Off-Reserve Aboriginal Inuit, Metis, Status, and Non-Status Indians in Canada.* Ottawa: CMHC.

Environics Analytics. 2010. *Wealthscapes 2010.* Toronto: Environics Analytics.

Ervin, A.M. 1968. *New Northern Townsmen in Inuvik.* Ottawa: Northern Science Research Group, Department of Indian Affairs and Northern Development.

FCM (Federation of Canadian Municipalities). 2001. *2001 Quality of Life Report.* Quality of Life Reporting System.

FCM. 2008. *Trends and Issues in Affordable Housing and Homelessness.* January.

FSIN (Federation of Saskatchewan Indian Nations) and SUMA (Saskatchewan Association of Urban Municipalities). 1993. *Options for Creating First Nations Urban Development Centres.* Saskatoon.

Findlay, I.M., and W. Wuttunee. 2007. *Aboriginal Women's Community Economic Development: Measuring and Promoting Success.* Saskatoon: CUISR.

Foss, E. 2004. *Affordable Housing and Home Ownership: Business Case Development for the Saskatoon Market.* Saskatoon and Region Home Builders' Association and Bridges and Foundations Project on Urban Aboriginal Housing.

FCPP (Frontier Centre for Public Policy). 2003. *Urban Reserves, a Temporary Stop-Gap. Special Laws Restrict Aboriginal Commerce. Why Not Special Laws to Promote It?* Regina: FCCP.

Gareau, M.M., with Saskatchewan Indian Institute of Technologies. 2002. *Effects of Urban Aboriginal Residential Mobility.* Ottawa: CMHC.

Gionet, Linda. 2008. *First Nations People: Selected Findings of the 2006 Census.* Ottawa: Statistics Canada.

Government of Canada. 1997. *Canada's Aboriginal Action Plan.*

Government of Canada. 1998. *Framework of Agreement on First Nations Land Management.*

Government of Canada. 1999. *Framework Agreement on First Nations Land Management: Executive Summary.*

Government of Canada. 2003. *Tri-Council Policy Statement – Ethical Conduct for Research Involving Humans.* Medical Research Council of Canada. Ottawa: Public Works Canada.

Government of Saskatchewan. 1992. *Synopsis of the Saskatchewan Treaty Land Entitlement Framework Agreement.*

Government of Saskatchewan. 2001. *A Framework for Cooperation: Policy Statement.*

Government of Saskatchewan. 2001–2. *Saskatchewan Municipal Affairs and Housing: Annual Report.* Regina.

Government of Saskatchewan. 2004. *A Framework for Cooperation – Saskatchewan's Strategy for Metis and Off-Reserve First Nations People: Building Our Future Together (Progress Report 2001–2 and 2002–3).*

Graham, Katherine, and Evelyn Peters. 2002. *Aboriginal Communities and Urban Sustainability.* Discussion paper, Canadian Policy Research Networks.

Grant, Gail. 1983. *The Concrete Reserve: Corporate Programs for Indians in the Urban Workplace.* Montreal: Institute for Research on Public Policy.

Grant, Gail, and Raymond Breton. 1984. *The Dynamics of Government Programs for Urban Indians in the Prairie Provinces.* Montreal: Institute for Research on Public Policy.

Green, D., and K. Milligan. 2007. *Canada's Rich and Poor: Moving in Opposite Directions.* Toronto: CCPA.

Green, Kathryn L. 2001. *Telling It Like It Is: Realities of Parenting in Poverty.* Saskatoon: Prairie Women's Health Centre of Excellence.

Green, Morgan. 2001. *Building Communities: First Nations Best Practices for Healthy Housing and Sustainable Community Development.* Ottawa: CMHC.

Grosso, P. 2003. *Uprooting Poverty and Planting Seeds for Social Change: The Roots of Poverty Project.* Saskatoon: CUISR.

Hammersmith, J., C. Littlejohn, and W. McCaslin. 2004. *Metis Student Housing Research Project: Housing That Supports Metis Student School Success.* Saskatoon: Bridges and Foundations Project on Urban Aboriginal Housing.

Hanna, Katriona, and Lori Hanson. 2004. *Aboriginal People and Housing: An Exploration of the Perceptions of Saskatoon Habitat for Humanity.* Saskatoon: Bridges and Foundations Project on Urban Aboriginal Housing.

Hanselmann, Calvin. 2001. *Urban Aboriginal People in Western Canada: Realities and Policies.* Calgary: Canada West Foundation.

Hanselmann, Calvin. 2002a. *Uncommon Sense: Promising Practices in Urban Aboriginal Policy Making and Programming.* Calgary: Canada West Foundation.

Hanselmann, Calvin. 2002b. *Enhanced Urban Aboriginal Programming in Western Canada*. Calgary: Canada West Foundation.

Hawthorn, H.B. 1966. *A Survey of the Contemporary Indians of Canada*. Ottawa: Department of Indian Affairs and Northern Development, Indian Affairs Branch.

Hagey, N.J., G.Y. Larocque, and C. McBride. 1989. *Highlights of Aboriginal Conditions, 1981–2001: Demographic Trends*. Ottawa: Indian and Northern Affairs Canada.

Health Canada. 1996. *HIV/AIDS Statistics to June 30, 1996 for Saskatchewan and Canada*. Ottawa.

Health Canada. 1998. *HIV/AIDS Epidemiology among Aboriginal People in Canada*; and *Research on HIV/AIDS in Aboriginal People: A Background Paper*. Ottawa and University of Manitoba.

Health Canada. 2009. *Indigenous Children's Health Report*. Ottawa: 30 March.

Health and Welfare Canada. 1983. *1983 Vital Statistics for the Registered Indian Population of Saskatchewan*. Regina: Health and Welfare Canada.

Heisz, A., and L. McLeod. 2004. *Low Income in Census Metropolitan Areas, 1980–2000*. Ottawa: Statistics Canada.

Howe, Eric. 2002. *Education and Lifetime Income for Aboriginal People in Saskatchewan*. Research report, Department of Economics, University of Saskatchewan, September.

Hughes, Marja. 1997. *Literature and Effective Practices Review of Municipal–Aboriginal Relations*. Ottawa: Centre for Municipal–Aboriginal Relations.

Hulchanski, J.D. 2002. *Housing Policy for Tomorrow's Cities*. Ottawa: CPRN.

Hull, Jeremy. 2001. *Aboriginal Post-Secondary Education and Labour Market Outcomes*. Winnipeg: Prologica Research.

Iheduru, Alex. 2004b. *A Quadrant of Poverty: Tracing the Spatial Divide between the Poor and Non-Poor in Saskatoon*. Research report, Department of Geography, University of Saskatchewan.

INAC (Indian and Northern Affairs Canada). 1996. *Guidelines for the Development of First Nations Housing Proposals*.

INAC. 1997a. *First Nation Taxation and New Fiscal Relationships*.

INAC. 1997b. *Gathering Strength: Canada's Aboriginal Action Plan*. Ottawa: INAC.

INAC. 2001. *Land Management and Procedures Manual: Additions to Reserves or New Reserves*. Ottawa: INAC, Land and Trust Services.

INAC. 2002. *Good Public Works Management in First Nations Communities*. Ottawa: INAC.

INAC. 2003. *Expanding the Reserve Base: An Overview of the Three-Phase Process to Add Land to Existing Reserves or Create New Reserves (ATR Process)*. INAC information brochure.

INAC. 2007. *Urban Aboriginal Strategy: Backgrounder*. Ottawa: INAC.

INAC. 2008. *Registered Indian Population by Sex and Residence, 2007.* Ottawa: First Nations and Northern Statistics Section, Strategic Policy and Research Branch, INAC.

Indian–Eskimo Association. 1971. *Final Report: Indians and the City.* Toronto: Department of the Secretary of State.

Indigenous Peoples Health Research Centre. 2004. *The Ethics of Research Involving Indigenous Peoples.* Report of the Indigenous Peoples Health Research Centre to the Interagency Advisory Panel on Research Ethics. Ottawa. July.

Innocenti Research Centre. 2008. *Report Card.* Florence, Italy: Innocenti Research Centre/UNICEF, 10 December.

IUS (Institute of Urban Studies). 2005. *An Examination of Hidden Homelessness among First Nations, Metis, and Inuit Peoples in Prairie Cities,* research proposal.

IUS (Institute of Urban Studies). 2009. *First Nations/Metis/Inuit Mobility and Service Needs Study.* Winnipeg: IUS.

Jackson, M. 2004. *Closer to Home: Child and Family Poverty in Saskatoon.* Saskatoon: CUISR.

Jewell, L., 1998. *Hidden Homelessness in Saskatoon: Proposed Methodology for Assessing the State of the Problem.* Saskatoon, SK: CUISR.

Johnson, Kristina. 2004. *Urban Aboriginal Housing Design Charrette: Final Report.* Saskatoon: Bridges and Foundations Project on Urban Aboriginal Housing.

Justice Canada. 1993. *Saskatchewan Treaty Land Entitlement Act.*

Keeling, M., L. Szejvolt, and J. Untereiner. 2004. *More Than Four Walls and a Roof.* Saskatoon: Quint Development Corporation and Bridges and Foundations Project on Urban Aboriginal Housing.

Kerr, D., A.J. Siggner, and J.P. Bourdeau. 1996. *Canada's Aboriginal Population, 1981–1991.* Ottawa: Canada Mortgage and Housing Corporation (CMHC) and Royal Commission on Aboriginal Peoples (RCAP).

Ketilson, Lou Hammond, M. Gertler, M. Fulton, R. Dobson, and L. Polsom. 1998. *The Social and Economic Importance of the Cooperative Sector in Saskatchewan.* Centre for the Study of Cooperatives, University of Saskatchewan.

La Prairie, Carol. 1995. *Seen but Not Heard: Native People in the Inner City.* Ottawa: Department of Justice.

Larbi, Patrick. 1998. *A Portrait of Municipal–Aboriginal Relations in Canada.* Centre for Municipal–Aboriginal Relations. Ottawa.

Larocque, G.Y., and R.P. Gauvin. 1989. *1986 Census Highlights on Registered Indians.* Ottawa: INAC.

Lemstra, Mark, and Cory Neudorf. 2008. *Health Disparity in Saskatoon: Analysis to Intervention*. Saskatoon Health Region.

Lynch, K., C. Spence, and I.M. Findlay. 2007. *Urban Aboriginal Strategy Database*. Saskatoon: CUISR.

MacDermott, W. 2003. *Child Poverty in Canada, Saskatchewan, and Saskatoon: A Literature Review and Voices of the People*. Saskatoon: CUISR.

Macdonald, D., and D. Wilson. 2010. Canadian Centre for Policy Alternatives report cited in *Saskatoon StarPhoenix*, 8 April.

Maidman, F. 1981. *Native People in Urban Settings: Problems, Needs, and Services*. Toronto: Ontario Task Force on Native People in the Urban Setting.

Manitoba. 2004. *A Reference Manual for Municipal Development and Service Agreements*. Winnipeg.

McCracken, Molly, and Gail Watson. 2004. *Women Need Safe, Stable, Affordable Housing: A Study of Social, Private and Co-op Housing in Winnipeg*. Winnipeg: Prairie Women's Health Centre of Excellence.

McKinnon, Nancy. 2003. *Report on Universal Accessibility in the Construction of the New Home*. Saskatoon: Bridges and Foundations Project on Urban Aboriginal Housing, June.

Mendelson, Michael. 2007. Report cited in Samyn, Paul. 2007. Study Busts Myths about Aboriginals. *Winnipeg Free Press*, 10 March, A5; and *Globe and Mail*, 6 July.

Merasty, R.A., and Associates. 2006. *Urban Aboriginal Strategy Saskatoon: Community Consultations on a Collaborative Planning and Granting Model*. Saskatoon: UAS.

Merasty, R.A. and Associates. 2007. *A Collaborative Community Model for Aboriginal Funding and Granting*. Saskatoon: UAS.

Micro-Economic Policy Analysis Branch and Aboriginal Business Canada. 1996. *Aboriginal Entrepreneurs in Canada: Progress and Prospects*. Ottawa: Industry Canada.

Molgat, Jean-Paul A. 1998. *Relations between Local, Regional, and First Nations Governments: The GVRD Experience*. Simon Fraser University.

Moloughney, B. 2004. *Housing and Population Health: The State of Current Knowledge*. Toronto: CIHI.

NAFC (National Association of Friendship Centres). 2001. *Urban Multipurpose Aboriginal Youth Centres Initiative*. Ottawa: NAFC.

Native Women's Association of Canada. 2010. *What Their Stories Tell Us*. April.

National Aboriginal Housing Association (NAHA). 2004. *A New Beginning: The National Non-Reserve Aboriginal Housing Strategy: Preliminary Report*. Ottawa: NAHA.

National Homelessness Initiative (NHI). Report. 2004.

Native Canadian Friendship Centre and Manpower and Immigration. 1976. *Report on the Needs of Native People in Metropolitan Toronto*, December.

Norris, M.J. 2002. *Registered Indian Mobility and Migration: An Analysis of 1996 Census Data*. Ottawa: Indian and Northern Affairs Canada.

Norris, M.J., D. Kerr, F. Nault, and A.J. Siggner. 1996. *Projections of the Populations of Aboriginal Identity, Canada, 1991–2016*. Ottawa: CMHC and RCAP.

Peters, Evelyn. 1984. *Native Households in Winnipeg: Strategies of Co-residence and Financial Support*. Winnipeg: Institute of Urban Studies.

Peters, Evelyn. 2007. *Urban Reserves*. Ottawa: National Centre for First Nations Governance.

Peters, Evelyn, with Oksana Starchenko. 2005. *Atlas of Urban Aboriginal Peoples*. Saskatoon: University of Saskatchewan, online.

PRI (Policy Research Initiative). 2005. *Housing Policy and Practice in the Context of Poverty and Exclusion: Synthesis Report*. Ottawa: PRI, August.

Poverty Free Saskatchewan. 2011. *Let's Do Something About Poverty*. October.

Prokop, S.T., and V. MacDonald. 2004. *First Nations University of Canada Saskatoon Campus Housing and Daycare*. Saskatoon: Bridges and Foundations Project on Urban Aboriginal Housing.

Pruden, Kelly. 2004. *Housing Strategy Policy and Procedures Manual*. Saskatoon: Central Urban Metis Federation Inc. (CUMFI) and Bridges and Foundations Project on Urban Aboriginal Housing.

Public Health Agency of Canada. 2010. Report cited in *Globe and Mail*, 11 March.

Radloff, K. 2006. *Community Resilience, Community Economic Development, and Saskatchewan Economic Developers*. Saskatoon: CUISR.

Redl, Lynn. 1996. *Muskeg Lake Urban Reserve Negotiations: A Precedent for First Nations / Municipal Relations*. INAC.

Richards, John. 2001. *Neighbours Matter: Poor Neighbourhoods and Urban Public Policy*. Toronto: C.D. Howe Institute, commentary no. 156, November.

Richards, John. 2008. *A Disastrous Gap – How High Schools Have Failed Canada's Aboriginal Students*. Toronto: C.D. Howe Institute, October.

Rivard, Ron, and Associates. 2000. *One Thousand Voices: Metis Homelessness Project*. Metis Urban Councils of Prince Albert, Regina, and Saskatoon.

Robillard, V., and E. Peters. 2007. *Service Needs and Perspectives of Hidden Homeless First Nations People in Prince Albert*. Research report, Department of Geography, University of Saskatchewan.

Ross, N.A. 2004. *Income Inequality and Population Health*. Toronto: CIHI.

RCAP (Royal Commission on Aboriginal Peoples). 1993. *Aboriginal Peoples in Urban Centres: Report of the National Round Table on Aboriginal Urban Issues*. Ottawa.

RCAP. 1996. *Report of the Royal Commission of Aboriginal Peoples*. Volumes III and IV. Ottawa: Department of Indian and Northern Affairs.

Saraswati, Jeea, and Ionna Sahas. 1996. *Building Bridges: Responding to HIV/ AIDS in Ethnocultural and Aboriginal Communities*. Ottawa: Health Canada.

SIIT (Saskatchewan Indian Institute of Technologies). 2000. *Urban First Nations People: Without Homes in Saskatchewan*. Saskatoon: SIIT.

SIIT. 2004. *Patterns and Influences of Home Ownership and Renting in Pleasant Hill*. Saskatoon: Bridges and Foundations Project on Urban Aboriginal Housing.

SRHBA (Saskatoon and Region Home Builders' Association). 2004. *Community Housing and Design Options*. Saskatoon: Bridges and Foundations Project on Urban Aboriginal Housing.

Seymour, David. 2009. Frontier Centre for Public Policy report cited in *Saskatoon StarPhoenix*, 29 January.

Siggner, A.J. 1977. *Preliminary Results from a Study of 1966–71 Migration Patterns among Status Indians in Canada*. Ottawa: Demography Section, Program Statistics Division, Indian and Eskimo Affairs Program.

Siggner, Andrew. 2002. *The Challenge of Measuring Demographic and Socio-economic Conditions of the Urban Aboriginal Population in Canada*. Ottawa: Statistics Canada.

Smylie, Janet. 2009. *Indigenous Children's Health Report: Health Assessment in Action, Health Canada*, cited in *Globe and Mail*, 31 March.

Soles, Kama. 2003. *Affordable, Accessible Housing Needs Assessment at the North Saskatchewan Independent Living Centre*. Saskatoon: CUISR.

Spence, C., and I.M. Findlay. 2007. *Evaluation of Saskatoon Urban Aboriginal Strategy*. Saskatoon: CUISR.

Sun, Yinshe. 2004. Development of Neighbourhood Quality of Life Indicators. Saskatoon: CUISR.

Trovato, F., A. Romaniuk, and I. Addai. 1994. *On- and Off-Reserve Migration of Aboriginal Peoples in Canada: A Review of the Literature*. Ottawa: Indian Affairs and Northern Development.

Tupone, Juliano. 2004. *The Core Neighbourhood Youth Co-op: A Review and Long-Term Strategy*. Saskatoon: Community–University Institute for Social Research.

UBCM (Union of British Columbia Municipalities). 1994. *Local Government and Aboriginal Treaty Negotiations: Defining Municipal Interest*.

UBCM. 2000. *Land Use Coordination, Servicing, and Dispute Resolution: Towards Certainty for Local Government through Treaty Negotiations*.

UBCM. 2003a. *Local Government Treaty-Related Interests in Land*. Policy Digest Paper 2, May.

UBCM. 2003b, 2004a. *Developing Good Neighbour Relations*. Local Governments and First Nations Technical Workshop Final Report.

UBCM. 2004b. *UBCM Comparative Analysis of 2003 Agreements in Principle and Local Government Interests*.

UAPS (Urban Aboriginal Peoples Study). 2010. Toronto: Environics Institute.

UAS (Urban Aboriginal Strategy). 1998, 2004, Planning reports.

UAS. 2006. *A Model for Aboriginal Collaborative Planning and Granting in the Saskatoon Community*. Saskatoon: UAS.

Vandale, Carol. 2004. *The Building Skills, Building Homes Project: A Community Education Study in Alternative Lifestyle Practice through Straw Bale Construction*. Saskatoon: Bridges and Foundations Project on Urban Aboriginal Housing.

Vanier Institute of the Family. 2010. *Annual Report*. 16 February.

Vincent, D.B. 1971. *The Indian–Metis Urban Probe*. Winnipeg: Institute of Urban Studies, University of Winnipeg, and Winnipeg Indian–Metis Friendship Centre.

Walker, R.C., and M. Barcham. 2007. *Comparative Analysis of Urban Indigenous Housing in Canada, New Zealand, and Australia*. Ottawa: National Aboriginal Housing Association (NAHA) and CMHC.

Walker, Ryan. 2008. *Social Housing and the Role of Aboriginal Organizations in Canadian Cities*. Montreal: IRPP.

Western Economic Diversification Canada. 2004, 2009. *Urban Reserves in Saskatchewan*.

Wiebe, Rhonda, and Paula Keirstead. 2004. *Surviving on Hope Is Not Enough: Women's Health, Poverty, Justice, and Income Support in Manitoba*. Winnipeg: Prairie Women's Health Centre of Excellence.

Wilkie, K., and L. Berdahl. 2007. *Hard Times: A Portrait of Street-Level Social Problems in Western Canada*. Calgary: Canada West Foundation.

Winnipeg Social Planning Council. 2004. *Urban Reserves: Exploring the Reality*.

Woods, F. 2003. *Access to Food in Saskatoon's Core Neighbourhood*. Saskatoon: CUISR.

## Graduate Dissertations

Atwell, P. 1969. Kinship and Migration among Calgary Residents of Indian Origin. MA thesis, University of Alberta.

Chu, J.W.L. 1991. Urban Native Housing: Problems, Policies, Programs, and Prospects. PhD diss., University of Michigan.

Drake, Deborah. 2003. Post-Incarceration Experiences: Listening to Aboriginal and Non-Aboriginal Ex-Prisoners. MA thesis in Sociology, University of Saskatchewan.

Gerber, Linda. 1977. Trends in Out-Migration from Indian Communities across Canada: A Report for the Task Force on Migrating Native People. PhD diss., Harvard University.

Guimond, Eric. 2009. L'éxplosion démographique des populations autochtones du Canada de 1986 à 2001. Dissertation de doctorat, Département de démographie, Université de Montréal.

Iheduru, Alex. 2004a. Aboriginal Residential Settlement Patterns in Saskatoon: Exploring the Relationship between Factors of Neighbourhood Preference and Residential Segregation. Research proposal, Department of Geography, University of Saskatchewan.

Lambert, Carmen. 1974. Identification et Integration Ethnique à l'Interieur d'une Ville Nordique: Whitehorse, Yukon. PhD diss., McGill University.

Nilson, Cathy. 2004. The FSIN-Province of Saskatchewan Gaming Partnership, 1995–2002. MA thesis in Political Studies, University of Saskatchewan.

Romanow, Carol-Anne. 2003. HIV/AIDS and Aboriginal Women in Saskatchewan: Colonization, Marginalization, and Recovery. MA thesis in Sociology, University of Saskatchewan.

Tota, Katarzyna B. 2002. Can Place-Based Collaborative Planning Work between First Nations and Local Governments in Nova Scotia? Defining the Context and Learning from Other Places. MA thesis in Urban Planning, Dalhousie University.

Vandale, C. 2004. The Building Skills, Building Homes Project: A Community Education Study in Alternative Lifestyle Practices through Straw Bale Construction. Report for the Bridges and Foundations Project on Urban Aboriginal Housing, based on MEd thesis, University of Saskatchewan.

Walker, Ryan. 2004. Urban Citizenship and Aboriginal Self-Determination in the Winnipeg Low-Cost Housing Sector. PhD diss. in Geography, Queen's University.

## Conference Papers/Proceedings

Anderson, Alan B. 1976. The Urbanization of Canadian Indians, Canadian Population Society meeting, Université Laval, May.

Anderson, Alan B. 1980. Urbanization of Canadian Native People. Canadian Sociology and Anthropology Association meeting, Université de Québec à Montréal, June.

Anderson, Alan B. 1985. Native Urbanization in Saskatchewan. Western Association of Sociology and Anthropology meeting, Winnipeg, February.

Anderson, Alan B. 1990. Reaching the People: Canadian Policing and Race Relations. Paper presented at the Joint Conference on Race Relations in the United Kingdom and Canada: Policies, Practice, and Research, York University, June.

Anderson, Alan B. 2004. Distinctive Housing Needs of Urban Aboriginals. PRI/SSHRC Policy Research Roundtable: Housing Research, Policy, and Practice in the Context of Poverty and Exclusion, Ottawa, October.

Aulinger, Maximilian. 2010. Research on Food Security. Meeting of the Urban Aboriginal Economic Development Network, First Nations University of Canada, Regina, 29–30 April.

Canadian Housing and Renewal Association. 2003. Annual Conference, Calgary, October.

CIHR (Canadian Institutes of Health research). 2007. Guidelines for Health Research Involving Aboriginal Peoples, workshop, University of Saskatchewan, 12 January.

Clatworthy, S.J. 2000. Patterns of Residential Mobility Among Aboriginal Peoples in Canada. Urban Aboriginal Strategy workshop, Regina, May.

Clatworthy, Stewart. J., E. Guimond, and M.J. Norris. 2002. Demography Workshop Proceedings, Aboriginal Policy Research Conference, Ottawa, November.

Clark, L., M. Gertler, K. Archibald, and L. Usiskin. 2003. Both Sides Now: Insider Perspectives on Community–University Research Collaboration in Community Economic Development, roundtable, CUExpo: Community–University Research: Partnerships, Policy, and Progress, Saskatoon, 8–10 May.

FNALM (First Nations Alliance for Land Management). 2003. Developing Good Neighbour Relations: Local Governments and First Nations Technical Workshop.

Guimond, E., N. Robitaille, and S. Senécal. 2008. *Definitions floues et éxplosion démographique chez les populations autochtones du Canada de 1986 à 2001.* Conférence sur les statistiques sociales, le Centre interuniversitaire Québecois de statistiques sociales et l'Institut national d'études démographiques (France).

Indigenous Peoples Health Research Centre with CIHR, NSERC, and SSHRC. 2005. Aboriginal Research Workshop, University of Saskatchewan, 21 March.

Jones, Darrell. 2004. Presentation as President of the Saskatchewan Housing Corporation, General Meeting of the Saskatoon and Region Home Builders' Association, Saskatoon, November.

Kerbow, David. 2002. Addressing the Causes and Consequences of High School Systems and Communities: A Forum Brief. American Youth Policy.

Lambert, Carmen. 1976. To Be or Not to Be Indian: A Question Concerning Indian Cultural Identity. National Conference on Ethnic Studies and Research, University of Regina, October.

Mawby, Russell. 2004. Engaging the Private Sector in Affordable Housing. PRI/SSHRC roundtable, 'Housing Research, Policy and Practice in the Context of Poverty and Exclusion,' 20 October.

Mendis, S., and M. Reed. 2003. What Is Community Capacity? A Framework for Discussion and a Tool for Community Assessment, roundtable, CUExpo, Saskatoon, 8–10 May.

Murphy, Brian. 2009. Thinking in the Active Voice. Expert Consultation on Guidelines on Poverty Reduction DAC/POVNET, Inter Pares, Ottawa, 12–14 September.

Norris, Mary Jane. 1985. Migration Patterns of Status Indians in Canada, 1976–81. Canadian Population Society, June.

Norris, Mary Jane. 2002. Aboriginal Mobility and Migration Within Urban Canada: Outcomes, Factors, and Implications. Aboriginal Policy Research Conference, Ottawa, November.

Norris, M.J., D. Beavon, E. Guimond, and M.J. Cooke. 2000. Migration and Residential Mobility of Canada's Aboriginal Groups: An Analysis of census Data. Annual Meeting of the Population Association of America, Los Angeles, March.

Peters, Evelyn. 1991. Family Values, Household Structure, and Housing Needs: Indian Households in Regina and Saskatoon, Saskatchewan, 1982. Canadian Population Society meetings, Queen's University, Kingston, ON.

Peters, Evelyn. 2009. Aboriginal Peoples in Cities: Myths, Realities, and Implications for Public Policy. Presented in a lecture series of the Johnson–Shoyama Graduate School of Public Policy, University of Regina and University of Saskatchewan, Regina and Saskatoon, February.

Siggner, Andrew. 2001. Demographic, Social, and Economic Profile of Aboriginal Peoples in Selected Western Canadian Cities. Policy Conference on Options for Aboriginal Canadians in Canada's Cities, Regina, May.

Siggner, Andrew. 2003. A Demographic and Socio-economic Profile of the Metis in Canada. The Metis People in the 21st Century conference, Saskatoon, June.

Siggner, A.J., J. Hull, A. Vermaeten, E. Guimond, and L. Jantzen. 2001. New Developments in Aboriginal Definitions and Measures. Annual Meeting of the Canadian Population Society, Université Laval, Quebec City.

Stanbury, W.T. 1972. British Columbia Indians Living Off Reserve: Some Economic Aspects. Fourth Annual Conference, Union of British Columbia Indian Chiefs, November, Prince Rupert, BC.

Stevenson, D., and G. Chu. 1970. Socio-economic Assimilation of Indians in Southwest British Columbia. Northwest Anthropological Conference, March.

Sully, Lorne, and Emmons, Mark. 2004. Urban Reserves: The City of Saskatoon's Partnership with First Nations. Pacific Business and Law Institute Conference, Calgary, 22 April.

Thakur, J. 2011. Habitat Housing Program. Sustainable Solutions for Housing Providers, National Aboriginal Housing Association National Conference, Regina, Sept. 15.

Totikidis, V., A. Armstrong, and R. Francis. 2005. The Concept of Community Governance. GovNet Conference, Melbourne, 28–30 November.

Walker, Ryan. 2010. Housing and Health: What Is the Link? What Can Be Done? Saskatoon Community Clinic, November.

# Contributors

**Alan B. Anderson** was Research Director of the Bridges and Foundations Project on Urban Aboriginal Housing. He is Professor Emeritus of Sociology at the University of Saskatchewan, where he is also Research Fellow (Ethnic and Indigenous Policy) in the Department of Political Studies, Research Associate of the Community-University Institute for Social Research, and an Associate Member of the Johnson-Shoyama Graduate School of Public Policy and the International Centre for Northern Governance and Development. An Honorary Associate Member of the National Aboriginal Housing Association, he has worked with Aboriginal Affairs and Northern Development Canada as well as the Australian Housing and Urban Research Institute.

**Kirsten Anderson**, the documentary photographer for the Bridges and Foundations Project, holds a BFA in photography and graduate diploma in journalism from Concordia University, Montreal. Her photographs of urban Aboriginal life have been exhibited at conferences in Ottawa, Winnipeg, and Saskatoon.

**Jim Durocher**, a Metis originally from northern Saskatchewan, has served as CEO of SaskNative Rentals and corporate owner of Chenew Holdings; he has long been active in Metis political issues and housing initiatives.

**Joseph Garcea** heads the Department of Political Studies at the University of Saskatchewan, where he has chaired the Public Administration Program, has been active in the Aboriginal Public Administration Program, and serves as a board member of the

Community–University Institute for Social Research. He is co-editor of *Urban Indian Reserves: Forging New Relationships in Saskatchewan*.

**Jerry Hammersmith**, long active in Saskatchewan provincial politics, holds a DEd in Comparative Education and was Managing Director of Broxbourne International, delivering community economic development programs (including housing) in indigenous communities in Canada, New Zealand, and Zimbabwe from 1973 to 1992.

**Allison Lachance**, from the Big River Cree First Nation, graduated from the University of Saskatchewan in Sociology and Aboriginal Justice and Criminology, later earning a law degree; she is currently a Policy Analyst for the Federation of Saskatchewan Indian Nations.

**Darlene Lanceley** has been Employment Development Consultant at the Saskatchewan Indian Institute of Technologies (SIIT) and is a board member of the Community–University Institute for Social Research and a doctoral student in Sociology at the University of Saskatchewan.

**Catherine Littlejohn** has more than three decades of experience working with Saskatchewan Metis on research projects and policy and institutional development. Holding an MEd in Indian and Northern Education and a PhD in educational policy and administrative studies, she is co-chair of the SaskNative Rentals Board. Her former research has included a study of Metis homelessness and the history of Metis communities in Saskatchewan.

**Wanda McCaslin**, a Metis from northern Saskatchewan, is the Law Foundation of Saskatchewan Research Officer, Native Law Centre, University of Saskatchewan, where she is editor of *Justice as Healing: Indigenous Ways* and editor of a newsletter on Aboriginal concepts of justice.

**Gail MacKay** is a Woodlands Metis originally from Sault Ste Marie, Ontario. She holds an MEd in Indian and Northern Education and is currently doing a PhD in Native Studies, Education Curriculum Studies, and Psychology at the University of Saskatchewan, where she lectures in the Department of Native Studies.

**Brenda Maire** did research with the Saskatoon Housing Initiatives Partnership and is now Research and Education Coordinator, Criminal Justice Division, Alberta Justice.

**Shelley Thomas Prokop** has been Assistant Professor in the School of Indian Social Work, First Nations University of Canada (Saskatoon Campus) and Manager of Representative Workforce, Human Resources Division, Saskatoon Health Region, and continues her own research consultant business.

**Carol Romanow** earned her MA in Sociology from the University of Saskatchewan, then became Health Planner and Researcher for the Health and Social Development Program of the Prince Albert Grand Council. Currently she is Health Promotions Manager, Community Services, Athabasca Health Authority, serving the northernmost communities and First Nations in Saskatchewan.

**Joan Sanderson**, a member of the James Smith Cree First Nation, is Associate Professor in the School of Indian Social Work, First Nations University of Canada, and on the Board of Directors for Tamara's House, serving women survivors of child sexual abuse.

**Cara Spence** formerly worked with the Race Relations Committee of the City of Saskatoon and was a research assistant with the Bridges and Foundations Project; then she worked as a Research Facilitator for the University of Saskatchewan College of Nursing. Currently she is a Research and Ethics Officer for the Regina-Qu'Appelle Health Region, a sociology instructor at Gabriel Dumont Institute, and an interdisciplinary doctoral student in global health at the University of Saskatchewan.

**Valerie Sutton** is Projects and Research Manager, Sun Ridge Group, Saskatoon; and has worked closely with the Bridges and Foundations Project.

**Alan Thomarat** is CEO of both the Saskatoon and Region Home Builders Association and the Canadian Home Builders Association-Saskatchewan, as well as President of the Saskatoon Housing Initiatives Partnership and the Galt Group (specializing in public policy research, market analysis, and business advisory services). He has been instrumental in founding the Bridges and Foundations Career Development Corporation.

**Brenda Wallace** has been Executive Director of the Saskatoon Housing Initiatives Partnership (SHIP) and Resource Planning Manager of the Meewasin Valley Authority; currently she is Manager of the Environmental Services Branch, City of Saskatoon.

# Index